D1602418

COGNITIVE SOCIAL PSYCHOLOGY

COGNITIVE SOCIAL PSYCHOLOGY

Edited by
ALBERT H. HASTORF
Stanford University

ALICE M. ISEN
University of Maryland

ELSEVIER / NORTH-HOLLAND
NEW YORK • AMSTERDAM • OXFORD

Elsevier North Holland, Inc.
52 Vanderbilt Avenue, New York, New York, 10017

Sole distributors outside the USA and Canada:
Elsevier Science Publishers B.V.
P.O. Box 211, 1000 AE Amsterdam, The Netherlands

Library of Congress Cataloging in Publication Data

Main entry under title:

Cognitive social psychology.

Bibliography: p.
Includes index.
Contents: Some perspectives on cognitive social psychology / Alice M. Isen and Albert H. Hastorf — Social knowledge / Nancy Cantor, Walter Mischel, and Judith Schwartz — Toward understanding the relationship between feeling states and social behavior / Margaret S. Clark and Alice M. Isen — [etc.] 1. Social psychology — Addresses, essays, lectures. 2. Cognition — Addresses, essays, lectures. I. Hastorf, Albert H., 1920– II. Isen, Alice M.

HM251.C644 320 81-12451
ISBN 0-444-00617-6 AACR2

Manufactured in the United States of America

CONTENTS

PREFACE

When George Mandler invited us to edit a volume on cognitive social psychology, we found the idea both tempting and a little frightening; tempting because we saw the area as not just a borderland (perhaps even a no man's land) between two areas of psychology, but an area that had the potential for providing both a theoretical and an empirical symbiosis between them. The frightening part is what appeared to us as an embarrassment of riches as a function of the vast amount of research activity that falls under this rubric.

It seemed to us that cognitive social psychology could be more than the study of the cognition of social events and more than the study of the influence of social factors on cognition. We hoped that this burgeoning field could be seen as a major step in the reunification of psychology.

After considerable debate, we concluded that it would be best to focus the volume on two major areas of concern, the first one being the exploration of areas of interaction between personality and social variables and cognitive functioning. This is represented in the chapters by Nancy Cantor, Walter Mischel, and Judith Schwartz; Margaret Clark and Alice Isen; Anthony Greenwald; and Leslie McArthur. The other focus centers on the exploration of practical topic areas where the methods and theories of cognitive social psychology have been brought to bear. This area is represented by chapters by John Carroll and Richard Wiener in regard to legal processes, Joanne Martin in regard to organizations, and Jerome Singer and Andrew Baum in regard to medicine.

We have undertaken to do an introductory chapter with the hope of casting some light on the history of, and some possible futures for, cognitive social psychology. We are aware that there are aspects of this chapter that are controversial, but it is our hope that the chapter will serve to encourage the unification of psychology rather than the partitioning of psychology. Of necessity we leave it to the reader to make judgment in regard to our success.

We would like to express our appreciation to the Boys Town Center for the Study of Youth Development at Stanford University which provided a hospitable setting for completing this work. We would especially like to thank Joyce Sanders, Pat Shallenberger, and Elsie Young for help in regard to a multitude of details in the preparation of the manuscript. Finally, we should like to thank the authors of the individual chapters. They have been cooperative beyond the call of duty.

Stanford, California

ALBERT H. HASTORF
ALICE M. ISEN

LIST OF CONTRIBUTORS

ANDREW BAUM, Uniformed Services University of the Health Sciences

NANCY CANTOR, Princeton University

JOHN S. CARROLL, Loyola University of Chicago

MARGARET S. CLARK, Carnegie-Mellon University

ANTHONY G. GREENWALD, The Ohio State University

ALBERT H. HASTORF, Stanford University

ALICE M. ISEN, University of Maryland

JOANNE MARTIN, Stanford University

LESLIE ZEBROWITZ McARTHUR, Brandeis University

WALTER MISCHEL, Stanford University

JUDITH SCHWARTZ, Princeton University

JEROME E. SINGER, Uniformed Services University of the Health Sciences

RICHARD L. WIENER, Loyola University of Chicago

COGNITIVE SOCIAL PSYCHOLOGY

ALICE M. ISEN   ALBERT H. HASTORF

SOME PERSPECTIVES ON COGNITIVE SOCIAL PSYCHOLOGY

In speaking to the 1976 annual meeting of the Society for Experimental Social Psychology as he received the group's Distinguished Senior Scientist Award, Fritz Heider remarked on the need for integration of ideas and concepts in social psychology and in psychology generally. Spreading the fingers of his hand in illustration, he described how, years before, he and his contemporaries had introduced "peninsulas" of thought and study that they hoped subsequent generations would extend and weld into a broad, solid foundation for the field. Instead of the hoped-for development, broadening, and integration of these ideas, however, he said softly, "it seems that the peninsulas have become"—and he paused, shrugged his shoulders, and smiled gently—"insulas."

In the years since Heider made this observation, a growing number of psychologists have expressed concern about the need for integration, not only within social psychology but in psychology generally, and even to some extent in social science and cognitive science more broadly. Many believe that various aspects of these fields can be brought to bear upon each other to their mutual benefit. One approach with potential for promoting this kind of integration is cognitive social psychology. This new perspective encourages the synthesis of social and cognitive psychology, and it embodies some ideas that have been gaining increasing acceptance in both of these fields in recent years.

At the same time, many people have asked whether this approach represents anything new in either cognitive or social psychology. They note that much of existing social psychology seems to have been "cognitive" in orientation all along, with little impact on cognitive psychology, and with little resultant integration or systematization of social psychology. In this chapter we will describe the evolution of cognitive social psychology, and we will try to clarify what is new about it. We will discuss the kind of contribution that one might expect from this new approach, pointing out its potential for integration and noting the suggestions that it makes for cognitive and social psychology, and perhaps for psychology as a whole, as well.

OVERVIEW

We begin with a brief description of what cognitive social psychology attempts to do and how it differs from existing social and cognitive psychology. Cognitive social psychology is an approach that stresses understanding of cognitive processes as a key to understanding complex, purposive, social behavior. At the same time that it calls attention to the importance of cognitive process for social interaction, however, it emphasizes the need to broaden our understanding of cognitive processes themselves. It proposes that cognitive processes are complexly influenced by variables such as feelings, frame of mind, context, and goals or purposes of the person, variables that are not usually studied in cognitive psychology.

What is distinctive about cognitive social psychology from a social psychologist's perspective, then, is its focus on (cognitive) process and its use of the concepts, accumulated knowledge, and, frequently, methods of cognitive psychology. What is distinctive about the field from a cognitive psychologist's point of view is its broadened conception of cognitive processes themselves. We will elaborate on these distinctions in the following sections.

Cognitive Social Psychology and Social Psychology

Much of social psychology has long been concerned with the role of what might be called cognitive elements—attitudes, perceptions, and attributions, for example—in producing interpersonal attitudes and behavior or even social movements. There have been relatively noncognitive foci in social psychology, such as the work on social facilitation (F. Allport, 1924; Triplett, 1897, Zajonc, 1965) and group processes (Cartwright & Zander, 1968). But, as many have noted, social psychology has devoted a large portion of its time and effort to what might be called a "cognitive" approach—cognitive in the sense that it is concerned with mental events or thoughts, or postulates these in accounting for behavior.

Definition of "Cognitive." In order to understand how modern cognitive social psychology differs from much of social psychology that has been called cognitive in approach, we must consider the definition of the term "cognitive." For an interesting illustration of the complexity of this definitional problem, try asking a few of your psychologist friends what "cognitive" means or what "cognitive psychology" is.

If your friends are like ours, you will discover a surprising degree of variation in the answers you receive. Some whom we queried replied that the term "cognitive" refers to anything unobservable, anything "going on in the head." For many people who use the term in this way, it is virtually synonymous with "mentalistic"; it signifies an unscientific approach because it deals with nonobservables. But for others who use the term in this way, it is simply to call attention to a broad class of events—those occurring in the mind of the social actor—that may influence behavior or other thoughts.

Others whom we asked about the definition focused on content and defined as "cognitive" anything intellectual—thought, knowledge, memory, sometimes perception, and any related elements (thoughts, bits of knowledge, and other items that can be called cognitions). Some gave answers implying or plainly stating that cognition must involve awareness. Others said that the word "cognitive" calls attention to process as well as intellectual content, and they defined it as referring to the processes involved in knowing and perceiving; thus awareness would not be implied, since one is often not aware of process, even process that results in conscious contents.

Some psychologists, basically subscribing to the latter view, added a focus on representation—the representation of knowledge. Still others stressed the distinction between modern cognitive psychology and "verbal learning"; some highlighting the changing, active, transformational, and constructive nature of cognition suggested early by Bartlett (1932) and others and more recently by Neisser (1967, 1976a), Jenkins (1974), and others. This last view suggests not only a focus on process and on representation, but also points to the interdependence of intellectual, motivational, and feeling processes that usually are not considered mutually influential.

Most cognitive psychologists to whom we spoke were in agreement that the most useful definition of "cognition" was one that reflected concern with process and was neutral with regard to the question of awareness or consciousness. In other words, most would agree with the statement that cognitive psychology is a field that is concerned with the processes by which knowledge is constructed, represented, and used.

Cognitive Social Psychology: A New Emphasis in Social Psychology. Given, thus, this perspective on the definitional problem, and if we adopt for cognitive social psychology a definition compatible with the one that the field of cognitive psychology has taken for itself, we can now better understand why there is a sense that social psychology has always been cognitive, but at the same time a sense that modern cognitive social psychology is somehow different in emphasis from much of the earlier work. It is the use of the term "cognitive" that has changed, especially in the past 15 years, as cognitive psychology has evolved and emerged as a distinct field. There is more stress now on understanding the processes involved in the representation and utilization of knowledge.

Early cognitive approaches in social psychology postulated mental intervening variables such as attitudes or sets to account for differences in behavior that could otherwise not be understood (Farr, 1976). In some instances psychologists studied certain aspects of these variables themselves, or rather noncumulatively provided demonstrations that such variables could interfere with the otherwise lawful working of memory and learning. Some, like that of Asch (1952), stressed the importance of a subject's interpretation of the situation, as a general framework. Later, cognitive approaches focused on more specifically determined attributions or other contents of the mind, as in the case of the social-perception literature, for example, where the focus is on what one knows or thinks about other people, or the thoughts one ascribes to them.

In the main, however, what earlier approaches did not undertake was a systematic consideration of the processes involved in these mental events.[1] This would be an important component of today's meaning of the term "cognitive," but the study of these processes has only recently been facilitated by developments in cognitive psychology itself. As cognitive psychology has developed its concern with processes such as organization in memory and the process of constructive representation of information or knowledge, a new emphasis in the field of social psychology based on these advances has similarly begun to develop.

Today's cognitive social psychology differs from other cognitive approaches in social psychology, then, in that, like contemporary cognitive psychology, it adopts a definition of "cognitive" that focuses on process, and it is concerned with cognitive process itself. It suggests that social behavior cannot be understood without understanding how people deal with and make use of information. It is concerned not only with *what* you know or think about people, but with *how* you come to know what you know, the processes by which you make use of it, and those by which it comes to influence other knowledge and behavior.

Cognitive Social Psychology and Cognitive Psychology

At the same time, cognitive social psychology can also be distinguished from cognitive psychology. Cognitive psychology, often of necessity and often with successful results, has tended to investigate cognitive phenomena in isolation from other aspects of existence and behavior, apart from the fabric of life. For this reason, however, although the field has accomplished much, it has not taken up certain important issues. Generally, it has not considered cognitive activity in affective and

[1]Some earlier approaches went so far as to consider "dynamics," that is, reaction to force, pressure, or stress—for example, in the study of attitudes and attitude-change. But, consideration of such dynamics (reactions to pressure) differs from a systematic study of process.

action-requiring contexts, and by and large it has not addressed the issue of applying its findings to complex situations of life.

Beyond this, however, the field of cognitive psychology has not seriously considered the role of interpersonally relevant (motivational and affective) variables in *cognitive processes themselves.* Sir Frederick Bartlett (1932) noted this problem nearly 50 years ago, saying,

> . . . The methods of the great physical and physiological pioneers, often brilliantly successful in the study of special sense reactions, and in the elucidation of certain psychophysical problems, have overspread the whole of psychological science. Yet all the while new problems, most of them concerned with conditions of response that have to be considered as resident within the organism—or the subject—itself have been forcing themselves to the front, and it is more than time that their implications were explicitly stated. (pp. 6 –7)

Despite this and other attempts to call for a more integrated approach to cognitive processes themselves, cognitive psychology, for the most part, has seemed reluctant to address these issues—to suggest that cognition itself cannot be fully understood without reference to the goals or frame of mind (which include task and situation variables) of the problem solver, for example. Cognitive social psychology adopts this perspective, and it is in this way that cognitive psychology and cognitive social psychology differ most clearly.

The question of affect, for example, has not received much attention in traditional cognitive psychology. Although we discuss the topic of affect more thoroughly later on, it is important for now to note the way in which affect *is* considered in cognitive psychology, on those occasions when it is discussed. Affect is treated as a thing apart, a separate force, a "spoiler," to otherwise lawful cognitive relationships.

For example, perhaps building on the positions of many motivational and physiological psychologists such as P. T. Young (1943, 1961) that emotion is "disorganizing" [see Easterbrook (1959), Leeper (1948, 1970), and Arnold (1970) for critical discussions of this issue], Abelson (1963) coined the phrase, "hot cognition," to refer to information processing when feeling emotion. Simon's (1967) suggestion of emotion as an "interrupt" in an otherwise goal-directed progam is another example of such a proposal. This kind of work had potential for broadening the field in its time because it discussed (or reintroduced) the concept of affect in the context of cognition. But it was only a beginning, and it was not pursued by cognitive psychology as a whole nor integrated theoretically into that field. Thus, it has promoted the corollary views that usually cognition is *un*affected by affect and motivation, that only strong (and perhaps negative) emotion influences cognition, and that somehow this influence is to interfere with a more basic and otherwise orderly process. We do not disagree with the view that strong emotion may interrupt behavior, but we would suggest that it is incomplete as a description of the relationship between affect and cognition.

Thus, what cognitive social psychology suggests for cognitive psychology is a broadening of focus to include the study of cognitive processing in complex situations or involving complex problems of the kind that people confront in their everyday lives. But, even more important, cognitive social psychology, drawing on earlier traditions within social psychology, suggests the integration of affective, motivational, and contextual variables in the study of cognitive process itself.

Summary and Implications

Let us now summarize and extend our definition of cognitive social psychology and the points of distinction between it and social psychology and cognitive psychology. (1) Cognitive social psychology suggests a stress on understanding cognitive process—the method by which information is represented and utilized—as a key to understanding complex social behavior. This is one way in which it differs from social psychology generally, much of which has often been thought of as "cognitive," but in a different sense. (2) These cognitive processes themselves are presumed to be complexly constructive and dependent on affective, motivational/contextual, and concurrent cognitive factors. This is a way in which cognitive social psychology differs from cognitive psychology generally. Each of these components has implications for the potential contribution of cognitive social psychology.

Process. First, the traditional cognitive approach in social psychology, social cognition, emphasizes the role of cognitive elements in social behavior but often assumes that cognition of social behavior is somehow different from cognitive processes generally. On the other hand, cognitive social psychology stresses a focus on the processes by which information comes to be known and used in decision-making regarding social behavior. Presumably these processes are the same as those operating when the person deals with other (nonsocial) kinds of information of equal complexity.

The assumption that social and nonsocial cognition are different may reflect the opinion that social situations may often involve more dimensions or levels of processing than do other kinds of tasks. In many cases it may be a reaction to the oversimplified view of cognition that has been prevalent in the field of cognitive psychology until recently. But the implication of cognitive social psychology's position is that the *same* processes are relevant in the processing of both social and nonsocial information of equal complexity.

Integration and Constructive Cognition. Second, in contrast with previous, relatively isolated, attempts to consider the role of context and social variables in cognition, or of people's perceptions of their circumstances in the production of isolated social behaviors, cognitive social psychology proposes a systematic approach to such questions. It attempts to understand them systematically and to relate them to process and the body of cognitive psychology, as well as to behavior. And it encourages both theoretical and organismic integration. By "organismic integration," we mean that affective, motivational, and cognitive factors can be considered together. (In addition, we will suggest that these processes may even be capable of representation in each other's terms, although the model does not require this particular form of integration. We will have more to say on this later.)

This perspective—that context, affective, motivational, and cognitive factors are mutually influential—suggests that cognitive processes are constructive and active, a point with implications for cognitive psychology (see, for example, Neisser, 1967, Ch. 11). It also suggests not just that it is possible to view affective, motivational, and cognitive processes together, but that it is misleading to do anything else. A recent paper by Tversky and Kahneman (1980) on the importance of the "framing" of a decision illustrates this point. Those authors found that, when confronting the same problem, framed differently (i.e., so as to highlight potential loss vs gain), decision-makers reached markedly different decisions, revealing differing goals or motives. Affect, decision-making, goal-setting, and behavior seem inevitably linked in context through constructive cognitive processes.

Purposiveness and an Implied Model. Finally, in cognitive social psychology, underlying the stress on context and on integrative constructive cognitive processes is the assumption of purposiveness. Purposiveness refers to the fact that behavior is intentional (or, where individual behaviors are not closely monitored, occurs against a background of intentions). Context, for example, is important because it influences the person's interpretation of her situation and the goals that she tries to accomplish or sees as possible and desirable in the situation.

Thus cognitive social psychology, assuming purposiveness and offering an opportunity for an integrated model of functioning in both social and nonsocial situations, may be seen by some as implying a theoretical orientation for psychology generally, rather than simply an alternative approach in social or cognitive psychology. In the model implied by cognitive social psychology, a person is viewed in social situations as attempting to think through the problems at hand in order to solve them and act on them. This purposive problem-solving, a so-called "cognitive" process, never occurs in the absence of the effects of feeling nor of the motivational or action component (requirements, goals, situational constraints, etc.) of behavior.

This model will not seem completely new to those familiar with the work of John Dewey and the functionalist school, to some extent of Edward Tolman, or of the personality theorist, George Kelly. It also draws upon the ideas of Sir Frederick Bartlett (themselves built upon and extending Johann Herbart's suggestion that ideas structure themselves into larger wholes and that the existing "apperceptive mass" then influences material to be perceived, through the process of assimilation, even when it is below consciousness or threshold) and the cognitive and social psychologists who noted and extended his suggestion of the constructive nature of cognition. It is distantly related to the Gestalt position, which stressed, for example, the integration of parts in the perception of the whole. And of course, it builds on earlier work by social psychologists, suggesting that thoughts and goals influence behavior.

This model regards persons as neither driven by internal needs nor tossed about by external stimuli, but as problem-solvers, who are evaluating situations, alternatives, and outcomes, planning actions, and trying to accomplish goals. They are actively and purposively attempting to choose appropriate courses of action for their circumstances. Understanding their behavior requires understanding the situation that they are in, what they are trying to accomplish, and how it all looks to them. How it all looks to them will be determined by how they construe their situations and options, and this will be determined by many interactive factors and processes.

The stress on purposiveness and cognitive process does not mean, however, that the focus in cognitive social psychology must be on the contents of conscious awareness as revealed through introspective report. It is important to note that the proposed approach stresses process rather than content; and process, even that which results in conscious contents, may not always be conscious. Even if the plan of the planner is conscious, this does not imply that all of the processes involved in the decision-making and the production of actual behavior are necessarily conscious. As Mandler (1975b) has pointed out in the context of people trying to describe their cognitive processes through introspection, "thoughts" of which we are aware are the *results* of the processes of cognition, not descriptors of the process.

Nonconscious cognitive processes such as "priming," where material related to a cue or presently utilized category, for example, becomes more accessible for use (see, for example, Brown, 1979; Neely, 1976, 1977; Posner & Snyder, 1975), may occur. In terms of our model they, like other processes, are of interest in an overall context of decision-making and action rather than for themselves. As a class they are neither less important nor more important than conscious factors. (By this we mean that we are not using the term "unconscious" or "nonconscious" in the motivational sense in which it is usually used. Nonconscious processes are simply cognitive processes of which one is not aware, for any of a number of possible reasons, such as the low level of cognitive effort required for their operation, for example.) Thus explicit awareness of variables is possible but neither necessary nor presumed in the analysis that we are suggesting for social behavior, even though the analysis is a cognitive one and assumes intentional, purposive behavior on the part of persons.

Thus, one might say that cognitive social psychology need not be different from social psychology or from cognitive psychology, but that it seems to be different because it attempts to be more integrative. Cognitive social psychology tries to address complex social behavior using information processing and cognitive problem-solving as the basis of an integrated framework for considering the full complexity of behavior, and it hopes to expand understanding of cognitive processes by considering the interactive role of social variables, feelings, frame of mind, context, and goals or purposes of the person, in cognitive process. Thus it tries to pull together cognitive and social psychology, and in the process it may present suggestions that have implications for psychology more broadly as well.

Let us now examine how the differences in approach that cognitive social psychology attempts to resolve may have come about and how the suggested integrative approach of cognitive social psychology evolved. In the process, we think, the compatibility of the fields of cognitive and social psychology will become clear.

A LOOK BACK

In the beginning, our great literature tells us, everything was one. And—the pattern is described apparently for all things and for all time—analysis and differentiation followed very soon thereafter. Likewise it was with psychology. In the beginning, there was monism, concern with mind as a unified whole, and in the process of development of the field, differentiation and specialization soon followed. Now we find a fairly marked degree of specialization in psychology and fairly extensive differentiation of mental or psychological processes, some distinctions probably rather arbitrarily drawn. In this section we review the beginning of this process of specialization and then trace the development of modern social and cognitive psychology. We hope that the reader will come away with a sense that the current demarcation lines between fields are to some extent matters of convenience that can be crossed, and actually changed, as the field progresses and a new integration becomes possible.

The Trilogy of Mind: Integrative or Segregative?

Hilgard (1980) points out, in a very informative paper, that the search for faculties, or differentiated powers of the mind—the stirrings of differentiation and specialization—was begun in the early 1700s. He suggests that occasional references in the writings of the Ancients to tripartite classifications of mind should not be overinterpreted. [Gordon Allport, for example, in his historical chapter in the *Handbook of Social Psychology* (1967) refers to Plato's tripartite division of forces in the body and to the tripartite division of society in ancient Greece as foreshadowing and paralleling the tripartite conceptualization of mind.] We choose the 18th century as our starting place: Leibnitz's *Monadology* was written in 1714, and Kant's *Critique of Pure Reason, Critique of Practical Reason,* and *Critique of Judgment,* which reflect not a unitary view of mind but the tripartite plan that had taken root by the middle of the 18th century, were published between 1780 and 1790.

Thus, the beginning of the search for differentiated powers or aspects of mind is usually placed in the 18th century. It is commonly associated with the *bipartite* division of mind into the two processes of (1) knowledge, and (2) desire, by Christian Wolff (who lived from 1679 to 1754). The first clear statement of the important *tripartite* division of mind into the once-dominant and now vaguely-familiar-to-us-all categories of Cognition, Conation, and Affection, appeared at midcentury in the writings of the philosopher and ethicist, Moses Mendelssohn (*Letters on Sensation,* 1755).

The three categories included (1) Cognition: knowledge, understanding, intellect (and some psychologists and philosophers of the day included "judgment" or sensation at least in part in this category); (2) Conation: desire, striving, will, motivation, action; and (3) Affection: pleasure and pain, feeling, "sensibility" (which included elements of perception or "sensitivity"), emotions, affect, affection, and "judgment."

It is sometimes difficult to understand the sense in which some of these words were intended (e.g., "judgment," "sensitivity"), but three things seem clear: (1) these were thought to be the basic, irreducible expressions of mental activity; (2) they were *not* generally viewed as separate agencies or active forces (except that it was difficult to maintain the distinction between this tripartite conception and Faculty Psychology), not factors that might interact with each other; and (3) this view was widely accepted in Europe and the United States for 150 years.

In sum, it can be said that the threefold classification was broadly accepted as representing not separate forces but the three basic expressions of mental life or mental activity, as illustrated in this quotation from the writings of William McDougall (1923):

> We often speak of an intellectual or cognitive activity; or of an act of willing or of resolving, choosing, striving, purposing or again of a state of feeling. But it is generally admitted that all mental activity has these three aspects, cognitive, conative, and affective; and when we apply one of these three adjectives to any phase of mental process, we mean merely that the aspect named is the most prominent of the three at that moment. Each cycle of activity has this triple aspect; though each tends to pass through three phases in which cognition, conation, and affection are in turn most prominent. . . . (p. 266)

Thus the complexity of mental events was appreciated. The different types of experience were recognized, but understanding of the unity or indivisibility of mental activity and the need to consider the implications for all three manifestations of experience in any process studied were assumed and preserved.

Note, however, the conceptual complexity of this position: alternative processes can be identified, yet they are all one. It is not surprising that by the mid-19th century, these reflections of the mind were beginning to be regarded as separate activities, or as unequal in "importance" or interest. Psychologists, for example, were beginning to emphasize one component or to restrict their investigation to only one of the three (usually the cognitive).

Even though an approach stressing only one of the three reflections of mind was considered inadequate even as late as the early part of this century, eventually concern with experimental method overtook concern with completeness, and these components began to be investigated separately without apology. Experimental methods were being developed, notably by Wundt, Ebbinghaus, and the Behaviorists, that were intended to make abstractions concrete and to help isolate "pure" psychological processes. (Consider, for example, the invention of the nonsense syllable for the study of cognitive processes and the orientation that underlies such a move.) In the excitement, and perhaps relief, of studying elementary processes (and somehow elements seem more "pure"), using a precise method, concern with completeness was submerged. And the above reference by McDougall to the three-part view of mind appears to be the last such reference to that formulation (Hilgard, 1980).

In presenting the foregoing history of the tripartite classification, we do not mean to idealize it. In fact, the specialization and differentiation that followed, the concern with methodology and with the pursuit of empirical evidence, were all essential to the development of a scientific psychology. It is doubtful that any field can progress without developing ways of disentangling variables and simplifying its focus of attention temporarily. A field must not oversimplify its subject matter, but neither can it follow itself to fall into "holistic paralysis"—to be demoralized and overwhelmed by the perceived need to deal with all variables at once. Sometimes complex situations must be simplified in order for study of them to begin.

With this point in mind, however, one must also remain aware of the need to broaden focus again as discoveries are made. This applies to both the relationship between areas—that discoveries made in one may be applied in others—and to the broader issue of the nature of psychological events. This is one reason that we have here alluded to the history of the tripartite conceptualization of mind: that formulation constituted an early appreciation of the complexity of psychological events. Now it may be possible and beneficial to incorporate both methodological technique and an appreciation of the complexity of behavior into the same endeavor.

At the same time, we wish to point out that appreciation of the complexity of psychological reality need not involve allegiance to the three-part view of mind that was proposed when differentiation was beginning 200 years ago. We presented some detail about this view because we sense a resurgence of interest in it, and because it dominated psychological thinking for 150 years and no doubt influenced even the theories of this century, which followed its period of hegemony. Proponents of the tripartite view of mind express awareness of the complexity of psychological events and generally call for an integrative approach in psychology. Yet, the three-part conceptualization does not appear to have served well as an integrative device.

The dominant theoretical orientations of the 20th century, which we describe in the following section, seem to focus on either cognition or conation (some would say that one focused on affect also). To some extent they may be seen as having abandoned the classic tripartite conceptualization because of such foci; yet, they also bear its imprint. Each appears to have selected one or another of the three elements of the trilogy for inordinate emphasis, but each also mentioned or showed awareness of the other elements in some ways. None, however, developed the other components to the extent that it developed the element that was its focus, and none produced a truly integrated system.

Perhaps the reason that cognition, behavior, and, to a lesser extent, feeling, have alternated as foci of attention in psychological theory is that these three truly are the bedrock of psychological reality and, as Kant said, "absolutely irreduceable." Perhaps there are no other units, and, if integration is to occur, these three "units" must be dealt with and integrated.

But perhaps the difficulty in holding these together as they are conceived in the tripartite view of mind is the very fact that they are seen as irreduceable and as basically different from one another. At best, they are as the novels of a trilogy—a set of three essentially separate and self-contained stories (or, in this case, domains or sets of processes) that comprise a larger unit only secondarily and only when viewed in the broadest perspective. While they represent experiences that must be integrated, the tripartite view does not provide the units or tools for relating them to one another. Thus, although the three-part conceptualization has served the function of not letting certain of the components slip from attention altogether, this view itself may not be the best model for integration. Perhaps new developments or a new perspective will provide the needed implement, and some new integrative plan will emerge out of consideration of the evolution of psychological knowledge and theory over the last century. Stranger things have happened.

The Beginning of Modern Psychology

As we have said, the first empirical psychologists chose to focus essentially, and despite brief mention of other components of experience, on "pure" processes, on one set out of the trilogy. Wundt founded his laboratory to study pure cognitive experience, devoid of affective or motivational (conative) components. (Affect was conceived as a separate system by Wundt and his followers, subject to the same analysis—into simple and compound elements—as cognition, however.) His primary subject matter was pure sensation, excluding even "perception," which he felt was contaminated by attitudes or interpretation. Moreover, he inaugurated an introspective method that involved no action component and minimized the effect of this aspect of conation as well. Weber's discovery of the relativity of discrimination, and Fechner's recognition that this discovery could be generalized into a psychophysical law, stimulated the development of experimental psychology in general and sensory psychology in particular. Ebbinghaus' creative invention of the nonsense syllable furthered the effort to study "pure" cognition. In addition, the British Associationist School had long since set the stage for the emerging experimental psychology of cognition, emphasizing sensation and the content-focused association of cognitive elements.

The Study of Thinking

Not only was thinking the subject matter of the Associationists, but sensations (and images) were the associational elements. Thomas Hobbes, for example, at the very founding of the approach in the mid-17th century, emphasized the empirical basis of mental life and held that all ideas originated in the senses and were "but the decaying remains of sensations" (Mandler & Mandler, 1964, p. 14). Although Hobbes himself also wrote about more complex and potentially integrative issues, such as the age-old problem of directed thinking (that is, the issue of what determines the train of thought), for about 200 years the field was generally dominated by a conception of mental life as associations of elementary sensations and ideas. This view was compatible with the field of psychology emerging from Wundt's laboratory in 1880 and, later, also with the Behaviorist position.

At the same time, however, pressures were building to conceptualize the units of thought more broadly and flexibly. Alexander Bain (c. 1855) is usually credited with the introduction of this more comprehensive approach to understanding thinking, even though others before him had made nods in the direction of comprehensiveness, and even though he stopped short of suggesting the new units. As we have noted, Hobbes commented on the problem of directed thinking, and James Mill noted the facility with which affect can direct thinking. But Bain proposed the concept of Compound Association, suggesting that more than one line of association (cue) can contribute to reviving a memory—a concept still of utility in the currently popular theory of "spreading activation"—and made a frontal attack on the problem of directed thinking. (It might also be noted in passing that Bain, also an adherent of the tripartite conceptualization of mind, exhorted his readers to recognize the importance of the noncognitive forces of Emotion and Will in the sphere of intellect, and in fact suggested that *affect* was the primary mark of mind. Still, we do not find affect and will integrated conceptually in Bain's contribution to the understanding of cognitive process.)

Another major impetus for change among the Associationists was no doubt the experience of members of the Würzburg School (A. Mayer, J. Orth, Henry Watt, and Narziss Ach) between 1880 and 1910. Their studies suggested the possibility of "imageless thought" and the importance of factors such as the task and determining tendency (set) on subjects' responses. Thus, this work indicated that introspection of conscious content could not deal with all of the issues that arose in conducting studies of thinking. Most notably, the problems of subjects' reports of "imageless thought" in a system where images were held to be the basic units of thought, the observed effects of the task and the effects of "determining tendency," brought into question the assumption that conscious experience provided access to the processes of thinking. Thus these problems undermined introspection as a method of study. Perhaps more importantly, though, these developments, summarized in a paper by Oswald Külpe in 1912, also advanced the movement toward adopting broader and more flexible units of thought as the basic units to be studied. (It is interesting that this same paper was probably also influential in stimulating Allport's work on attitudes, although the focus of the latter was on social application rather than on the cognitive theoretical question of the appropriate units to employ.)

In the United States William James (1890) was suggesting, similarly, that elemental associationist processes would not turn out to be the way of understanding complex processes of thinking, that somehow the response (thought) in a complex event was not a separate, interchangeable element but was part of the event (i.e., that the units of thought were more complex, constructive, and changing or dependent on context). John Dewey became heir to this position in America and incorporated it into his purposive, functional psychology. This is somewhat ironic because what we are suggesting now, in discussing the field of cognitive social psychology, is the inverse of the situation that attended Dewey's adoption: We are suggesting that the field of cognition, which is by now perfectly used to dealing with flexible (rather than elementaristic) cognitive units, incorporate a variant of Dewey's purposive, functional orientation into its cognitive psychology.

The important step of broadening the units of cognition was not actually taken, however, until the work of Otto Selz, which Mandler and Mandler (1964) have termed the major turning point in the history of thinking. Selz had studied with the Würzburg psychologists, but was also influenced by the Act Psychology of Brentano and Meinong. These two influences were both evident in the suggestions he made for cognitive psychology. He not only proposed, as the Würzburgers were tending to propose, that the basic cognitive units could be whole sets of relationships, trains of thought, or schemata, rather than atomistic particles or sensations; but he also emphasized that thinking was an active process, and he called for attention to process rather than content in the effort to understand thinking. He anticipated modern cognitive psychology in this stress on process and in his concept of larger units of response that, like schemata, for example, are in essence specific to or integrally related to the act or task before the subject. Indeed, his ideas, published in 1927, seem surprisingly current, and it is reasonable to suppose, as Mandler and Mandler (1964) do, that cognitive psychology might have advanced more quickly if Selz's work had been given proper recognition. They note that Selz spent his career in a minor academic position at Mannheim and was killed in a German concentration camp in the 1940s.

The final blow to introspection as a technique for the scientific investigation of thinking came from the Gestalt school. Koffka, for example, noted the difference between functional and descriptive concepts, between knowledge of process and conscious awareness of one's state, which is the outcome of that process. In many other ways as well the contributions of the Gestalt school to the study of thinking were marked. It opposed the Wundtian and Associationist tradition of focusing on basic elements, stressing instead the importance of organization or integration of parts in the perception of an object or stimulus (a whole or form). And it opposed the Behaviorist position that was dominant in American psychology and that denied the importance of complex mental organization and cognitive processes. It influenced Edward Tolman's formulation of his antiassociationist "purposive behaviorism," and through Tolman's work, it had influence on the revision of behaviorism, which, according to some, eventually enabled the emergence of cognitive psychology (Ash, 1980; Mandler & Mandler, 1968).[2]

Behaviorism and Psychoanalysis

As we have seen, then, by the end of the first decade of this century, introspection was proving inadequate and losing ground as the accepted method for studying thinking. After the death of Titchener, who had been an overwhelming proponent of introspectionist sensory psychology in the United States, concern that psychology develop as an experimental field led to the eventual rejection of introspection as a method of investigation. The work of Pavlov, Thorndike, and Watson helped to ensure that in the United States the method that replaced introspection would be that of observation of behavior or of physiological response. In terms of the trilogy of mind of which we have been speaking, however, the change from introspection to behavior analysis represented not only a methodological shift but also a theoretical and subject matter change of emphasis from cognition to conation.

As Behaviorism developed, it rejected—and then in some variants gradually reintroduced—certain aspects of conation (motivation, drive) in its effort to deal strictly with observables. But basically the system stressed conation (action, behavior) to the exclusion of cognition and affect. Behavior as a function of observable stimulation became the dependent measure of interest. Behaviorism rose to prominence among schools of thought in American psychology, and even other schools came to be influenced by its refusal to conceptualize complex mental structures or processes. Mandler and Mandler (1968) suggest that Behaviorism "subverted" the budding Functionalist school of John Dewey,

[2]Gestalt psychology would probably not be considered part of modern "cognitive psychology" because it did not stress the activity of cognition and cognitive organization. Although it spoke of organization, it saw this as innately given and a function of the stimulus and thus did not focus on the process of this organization and its changing nature. Nonetheless, Gestalt influenced the field of modern cognition substantially, if indirectly, through cognitive psychologists whom it stimulated (such as Ulrich Neisser, who studied at Swarthmore College, an important center of Gestalt activity in the middle third of this century), and through the exhilarating sense of optimism and faith in the positive side of man's thinking processes that many report its proponents to have stressed (see, for example, Asch, 1980, and Neisser, 1980).

James Rowland Angell, and Harvey Carr, and, combining with the Pavlovian approach, "reinstated a naive empiricism and associationism which had already been rejected by some of the more sophisticated associationists . . . such as Alexander Bain and G. E. Muller." (p. 374). They argue that Behaviorism's effect was to delay investigation of cognitive processes, and of course, Behaviorism had little time for affect, either.

Some might argue that the Behaviorists were not ignoring affect and cognition but that they sought (and the Skinnerians still seek) to describe all of psychology in the coin of one of the tripartite components of mind, conation. They simply chose conation (behavior), where we would now choose cognition instead. If this was their goal, it is fair to say that they did not go to great lengths to make it clear; and their open abhorrence of terms referring to cognition or feeling led many of their own number, as well as others, to the inference that they had no interest, even ultimately, in such experience.

In Europe during this same period, Freud's system, Psychoanalysis, was being developed. Psychoanalysis would reject the narrowness of the Behavioristic position that only observables were appropriate for study or theoretical use. Some might suggest that, of our three variables of the trilogy, the emphasis in Freud's theoretical system was on affect. We would acknowledge that Freud considered affect of importance, especially in his clinical work. In his theory, too, he discussed affect (especially anxiety) and gave an important place to powerful *drives* resulting from what might seem to be feeling-related processes or emotions. But the essence of Freud's theoretical system was really motivational—it was a description of motivational processes and the interplay of forces determining motives and behavior—and concern with affect independent of motivation was secondary.

While it is true that one can quote Freud as having said that "affect is primary," one can also quote Wundt (as noted by Zajonc, 1979) as having said the very same thing, even though one would hardly characterize Wundt's system as placing primary stress on feelings. And, as we have seen, Alexander Bain said something similar, as did James Mill, and so on. Freud acknowledged the importance of how things feel, but he did not undertake a systematic consideration of affect as he did motivation. Beginning with a concept of innate motivation and discussing the ways in which this motivation comes to be civilized, adapted, distorted, or whatever, the system addresses feelings only as related to motivation. Finally, of course, feelings are too available to consciousness to be of central theoretical importance in Freud's system. In very important ways, then, motivation determines both affect and, as we shall see shortly, cognition. So, all in all, we would say that Psychoanalysis is an example of a theoretical system that parallels Behaviorism in its stress on the conative. It foregoes, however, the discipline (limitation or narrowness, if you're inclined to call it that) of the latter, which restricts itself to observables, in favor of the license to postulate hypothetical structures and processes within the mind and simply to assert their operation.

Psychoanalysis and Behaviorism could not have been more different in their criteria of evidence, in their theoretical stress on observables vs inferables; but, strangely enough, what emerged in the 1940s was a marriage of the two theoretical systems in the work of Behaviorists, primarily at Yale University (Neal Miller, for example, and Dollard and others). Perhaps it was their shared stress on the conative, their disdain for viewing cognitive processes as important determinants of behavior (or feelings), or simply their contiguity in time, that led to this paradoxical union; but whatever the reason, there it was.

The Rise of Social Psychology

Enter social psychology. Actually social psychology has been running alongside for some time now, occasionally making brief appearances. Although much of early social psychology was anthropological/comparative rather than experimental in nature (Farr, 1976), as early as 1897 Triplett had begun a series of experimental studies of the effect of being alone or with others on task performance. Study of the influence of the presence of others continued during the 20th century (e.g., F. H. Allport, 1924; Dashiell, 1935; Zajonc, 1965), but in the main, social psychology diverged from this behavioristic approach, and its major focus and influence were to be in other contexts, as social psychology paralleled and utilized each of several major theoretical systems.

Social psychology has been flexible (some might say fickle) and has often adopted, or adapted itself to, the several theoretical systems in psychology, and to some extent in sociology as well, that have been influential at various times during the 20th century. This has made it seem always changing and always current. But through all of these changes, in general, social psychology has remained true to two concerns that have given it a kind of continuity, a degree of uniqueness, and the peculiarly "cognitive" cast that we noted earlier. (We say "peculiarly" because, from its name, one might expect social psychology to be concerned with the behavior of people in groups, not with the cognition of individuals.)

As explained by Farr (1976), at least one impetus for experimental social psychology to embrace cognitive hypotheses occurred when the behaviorally oriented social facilitation studies began to produce contradictory results ("social inhibition," on some occasions) that defied behavioral explanation. Researchers were led to postulate mental elements (e.g., thoughts or interpretations), events, or processes, as intervening variables to explain the observed differences in behavior. Consideration of such cognitive contents was relatively compatible with the theoretical orientations of some, as well, and psychologists such as Asch, Lewin, Sherif, and others, formulated approaches emphasizing the importance of the subject's *understanding* of the experimental situation and goals formulated on that basis.

Steiner (1979) provides an interesting alternative perspective on this issue of how social psychology "became cognitive." He proposes that this development emerged out of the question of whether the individual or the group was the appropriate unit of analysis of social behavior. McDougall's early work and that of F. H. Allport, although the two men differed on the issue of whether behavior patterns were innate or learned, agreed in stressing the idea that the fundamental causes of actions lay within individuals, even in group settings. On the other hand, G. H. Mead suggested that the group itself was the appropriate unit for analysis. His view was that the behavior of individual members of a group is a result of an interaction process that involves interdependence with other group members.

This view of the basic interdependence of group members fostered the notion that people infer one another's thoughts, feelings, and intentions, that each person in an interaction situation mentally puts himself "in the other's shoes" so that he can anticipate what response will be needed or appropriate. It is easy to see that this idea is closely related to those basic to "attribution," person perception, and other traditional "cognitive" approaches in social psychology. Thus, somewhat paradoxically, the position that the group is not the sum of its members, that it cannot be understood by simply understanding the behavior of individuals, led to the adoption of the cognitive focus in social psychology, a seemingly individualistic orientation. But note that this cognitive focus stems from the field's concern with appropriately representing the full complexity of the interaction situation.

Thus, social psychology, in its concern with social relations and variables affecting social relations, has consistently called for research relevant to real-life problems and situations. In addition, the second concern that has characterized social psychology is that from the beginning it has been troubled that attempts to study "pure" processes were truncated and incomplete, rather than "pure." One of the earliest issues that social psychology addressed in a sustained manner, probably much influenced by Külpe's suggestion, that set or attitude might influence the results of experiments being conducted by the sensory psychologists attempting to study "pure" cognition, was in the work of Gordon Allport on attitudes. This work was, in a way, a call not to study "pure" cognition, but to study "real" cognition—cognition as it actually occurs—and a call to be more aware of the complexity of factors that might influence phenomena of interest. But it was at that time a small voice in an otherwise noisy environment. Its time was yet to come.

By the 1940s, when the courtship of Hullian and Freudian theories was occurring in the behavioral laboratories, social psychologists joined the ranks of those translating Freudian concepts into Hullian language, or into experience-based (as contrasted with innate) concepts. In particular, in addition to the "frustration-aggression" hypothesis, where frustration was substituted for Freud's innate drive mechanism (Dollard, Doob, Miller, Mowrer, & Sears, 1939), social psychologists of the Yale group somewhat later addressed the question of attitude change. They based their work on the premise, derived from the Behavioral and Psychoanalytic conceptualizations, that motive determines attitude (which might be considered affect). In addition, a theoretical newcomer on the scene, the "new look in perception" (e.g., Bruner & Goodman, 1947; Bruner & Postman, 1947; McGinnies, 1949), was also based on the assumed primacy of motivation and suggested the proposition that motive can determine cognition, as well. This is just what one would expect during the hegemony of theoretical systems that stressed conation, as the Behavioral and Freudian did.

In opposition to this irresistible zeitgeist, Gestalt psychology stood as the theoretical outlier of the times. Initiated in Europe at the same time that Behaviorism was founded in the United States (Wertheimer's paper on apparent movement appeared in 1912, one year prior to the publication of Watson's "Psychology as the Behaviorist views it."), Gestalt psychology did not become well-known in the United States until the 1930s and 1940s, when the phenomenon that the Mandlers (1968) have called the "diaspora of experimental psychology" resulted in many European psychologists emigrating to the United States, to save their integrity and their careers, if not their lives. But, contemporaneously with Behaviorism and Psychoanalysis, though later in the United States, the Gestalt school was being developed, first by Wertheimer, Koffka, and Köhler and their students, and then extended and applied by the social psychologists Lewin and Heider. As we have seen in the study of thinking, in addition to opposing the introspective and elementarist associationist traditions, the Gestalt school opposed the Behaviorist position that ignored conscious experience entirely.

In terms of the trilogy of which we have been speaking, the Gestalt perspective turned the behavioral–psychoanalytic position on its head: its position was that, of the three types of content, cognition was the primary, arising out of the nervous system, as a function of the stimulus presented. Thus cognition is given and is pure, in the sense that it is unaffected by so-called "needs" or "drives." Affect and motive do not cause cognition, as the Freudians and the Freudian–Behaviorists would argue. To be sure, affect and motivation are considered in Gestalt systems—as, for example, in the concept of valence—but they are not presumed to cause or determine cognition. The three are essentially separate systems. However, if a relationship between them can be inferred, it would be that cognition is primary and that motivation and affect might be influenced by cognition more readily than the other way around.

In fact, although Gestalt psychologists did not themselves propose that cognition influenced motivation and affect, their heirs came right to the doorstep of such statements. The Laws of Good Figure and Grouping, the Balance principle, implied that certain configurations could produce affect. When Heider applied this principle to interpersonal perception and interaction, it appeared that from the Gestalt position one could derive the proposition that cognition might produce not only affect but also motivation. The clearest examples of these positions regarding the influence of cognition on motivation and affect are to be seen in the work of two of Lewin's students: in Festinger's

Theory of Cognitive Dissonance (cognition produces motivation and subsequently feelings or attitudes), and in Schachter's work with Singer on the cognitive determination of affect and behavior (cognition determines affect and subsequently, sometimes, behavior).

In a sense these positions, so central to social psychology, may seem some distance away from the Gestalt position itself, with its stress on nativism, on the holistic nature of perception, on the importance of the stimulus in the perception process. At the same time their roots can be traced to the Gestalt tradition. Likewise, Lewin, whom many consider to have been the most influential social psychologist of all, is often considered a representative of the Gestalt approach. While several historians and contemporaries of Lewin's have pointed out that he was not technically a Gestalt psychologist (e.g., Mandler & Mandler, 1968; Ash, 1980), still, it is generally accepted that he met with the Gestalt group in this country frequently and that they had mutual influence on each other. Thus many people, sensing the role of Gestalt ideas in much of this social psychological work and also tracing the origin of the early cognitive orientation in social psychology to the Gestalt approach, suggest that the Gestalt school had enormous, if indirect, influence on social psychology.[3]

IMPLICATIONS

Implications with Regard to Integration

The Trilogy. The first point that seems striking to us, as we review this brief history, is the ambivalence that most psychologists of the 20th century showed regarding integration of the trilogy of processes proposed 200 years ago. This ambivalence was reflected more in their work than in their statements. Statements regarding the importance of integration can be found in the writings of most of the theoreticians of this century as well as the last. But implementation of those statements has been another question.

Most theories, as we have seen, stressed one out of the proposed trilogy of processes; still their authors often felt obliged to consider the other aspects of experience, as well. These attempts, however, were not well-integrated into the theoretical structure. Sometimes, for example, this took the form of proposing that occasionally the central process might "spill over" to intrude upon the other spheres (as when motivation spills over into the cognitive sphere to influence perception and one notes "defensive" perception). Other times, the remaining domains

[3]In addition, Wertheimer's position on social psychology, reported by Asch (1980) from notes taken at some of Wertheimer's seminars, reveals a conception compatible with that of the cognitive social psychology model that we are proposing here. He stressed the positive side of human nature and took as his starting point a person capable of understanding and discovering things about the world and motivated to become clear about his situation. He proposed an integrated view of affect, motivation, and thinking as inseparable. It is unfortunate that these views were not published and systematically developed over the years, although they can be seen as having gained representation in Asch's (1952) work and in much of the other work mentioned here.

were dealt with separately. But, in any case, most often there were not sustained attempts at real integration of the three types of processes.

Having presented this history of what may be viewed as essentially attempts to address psychological experience from within the framework of the trilogy, and with the benefit of hindsight, we can now see that perhaps there is something self-contradictory about the form in which the trilogy has come down to us. It exhorts psychologists to be integrative and to speak to the unity of mind and of experience, but at the same time it maintains that the three types of experience are irreduceable—that they cannot be reduced to a common denominator or to common terms in which they can be addressed or considered simultaneously. It seems unlikely that they can be integrated if they can only be dealt with sequentially.

Cognitive Social Psychology and the Integration of Motivation, Affect, and Cognition. As we have seen, the tripartite view itself has not been a helpful integrator, but clear alternatives have not taken hold. As we have also seen, cognitive social psychology proposes an integrated view of these cognitive, motivational/behavioral, and affective components of mind and thus may have something to contribute regarding the general question of integration.

The view fostered by cognitive social psychology emphasizes the mutuality and simultaneity of these three processes. This is *not* necessarily the same as saying that they interrelate or interact. One possible form of integration is that of interaction or mutual influence. But we would like to suggest another—that these three components of experience can be understood in each other's terms, and in this case, more specifically, that they can be understood in terms of cognitive processes.

How can affect and motivation be understood as the results of cognitive processes? Feelings, motivations, and situational constraints of which we are aware are, by definition, conscious and are experienced consciously as affect, motivation, etc. (These, like cognitive elements such as thoughts or interpretations, might be called "content.") But, just as we pointed out earlier for "thoughts" of which people are aware, these awarenesses are the *results* of process. They are the end states in which we find ourselves. Though the states involve feelings, desires, etc., rather than the more "intellectual" or "cognitive" content represented by thoughts, evaluations, or estimates, the processes that produce them can be described as cognitive processes. Actually, an integrative view of these expressions of psychological experience (cognition, motivation/behavior, and affect) would hold that any one can be understood in the terms of any other. Our model, while acknowledging this in principle, expresses a preference for the cognitive as a set of processes by which to understand behavior.

One reason for choosing the cognitive set of processes is their apparent centrality in human life and activity, and in the definition of being human. It is almost a truism to point out that many regard cognitive activity as the essential mark of humankind (*Homo sapiens*).

Another reason for choosing the cognitive as a set of processes in which to attempt the understanding of behavior, however, is that much more is known about them than about alternative processes. In part this is because, through centuries of thought and integrative interaction with other fields, the study of cognition has begun to develop the flexible units and conceptualizations of psychological process that lend themselves to integrative use.

We are aware that entirely alternative approaches to integration are available. For example, one could propose simply that these processes interact with each other. The problem then becomes, however, one of how to formulate and study such interaction systematically. Ulrich Neisser, in his groundbreaking book, *Cognitive Psychology* (1967), recognized the importance of affective and motivational processes in cognition and the need to consider all three at once; but he stopped short of proposing the full integration that we are suggesting is possible. For example, although he noted the importance of motivation and context in cognitive processes, still he defined motivation out of the cognitive sphere, ascribing it to a realm that he called "dynamic," and he was then not able to suggest a means of integrating such factors.

While we applaud the vision expressed in Neisser's book, we would suggest that motivation (and affect) can be viewed as a part of the cognitive process rather than as an outsider knocking at the door to disrupt the feast. We would propose that one can think of motives as goals and plans, for example, that vary with circumstances. They can be influenced by representational (cognitive) processes—interpretation of context, coexisting goals, organization in memory, etc.—and they can influence perception and evaluation cognitively, via some of these same processes. Thus they can be conceptualized fully as cognitive processes. They need not be thought of as arising in some other domain and merely interacting with cognitive processes in ways that then are difficult to specify; they are part of the cognitive process.

From a slightly different perspective, Irwin (1971) has proposed a cognitive theory of motivation based on Tolman's principles of purposive behavior. Here, too, affect and motivation are conceptualized as part of the overall cognitive formulation. This provides a tool that may aid in the eventual understanding of these processes as well as of the cognitive. Likewise, we are suggesting that all aspects of experience are expressed at once, have cognitive representation and impact, and can be understood as cognitive processes. (In addition, however, we are proposing that attention be paid directly to understanding these cognitive processes.)

A final example of the utility of this proposed form of integration is provided in response to Hilgard's call for integration of cognitive, affective, and motivational aspects of experience in the study of behavior (1980). He points out that when we become caught up in understanding, for example, a child's cognitive processes, ". . . we are apt to forget that children's lives are affected by sibling rivalries as well as by stages in cognitive growth" (p. 115). Still, it is not clear from this suggestion how one should go about integrating these components. Some might infer from this observation that the processes must be dealt with sequentially, that in order to attend to "sibling rivalry" one must abandon attention to cognition. We would propose, to the contrary, that while the warning that we not forget the domains of affect and motivation is helpful, the implication that these must be studied separately from cognition need not be drawn.

Rather, we would suggest that "sibling rivalry" can be viewed and addressed within a cognitive framework—as a certain set of goals, expectations, and perceived behavioral alternatives, given a certain set of circumstances. By looking at how the child views his situation, what his goals are, and what he sees as options, we can come to "understand" his feelings and behavior. As has been suggested by cognitively oriented personality theorists and therapists from George Kelly to Meichenbaum and Goldfried more recently, this understanding may be more useful than that obtained by simply labeling his feelings and behaviors as the result of "sibling rivalry" or some other "basic motive" that one can then only accept or suppress. If we know how the situation looks to the child and the cognitive processes that contribute to his view, we may be able to help him address the situation differently and possibly, if conditions are right, resolve the problem. Sometimes, for example, this may involve parents changing their behavior as they come to realize how it appears to the child.

Implications with Regard to Affect

The second point that emerges from consideration of the history that we have presented is the relative neglect of affect over the centuries. There were zeitgeists that stressed cognition, and individual cognitive theories arose during these times; and there was a movement for motivation or conation, with appropriate theories dominating the scene during those times. But there was never even a single theory, much less a zeitgeist, that postulated the centrality of affect and encouraged the systematic study of affect. Even those theories that did mention affect either cast it in the role of an epiphenomenon or treated it unsystematically.

Why affect has received for the most part only indirect consideration is something of a mystery. People seem not to have been able to define it satisfactorily, and perhaps this has had a lot to do with its relative neglect. Affect overlaps both cognition and conation: it seems constantly in danger of being confused with motivation and, frequently, even with cognition (as in the case of attitudes, for example). How should affect be defined and studied?

Attempts to define feeling states physiologically have not met with clear success, to say the least. When all is said and done, despite sustained and repeated efforts to uncover specific physiological states associated with specific emotional states, and despite some promising leads (e.g., Ax, 1953), Cannon's 1927 statement that we have not achieved a set of independent physiological definitions of feeling states seems as true today as it seemed 50 years ago (Cannon, 1927; Grossman, 1973; Hassett, 1978; Lacey, 1975; Woodworth & Shlosberg, 1954). At the same time, attempts to define affect in terms of general arousal or activation (Duffy, 1934; Lindsley, 1951), in accord with Cannon's formulation, have likewise proved disappointing (Lacey, 1959, 1967, 1975; Lacey, Kagan, Lacey, & Moss, 1963). Attempts to understand affective states as generalized arousal coupled with specific labels on the basis of external conditions (e.g., Schachter & Singer, 1962) or more generally in terms of misattribution of "arousal" (e.g., Valins, 1966) have come under recent criticism as well (e.g., Lacey, 1975; Leventhal, 1979).

Thus, the attempt to define emotional states physiologically has proved maddeningly complex, and the cognitive labeling hypotheses have still to be refined. And otherwise, with a few exceptions, despite remarkably sensitive insights on the part of many of those who write about emotion, the study of emotion seems in a relatively early stage of development. Its subject matter is not yet agreed upon, nor are the units of analysis well worked out. Only recently has research on emotional states begun to develop definitions and units other than those rooted in the common language and, in many cases, in introspection [for an example of an alternative approach, see Leventhal (1974, 1979)]. In some systems, for instance, joy and sorrow are considered "opposites" in a symmetrical system that resembles a color wheel. Thus they are considered in some sense equal except for sign. Anger and fear are likewise "opposites," although of the same sign. Yet the basis of these assumptions is not clear,[4] and their adequacy and utility are essentially untested.

As Mandler (1975b) points out, there is no reason to expect that the common language terms for emotions will serve as adequate tools for the scientific analysis of affect. These terms may not lead us to the kinds of units and levels of analysis that will allow us to develop powerful formulations. The question is even more basic than that of whether "joy" and "sorrow" or "anger" and "fear" are opposites. The question is whether such terms as "joy" and "sorrow" are the appropriate ones for analysis. We suspect that the answer to the question of how to represent affect in order to be able to study it will require the same kind of attention to the problem, over a period of decades, that was required before sophisticated flexible definitions of cognitive processes began to emerge. Perhaps the task will be even more difficult for affect because it is so volatile.

A New Emphasis on Affect. Even now, however, there seems to be increasing interest in affect as a subject for investigation in psychology. Social psychology, in particular, seems to be making a place for affect in its research and theory. Cognitive social psychology, with its emphasis on integration and the realistic representation of decision-making con-

[4]The conceptualization of anger and fear as opposites has been said to be based on Cannon's stress on the body's preparation for fight or flight. Yet, as we have seen, Cannon's position was that the *same* physiological changes occurred in many emotions, and he would not likely have argued for defining these states as "opposites" on a physiological basis. Moreover, other authors (e.g., Woodworth & Shlosberg, 1954) have suggested that anger and fear, or at least the facial expressions accompanying these states, are seen as closely related rather than "opposites."

texts, is especially concerned with development of the study of affect and inclusion of this perspective in the field. Its proposal that affect, cognition, and motivation be considered together, and possibly in a single set of terms, encourages (and may facilitate) the study of affect.

As we see it, psychology's attention to affect may take any of a number of forms. First, it is possible that affect will continue to be regarded essentially as an epiphenomenon and that its investigation will be unsystematic, even haphazard. This will occur, for example, if one or another moribund theories is resurrected as a device for addressing questions concerning affect; or even more likely, if affect is breathed into a dying theoretical system in an attempt to save it—as, for example, if evidence of the importance of affect were used to conclude that "Freud was right" (affect is primary) and thus to spur studies dictated by psychoanalytic theory and designed to promote it. We hope that this will not be the path that the field will follow because this will again relegate affect to the status of epiphenomenon, by-product, or derived construct in an existing formulation that has already given all it has to give. But we are encouraged because there is already some indication that attention will focus on affect as an important issue in its own right.

This brings us to the second possibility. That is, that affect will become the new "first cause," the new basis of some limited, ad hoc, and loosely organized set of postulates, in which affect will be cast in the role of "driver." Where, previously, motivation was seen as driving cognition, and then cognition was seen as driving motivation, now will affect come to be seen as the cause or shaper of cognition and motivation? Perhaps this will be the road that affect travels, but we hope not. Such a conceptualization seems just as incomplete as those that preceded it. Surely, if we have learned one thing in the past 80 years, it is that all of these three processes can be demonstrated to affect each other under at least some conditions.

Cognitive Social Psychology and Affect. In contrast, and in keeping with what we have described throughout this chapter as the orientation of cognitive social psychology, what we would see as most welcome would be, first, attention to the processes themselves involved in affect. Second, to the extent that people address the question of the influence of affect on cognition or motivation, we would encourage attention to their simultaneous influence on each other and on actions. Third, we would suggest that these influences can best be addressed through a systematic consideration of the conditions under which each of various types of relationships occurs, in the unifying context or perspective of intentional behavior.

This proposition for the study of affect is integrative and based on the assumption that the tripartite components of mind are mutually interactive and can be viewed simultaneously. It even welcomes the proposal that they can be understood in one set of terms, for the time being the cognitive. It is thus incompatible with the concept of the trilogy of mind as irreduceable faculties or components of experience.

An alternative possibility, however, is that the three systems are not freely interactive but are, as originally proposed, truly irreduceable. If this is the case, then another possibility for today's attention to affect is that it may produce an entirely new theoretical system, one based on affective process rather than cognitive or behavioral process. This would be compatible with all of the basic assumptions of cognitive social psychology (e.g., focus on process, broadened conceptualization of the action situation), differing only with the suggestion above that the systems can be represented in each other's terms. Indeed, the current work of Zajonc (1979), proposing that affect is distinct from cognition and is processed distinctively, may be a step in that very direction. And Howard Leventhal's (1974, 1979) papers on the topic, proposing an innate perceptual mechanism for the generation and processing of affect, may contribute to that development as well.

COGNITIVE SOCIAL PSYCHOLOGY APPLIED

Our final note is that the approach suggested by cognitive social psychology has something to contribute in the important growing trend among psychologists to involve themselves in the study of complex problems as they occur in life and society. Many, but especially social psychologists, in increasing numbers are working in such settings as the criminal justice system, the medical care system, and the educational system, to name just a few examples, trying to address the life and societal problems that press us for solutions. Also increasing is the sophistication of these psychologists regarding the need to represent the problems that they confront in those settings fully and accurately. The need for an integrated approach, such as that fostered by cognitive social psychology, one that takes cognizance of the importance of context, of framing, and of actors' perceived goals, is nowhere more apparent than it is in these applied settings.

For an example of this need, consider the following: Cross-cultural psychologists such as Cole and his associates (Cole & Scribner, 1974; Scribner, 1978) have recently pointed out and described a phenomenon that they discovered in the course of their studies of the intelligence or cognitive processes of unschooled peoples. Referred to as the "empirical bias" of such people, this phenomenon calls attention to the need to consider the respondent's perspective or goals, in evaluating his or her behavior. It is illustrated in the following two excerpts:

1. EXPERIMENTER: Flumo and Yakpalo always drink cane juice (rum) together. Flumo is drinking cane juice. Is Yakpalo drinking cane juice?

   SUBJECT: Flumo and Yakpalo drink cane juice together, but the time Flumo was drinking the first one Yakpalo was not there on that day.

   EXPERIMENTER: But I told you that Flumo and Yakpalo always drink cane juice together. One day Flumo was drinking cane juice. Was Yakpalo drinking cane juice that day?

SUBJECT: That day Flumo was drinking the cane juice Yakpalo was not there on that day.

EXPERIMENTER: What is the reason?

SUBJECT: The reason is that Yakpalo went to his farm on that day and Flumo remained in town on that day (Cole, Gay, Glick, & Sharp, 1971, 187 – 188).

2. EXPERIMENTER: All Kpelle men are rice farmers.
Mr. Smith is not a rice farmer.
Is he a Kpelle man?

SUBJECT: I don't know the man in person. I have not laid eyes on the man himself.

EXPERIMENTER: Just think about the statement.

SUBJECT: If I know him in person, I can answer that question, but since I do not know him in person I cannot answer that question.

EXPERIMENTER: Try and answer from your Kpelle sense.

SUBJECT: If you know a person, if a question comes up about him you are able to answer. But if you do not know the person, if a question comes up about him, it's hard for you to answer it. (Scribner, 1978, p. 490)

In the second example, because the respondent explains his perspective to us, it is clear that he is not engaging in the reasoning task at all and regards the problem as unanswerable or perhaps "improper." But in the first example, the distraction provided by the empirical bias comes across more subtly, and if the experimenter is not careful to take the respondent's perspective and goals into account as a matter of course, she may make serious errors regarding the subject matter—the respondent's "intelligence" or reasoning process. As Cole and Scribner (1974, p. 166) say, "It is quite clear that we cannot draw conclusions about reasoning processes from the *answers* people give to logic problems. We have first to ask: 'What is their understanding of the task? How do they encode the information presented to them? What transformations does the information undergo, and what factors control these?' "

The relevance of this illustration to cognitive social psychology and to the utility and importance of its approach in applied settings should be apparent. These excerpts illustrate, as many cross-cultural researchers have pointed out, that cognitive processes are situation-dependent (for example, Scribner & Cole, 1973). They also show, as Neisser (1976b) has noted, that the experimenter's and respondent's interpretations of the task may differ. They indicate that one is likely to go entirely wrong in understanding interactions and in drawing conclusions regarding even concepts such as intelligence if one does not look at the task as the respondent sees it and interpret the respondent's behavior in terms of what she or he is trying to do in the situation. We suggest that the same process is advisable generally and that it will be especially crucial not only in officially "cross-cultural" studies such as Cole and Scribner's, but in any applied setting where one is likely to encounter people from differing molds and in unaccustomed contexts.

At the same time, the need for vigorous scientific orientation and method is not in the least bit diminished in applied settings. Unfortunately, it is sometimes obscured by the complexity and urgency of the problems to be resolved. The dreaded "holistic paralysis" (or inability to take action because of perceived complexity) found in laboratories and universities has an equally dangerous field-setting counterpart, "desperation's disease." The major sequella of this malady is succumbing to the pressure to conduct methodologically incomplete and inadequate research or to take action even when one has no basis for action. This is very likely a response to complexity, just as paralysis is, but it is a variant that results under the pressure for action that is endemic to applied settings. The approach offered by cognitive social psychology may help researchers and practitioners to maintain their scientific perspective and standards, because it provides them with an orientation and additional tools for systematically addressing the complexity encountered in these settings. Thus it may enable them to plan and carry out meaningful, large-scale research and intervention efforts rather than desperate shots in the dark.

CONCLUSION

Cognitive social psychology represents a confluence of the foci and developments that have been influential in the evolution of modern cognitive and social psychology. It contains elements of each of these fields, but it differs from each as well. It draws on their shared ancestry (as, for example, in the work of people such as the Würzburg psychologists and Sir Frederick Bartlett) and on their distinctive accomplishments to suggest not a revolutionary new approach, but an integrative new approach. More specifically, this new field attempts to understand cognitive processes more broadly, and attempts to understand social behavior systematically in terms of the cognitive processes involved in purposive social behavior. It adopts the social psychologist's traditional concern with complex social behavior, the unifying perspective of purposive behavior as a context in which both social and nonsocial psychological events occur, and the cognitive psychologist's tools, accumulated knowledge, focus on process, and model that addresses questions of cognitive representation and constructive process.

Our hope is that cognitive social psychology, being not just in name but in a very real sense a product of these two subfields of psychology, will contribute to integration in the field and to improved communication between its subfields. We also hope that the approach embodied in cognitive social psychology will help our field to address some of the major societal and life problems with which people are faced. The chapters included in this volume illustrate only part of the range of topics that are encompassed by the field, only some of the issues that can be addressed by it, and only a sampling of the approaches that are fostered by it.

REFERENCES

Abelson, R. P. Computer simulation of "hot" cognition. In S. Tomkins and S. Messick (Eds.), *Computer simulation of personality.* New York: Wiley, 1963.

Allport, F. *Social psychology.* Boston, Mass.: Houghton Mifflin, 1924.

Allport, G. The historical background of modern social psychology. In G. Lindzey and E. Aronson (Eds.), *Handbook of social psychology,* Vol. 1. Reading, Mass.: Addison-Wesley, 1967.

Arnold, M. B. *Feelings and emotions.* New York: Academic, 1970.

Asch, S. *Social psychology.* Englewood Cliffs, N.J.: Prentice-Hall, 1952.

Asch, S. Max Wertheimer: Memories and reflections. Address delivered as part of the symposium, "Gestalt theory: Celebrating the centenary of Max Wertheimer's birth," annual meeting of the American Psychological Association, Montreal, 1980.

Ash, M. G. Gestalt theory in two cultures: Thesis for discussion. For the symposium, "Gestalt theory: Celebrating the centenary of Max Wertheimer's birth," at the Annual Meeting of the American Psychological Association, Montreal, 1980.

Ax, A. F. The physiological differentiation between anger and fear in humans. *Psychosomatic Medicine,* 1953, *15,* 433 –442.

Bartlett, F. C. *Remembering: A study in experimental and social psychology.* New York: Cambridge University Press, 1932.

Brown, A. Priming effects in semantic memory retrieval processes. *Journal of Experimental Psychology: Human Learning and Memory,* 1979, *5,* 65 –77.

Bruner, J. S. & Goodman, C. C. Value and need as organizing factors in perception. *Journal of Abnormal and Social Psychology,* 1947, *42,* 33 –44.

Bruner, J. S., & Postman, L. Emotional selectivity in perception and reaction. *Journal of Personality,* 1947, *16,* 69 –77.

Cannon, W. B. The James –Lange theory of emotions: A critical examination and an alternative. *American Journal of Psychology,* 1927, *39,* 106 –124.

Cartwright, D., & Zander, A. *Group dynamics: Research and theory.* New York: Harper & Row, 1968.

Cole, M., & Scribner, S. *Culture and thought: A psychological introduction.* New York: Wiley, 1974.

Cole, M., Gay, J., Glick, J., & Sharp, D. *The cultural context of learning and thinking.* New York: Basic Books, 1971.

Dashiell, J. F. Experimental studies of the influence of social situations on the behavior of individual human adults. In C. A. Murchison (Ed.), *Handbook of Social Psychology,* Vol. 2. Worcester, Mass.: Clark University Press, 1935.

Dollard, J., Doob, L., Miller, N., Mowrer, O. H., & Sears, R. *Frustration and aggression.* New Haven, Conn.: Yale University Press, 1939.

Duffy, E. Emotion: An example of the need for reorientation in psychology. *Psychological Review,* 1934, *41,* 184 –198.

Easterbrook, J. A. The effect of emotion on cue utilization and the organization of behavior. *Psychological Review,* 1959, *66,* 183 –201.

Farr, R. M. Experimentation: A social psychological perspective. *British Journal of Social and Clinical Psychology,* 1976, *15,* 225 –238.

Grossman, S. P. *Essentials of physiological psychology.* New York: Wiley, 1973.

Hassett, J. *A primer of psychophysiology.* San Francisco, Calif.: Freeman, 1978.

Hilgard, E. R. The trilogy of mind: Cognition, affection and conation. *Journal of the History of the Behavioral Sciences,* 1980, *16,* 107 –117.

Irwin, F. *Intentional behavior and motivation: A cognitive theory.* Philadelphia, Pa.: Lippincott, 1971.

James, W. *The principles of psychology.* New York: Dover, 1890.

Jenkins, J. J. Remember that old theory of memory? Well forget it! *American Psychologist,* 1974, *29,* 785 –795.

Lacey, J. I. Psychophysiological approaches to the evaluation of psychotherapeutic process and outcome. In E. A. Rubenstein and M. B. Parloff (Eds.), *Research in psychotherapy.* Washington, D.C.: American Psychological Association, 1959.

Lacey, J. I. Somatic response patterning and stress: Some revisions of activation theory. In M. H. Appley and R. Trumbul (Eds.), *Psychological stress: Issues in research.* New York: Appleton-Century-Crofts, 1967, 14 –44.

Lacey, J. I. Psychophysiology of the autonomic nervous system, In J. R. Nazzaro (Ed.), *Master lectures on physiological psychology.* Washington, D.C.: American Psychological Association, 1975.

Lacey, J. I., Kagan, J., Lacey, B. C., & Moss, H. A. The visceral level: Situational determinants and behavioral correlates of autonomic response patterns. In P. H. Knapp (Ed.), *Expressions of the emotions in man.* New York: International Universities Press, 1963.

Leeper, R. W. A motivational theory of emotion to replace "emotion as disorganized response." *Psychological Review,* 1948, *55,* 5 –21.

Leeper, R. W. The motivational and perceptual properties of emotions indicating their fundamental character and role. In M. B. Arnold (Ed.), *Feelings and emotions.* New York: Academic, 1970.

Leventhal, H. Emotions: A basic problem for social psychology. In C. Nemeth (Ed.), *Social psychology: Classic and contemporary integrations.* New York: Rand McNally, 1974.

Leventhal, H. A perceptual-motor processing model of emotion. In R. Pliner, K. R. Blankenstein, & I. M. Spigel (Eds.), *Advances in the study of communication and affect,* Vol. 5. New York: Plenum, 1979.

Lindsley, D. B. Emotion. In S. S. Stevens (Ed.), *Handbook of experimental psychology.* New York: Wiley, 1951.

McDougall, W. *Outline of psychology.* New York: Scribner, 1923.

Mandler, G. *Mind and emotion.* New York: Wiley, 1975. (a)

Mandler, G. Consciousness: Respectable, useful, and probably necessary. In R. L. Solso (Ed.), *Information processing and cognition.* The Loyola Symposium. Hillsdale, N.J.: Erlbaum, 1975. (b)

Mandler, J. M., & Mandler, G. *Thinking: From association to Gestalt.* New York: Wiley, 1964.

Mandler, J. M., & Mandler, G. The diaspora of experimental psychology: The Gestaltists and others. In *The intellectual migration: Europe and America, 1930 –1960.* Cambridge, Mass.: Harvard University Press, 1968, 371 –419.

McGinnies, E. Emotionality and perceptual defense. *Psychological Review,* 1949, *56,* 244 –251.

Mendelssohn, M. *Letters on sensation,* 1755. Referenced in J. E. Erdmann, *A history of philosophy,* Vol. 2. London: Swan Sonnenschein, 1892.

Neely, J. H. Semantic priming and retrieval from lexical memory: Evidence for facilitory and inhibitory processes. *Memory and Cognition,* 1976, *4,* 648 –654.

Neely, J. H. Semantic priming and retrieval from lexical memory: Roles of inhibitionless spreading activation and limited capacity attention. *Journal of Experimental Psychology,* 1977, *106,* 226 –254.

Neisser, U. *Cognitive psychology.* New York: Appleton-Century-Crofts, 1967.

Neisser, U. *Cognition and reality: Principles and implications of cognitive psychology.* San Francisco, Calif.: Freeman, 1976. (a)

Neisser, U. General, academic, and artificial intelligence. In L. Resnick (Ed.), *The nature of intelligence.* Hillsdale, N.J.: Erlbaum, 1976. (b)

Neisser, U. Discussion. Part of the symposium, "Gestalt theory: Celebrating the centenary of Max Wertheimer's birth," at the annual meeting of the American Psychological Association, Montreal, 1980.

Posner, M. I., & Snyder, C. R. R. Attention and cognitive control. In R. L. Solso (Ed.), *Information processing and cognition: The Loyola symposium*. Hillsdale, N.J.: Erlbaum, 1975.

Schachter, S., & Singer, J. L. Cognitive, social, and physiological determinants of emotional state. *Psychological Review*, 1962, *69*, 379 –399.

Scribner, S. Modes of thinking and ways of speaking: Culture and logic reconsidered. In Johnson Laird (Ed.), *Thinking*. London: Cambridge University Press, 1978.

Scribner, S., & Cole, M. Cognitive consequences of formal and informal education. *Science*, 1973, *182*, 553 –559.

Simon, H. A. Motivational and emotional controls of cognition. *Psychological Review*, 1967, *74*, 29 –39.

Steiner, I. Social Psychology. In E. Hearst (Ed.), *The first century of experimental psychology*. Hillsdale, N.J.: Erlbaum, 1979.

Triplett, N. The dynamogenic factors in pace-making and competition. *American Journal of Psychology*, 1897 –98, *4*, 507 –533.

Tversky, A., & Kahneman, D. The framing of decisions and the rationality of choice. Unpublished manuscript, Stanford University, Palo Alto, Calif., 1980.

Valins, S. Cognitive effects of false heart rate feedback. *Journal of Personality and Social Psychology*, 1966, *4*, 400 –408.

Woodworth, R. S., & Shlosberg, H. *Experimental psychology*. New York: Holt, Rinehart and Winston, 1954.

Young, P. T. *Emotions in man and animal*. New York: Wiley, 1943.

Young, P. T. *Motivation and emotion*. New York: Wiley, 1961.

Zajonc, R. B. Social facilitation. *Science*, 1965, *149*, 269 –274.

Zajonc, R. B. Feeling and thinking: Preferences need no inferences. Distinguished Scientific Contribution Award address, presented at the annual meeting of the American Psychological Association, New York, 1979.

NANCY CANTOR WALTER MISCHEL JUDITH SCHWARTZ

SOCIAL KNOWLEDGE:

STRUCTURE, CONTENT, USE, AND ABUSE

This chapter is organized around the following five general questions about the study of social knowledge and cognition:

1. *The Multiple Focus Question:* What are the various different overarching schemes that people use to organize and categorize social experience?
2. *The Accessibility Question:* Are some organizations and constructions very accessible and frequently and easily used to structure and encode social experience?
3. *The Structure Question:* How orderly, complex, and consensually agreed upon are the internal, cognitive representations of social experience?
4. *The Content Question:* What kinds of information do we represent and store about social experience?
5. *The Function Question:* How and under what conditions is social knowledge used in generating and planning social behavior?

First, we will take up the cognitive categorization schemes that people use to structure social experience; then we will consider factors that influence the accessibility and use of these various organizational schemes. Next, we will examine research about the structure and content of social knowledge. Finally, we will consider perhaps the most difficult question: how does social knowledge function in the generation of social behavior?

CATEGORIZATIONS: ON WHAT DO WE FOCUS?

A fundamental quality of cognition is the tendency to categorize both objects and people into groups, types, or other categories so that nonidentical stimuli can be treated as if they were equivalent (Rosch, Mervis, Gray, Johnson, & Boyes-Braem, 1976). To simplify the complex flood of information from the world, people sort things and other human beings according to similarities in their essential features, forming natural categories and communicating about the similarities and differences between these "kinds" or "types" (of tables, of clothes, of friends) through shared category labels. Categorization schemes allow us to structure and give coherence to our general knowledge about people and the social world, providing expectations about typical patterns of behavior and the range of likely variation between types of people and their characteristic actions and attributes. Every social experience serves to enrich one's knowledge of the probable behavior and attributes of different types of persons in different social contexts.

A great deal of research on social cognition has focused on the consequences of categorization (for example, in the form of "stereotyping"). Much less attention has been devoted to the structure and genesis of people's natural categories about the social world. We know much more about the end results of the categorization process than about its initial stages. What are the salient units for the categorization of people? At what level of abstraction do we find and/or perceive coherent, meaningful "person types"? What configurations of behavioral evidence tend to activate a particular person category? What rules underlie how we naturally categorize people? Questions of this kind have recently begun to receive increasing attention (e.g., Higgins, Herman, & Zanna, 1980) and have been central in our explorations of natural categories in social cognition (e.g., Cantor & Mischel, 1979). We began by studying natural categories about types of persons (introverts, used-car salesmen) and then turned to the ways in which people categorize types of psychological situations (parties, libraries).

The Categorical-Prototype Approach

Our studies of social knowledge have been guided by a *categorical-prototype* approach, which we will illustrate over the course of this chapter. This approach begins with the realization that, while the borders of categories may be fuzzy [as Wittgenstein (1953) first noted], the central, clearest examples of each category may be quite distinct from those in other categories. Just as recent efforts in cognitive psychology have focused on studying the "clear" or prototypical examples of categories rather than on the fuzzy, borderline ones, students of social knowledge need to identify the prototypical cases and the rules used to judge prototypicality in the categorization of people and psychological situations.

The search for prototypes, rather than for trait dimensions, avoids some of the central assumptions of classical trait psychology and therefore, it is hoped, also avoids some of its pitfalls and empirical limitations (Mischel, 1968).

Briefly, our approach draws an analogy between the properties of categories used to label and describe common objects (like tables and chairs) and those used to classify people and everyday situations (Cantor & Mischel, 1979). In particular, we have borrowed extensively from recent "revisionist" perspectives on natural language classification (cf. Smith & Medin, 1979). According to the revisionist position, knowledge about any given category is structured around, and represented in, long-term memory as a *prototype* that captures the meaning of the category. The prototype serves as a symbol and reference point for the category. The category prototype can take on many forms depending on the domain: for instance, prototypes have been variously defined as (1) the central tendency of a set of geometric forms, defined as the mean value of the set of stimulus objects on each relevant feature dimension (see, for example, Posner & Keele, 1968; Reed, 1972); (2) a representative set of exemplars of the category (see, for example, Ebbesen & Allen, 1979; Medin & Schaffer, 1978; Smith & Medin, 1979; Walker, 1975); or (3) an abstract set of features commonly associated with members of a category, with each feature assigned a weight according to degree of association with the category (see, for example, Cantor & Mischel, 1979; Cantor, Smith, French, & Mezzich, 1980; Rosch & Mervis, 1975; Smith & Medin, 1979). This abstract feature set prototype has been the one most extensively studied and used in investigations of natural language categorization (cf. Rosch, 1978; Rosch et al., 1976). Cantor and Mischel (1979) and Cantor et al. (1980) have also found this form of the prototype model to be useful in characterizing the naive observer's beliefs about different categories of persons like extraverts, manic-depressives and comic-jokers.

In our first applications of this approach to person taxonomies, we examined the characteristics of person categories at different levels of inclusiveness or abstraction and searched for rules used to identify prototypical exemplars of person categories (Cantor & Mischel, 1979). These efforts allowed us to explore the similarities and differences between person and object categorization, as well as shedding some light on the nature of different kinds of conceptual units commonly used to construe people's personalities and social behavior. Our investigations included the lay perceiver's categorical knowledge about types of personalities and everyday social situations, and the nature and richness of the features commonly associated with different kinds of people and situations (e.g., Cantor, 1980; Cantor & Mischel, 1979).

Our initial studies adhered to the traditional distinction between social knowledge about persons (extraverts and knee-jerk liberals) and situations (parties and election nights). Therefore we sought separate taxonomies of types of persons and types of everyday situations. Sam-

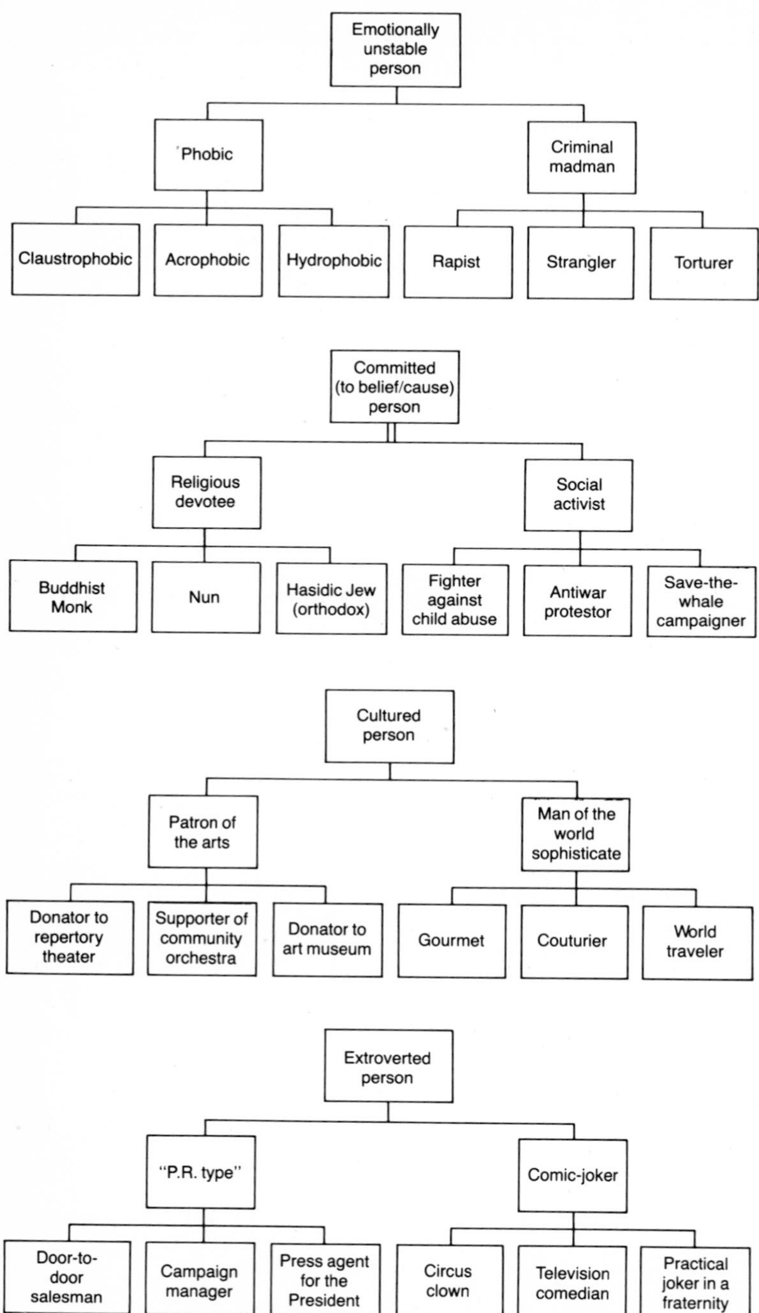

FIGURE 1. Three-level person taxonomies.

IDEOLOGICAL	SOCIAL	STRESSFUL	CULTURAL
Being in an Ideological[a] Situation	**Being in a Social Situation**	**Being in a Stressful Situation**	**Being in a Cultural Situation**
Being at a Demonstration for a Cause[b]	Being at a Party	Being Imprisoned	Being on a Tour
being at an antiwar demonstration[c]	being at a fraternity party	being in a county jail	being on a tour of old English castles
being at a save-the-whales sit-in	being at a cocktail party	being in a state penitentiary	being on a tour of European museums
being on a union picket line	being at a birthday party	being in a hospital for the criminally insane	being on a tour of Roman ruins
Being at a Religious Ceremony[b]	Being on a Date	Being at an Interview	Being at the Performing Arts
being at Sunday Mass[c]	being on a first date	being at a job interview	being at the symphony
being at a revival meeting	being on a double date	being at an admissions interview	being at the ballet
being at a barmitzvah	being on a blind date	being at a psychiatric interview	being at the theater

[a]Superordinate level. [b]Middle level. [c]Subordinate level.

FIGURE 1. Three-level situation taxonomies *(continued)*

ple person taxonomies and situation taxonomies are illustrated in Figure 1. Before directly considering our findings on these cognitive-social schemes, we must summarize the methodology of our categorical-prototype approach.

Methodology of the Categorical-Prototype Approach

The prototype view [as articulated by Rosch (1978) and Smith and Medin (1979)] has provided a research strategy that can be readily adapted to study the naive observer's categorical knowledge of situations and persons. Our investigations generally involve the following steps (see, for example, Cantor, 1980; Cantor & Mischel, 1979; Cantor et al., 1980). First, we establish taxonomies of commonly used categories in the particular domain under consideration—be it taxonomies of personality categories, categories of psychiatric disorders, or categories of situations. To establish the taxonomies, we generally turn first to professionals in the particular field—personologists for person taxonomies and psychiatrists for psychiatric ones—and obtain widely used category labels. For exmple, the person taxonomies illustrated in Figure 1 were obtained from many factor analytic studies in the field of personality (see Norman, 1963). Next, we verify that these are meaningful taxonomies for the "naive" perceiver by asking untrained undergraduates to perform a card-sorting task. Each student receives a shuffled deck of cards, each card containing one category label, and must create his/her own hierarchical taxonomies. These card-sorting data are then submitted to cluster analyses (using a hierarchical clustering program) to verify that the naive and professional psychologists agree on the same hierarchies.

After verification of the taxonomies, the next step is to obtain prototypes for each category in each taxonomy. In our research, the category prototype is taken to be a list of attributes that people generally agree upon as common to and characteristic of members of the category. (The list of attributes is only "roughly correlated" with category membership—not every category member will have *all* of these attributes, and not every perceiver will see *all* of the attributes as relevant to the category.) To generate these prototypes, we ask our subjects to list the attributes that they see as characteristic of members of a category. (Each subject generally lists attributes for only one category from each taxonomy, all of these categories being taken from the same level of abstraction—e.g., a particular subject might generate a prototype for Interview, for Party, for Tour, and for Demonstration for a Cause.) In generating these attribute lists, subjects are completely free to include anything and everything they see as associated with the category—no guidelines or restrictions are provided by the experimenter.

At the end of this stage, we have several separate attribute lists for each category. To obtain a single prototype list for each category, we extract the attributes listed in at least 2 or 3 or 4 of these (10 −13) individual lists and thus combine these lists to obtain a (loosely) *consensual prototype* for each category. So, we look at the 10 *party* lists and include in the prototype list only those attributes that had been listed by at least 2 of the 10 subjects. Frequently, we also ask new judges to estimate the percentage of category members that would have each attribute in the consensual prototype list. For example, judges estimate the percentage of *parties* with *dancing*. These percentage weights can be used as a further criterion for inclusion in the final consensual prototype; for example, only those attributes estimated to be true of 50% or more of the members of a category would be included in the consensual prototype for that category. This procedure, then, provides a freely generated prototype for each category in each taxonomy. [For further details the reader can consult our empirical papers (Cantor, Smith, French, & Mezzich, 1980; Cantor, Mischel, & Schwartz, 1981).] These (consensual) prototypes can then be examined to test hypotheses about the *richness* of situation or person prototypes, the *hierarchical well-formedness* of these taxonomies, and the *content* of the attributes commonly associated with everyday situation and person categories. Examples of such work will be considered throughout the chapter (see the sections on accessibility and utility, structure, and content).

Person-In-Situation Prototypes

As mentioned above, and illustrated in Figure 1, we began our studies intending to examine natural categories for persons and for situations separately. Traditionally, professional psychologists tended to partition the social world into persons and situations, viewing each as distinct sources of variance whose relative contributions to the genesis of social behavior could be and should be separately assessed and partitioned (e.g., Endler & Hunt, 1969). Indeed, the relative potency of persons versus situations as independent causes of human behavior has been debated hotly (e.g., Bowers, 1973; Carlson, 1971). While the person-situation distinction may have been useful in some studies of social knowledge, it is by no means clear that natural social cognition follows such a dichotomy. Naive knowledge systems may not be organized around such discrete entities as "persons" and "situations." Rather, the richest, most lifelike and useful cognitive-social structures may be compound in nature; amalgams of generalizations about people-in-situations or life-goals-I-have-in-situations or scripts-for-behavior-in-situations. Indeed, we found that analysis of situation prototypes revealed substantial numbers of features describing the *people* and social behavior typically found in these social situations. Apparently, when lay perceivers carve up the social world, they do not always adhere to the traditional person-situation divisions established by psychologists. Consequently, we turned next to investigating more fully the prototypes for compound person-situation categories (see Cantor, Mischel, & Schwartz, 1981). We found that such structures combine a focus on people and on situations, on the self and the external world, and on objective social roles and subjective personal goals. Such compound cognitive schemes seem to capture both the subjective and dynamic quality of current goals and plans and the more archival, stable components of knowledge about the social world in the abstract.

In one study, for example, we examined the hypothesis that people share prototypic images of the person who best fits each of a variety of different kinds of everyday situations. Princeton University undergraduates were asked to describe the features of the kinds of persons whom they saw as "ideal" for a variety of everyday social situations, e.g., the prototypic person for a party. Ten subjects described the prototypic person for each of four superordinate situation categories (SOCIAL, CULTURAL, IDEOLOGICAL, and STRESSFUL SITUATIONS) and ten other subjects described the characteristics of the person who would function best in each of four (less abstract) middle level situations (PARTY, TOUR, INTERVIEW, and DEMONSTRATION FOR A CAUSE). Subjects' lists were then coded for consensus; any feature listed by two or more subjects for a particular category was included in the consensual *person-for-a-situation prototype* for that category. These person-for-a-situation prototypes indicated that people do share substantial amounts of knowledge about the prototypic person for a wide variety of situations. The average number of features in the consensual person-for-a-situation prototype was 18.5; rich person-for-a-situation prototypes were obtained. Moreover, in all cases the compound prototypes contained as many features as the separate person or situation prototypes obtained in earlier research (Cantor, 1980; Cantor & Mischel, 1979).

We also examined the content of these person-for-a-situation prototypes. For this purpose we used a coding scheme similar to one developed in earlier studies of simple person prototypes (see Cantor & Mischel, 1979). The coding scheme contained five content categories: (1) Dispositional features describing feelings, traits, attitudes of the person. (2) Behavioral features describing the person's behavior. (3) Physical features describing the person's appearance. (4) Situation features mentioning places in which the person is likely to be seen. (5) Social features mentioning the person's group affiliations, nationality, socioeconomic class status, or social roles. A naive coder categorized each feature in each prototype list as fitting one of these five content categories. Only one feature from a total of 148 features (across the eight consensual prototypes) did not fit in any of these five content categories. The mean number of features of each type for the four superordinate and the four middle level categories are presented in Table 1.

Two noteworthy points emerged from this analysis. First, dispositonal and behavioral characteristics dominated these person-for-a-situation prototype descriptions. Second, the prototypes for the middle level categories were more concrete (and vivid) because they contained greater numbers of behavioral and physical appearance characteristics than did the prototypes for the superordinate categories. As observed in previous studies, the gain in prototype richness from the superordinate to the middle level categories was primarily due to increasing numbers of concrete behavioral and physical appearance features in the prototypes for the middle level categories. Reassuringly, this finding replicates an earlier one for simple personality prototypes (Cantor & Mischel, 1979).

Another source provides further support for the availability and richness of these compound person-situation prototypes (Cantor, Mischel, & Schwartz, 1981). Princeton undergraduates were asked to form images, as quickly as possible, of either different types of persons (e.g., "super-jocks"), different persons-in-situations ("super-jocks at an athletic game"), or different situations ("athletic game"). After forming the image and pressing a reaction time button, subjects described their image. Not only were the person-in-situation images again rich in content; they also were formed more quickly than simple person images alone. This study will be described in more detail in the next major section. For the present, suffice it to say that lay perceivers can and do operate well (generate prototypes easily, generate rich images, agree on the relevant features) with social categories that label types of persons with the situations they typically inhabit and describe situations by the people and behavior most appropriate and/or typical for those kinds of situations.

Summary

In this section we considered some of the multiple organizational schemes available for structuring social experience. We focused on cognitive schemes that integrate knowledge of persons and situations in compound person-situation prototypes, as revealed by the categorical-

TABLE 1. The Content of Person-for-a-Situation Prototypes: Number of Features of Each Content Type

	Dispositions	Behaviors	Physical Appearance	Situations	Social Attributes	Miscellaneous	Total
Superordinate categories	M = 9	3.75	.75	1.25	1.75	0	16.5
	SD = 1.83	1.9	.96	1.89	1.5	0	3.79
Middle categories	M = 9.5	6	2.5	1.25	1.00	.25	20.5
	SD = 3.7	.82	1.29	1.5	2.00	.5	2.65

prototype approach. Our applications of the categorical-prototype approach to the study of social knowledge suggest the availability of rich and consensual compound knowledge structures that bridge the person-situation dichotomy and place prototypic persons within particular relevant situations. These person-for-a-situation compound prototypes may be central to the layperson's everyday "natural" categorical knowledge about persons and situations.[1] A related intriguing possibility that we plan to explore is that situations may also be naturally categorized with reference to the ideal person (prototype) for that situation.

ACCESSIBILITY AND UTILITY OF VARIOUS CATEGORICAL SCHEMES

Given the availability of multiple categorical schemes for sorting social knowledge, we must consider their accessibility and utility. Are people generally more likely to use one particular organizational structure than another? What makes a specific categorization strategy easier to access and use than any of a large array of possible alternative strategies? Is one categorical scheme more useful than another for performing one or more common social-cognitive tasks? If so, how adaptive is the lay perceiver in the selection of construal strategies? Does the perceiver select the "right" scheme for the task at hand? In order to characterize accurately the inevitable selectivity the social categorizer must exercise in choosing among these possibilities, psychologists must address questions regarding the accessibility and utility to the perceiver of various schemes for organizing the social world.

Certain classes of beliefs or cognitive structures may simply be easier to retrieve (access, think about, bring to mind) than others, under most circumstances. For example, information about one's *own* experience may always be more salient—and thus more influential in shaping interpretations of social experience—than are generalizations stored in memory about people and social life in the abstract (cf. Bower & Gilligan, 1979; Rogers, Kuiper, & Kirker, 1977; Rogers, 1980). Interpretations of other people's behaviors and of social interactions may be filtered through a set of beliefs about the self; self-schemata may anchor perceptions of others (Kuiper & Derry, 1980; Markus & Smith, 1980).

Recent research on causal attribution (cf. Jones, Kanouse, Kelley, Nisbett, Valins, & Weiner, 1972; Ross, 1977) and social judgment (cf. Nisbett & Ross, 1980; Tversky & Kahneman, 1974) suggests another potential accessibility difference between two broad classes of categorical knowledge structures, namely, person knowledge and situation knowledge. The findings from these studies point toward a characterization of the lay perceiver as an inveterate trait theorist, a staunch believer in enduring *personal* causes of behavior who, at worst, completely ig-

[1]Pervin's (1976, 1977) studies illustrate an alternative route that also yields some evidence of compound self-situation knowledge. He factor-analyzed free responses obtained when four subjects were asked to generate their own lists of "current life situations" and to describe their feelings and behaviors in them.

nores situational factors and, at best, adjusts his or her perceptions only insufficiently for the influence of such factors. People seem strongly to prefer to organize the world in terms of persons.

Does this preference on the part of the naive psychologist reflect a difference in the amount of knowledge he or she has about person categories and situation categories, respectively? It is *not* plausible that the lay perceiver's trait-oriented bias reflects an absence of rich, well-organized, normative knowledge structures about situations. The data from our studies of situation taxonomies (Cantor, 1980) undermine such an explanation. What, however, can we say about the relative *accessibility* of cognitive generalizations about persons and situations? Perhaps both person and situation knowledge exist in the head of the perceiver, but person prototypes are easier to access, and therefore are used more often, then are situation knowledge structures.

The Accessibility of Person and Situation Knowledge

We used an imagery-RT paradigm to address the relative accessibility of three types of category prototype-images—images of person types (e.g., "Super-jock"), situation types (e.g., "Athletic game") and of compound person-in-situation units (e.g., "Super-jock at an athletic game"). To investigate the accessibility of knowledge classified in these three ways, we compared the speed of forming images associated with typical exemplars of each of these three kinds of categories (Cantor, Mischel, & Schwartz, 1981). (In addition, we asked subjects to describe the contents of their prototype-images so as to provide data on the comparative richness of categorical knowledge about classes of persons, situations, and persons-in-situations).

The category labels (phrases) used to elicit Person, Situation, and Person-in-Situation image formation are listed in Table 2, which also contains the mean-RT data. Most of these categories were taken from the middle level of the three-level Person and Situation taxonomies used in our previous research (see Figure 1 or Cantor & Mischel, 1979). A few labels were devised for use in this study. The Person-in-Situation image phrases were always constructed by combining a Person label with its corresponding Situation label.

In the instructions, *Ss* were told that "we don't mean to use the word 'image' in a strictly visual sense—when we ask you to image a person (situation/person in a situation), we'd like you to form as complete and detailed an image as you can."[2] Each *S* formed a series of seven Person,

[2]Rough guidelines were provided as to the possible nature of these images. For *Ss* in the Person condition, it was suggested that Person images might include components such as physical appearance, personality characteristics, opinions, attitudes, beliefs, and typical behaviors, actions, and interactions engaged in by the Person. Instructions for the Situation *Ss* suggested that Situation images might contain information about things like physical setting and surroundings, etiquette, expectations and rules for how to act in the situation, and behaviors, actions, and interactions going on in the situation. Person-in-Situation *Ss* were told that some of the components of a Person-in-Situation image might be the person's physical appearance in the situation, the way the person acts in the situation (behaviors, actions, and interactions in the situation), and the way the person thinks and/or feels in the situation. Of course, subjects were aware that these were only rough guidelines and that they were free to emphasize anything they wished in their images.

TABLE 2. Mean RT in Seconds for Each Image-Stimulus Phrase

Person	Religious devotee	Criminal madman	Patron of the arts	Comic-joker	Super-genius	Super-jock
	31.8	29.9	42.6	30.3	31.1	28.6
Person-in-Situation	Religious devotee at a religious ceremony	Criminal madman at the scene of a crime	Patron of the arts at a performing arts opening	Comic-joker at a party	Super-genius at a class meeting	Super-jock at an athletic game
	17.3	18.9	17.4	14.9	21.2	15.3
Situation	Religious ceremony	Scene of a crime	Performing arts opening	Party	Class meeting	Athletic game
	8.7	9.4	10.1	7.4	7.5	7.1

Situation, or Person-in-Situation images. (The first image was designated as a "Practice" trial; data were therefore analyzed for only six images.) The image-stimulus phrases were presented one by one on a computer console screen, and the *S* was instructed to begin forming his/her image as soon as the phrase appeared. When the *S* considered his/her image complete, s/he pressed a key on the computer console, resulting in a record of the RT (speed of formation) for that stimulus phrase. The *S* was then given one minute to write down the components of the image just formed.

To examine the relative accessibility of Person, Situation, and Person-in-Situation knowledge, the RT data were analyzed to determine whether these three kinds of images differed in the ease, or speed, of formation. Table 2 presents the mean RT's in seconds for the different images. As is clear from this table, the three conditions did differ significantly (F' (2,46) = 5.41, $p < .01$) in speed of formation, with Situation images formed the most quickly ($\bar{x}$ = 8.4 sec), Person-in-Situation images formed somewhat more slowly ($\bar{x}$ = 17.5 sec), and Person images formed the most slowly ($\bar{x}$ = 32.4 sec). This is a rather surprising finding, in light of the abundant evidence for person-oriented biases in the processing of social information. Moreover, this effect of categorical scheme on RT was consistent across all six individual comparisons between the three stimulus conditions. In no case did a Person Image phrase yield a faster mean RT than its corresponding Person-in-Situation phrase; nor did a Person-in-Situation phrase ever yield a faster mean RT than its corresponding Situation phrase. The data, then, seem to reveal a very clear and remarkably stable hierarchy of ease-of-imagery-formation. Since this hierarchy suggests that Situation prototypes may in fact be quicker and easier to access than are Person prototypes, the RT data from this study certainly discourage a "cognitive accessibility" explanation for the apparently stubborn trait-orientedness of the lay perceiver.

Recall that we argued in the previous section for the richness and availability of compound person-situation prototypes. Consequently, the reader may be surprised by the finding that simple Situation prototypes are easier to access than are Person-in-Situation prototypes. Indeed, this is a rather surprising finding. Content analyses of the protocols from this study may provide some clues about the reasons for this result. These content analyses revealed that approximately 60% of the information in the Situation images was descriptive of *persons* present in the situation. Thus information accessed via "Situation" labels seems naturally to straddle the traditional Person-Situation distinction. In addition, the present RT data support the notion that compound Person-in-Situation prototypes are more accessible than are simple Person prototypes devoid of context.

How much information is actually present in the prototypes-images produced by our *Ss* in this RT study? Our RT data can only be interpreted as suggestive of the greater accessibility of situation information *if* the more quickly formed Situation images are as rich and complete (contain as much information) as the other two types of images—i.e., if no speed-richness trade-off is observed—the data from this study can be taken as suggestive of the accessibility (and potential usefulness) of information organized by a situation scheme.

First, in order to determine whether the three image-type conditions differed in sheer volume of written material produced, we counted the number of words written by *Ss* in these three conditions. There were no significant differences in number of words written ($\bar{x}$ = 22.5, 24.7, 22.7 words, Person, Situation, and Person-in-Situation images, respectively; F' (2,47) < 1, n.s.

Moreover, *Ss* who imaged Situations actually seemed to squeeze *more* nonredundant attributes or pieces of information into approximately the same amount of written material as was produced by Person and Person-in-Situation *Ss*. A naive coder counted the number of components (features, attributes) in each imagery protocol. A component was defined as a word or phrase which adds information to, or fills out, the image in some way. The three Image types differed significantly in number of components (F' (2,43) $= 7.95$, $p < .001$), with situation images the richest ($\bar{x} = 10.48$ components), and Person and Person-in-Situation images roughly equivalent ($\bar{x}$'s = 8.17 and 8.13 components, respectively). While this finding should be interpreted with some caution, given the inherent difficulties in making richness comparisons among qualitatively different kinds of information, it is clear that no obvious speed-richness trade-off can account for the large RT differences observed in this study. We can say with some confidence, then, that information organized according to "Situation" categories is not only rich, and well-organized, but also quite accessible. The richness and accessibility of situation knowledge units imply that such units are potentially very useful for structuring social information (though the utility or consequences of using situation schemes still needs to be assessed directly).

Surely the choice to categorize according to one organization scheme as opposed to another is based on more than general accessibility differences which persist across most circumstances and across most individuals. There may certainly be individual differences in the content and structure of knowledge that people characteristically access and use in organizing social perception. For example, Snyder & Cantor (1980) have argued that for some individuals (Low Self-Monitoring individuals, Snyder Scale, 1974), self-knowledge is particularly easy to access, while other individuals (High Self-Monitors) more easily generate informative descriptions of people-in-the-abstract, prototypic people for different situations. Thus the relative accessibility and utility of different cognitions and cognitive structures may be subject to consistent variations across individuals (cf. Higgins & King, 1980).

Further, the accessibility of any given category at any given time may be affected by a multiplicity of factors. These factors might include the recency and frequency of exposure to instances of the category, the salience of the category in memory, the relation of the category to other accessible categories, the expectations of the perceiver, and the motivational state (goals, purposes, needs, etc.) of the perceiver. [See Higgins and King (1980) for a discussion of these factors as determinants of construct accessibility.]

The Effects of Goals and Purposes on Accessibility

The perceiver's *purpose* or *goal* also may influence the choice of a strategy by which to organize an ongoing stream of social information. For example, Cohen and Ebbesen (1979) found that subjects tend to "unitize" (chunk or divide) a videotaped sequence of behavior differently (using different size units and adopting a different focus within each unit) under instructions to form an impression of the person rather than under instructions to learn the task being performed. The particular organizational structure that is most accessible is determined by the "observational goal" of the perceivers in each condition.

Two sets of studies (Hoffman, Mischel, & Mazze, 1980; Jeffery & Mischel, 1979) have demonstrated and clarified the effects of purpose on the accessibility of various categorical schemes. In one series of studies (Jeffery & Mischel, 1979), it was shown that "personality impression" and "behavior prediction" sets led to categorizations of behavioral episodes based primarily on traits, while a "recall" set resulted in categorizations which paralleled the built-in structure of the stimulus information, based about equally on traits and on situational features. In another set of experiments (Hoffman et al., 1980), subjects whose purpose was either to recall behavioral episodes about a person or to empathize with (take the perspective of) the person, tended to organize the information in terms of the target person's *goals*, while subjects with "personality impression" and "behavior prediction" sets again chose *trait-based* categorical schemes.

What is particularly interesting about these two sets of studies is that they go beyond the accessibility effects summarized above to establish a link between accessibility and *utility* of categorical schemes. In both cases it was shown that the categorizations made by subjects with the goal of recalling the stimulus information actually did facilitate recall by new subjects, relative to the categorizations generated by subjects with other goal sets. In other words, recall *Ss* showed an adaptive tendency to use the best available categorization scheme for their assigned purpose—for recall *Ss*, the most accessible cognitive organization was also the most useful.

Summary

This section considered the relative accessibility of different organizational schemes and a few of the factors that influence cognitive accessibility. In particular, we compared the accessibility of "person" units and "situation" units. We also considered individual difference factors affecting accessibility and concluded that goals and purposes may importantly influence how the perceiver construes and structures the social world.

STRUCTURE: IS THERE ONE? IS IT ORDERLY? IS IT SHARED?

In the study of social knowledge, investigators often try to determine the basic units, the underlying dimensions or factors, the primitive building blocks organizing knowledge about a given subarea (e.g., the person, the self, the situation). Examples are factor analytic studies of people's implicit personality theories (Schneider, 1973), and of their perceptions of situations (see Magnusson, 1979). A categorical, as opposed to dimensional, approach leads to a search for "basic" categories that are cognitively represented by rich and distinctive consensual beliefs, prototypes or stereotypes (e.g., Ashmore & Delboca, 1979; Cantor & Mischel, 1979; Cantor et al., 1980; Taylor, 1979). Yet another approach is represented by computer simulation attempts, as in the work of Schank and Abelson (1977) on social scripts and the primitive building blocks of scenario comprehension.

The particular underlying structure one discovers depends on the particular discovery technique employed: factor analytic and multidimensional scaling techniques reveal basic dimensions of person and situation perception; taxonomic studies suggest basic levels of personality categories; and computer simulations demonstrate primitive procedures and social scripts. It may be a useless enterprise to search for the one basic cognitive representation or structure (cf. Anderson, 1978); cognitive structure may be more fluid and flexible than such a search assumes, and many different structures (e.g., category prototypes, scripts, bipolar dimensions) may simultaneously or equivalently fulfill the same cognitive needs of the perceiver. Just as we have multiple, overlapping knowledge in different social domains (constructive alternativism), the same knowledge may be internally represented in different structures simultaneously (structural alternativism). But such structural alternativism does not negate the utility of studies of cognitive structure in any given social domain. Given the complexity of social knowledge, structural investigations have utility to the extent that they reveal underlying consistencies in the organization of social experience.

Assuming that it is unproductive to search for a single, most fundamental structure for social knowledge, what, then, are interesting structural questions to be investigated? The following three general and interrelated goals seem promising candidates for research:

1. Finding "economic" structures for representing social knowledge
2. Evaluating the degree of orderliness of those structures
3. Estimating the degree of consensus across perceivers about those structures

Next we will consider each of these questions in succession.

"Economic" Structures?

Within any particular structural model or representation there are more and less efficient, "economic" ways to organize the relevant information. The perceiver's aim is to reduce the complexity of the information by abstracting the central gist, yet to avoid oversimplification that sacrifices too much of the inherent richness of our knowledge and perceptions of people, events, objects. Consequently, regardless of the particular form of the representation, the perceiver faces a trade-off between complexity-intricacy of the structure and economy of representation. This often reduces to a question of numbers: How many category cuts shall one make in sorting a given set of objects or people or events? How many dimensions are required to capture the relations between objects in a multidimensional space? The number question is actually an "abstraction" question in disguise: How generalized, abstract, inclusive should the representation be or, conversely, how intricate, finely tuned, specific should it be?

Consider, for example, the taxonomic-categorical approach illustrated in the work of Eleanor Rosch on object perception (Rosch, 1978) or in our own work on person perception (Cantor & Mischel, 1979). The same set of objects or persons can be categorized with a few very inclusive, abstract categories or with many, very specific and finely tuned ones. Thus, we can represent our knowledge of all "Social Situations" with one category or, instead, with a few less inclusive categories such as "Parties" versus "Dates" versus "Family Events." Alternatively, we can categorize "Social Situations" at an even more specific level, and separately represent our knowledge about "Blind Dates" and "Double Dates" and "Formal Dates." Which level of abstraction can represent our rich social knowledge in a nonredundant, structurally efficient manner? The Rosch prototype approach provides one answer to this structural question in the domain of categorical representations [see Rosch et al. (1976) on basic level categories].

When we examine consensual prototypes in a variety of different social and nonsocial taxonomies (e.g., taxonomies of personality types: Cantor & Mischel, 1979; taxonomies of psychiatric disorders: Cantor et al., 1980; taxonomies of man-made objects: Rosch et al., 1976), we find the following pattern of data. First, the consensual prototypes are richer (contain more features) the less abstract the category. Moreover, categories at a middle level in these three-level taxonomies (categories such as Party or Date; Car or Table; Schizophrenia or Affective Disorder) seem to have both rich and relatively nonredundant prototypes. These middle-level categories with their attendant prototypes seem to comprise an "economic" structural representation for categorical knowledge. Furthermore, at least in the domains of man-made objects and biological classes (the domains of tables and cars, birds and trees), there are differences in the case of using these different categories (see Rosch et al., 1976). For example, children tend to use these "basic level" labels to name objects at an earlier age than they use either the more general or more specific labels; similarly, adults label objects with these basic level terms more quickly than they use the superordinate or subordinate terms for the same objects. Adults also find it easier to form a single visual image to represent the whole category for basic level categories as compared to either more or less inclusive categories in the same taxonomies. There seem to be consequences to categorizing at different levels of abstraction (see Cantor & Mischel, 1979; Rosch, 1978).

As Wiggins (1980) points out, the most economic level of abstraction to represent categorical knowledge will depend heavily on the *expertise* of the perceiver-user and the *purpose* of the categorization. A researcher in the field of personality may be able to make rich, nonredundant distinctions between 16 different interpersonal trait categories and keep in mind all of these categories when he/she analyzes individual behavior. However, the more "naive" perceiver may find it easier and more economic to represent only eight or so main types of interpersonal interaction styles. Wiggins' (1979, 1980) studies of circumplex models in the interpersonal trait domain provide an excellent source for investigation of the utility of different structural representations of social knowledge. Just as the relative accessibility of different organizational schemes is affected by the perceiver's goals (see p. 47), the utility of various levels of structural representation seems also to depend upon purpose.

Orderly Structures?

In addition to considering the most efficient level of structural complexity for representing social knowledge, it is also interesting to evaluate the degree of orderliness in these social-cognitive structures. In a model that represents knowledge as organized along multiple dimensions in a geometric space, for example, can the stimuli be adequately represented in a few basic dimensions? For factor analytic or multidimensional scaling approaches, it is useful to determine whether the solutions account for a reasonable proportion of the variance in people's ratings of the stimulus objects. For example, Wiggins (1979) had three different large samples of subjects rate the applicability of 128 trait terms to their own personalities. He found that a relatively simple circumplex structure (with eight dimensions) repeatedly emerged and accounted for these ratings very well indeed [see Wiggins (1979) for details]. Self-ratings (and the cognitive structures derived from them) in the interpersonal domain seem quite orderly.

Similar analyses of order in a taxonomic-categorical approach also come to the conclusion that social taxonomies are as well-structured and coherent as their nonsocial counterparts (e.g., Cantor, 1980; Cantor et al., 1980). Degree of taxonomic order can be measured by comparing the similarity of the prototypes for pairs of categories that are close together with the similarity of the prototypes for categories far apart in a particular taxonomy. For example, consider the situation taxonomies in Figure 1. We (Cantor, Mischel, & Schwartz, 1981) had independent groups of subjects generating prototypes for these different categories. Then we computed the degree of overlap in features across all pairwise combinations of prototypes within each taxonomy. If a taxonomy is orderly, then the prototypes for categories at the same level of abstraction and close together in the taxonomy (e.g., job interview and psychiatric interview) should be more similar (more feature overlap) than those at the same level but farther apart (e.g., job interview and county jail). This pattern of results consistently occurred in the four different situation taxonomies, as well as in other domains [e.g., psychiatric taxonomies (Cantor et al., 1980)]. Moreover, these taxonomies also were quite orderly on another measure of taxonomic structure: category prototypes had significantly more features in common with prototypes for the more inclusive categories in which they were nested (e.g., Cocktail party is nested in Party) than for those in which they were not nested (e.g., Cocktail party is not nested in the more inclusive category Date). Again, this orderliness has also been observed in other domains of social knowledge, such as psychiatric taxonomies (see Cantor et al., 1980). The degree of orderliness is by no means perfect; for example, in a perfectly structured taxonomy, all of the features in the Date prototype would be found in the prototype for Double Date. But the obtained orderliness is clearly beyond chance and quite similar to that observed in nonsocial domains such as taxonomies for animals or furniture or colors (see Lehrer, 1974: Rosch et al., 1976).

Consensual Structures?

A final question about structure that seems worthy of attention concerns the degree of consensus about everyday social knowledge. This question has at least two identifiable subparts: (1) Can the same general structure be derived to account for different people's perceptions of the social world? (2) Do different people agree as to the contents of these structures? Let us illustrate this once again using Wiggins' (1979) work on self-ratings in the interpersonal trait domain. Wiggins found a high level of structural consensus in these ratings. Not only did a general circumplex model fit many different people's ratings; but a particular one, illustrated in Figure 2, also emerged repeatedly in these data. Similarly, in our taxonomic-categorical studies of person and situation per-

FIGURE 2. Wiggins' (1979) circumplex model.

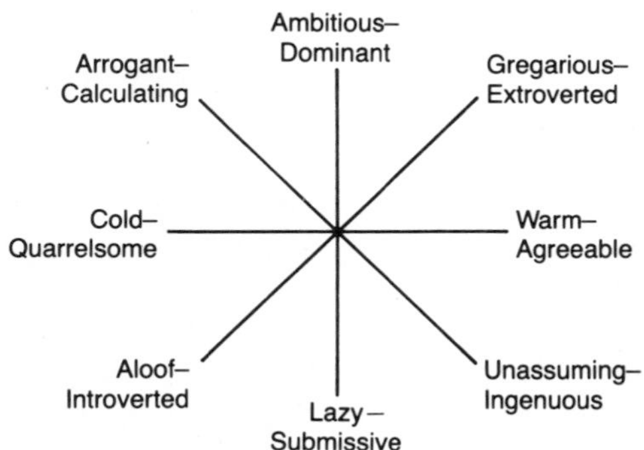

ceptions, we find that people consistently agree as to the hierarchical relations in these different taxonomies (see, for example, Cantor & Mischel, 1979). Moreover, analyses of the actual prototypes for any given category usually reveal a substantial number (10 −15) of features that at least 3 or 4 out of 10 −13 people will have spontaneously and independently generated to describe members of that category. While the greatest proportion of features are usually unique to one person's list, it is possible to extract consensual prototypes for a wide variety of social categories. (We will return to issues of consensus later in the next major section.)

Summary

In this section we discussed the difficulty of finding the one most basic structural representation for social knowledge but argued for the utility of asking other questions about the "economic," orderly, and consensual properties of structural representations. For different structural models, economy, order, and consensus in the representation of social domains may be demonstrated readily.

CONTENT OF SOCIAL KNOWLEDGE AND PERCEPTION: WHAT KINDS OF INFORMATION DO WE REPRESENT AND STORE?

What kinds of information are contained in our stored generalizations (prototypes, scripts, etc.) about social entities, and in our specific, on-the-spot perceptions of persons and social events? In attempts to answer this question, researchers have asked about the kinds of attributes commonly associated with various categories of social knowledge—for example, the contents of sex-role stereotypes (e.g., Spence & Helmreich, 1978), political attitudes (e.g., Judd & Kulik, 1980), occupational stereotypes (e.g., Cohen, 1977), behavioral scripts (e.g., Schank & Abelson, 1977), and generalizations about social situations (e.g., Cantor, 1980). These content analyses address both the *general kinds* of elements that make up social knowledge structures (for example, the proportions of physical appearance and trait-dispositional attributes in an occupational stereotype) and the *specific* features that comprise a given prototype, script, or stereotype (for example, a cheery disposition and chewing gum for a waitress stereotype).

Free-Response Approaches to the Content of Stored Social Knowledge

Free-response descriptive techniques provide rich, relatively naturalistic material that can be subjected to content analyses. Fiske and Cox (1979) recently used free-response descriptions to provide evidence about the kinds of attributes in person knowledge. They proposed that people tend to define persons in terms of six broad categories: physical appearance, behavior, social relationships, typical contexts, personal origins, and internal properties. Content analyses of the free-response descriptions they collected offered support for this taxonomy. Four of the proposed categories figured importantly in their subjects' person descriptions. Appearance attributes were used most commonly, followed by internal properties (personality characteristics) and relationships, with behaviors also contributing substantially to description content. Analyses that broke the descriptions down into temporal stages revealed that the various attribute categories were used differentially over stages of the description. Appearance information dominated at the beginning, and behavior and personality descriptors emerged later. Relationship and context information, when used, appeared early, while origins emerged late.

Given the role of goals in person perception (see the section entitled Accessibility and Utility of Various Categorical Schemes), it is not surprising that the writer's purpose also affected the content of these person descriptions. Descriptions written for the purpose of helping someone to "pick the person out in a crowd at Grand Central Station" contained far more appearance features than did descriptions written to convey "what it is like to be around the person." In-depth "what it's like to be around the person" descriptions focused more on personality and relationship information.

Cantor and Mischel (in Cantor, Mischel, & Schwartz, 1981) have recently used free-response techniques to investigate the content of prototypes of everyday situations. Using the techniques described in the section on categorizations, we analyzed the content of consensual prototypes generated for categories in four situation taxonomies (see Figure 1). The greatest proportion (averaging over 50%) of the attributes in these consensual situation prototypes were descriptors of the dispositions and behaviors of *persons* typically present in these situations (e.g., solemn people at religious ceremonies who sing and listen to priests). As expected, the situation prototypes also contained physical and atmospheric descriptions of settings in which the situations occurred and references to events and places associated with the situations. But the person-orientedness of the situation prototypes was most striking. Cognitive generalizations about situations apparently include numerous details about the most appropriate behaviors for a situation, the feelings associated with being in a situation, and the appearance, dispositions, reactions, and behaviors of others typically present in the situation.

The previously described imagery-RT study by Cantor, Mischel, and Schwartz (1981) also included content analyses of the Person, Situation and Person-in-Situation imagery-prototypes generated by the subjects. The imagery protocols in all three conditions were coded for four broad content categories:

1. *Person-Nonphysical* (i.e., personality traits, feelings, attitudes, behaviors, socioeconomic status, social relationships, voice quality), e.g.,

snob; socially inept; gets women; says "Hi Ya Fellow" a lot; bores friends with proselytizing; firm voice; has four kids.

2. *Person-Physical* (i.e., anything referring to physical characteristics of a person—appearance, physical movements, sex, age, race), e.g., male; very good-looking; medium height; muscular; hairy body; neatly dressed; middle-aged.
3. *Situation-Nonphysical* (i.e., place or event names, time of day, year, season, atmosphere of situation,), e.g., very frantic atmosphere; gloomy night; church; soccer game; serious; reverent mood; sunny day.
4. *Situation-Physical* (i.e., physical surroundings, objects present in the situation), e.g., white tablecloth; candles on altar; dark wood rooms; beer and hot dogs; windows on one side; elegant stage.

In order to produce an index of the prominence of each of these four content categories in each type of imagery protocol, we computed the percentage of the total number of components in a protocol accounted for by each content category, as summarized in Table 3. The content analyses from this study reinforce the conclusions suggested by the Cantor and Mischel Situation-prototype content analysis—namely, the naive perceiver's categorical knowledge about situations seems to be heavily person-oriented, focusing (62% of the Situation-protocol content) on various characteristics and typical behaviors of the persons who inhabit those situations. This apparent social, behavioral bent in perceiving and interpreting situations seems potentially very useful in planning and guiding social behavior. The data of Price and Bouffard (1974), demonstrating substantial consensus among individuals about the degree of appropriateness of specific behaviors to various situations, are also relevant. These data too strongly suggest scriptlike, behavioral guidelines in the naive perceiver's situation knowledge stores.

TABLE 3. Proportion of Total Components of Each Image Type Represented by Each Content Category

	Image Type		
Content Category	**Person**	**Situation**	**Person-in-Situation**
Person-Nonphysical	.72	.54	.62
Person-Physical	.26	.08	.35
Situation-Nonphysical	.02	.15	.02
Situation-Physical	.002	.23	.009

Degree of Consensus

In addition to revealing the kinds of attributes represented in various types of social categorical knowledge, content analyses are useful for assessing the degree of consensus across individuals in their constructions of the social world. Cantor and Mischel's prototype-generation studies, described in the section on categorizations, provide an example of the use of content analysis for gauging the consensuality of social knowledge content.

Consider the "number of subjects" by "number of features" frequency distribution shown in Figure 3. This schematic diagram illustrates the typical pattern of consensuality observed in these social prototype studies and in prototype studies in the object domain (e.g., Cantor, Smith, French, and Mezzich, 1980; Rosch et al., 1976). As can be seen from the graph, there are typically many idiosyncratic features—features listed by only one subject—a substantial number of features listed by a few to several subjects, and practically no features listed by all subjects generating feature lists. Note that this pattern of agreement/disagreement among subjects is consistent with the view of categories as fuzzy feature sets organized around prototypes. If categories were "well-defined" (that is, if an entity were required by the perceiver to exhibit an entire set of necessary and sufficient defining features in order to be classified as a category member) then one would expect complete (or almost complete) consensus among subjects. In that case, the lists would contain all of these necessary and sufficient features, and little, if any, variability among subjects would be observed. But the data pro-

FIGURE 3. Schematic diagram illustrating degree of consensus in prototype-generation studies.

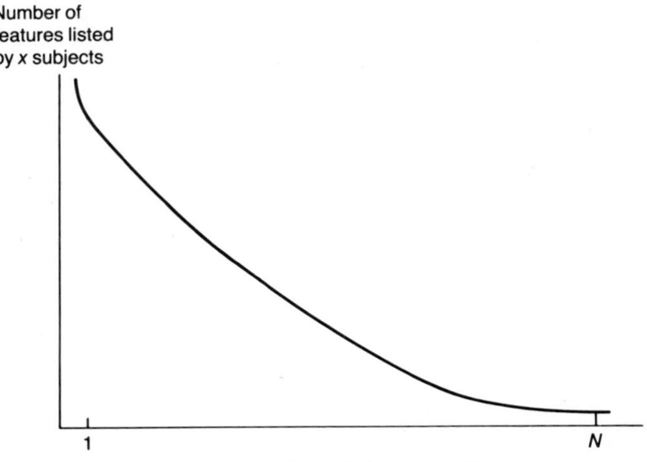

vided by those free-response studies are not consistent with this classical view of categories. Rather, consensus analyses indicate that categories are characterized by a set of features imperfectly correlated with category membership: some of these features (i.e., those listed by many subjects) are highly associated with the category, and other features less so.

The Content of Ongoing Social Perception

In addition to clarifying the content of prior knowledge about the social world, content analyses also can address questions about the content of ongoing, immediate social perception. Such analyses can focus on the kinds of information attended to and encoded in an ongoing social interaction, and also can illuminate the nature of the impressions, social judgments, and memory formed under such circumstances.

Assuming some limitations on our ability to process all available social (and nonsocial) stimuli, it is likely that people develop proclivities to pay special attention to certain kinds of information at the expense of other stimuli. Indeed, much recent research has identified the kinds of information perceivers attend to and the kinds of data they ignore (e.g., Kahneman & Tversky, 1973; Nisbett & Borgida, 1975; Nisbett & Ross, 1980). The results convincingly demonstrate that, in making predictions, probability estimates, and choice decisions, people often ignore statistical base rate information in favor of "case data" about the experiences or attributes of known target individuals, and they do this even when these case data are totally nondiagnostic with respect to the prediction or decision. Similarly, attribution theorists, such as Jones (1979) and Ross (1977) have repeatedly demonstrated the intuitive psychologist's affinity for person-oriented, dispositional, as opposed to situational, explanations for the causes of observed behaviors. Case data and personality information, then, seem to be more prominent in the content of social information processing than are base rate data and cues about situational content.

Next, consider the content of person memory and impressions of *particular* target persons (as distinguished from cognitive generalizations about *classes* of persons). Is memory "biased" toward the perceiver's first impressions or prior expectations about the target person? That is, does the perceiver strive for consistency in processing information about another person; does she/he preferentially remember information consistent with his/her first impression? The evidence on this question is somewhat mixed. For example, information consistent with a previously established expectancy is better recalled than information inconsistent with the prior expectancy (Rothbart, Evans, & Fulero, 1979). Similarly, Snyder and Uranowitz (1978) and Darley and Akert (1980) also have found that subjects tend to reconstruct or reinterpret retrospectively; an ambiguous body of information about a target person is reinterpreted to make that information consistent with new information (Hayden & Mischel, 1976). In contrast, a series of other studies shows superior recall for behavioral information which is *incongruent* with a prior personality trait-based impression of a hypothetical character (Hastie & Kumar, 1979).

In view of these (and other) apparently conflicting data [for review, see Taylor and Crocker (1980) and Hastie (1980)] it seems likely that the relationship between the memorability of information and its degree of consistency with a prior expectancy is not a simple one. In an extremely thorough review of the relevant research, Hastie (1980) has recently speculated that memory for expectancy-congruent and incongruent information is differentially favored at different stages of information-processing. Specifically, acquisition processes may favor memory for incongruent events, while processes occurring during the retrieval phase may favor memory for impression-congruent information. Further research is required to sort out these possibilities and test Hastie's hypothesis.

Summary

In this section, we discussed research on the content of stored social knowledge, focusing on free-response prototype-generation studies. We emphasized the person-oriented content of knowledge about situations, and considered the degree of consensus about prototype content. Finally, biases in the content of ongoing social perception were described.

FUNCTION: RELATIONS BETWEEN BELIEF, THOUGHT, AND ACTION

The relations between belief, cognition, and action raise an especially complex and challenging set of issues for students of social cognition. What functions do our beliefs and social knowledge serve in generating interpersonal behavior? How "thoughtful"—or "mindless"—is action (Langer, 1978)? Do people have accurate introspective insight into the causal determinants of their own behavior (Nisbett & Wilson, 1977)? For the moment we will approach these questions through illustrative research examples; later a more theoretical discussion of the same issues will be presented (see pp. 62 –68). We have chosen as empirical illustrations in this section two research programs that address the role of knowledge and cognition in behavioral planning. In the first instance (Snyder's self-monitoring work), the relation between belief (knowledge, goals) and action is investigated independent of the role played by "conscious," "strategic" cognition. By contrast, investigations of self-regulation have explicitly studied the relation between cognitive strategies and behavior (Mischel, 1980).

Self-Monitoring: Social Knowledge and Social Behavior

Using an individual differences approach [see Snyder (1979) for a review of this work], Snyder has isolated two patterns of social behavior that seem to have corresponding patterns of social knowledge. High self-monitoring individuals (identified by self-reports on the Snyder Self-Monitoring Scale, 1974) exhibit a consistent pattern of interest in, and adherence to, socially defined norms. They report attentiveness to social cues, use of social comparison information and modulation of self-presentation to fit the apparent requirements of each individual situation (Snyder, 1974; Berscheid, Graziano, Morison, & Dermer, 1976). Moreover, they are discriminative in behavior from situation to situation, as one would expect on the basis of their self-reports (Snyder & Tanke, 1976; Snyder & Swann, 1976). By contrast, low self-monitoring individuals have a very different pattern of self-report and social behavior; they report an interest in "being true to their own attitudes and dispositions" and generally act in a manner that consistently reflects these stated predispositions, even when this entails ignoring social cues for appropriate behavior (Snyder, 1974; Snyder & Monson, 1975). Hence, the literature on self-monitoring suggests that two rather distinct patterns of self-reports are coordinated with two (frequently divergent) styles of social behavior.

Of particular interest for the present purposes is the claim that, in addition to these patterns of coordinated self-reports and social behavior, there also may exist corresponding patterns of social knowledge. Snyder and Cantor (1980) have argued that the particular orientation of low self-monitoring individuals, as well as their behavioral style, may be associated with extensively developed and easily accessible stores of self-knowledge. Having frequently focused on their own attitudes and predispositions, low self-monitoring individuals may acquire correspondingly well-developed knowledge in that domain. High self-monitoring individuals, on the other hand, having frequently considered social comparison information to guide their behavior, may have correspondingly rich knowledge about a variety of different person prototypes in the abstract. Snyder and Cantor (1980) demonstrated this pattern of links between self-monitoring style and social knowledge in two converging studies. In both a structured and free response format,

> high self-monitoring individuals were particularly skilled at constructing informative images of individuals who are prototypic examples of diverse trait domains. Low self-monitoring individuals were particularly adept at constructing informative images of their characteristic selves in these same trait domains.
>
> M. Snyder and N. Cantor (1980, p. 18)

Extending the logic of this argument beyond the domain of dispositional (trait) knowledge; high self-monitoring individuals would be expected to have more highly developed conceptions of the prototypic-person-for-a-situation (see the section on categorizations) than would their low self-monitoring counterparts. Similarly, low self-monitoring individuals should be very clear on how they act and what kind of a person they are in their important life situations. Research investigating this hypothesis is currently underway.

The pattern of data on self-monitoring clearly illustrates the potential for coordination between social knowledge and social behavior. It remains to concretize the actual function assumed by that knowledge in *generating* that behavior. For example, how might compound self-in-situation or prototype-for-situation images be used by low and high self-monitoring individuals, respectively, to choose and shape their behavior? Snyder (1979, pp. 106 –107) suggests:

> The behavioral orientations of individuals who differ in their self-monitoring propensities may be reflections and manifestations of their characteristic modes of thought. Specifically, person-in-situation scenarios involving characteristic selves or prototypic others may be involved fundamentally in the process by which individuals plan and guide their actions in social contexts. Low self-monitoring individuals seem to be particularly skilled at constructing cognitive images involving their characteristic selves. Their self-images seem to be particularly rich sources of information that would be of considerable utility in choosing behaviors in social situations. In fact, as research on the behavioral consequences of self-monitoring makes clear, their social behavior demonstrates precisely the correspondence between public behavior and private self-conception and the cross-situational consistency that the habitual enactment of such scenarios would produce. High self-monitoring individuals, in contrast, seem to be particularly skilled at constructing informative cognitive images involving other individuals who are prototypic examples of a wide variety of behavioral domains. Indeed, their social behavior reflects the marked cross-situational specificity that the continuing behavioral enactment of such scenarios would generate.

Considerable work will be required to demonstrate conclusively this *active* and *dynamic* role posited by Snyder (1979) and by the present authors for compound person-situation social knowledge in the generation of social behavior. One step in this direction has been taken by Snyder (1980) in his recent work on self-monitors' varying proclivities for choosing to enter social situations. Snyder gave his high and low self-monitoring subjects the "choice of entering or not entering a social situation that called for the expression of extraversion" (Snyder, 1980). However, for half of his subjects the situational requirement of extraversion (the prototype-for-the-situation) was clearly conveyed. For the remaining subjects, "the extraverted character called for by the situation was defined in only the vaguest of terms" (Snyder, 1980). The results supported the view that high self-monitoring individuals are sensitive to and plan behavior according to situational prototypes. High self-monitors were willing to enter the clearly defined situation and unwilling to enter the vaguely defined one, regardless of their own prior self-reports of extraversion or introversion. Similarly, these data also supported a view of the low self-monitor as relatively self-oriented, checking the fit between general situational requirements and personal characteristics. Low self-monitors were unaffected by the clarity of the situation prototypes (equally willing to enter either situation). But while extraverted low self-monitors were willing to enter either situation, introverted low self-monitors would not enter either the clearly or vaguely defined extraverted situation. The high self-monitors' sensitivity to the explicitness of situational requirements affects their choices of situations; the low self-monitors' adherence to their self-images influences their situational choices.

While only preliminary, this work begins to address the crucial question of the function played by different social information in the generation of behavior. In a similar vein, Cantor (1980) is currently investigating the choice of information (about self, partners, or task-situations) that subjects want in order to prepare themselves for social interactions. Research in this area now seems ripe to move from associational statements to more exactly specifying the utility of social knowledge in specific social interactions.

Self-Regulation: Cognition and Social Behavior

The second relevant program of research that we use illustratively here investigated the role of conscious thought and attention in a delay of gratification paradigm (Mischel, 1980). In this paradigm children attempt to wait for a preferred but delayed reward over a less preferred but immediately available one. A number of studies showed the dramatic role of attention to the rewards in self-imposed delay of gratification. Specifically, initial theorizing (reviewed in Mischel, 1974) suggested that during delay of gratification attention to the rewards should serve a "time-binding" function and facilitate the child's ability to wait for them. These expectations proved to be exactly wrong: preschool children were able to wait ten times longer when the rewards in the contingency were *not* available for attention during the delay period than when they were in view (Mischel & Ebbesen, 1970). In contrast, attention to symbolic representations (pictures) of the rewards in the contingency ("relevant rewards") made it much easier for preschool children to delay gratification (Mischel & Moore, 1973, 1980). More interesting for the present argument, the effects of the actual rewards physically present or absent in the situation could be completely overcome and even totally reversed by changing how the child represented those rewards mentally during the delay period. For example, when preschoolers ideate about the rewards for which they are waiting in consummatory or "hot" ways (for instance, focusing on their taste) they can hardly delay at all; but if they focus on the "cool" qualities of the rewards (on their abstract or nonconsummatory qualities) they can wait for them easily and even longer than if they distract themselves from the rewards altogether (Mischel, 1974; Mischel & Baker, 1975). Thus "hot" reward-oriented ideation decreased delay by making it more aversively frustrative and arousing. In contrast, delay is facilitated by ideation about the task-contingency, and by "cool" ideation focusing on the abstract (rather than consummatory) features of the rewards. In sum, the "overall findings on cognitive stimulus transformations clearly reveal that how children represent the rewards cognitively (not what is physically in front of them) determines how long they delay gratification" (Mischel, 1980, pp. 21–22).

The findings also illustrate how even young children can and do increase their own power to control what stimuli do to them by changing how they think about those stimuli. Once people recognize how their own ideation makes self-control either hard or easy, the option to engage in such control becomes truly their own: they know *how* to regulate their behavior effectively and thereby gain the choice of whether or not to do so. In this sense, the person's knowledge of the variables that allow "stimulus control" in given situations provides him or her potential power over those situations and can enhance the individual's ability to control stimuli purposefully rather than be controlled by them.

This stream of research thus demonstrates the potential role of cognition and self-instructional strategies in directly controlling behavior and overcoming external stimulus control. Similar self-instructional processes are at the heart of the cognitive-behavioral therapies of Meichenbaum (1977) and others (Agras, Kazdin, & Wilson, 1979) who teach people to use cognition as a mediator in changing and shaping their social behavior more adaptively. It is less clear, however, to what degree cognitive strategies play a determining role in spontaneous social behavior. (This issue is similar in principle to the one raised in reference to Snyder's self-knowledge and self-monitoring findings.) In the case of self-regulation, children do seem to exhibit increasingly accurate spontaneous knowledge of efficient delay rules during the course of development (Mischel, 1981). For example, by age seven years, they are quite aware of the utility of self-distraction techniques (as opposed to exposure to the rewards) in enhancing the capacity to "time-bind" or delay, although before the age of four years they either do not know the better strategy or even systematically choose the worst one. A central part of the cognitive competency underlying all successful forms of self-regulation (for adults as well as children) involves knowledge of the appropriate cognitive techniques to use and the conditions under which to draw on these cognitive strategies (Brown, 1978). Social (self and generalized) knowledge and cognitive strategies *can* directly aid social behavior; but even when these resources are available, people may not always use them (cf. Langer, 1978).

Summary

In this section we have considered the very complex issues of the relations between social knowledge and social behavior. Work on self-monitoring processes was cited as one body of evidence documenting the coordination of particular kinds of social knowledge with specific styles of social behaivor. Work on self-regulation demonstrated the potential utility of cognitive, self-instructional strategies for controlling otherwise difficult behavior and overcoming stimulus control through cognitive self-control. But how frequent and pervasive is spontaneous cognitive mediation in social interactions? We turn next, in the concluding section of this chapter, to some speculations on this issue.

SOME CONCLUDING SPECULATIONS

Interrelations Between Knowledge, Cognitive Work, and Behavior

In this chapter we have seen that everyday social knowledge is substantial and varied in content (sections on categorizations and content), easily brought to mind (section on accessibility and utility), and orderly and efficiently structured (section on structure), providing a wealth of facts and rules-of-thumb potentially useful for generating social behavior (section on function). How, then does this store of social knowledge actually inform our everyday behavior? In this concluding section, we indulge in some speculations about the interrelations between social knowledge, cognitive work (processes such as attention and memory) and social behavior. We will briefly consider four interrelated issues of enduring interest to social and personality psychologists.

1. How much social behavior involves "conscious," "strategic" cognitive work as opposed to relatively "mindless" and "automatic" action?
2. What role is played by social knowledge in the generation of overt social behavior and under what conditions is this contribution maximized?
3. How much of our perceptions and behaviors are created "in the head" and biased toward preexisting expectancies? When do we actually accommodate to "objective" environmental contingencies and stimuli?
4. What is the nature and accuracy of our introspective access to the processes by which behaviors are shaped and executed?

To consider these issues properly, it is necessary to establish, at least tentatively and in schematic form, a model of possible interrelations between knowledge, cognitive work, and behavior. Figure 4 presents such a model, intended to represent the activity of the lay observer-actor at any particular moment. [This model has been abstracted from models provided by various cognitive psychologists, e.g., Norman and Bobrow (1975), Klatzky (1975), and many others.]

Three components in the slice of current activity are represented along the y-axis of Figure 4: stimulus inputs, cognitive work, and overt behavioral outputs. The x-axis is intended to represent variations in the degree to which each component would generally be in the "foreground" (in conscious focus) at a particular point in time. The current stimulus input consists of a foreground component in the actually impinging events in the external situation and a more stable background component of long-term social knowledge (e.g., scripts, prototypes, causal theories). Similarly, current cognitive work can be considered as including both a limited supply of conscious working memory (or focused attention) and

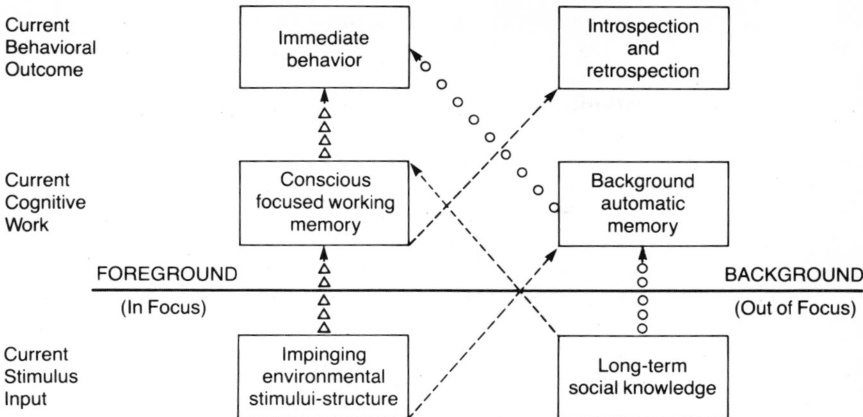

FIGURE 4. Schematic diagram of interrelations between knowledge, cognition, and behavior. (See text for explanations of the illustrative links between components.)

a more extensive capacity to process information automatically (see Klatzky, 1975, or Shiffrin & Schneider, 1977). Finally, there are the very immediate, overt actions of the person and the more distanced introspections and retrospections in which he/she engages (see White, 1980).

Of central concern here are the interrelations between these various components in the "current action space" of the individual. We would make a number of suggestions in this regard [see Norman and Bobrow (1975) for similar discussion]. First, both environmental stimuli and long-term social knowledge serve as input to both working memory and automatic memory, with both memories contributing to the immediate overt behavior. Second, introspection and retrospection have access only to the contents of conscious working memory [both process and product; see White (1980)] and not to those of automatic memory. Finally, as one level in this diagram feeds into the next (e.g., stimulus input level feeds to the cognitive work level, which feeds to the behavioral outcome level), there is a trade-off between the relative contributions from the "focused" and the "distanced" components at each level. In other words, any particular product at any given level (such as a behavioral outcome) is almost always the result of input from both the focused and more distanced components at an earlier level. But the product is also likely to be more heavily determined by either the focused or the distanced aspects. Thus overt behavior, at any particular point in time, is likely to be shaped by both conscious and automatic cognitive work, which, in turn, are fed by stimuli both "in the head" (social knowledge) and "in the environment" (impinging stimuli). However, the greater the contribution at any given moment of, for example, social knowledge to conscious working memory, the less conscious capacity is allotted to scanning and working on environmental input.

These assumptions, of multiple input relations between levels and trading relations within any given level, are central to consideration of the issues outlined at the outset of this discussion. We turn now to ways in which this schematic model may shed some light on those issues.

To consider such issues, it is helpful to outline two extreme or paradigmatic cases of interrelations between knowledge, cognitive work, and behavior within the present model. These are paradigmatic cases in that they represent extremes of the trade-offs possible at any one of the three main levels (input, cognitive work, behavior).

Paradigmatic Case A: Scripted Behavior. In Case A, we are considering *overt behavior* as shaped mainly by contributions from *automatic memory*. An example is walking into a restroom and executing "the restroom script" (see Langer, 1978; Schank & Abelson, 1977). If the restroom environment presents no surprises (such as a woman and her dog in the men's room), then the predominant contribution to *automatic memory* and, in turn, to *overt behavior*, will be from the stores of *social knowledge* comprising the restroom script. Of course, in addition to social knowledge, environmental input will also feed into automatic memory (e.g., the actor scans the restroom for the expected situation). However, the main burden of behavior planning and execution will be accomplished through relatively automatic activation of the "default" material in the restroom script—the cognitive generalizations that tell one to do whatever one "normally" does in "normal" restrooms. (The *major* relations underlying Case A are illustrated in Figure 4 by lines comprised of circles.)

Paradigmatic Case B: Conscious Behavior. In Case B, we are considering *overt behavior* as shaped primarily by contributions from *conscious working memory*. Returning to the restroom situation, suppose the normal men's room were suddenly transformed by the presence of a woman casually leaning against a wall as her dog drank from a toilet. In this case, we suggest the *environmental stimuli* overwhelm, by violating the script-expectations, the contribution of the social knowledge component. In turn, the contribution of conscious working memory (to overt behavior) overpowers that of automatic memory and the normal, mundane scripted behavior is blocked as the actor works to salvage the situation. (The *major* relations underlying Paradigm B are illustrated in Figure 4 by lines comprised of triangles.)

We turn now to some implications of these two paradigmatic cases and the accompanying schematic model for the four issues raised earlier.

Issues 1 and 2: "Consciousness versus Mindlessness" and the Role of Social Knowledge in Overt Behavior

The existence of "mindless," scripted behavior is often viewed as equivalent to the demonstration that social knowledge (and cognition in general) is not involved in shaping the overt behavior ([though, it should be noted, this was *not* Langer's intention in introducing the term; see Langer (1978)]. However, and paradoxically, it is clear from Case A that, under the assumptions of the present model, the contributions to behavior of schematic social knowledge (such as that under consideration in the present chapter) are actually maximized under conditions of scripted behavior and certainly are greater in Case A than in Case B. This is an important, though simple, point that is often ignored: mindless behavior (i.e., behavior with a heavy automatic memory component) makes great use of the mind (i.e., relies primarily on input from stored, relatively stable schematic knowledge). Moreover, scripted behavior certainly relies on a great deal of cognitive activity, however fast and painless the workings of automatic memory may be. The execution of a script involves complex activation-of-knowledge and inferential processes; automatic processing should not be confused with *no processing*. To do so would undervalue the mental accomplishments of the man in the woman-free restroom.

Issues 3 and 4: Biases in Perception and Introspection

Personality and social psychologists also have given much attention lately to problems of the biased perception and introspection presumed to accompany the perceiver's reliance on schematic knowledge. Personality psychologists (e.g., Block, 1977; D'Andrade, 1974; Schweder, 1977) debate whether traitlike consistencies in behavior actually exist or are simply "fictions" created by the observer who expects them to exist (e.g., by the lay psychologist who organizes social experience around trait categories). Similarly, Nisbett and Wilson (1977) have raised the point that people's introspections and explanations of their own behavior are often of limited accuracy because they rely too heavily on metatheories of "how the world works," on scripts and social schemata that are insensitive to actual causal contingencies. In both of these arguments, an underlying question is the degree to which schematic knowledge may be efficient to use (i.e., automatically retrieved from memory) but easily abused (by frequently providing the lay perceiver with an inaccurate, biased view of reality).

While we surely cannot provide a definitive answer to these complex questions, the schematic model presented above can stimulate further speculation and supports an unextreme, neither-nor, matter-of-degree, interactionist position. Consider, first, the question of whether perceptions primarily reflect the perceiver's biases and expectations or mirror reality. Given the assumption that there are always multiple inputs from the environment, from schematic knowledge and from both working and automatic memory, the interactionist answer seems as mandatory as it is undramatic (cf. Cantor & Mischel, 1979, and Rosch et al., 1976). As we see in Case A, schematic knowledge will be used to the extent that the environmental structure is sufficiently orderly to warrant its use. Because it is in some sense easier to use schematic knowledge and heavily automatic processing, the lay perceiver's threshold or cutoff criterion for "order in the environment" may be lower than that of the personologist. The lay perceiver may be willing to conclude that traitlike consistency exists in a particular person's behavior, even though as trained personologists we would only observe a .30 consistency coefficient. But as Paradigm B illustrates, environmental structure and contingencies do not go unnoticed. Clear violations of expectations trigger conscious strategies and adaptive responses. Just as it was necessary to build trading relations at all levels in the model, it is important to recognize the existence of a continuous trade-off between speed/accuracy or economy/bias in human social perception and behavior. Dependence on schematic knowledge illustrates this delicate balance.

Nisbett and Wilson (1977) and others (e.g., Smith & Miller, 1978; White, 1980) have called attention to biases resulting from reliance on schematic social knowledge, in the domain of introspection. Without entering into this complex argument deeply, note that our schematic diagram also speaks to the introspection issue. First, a main assumption of our model (and of the Nisbett and Wilson position) is that we do not have direct introspective access to the process or content of automatic memory. Consequently, to the degree that overt behavior is determined by a chain primarily feeding through automatic memory, we will not have direct access to the determinants of our own behavior, regardless of whether the primary input to automatic memory came from schematic social knowledge (as in Case A) or from environmental input (as in current theories of automatic visual processing). In the event that behavior was primarily influenced by automatic processing, our introspection will be forced to resort to a consideration of schematic knowledge about plausible causal chains and metatheories about "how the world works" (Nisbett & Wilson, 1977). In contrast, to the degree that impinging environmental stimuli or an absence of appropriate scripts force us to direct behavior primarily through conscious strategies (Paradigm B), then introspective access to this process will be available and used. However, as White (1980) cogently points out, the greater the intervening time and events between the actual cognitive work leading to behavior and the introspection about that process, the more likely it is that the contents of working memory have shifted and introspective access will be lost. In that case (which we may want to call retrospection rather than introspection) the input is again likely to be primarily schematic about "how the world works."

This sketch of the introspective process is not fundamentally different from Nisbett and Wilson's (1977) characterization of that process. However, they concluded that such a model suggests that the lay perceiver will have quite poor accuracy in his/her introspections. Our speculations lead us to somewhat different emphasis in thinking about introspective accuracy. First, Nisbett and Wilson's conclusion seems to rest on the assumption that the schematic knowledge used as input to introspection when automatic processing has gone on (e.g., Case A) will not be an accurate reflection of the input that was involved in the execution and planning of the original behavior. However, the present model suggests that frequently under automatic processing conditions, the main input to the cognitive-behavioral chain will, in fact, have been schematic social knowledge. In other words, in the case of automatically executed social behavior, the actor's generalized scripts *do* serve as the basis both for behavior *and* for introspective explanations of that behavior. To the extent that the *same* script (or script element) has been invoked for both these purposes in a given instance, we can say that the actor's introspection has been accurate in some practical, meaningful sense. It seems likely to us that these conditions of "practical accuracy" are quite prevalent in the social world.

Consider, for example, a subject who complies in response to "placebic" information in the Xerox machine situation staged by Langer and her colleagues (Langer, Blank, & Chanowitz, 1978). Having observed the subject's automatic compliance with a request to allow the experimenter to use the machine first "because I have to make copies," suppose one were to ask this subject to introspect about the cause of his/her compliance. After consulting a "doing favors for strangers" script, the subject would most likely report having complied because the requester "was in a hurry," or for some other seemingly justifiable reason. While this reason is not supplied by the actual behavioral interaction (it is not conveyed in the experimenter's request), it *is* supplied by the script invoked for causal explanation. That is, a typical element of "doing favors for strangers" situations is the assumption that the person asking the favor has a real or good reason for doing so. Moreover, given that this "favor-doing" script is the very schema that in fact activated the subject's automatic compliant behavior, it is hardly inaccurate for the subject to cite the "good reason" aspect of this script as the cause of his/her behavior. The automatic, scripted *assumption* that a good reason existed *was* the basis for compliance with the request. The fact that this inference has been *automatically* fed into overt behavior (because the "favor-doing" script was activated) rather than given by the environmental stimuli (the request) does not seem a sufficient reason to label the subject's introspective causal explanation inaccurate. In a practical sense, the subject *has* cited the correct influential factor; the inference that the request was justified by a good reason. Introspective consultation of schematic social knowledge has served this subject rather well.

Second, consider the conditions when the schematic knowledge would probably not provide a good match with the original input to the cognitive-behavioral process (and thus would provide for inaccurate introspections). The present model suggests that naturally occurring social behavior will be determined primarily by environmental stimuli and contingencies—reflected through conscious working memory—under two conditions: when the environmental structure grossly violates schematic expectations or when no appropriate schema exists. Under these conditions we would expect the accuracy of the perceiver's introspections to be primarily a function of the availability in working memory of the actually operative environmental events and stimuli—and this, in turn, will be a matter of intervening time and events. Consequently, as

White (1980) suggested, we expect that the closer the conditions of introspection are to retrospection, the less accurate these introspections will be. White (1980) provides data that support this claim. As elapsed time and number of intervening events increase, the perceiver is more likely to fall back on less accurate explanations of his/her behavior, explanations based on schemata that are inappropriate to this "nonscripted" circumstance. So, the accuracy of introspection in this case will depend on the ecology of the social world, on the frequency with which introspective conditions approximate those of retrospection.

Summary

We speculated about the role of social knowledge in the generation of behavior and introspection. Some interpretations of "mindlessness" in social behavior, in our view, may have undervalued the important functions of social knowledge in shaping everyday interactions. An emphasis on bias and inaccuracy associated with the use of schematic social knowledge may grossly exaggerate the costs and obscure the benefits of having such knowledge. The research reported in this chapter suggests that schematic social knowledge is multifaceted, well-structured, and easily accessed. Our speculations in the last section suggest that such knowledge is also heavily implicated in social behavior (in both immediate overt behavior and in introspection). Rather than being necessarily biased or inaccurate, social knowledge is frequently economic, efficient, and adaptive.

REFERENCES

Agras, W. S., Kazdin, A. E., & Wilson, G. T. *Behavior therapy: Toward an applied clinical science.* San Francisco, Calif.: Freeman, 1979.

Anderson, J. Arguments concerning representations for mental imagery. *Psychological Review*, 1978, *85*(4), 249 –277.

Ashmore, R., & Delboca, F. Sex stereotypes and implicit personality theory: Toward a cognitive-social psychological conceptualization. *Sex Roles*, 1979, *5*(2), 219 –248.

Berscheid, E., Graziano, W., Morison, T., & Dermer, M. Outcome dependency: Attention, attribution, and attraction. *Journal of Personality and Social Psychology, 34,* 1976, 978 –989.

Block, J. An illusory interpretation of the first factor of the MMPI: A reply to Shweder. *Journal of Consulting and Clinical Psychology*, 1977, *45*(5), 930 –935.

Bower, G. H., & Gilligan, S. G. Remembering information related to one's self. *Journal of Research in Personality*, 1979, *13*, 420 –432.

Bowers, K. Situationism in psychology: An analysis and a critique. *Psychological Review*, 1973, *80*, 307 –336.

Brown, A. Development, schooling and the acquisition of knowledge about knowledge. In R. Anderson, R. Spiro, and W. Montague (Eds.), *Schooling and the acquisition of knowledge.* Hillsdale, N.J.: Erlbaum, 1978.

Cantor, N. Perceptions of situations: Situation prototypes and person-situation prototypes. In D. Magnusson (Ed.), *The situation: An interactional perspective*, Hillsdale, N.J.: Erlbaum, 1980.

Cantor, N., & Mischel, W. Prototypes in person perception. In L. Berkowitz (Ed.), *Advances in experimental social psychology*, Vol. 12. New York: Academic, 1979, pp. 3 –52.

Cantor, N., Mischel, W., & Schwartz J. A prototype analysis of psychological situations. *Cognitive Psychology*, 1981, in press.

Cantor, N., Smith, E. E., French, R., & Mezzich, J. Psychiatric diagnosis as prototype categorization. *Journal of Abnormal Psychology*, 1980, *89*(2), 181 –193.

Carlson, R. Where is the person in personality research? *Psychological Bulletin*, 1971, *75*, 203 –219.

Cohen, C. Cognitive basis of stereotyping. Paper presented at the meetings of the American Psychological Association, San Francisco, Calif., August, 1977.

Cohen, C., & Ebbesen, E. Observational goals and schema activation: A theoretical framework for behavior perception. *Journal of Experimental Social Psychology*, 1979, *15*, 305 –329.

D'Andrade, R. G. Memory and the assessment of behavior. In H. M. Blalock (Ed.), *Measurement in the social sciences*. Chicago, Ill.: Aldine, 1974.

Darley, J., & Akert, R. Biographical interpretation: The influence of later events in life on the meaning of earlier events. Unpublished manuscript, Princeton University, Princeton, N.J., 1980.

Ebbesen, E. B., & Allen, R. B. Cognitive processes in implicit personality trait inferences. *Journal of Personality and Social Psychology*, 1979, *37*, 471 –488.

Endler, N. S., & Hunt, J. McV. Generalizability of contributions from sources of variance in the S-R inventories of anxiousness. *Journal of Personality*, 1969, *37*, 1 –24.

Fiske, S. T., & Cox, M. G. Person concepts: The effect of target familiarity and descriptive purpose on the process of describing others. *Journal of Personality*, 1979, *47*(1), 136 –161.

Hastie, R. Memory for information that is congruent or incongruent with a conceptual schema. In E. T. Higgins, C. P. Herman, & M. P. Zanna (Eds.), *Social cognition: The Ontario symposium on personality and social psychology*. Hillsdale, N.J.: Erlbaum, 1980.

Hastie, R., & Kumar, A. P. Person memory: Personality traits as organizing principles in memory for behaviors. *Journal of Personality and Social Psychology*, 1979, *37*, 25 –38.

Hayden, T., & Mischel, W. Maintaining trait consistency in the resolution of behavioral inconsistency: The wolf in sheep's clothing? *Journal of Personality*, 1976, *44*, 109 –132.

Higgins, E. T., & King, G. Accessibility of social constructs: Information-processing consequences of individual and contextual variability. In N. Cantor & J. Kihlstrom (Eds.), *Personality, cognition and social interaction*. Hillsdale, N.J.: Erlbaum, 1980.

Higgins, E. T., Herman, C. P., & Zanna, M. (Eds.) *Social cognition*. Hillsdale, N.J.: Erlbaum, 1980.

Hoffman, C., Mischel, W., & Mazze, K. The role of purpose in the organization of information about behavior: Trait-based versus goal-based categories in person cogniton. Unpublished manuscript, Stanford University, Palo Alto, Calif., 1980.

Jeffery, K. M., & Mischel, W. Effects of purpose on the organization and recall of information in person perception. *Journal of Personality*, 1979, *47*, 397 –419.

Jones, E. E. The rocky road from acts to dispositions. *American Psychologist*, 1979, *34*, 107 –117.

Jones, E. E., Kanouse, D., Kelley, H. H., Nisbett, R. E., Valins, S., & Weiner, B. (Eds.). *Attribution: Perceiving the causes of behavior*. New York: General Learning Press, 1972.

Judd, C. M., & Kulik, J. A. Schematic effects of social attitudes on information processing and recall. *Journal of Personality and Social Psychology*, 1980, *38*(4), 569 –578.

Kahneman, D., & Tversky, A. On the psychology of prediction. *Psychological Review*, 1973, *80*, 237 –251.

Klatzky, R. L. *Human memory: Structures and processes*. San Francisco, Calif.: Freeman, 1975.

Kuiper, N., & Derry, P. A. The self as a cognitive prototype. An application to person perception and depression. In N. Cantor & J. Kihlstrom (Eds.), *Personality, cognition and social interaction*, Hillsdale, N.J.: Erlbaum, 1980.

Langer, E. J. Rethinking the role of thought in social interaction. In J. Harvey, W. Ickes, & R. Kidd (Eds.), *New directions in attribution research*, Vol. 2. Hillsdale, N.J.: Erlbaum, 1978.

Langer, E. J., Blank, A., & Chanowitz, B. The mindlessness of ostensibly thoughtful action: The role of "placebic" information in interpersonal interaction. *Journal of Personality and Social Psychology*, 1978, *36*(b), 635–642.

Lehrer, A. *Semantic fields and lexical structure*. Amsterdam: North-Holland Publishing, 1974.

Magnusson, D. *The situation: An interactional approach*. Hillsdale, N.J.: Erlbaum, 1979.

Markus, H., & Smith, J. The influence of self-schemas on the perception of others. In N. Cantor & R. Kihlstrom (Eds.), *Personality, cognition and social interaction*, Hillsdale, N.J.: Erlbaum, 1980.

Medin, D., & Schaffer, M. Context theory of classification learning. *Psychological Review*, 1978, *85*, 207–238.

Meichenbaum, D. *Cognitive behavior modification*. New York: Plenum, 1977.

Mischel, W. *Personality and assessment*. New York: Wiley, 1968.

Mischel, W. Processes in delay of gratification. In L. Berkowitz (Ed.), *Advances in experimental social psychology*, Vol. 7. New York: Academic, 1974.

Mischel, W. Objective and subjective rules for delay of gratification. Paper presented at symposium on "Cognition in Human Motivation," Louvain, 1980.

Mischel, W. Metacognition and rules of delay. In J. Flavell & L. Ross (Eds.), *Cognitive social development: Frontiers and possible futures*. New York: Cambridge University Press, 1981.

Mischel, W., & Baker, N. Cognitive appraisals and transformations in delay behavior. *Journal of Personality and Social Psychology*, 1975, *31*, 254–261.

Mischel, W., & Ebbesen, E. Attention in delay of gratification. *Journal of Personality and Social Psychology*, 1970, *16*, 329–337.

Mischel, W., & Moore, B. Effects of attention to symbolically presented rewards upon self-control. *Journal of Personality and Social Psychology*, 1973, *28*, 172–179.

Mischel, W., & Moore, B. The role of ideation in voluntary delay for symbolically presented rewards. *Cognitive Therapy and Research*, 1980, *4*, 211–221.

Nisbett, R. E., & Borgida, E. Attribution and the psychology of prediction. *Journal of Personality and Social Psychology*, 1975, *32*, 932–943.

Nisbett, R. E., & Ross, L. *Human inference: Strategies and shortcomings of social judgment*. Englewood Cliffs, N.J.: Prentice-Hall, 1980.

Nisbett, R. E., & Wilson, T. D. Telling more than we can know: Verbal reports on mental processes. *Psychological Review*, 1977, *84*, 231–259.

Norman, W. T. Toward an adequate taxonomy of personality attributes: Replicated factor structure in peer nomination personality rating. *Journal of Abnormal and Social Psychology*, 1963, *66*, 574–583.

Norman, W. T., & Bobrow, D. G. *On the role of active memory processes in perception and cognition*. Technical Report No. 50. San Diego, Calif.: Center for Human Information Processing, 1975.

Pervin, L. A. A free-response description approach to the analysis of person–situation interaction. *Journal of Personality and Social Psychology*, 1976, *34*, 465–474.

Pervin, L. A the representativae design of person–situation research. In D. Magnusson & N. S. Endler (Eds.), *Personality at the crossroads: Current issues in interactional psychology*. Hillsdale, N.J.: Erlbaum, 1977.

Posner, M., & Keele, S. On the genesis of abstract ideas. *Journal of Experimental Psychology*, 1968, *77*, 353–363.

Price, R., & Bouffard, D. L. Behavioral appropriateness and situational constraint as dimensions of social behavior. *Journal of Personal and Social Psychology*, 1974, *30*, 579–586.

Reed, S. K. Pattern recognition and categorization. *Cognitive Psychology*, 1972, *3*, 382–407.

Rogers, T. A model of the self as an aspect of the human information processing system. In N. Cantor & J. Kihlstrom (Eds.), *Personality, cognition, and social interaction*. Hillsdale, N.J.: Erlbaum, 1980.

Rogers, T., Kuiper, N. A., & Kirker, W. S. Self-reference and the encoding of personal information. *Journal of Personality and Social Psychology*, 1977, *35*, 677–688.

Rosch, E. Principles of Categorization. In E. Rosch & B. B. Lloyd (Eds.), *Cognition and categorization*. Hillsdale, N.J.: Erlbaum, 1978.

Rosch, E., & Mervis, C. Family resemblances: Studies in the internal structure of categories. *Cognitive Psychology*, 1975, *7*, 573 –605.

Rosch, E., Mervis, C., Gray, W., Johnson, D., & Boyes-Braem, P. Basic objects in natural categories. *Cognitive Psychology*, 1976, *8*, 382 –439.

Ross, L. The intuitive psychologist and his shortcomings: Distortion in the attribution process. In L. Berkowitz (Ed.), *Advances in experimental social psychology*, Vol. 10. New York: Academic, 1977.

Rothbart, M., Evans, M., & Fulero, S. Recall for confirming events: Memory processes and the maintenance of social stereotypes. *Journal of Experimental Social Psychology*, 1979, *15*, 343 –355.

Schank, R., & Abelson, R. *Scripts, plans, goals, and understanding*. Hillsdale, N.J.: Erlbaum, 1977.

Schneider, D. J. Implicit personality theory: A review. *Psychological Bulletin*, 1973, *79*, 294 –309.

Shiffrin, R. M., & Schneider, W. Controlled and automatic human information processing: II. Perceptual learning, automatic attending and a general theory. *Psychological Review*, 1977, *84*, 127 –190.

Shweder, R. A. Illusory correlation and the MMPI controversy. *Journal of Consulting and Clinical Psychology*, 1977, *45*(5), 917 –924.

Smith, E. E., & Medin, D. Representation and processing of lexical concepts. Unpublished manuscript, Stanford University, Palo Alto, Calif., 1979.

Smith, E. R., & Miller, E. R. Limits on perception of cognitive processes: A reply to Nisbett and Wilson. *Psychological Review*, 1978, *85*, 355 –362.

Snyder, M. The self-monitoring of expressive behavior. *Journal of Personality and Social Psychology*, 1974, *30*, 526 –537.

Snyder, M. Self-monitoring processes. In L. Berkowitz (Ed.), *Advances in experimental social psychology*, New York: Academic, 1979.

Snyder, M. On the influence of individuals on situations. In N. Cantor & J. Kihlstrom (Eds.), *Personality, cognition, and social interaction*, Hillsdale, N.J.: Erlbaum, 1980.

Snyder, M., & Cantor, N. Thinking about ourselves and others: Self-monitoring and social knowledge. *Journal of Personality and Social Psychology*, 1980, *39*, 222 –234.

Snyder, M., & Monson, T. C. Persons, situations and the control of social behavior. *Journal of Personality and Social Psychology*, 1975, *32*, 637 –644.

Snyder, M., & Swann, W. B., Jr. When actions reflect attitudes: The politics of impression management. *Journal of Personality and Social Psychology*, 1976, *34*, 1034 –1042.

Snyder, M., & Tanke, E. D. Behavior and attitude: Some people are more consistent than others. *Journal of Personality*, 1976, *44*, 510 –517.

Snyder, M., & Uranowitz, S. W. Reconstructing the past: Some cognitive consequences of person perception. *Journal of Personality and Social Psychology*, 1978, *36*, 941 –950.

Spence, J. T., & Helmreich, R. L. *Masculinity and femininity: Their psychological dimensions, correlates and antecedents*. Austin, Tex.: University of Texas Press, 1978.

Taylor, S. E. A categorization approach to stereotyping. In D. L. Hamilton (Ed.), *Cognitive processes in stereotyping and intergroup behavior*. Hillsdale, N.J.: Erlbaum, 1979.

Taylor, S. E., & Crocker, J. C. Schematic bases of social information processing. In E. T. Higgins, P. Herman, & M. P. Zanna (Eds.), *The Ontario Symposium on Personality and Social Psychology*, Vol. 1. Hillsdale, N.J.: Erlbaum, 1980.

Tversky, A., & Kahneman, D. Judgment under uncertainty: Heuristics and biases. *Science*, 1974, *185*, 1124 –1131.

Walker, J. H. Real-world variability, reasonableness judgments and memory representations for concepts. *Journal of Verbal Learning and Verbal Behavior*, 1975, *14*, 241 –252.

White, P. Limitations on verbal reports of internal events. A refutation of Nisbett and Wilson and of Bem. *Psychological Review*, 1980, 87(1), 105 –112.

Wiggins, J. S. A psychological taxonomy of trait-descriptive terms: The interpersonal domain. *Journal of Personality and Social Psychology*, 1979, *37*(3), 395 –413.

Wiggins, J. S. Circumplex model of interpersonal behavior in personality and social psychology. In L. Wheeler (Ed.), *Review of personality and social psychology*. Beverly Hills, Calif.: Sage Press, 1980.

Wittgenstein, L. *Philosophical investigations*. New York: Macmillan, 1953.

MARGARET S. CLARK ALICE M. ISEN

TOWARD UNDERSTANDING THE RELATIONSHIP BETWEEN FEELING STATES AND SOCIAL BEHAVIOR

Have you ever had an experience similar to this: You are walking down a street, on a clear, bright day, when suddenly you come upon a $5.00 bill lying right there in your path, looking up at you, so to speak; and no one is there to claim it but you? You stare, blink, and determine in a split second that it really is money; you look around again and see no one. And so you pick up the $5.00 bill, give a thought to your good fortune, feel a lift in your spirits, and perhaps think about how you will spend the money or what recent expenditure it "covers." Chances are that we have all had an experience something like this at one time or another. Now, we would like to ask you what effect you think this "find" and its resultant elation had on your cognitions and behavior.

Next, consider the following excerpt from a short story by Katherine Mansfield, in which she describes a young woman, Bertha, who is experiencing a "feeling of bliss. . . ." Bertha reflects on her life thinking,

> Really—really—she had everything. She was young, Harry and she were as much in love as ever, and they got on together splendidly and were really good pals. She had an adorable baby. They didn't have to worry about money. They had this absolutely satisfactory house and garden. And friends—modern, thrilling friends, writers and painters and poets or people keen on social questions—just the kind of friends they wanted. And then there were books, and there was music, and she had found a wonderful dressmaker and they were going abroad in the summer, and their new cook made the most superb omelettes. . .
>
> From *Bliss*, Katherine Mansfield

Bertha's state, like the one we asked you to imagine at the very beginning of the chapter, is typical of what we would call a positive feeling state, and we suggest that such states have extensive effects on general cognition, social judgment, and behavior. Perhaps the cognitive effects are difficult to discern on the basis of the first illustration, in part because it is not written in such detail as the excerpt, and the exercise produces only a shadow of the original experience. The train of thought detailed in the Mansfield excerpt, however, demonstrates nicely the kind of cognitive effects we are suggesting: Bertha's thoughts go from being in love, to having exciting friends, to going abroad, and to delicious omelettes. We will be presenting evidence that such feeling states, negative as well as positive, influence what people think about and the judgments they make, and thus have important effects on social behavior; we will also suggest a cognitive interpretation of how feeling states have these effects. Thus the relevance of this chapter to a book on cognitive social psychology should become evident, for we will propose that the impact of feeling states on perception and social behavior can best be understood as functions of the cognitive processes through which people organize and utilize knowledge of the world and, on that basis, make judgments and choices of actions in both social and nonsocial contexts.

THE NATURE OF FEELING STATES

The literature in social psychology contains many studies in which terms such as "feelings," "emotions," "moods," and, more generally, "affect," are used. Since many of these words are used interchangeably, we will define what we mean by "feeling states," and distinguish this term from "emotion."

Feeling states or moods are induced by pleasant or unpleasant experience—pleasing music, noise, a beautiful scene, something positive or negative happening to a person—or by recall of positive or negative experiences from memory (although the latter may constitute a special, attenuated, case). Many authors argue that feeling states involve labeling or interpretation (e.g., Schachter & Singer, 1962), but others propose alternative models of how feelings are generated. Leventhal (1974), for example, suggests that feelings of pleasantness and unpleasantness may be basic perceptual reactions, produced when innate perceptual mechanisms sensitive to specific, emotion-producing features of a display are stimulated. In either case—and we suspect, as Leventhal proposes, that there are conditions under which each of these potentialities predominates—we suggest that the feelings, once induced, are prolonged because positive or negative thoughts tend to lead to other, similarly toned thoughts and behavior. This, we suggest, creates a feeling state or mood. We would also propose that feeling states actually consist in thinking positive (or negative) thoughts and in having easy access to a substantial amount of additional positive (or negative) material in memory.

The first point we would make regarding the kind of state we are describing is that feeling states are pervasive (Ryle, 1950; Nowlis, 1970; Brady, 1970). They are not directed toward any particular subject and cannot be identified with any specific set of behaviors. Bertha's state is an example of a positive feeling state; thoughts about a wide variety of topics are generated—the attractiveness of the baby, good music, superb omelettes, and so forth. For another example, a positive feeling state produced by receiving an unexpected gift may lead not only to thoughts of how pleasant the giver is, but to thoughts of how satisfied one is with one's life, and to recalling of what a great time one had at the party last night. One can easily think of negative feeling states as well. Just imagine a woman who has completed an interview for a job. She thinks she did poorly and, consequently, that she will not get the job. This leads her to think about how incompetent she is, how disappointed her husband will be, and how much she needs the income. Soon she may also be thinking about how poorly she and her husband have been getting along, and of what a miserable winter they've been having. Note that in this illustration again, the feeling state is pervasive, and one thought associated with negative feeling leads to similarly toned thoughts on many different topics—lack of money, a bad winter, and personal incompetence.

Likewise, the cause of a person's feeling state does not necessarily become the target of the behavior affected by it. A given feeling state may affect a great variety of judgments and behaviors. Thus we can understand the finding that a person put in a positive feeling state by receiving the news that he or she has just succeeded on a task, for example, is more likely than a control subject to help some third person (e.g., Isen, 1970). In other words, feelings have neither specific behavioral impulses nor specific targets associated with them. Rather, the behavior affected by feeling states is likely to be determined by what in the environment a person's attention is directed to after the feeling state has been induced. If a person is given a free gift, which induces a positive mood, and that person subsequently comes across someone in need of help, the person's decision about whether or not to help is what will be affected by the feeling state (Isen, Clark, & Schwartz, 1976). If the same person instead is asked how his or her car is running, that judgment is what will be affected by the feeling state (Isen, Shalker, Clark, & Karp, 1978).

Note that our examples above imply that in most cases, unlike "emotions," feelings are not attention-getting, nor do they interrupt ongoing behavior to result in an abrupt change in activity. Rather, whatever induces a feeling state tends gently to redirect ongoing thinking and behavior and/or to affect what behavior or thoughts will occur next, but within the existing context. This means that the impact of feeling states on behavior is not immediately obvious, and it may be this factor that has led some others (e.g., Brady, 1970) to feel that affect has little influence on interaction or behavior. This may also account, in part, for the neglect of feeling states in psychology, generally. Brady (1970, p. 70), for example, has stated that

> Although both feelings and emotional behavior involve psychological interactions between the organism and environment, a useful and important distinction between the two can be made on the basis of the localizability of their principal effects or consequences. *Emotional behavior* seems most usefully considered as part of a broad class of *effective* interactions, the primary consequences of which appear to change the organism's relationship to its *external* environment. *Feelings* or *affective* behavior, on the other hand, can be distinguished as a generic class of interactions, the principle effects of which are localizable *within* the reacting organism rather than in the exteroceptive environment.

In other words, Brady focuses on the feeling tone of these states (the subjective experience of feeling) but suggests that, unlike emotions, they do not have notable effects on a person's interactions with people or objects in the environment.

In contrast, we suggest that feelings have important effects on cognition and behavior, and we would even argue that, because these states occur so frequently, understanding of their effects is extremely important to our understanding of behavior. Powerful emotional experiences may interrupt behavior and may be more dramatic and attention-getting when they occur (Simon, 1967; Mandler, 1975). But the subtle, pervasive, and almost irresistible effects of low-level affective states are so often with us that their potential influence may be very great, and they are deserving of study in their own right, distinct from high-intensity emotion.

It is for this reason, that we believe it is important to study feeling states in their naturally occurring forms and contexts. Some authors have attempted to study affect in a more context-free manner, as induced via hypnosis (Bower, Monteiro, & Gilligan, 1978) or by means of feedback from a meter (Forest, Clark, Mills, & Isen, 1979), for example, in an effort to study the "pure" emotion or an intense form of the emotion or feeling state. While the latter is appropriate for studying certain aspects of emotions or other states, we propose that in studying feeling states (1) there is an advantage to recreating as nearly as possible the feelings that one wishes to study, and (2) context and the process of constructing the feeling state naturally is an integral part of the experience. The feeling states induced in an experiment that arranges for its subjects to experience good fortune or success or pleasant social interactions, for example, if these are the experiences that one presumes to be influential in determining behavior, are probably more likely to duplicate the influential feeling states that people experience than are the feeling states induced more "purely." (Of course one cannot duplicate every possible individual mood-inducing circumstance; nor is this necessary if one uses a range of situations broad enough to allow triangulation on the construct of affect and to provide the basis for confidence that the situations used are representative of those that affect people naturally.)

In summary, then, we have said that feelings are general and pervasive, having no inherent targets, and they usually do not interrupt ongoing behavior. They are relatively transitory, they can occur frequently, often in the normal course of everyday life, and they consist in thinking about positive or negative material and in having easy access to a substantial amount of additional compatible material in memory. We tend to think that physiological arousal is not a necessary condition for the existence of a feeling state, although it can certainly accompany feelings; however, we are not ready to decide this issue, since evidence on it is lacking.

Feeling states or "moods" are thus distinguished from "emotions," which, in contrast, are usually more intense (Wessman & Ricks, 1966; Nowlis, 1970) and do involve arousal as well as a cognitive component that is usually thought to provide the interpretation and the positive or negative valence of the emotion (Mandler, 1975; Schachter & Singer, 1962). Further, the intensity of emotions, combined with the fact that emotions are closely tied to specifiable behavior, means that emotions are likely to disrupt ongoing behavior and to result in behavior directed toward a different goal (Brady, 1970). As Brady (1970, p. 70) has stated, ". . . emotional behavior seems uniquely definable in terms of a change or perturbation, characteristically abrupt and episodic, in the ongoing interaction between organism and environment."

Finally, despite the differences that we have noted between emotions and feeling states, it is probably not the case that they can be entirely separated from each other. Feeling states and emotions often occur together because the conditions that elicit emotions may also elicit a feeling state. For example, a personal insult may elicit anger, which leads to a counterattack, and the same insult and/or the counterattack may also elicit an ongoing negative feeling state.

All one need do in order to see this point is to remember one's last real argument with one's spouse, parent, sibling, or whomever. After the argument (and before making efforts to feel better), one may have felt "cross" or irritable. One's children may have seemed more "underfoot" than at other times, one's responsibilities at work or at home may have seemed more burdensome than usual, and one may have felt like a fire-breathing dragon apt to "pounce" on whatever unsuspecting soul entered the room or called on the phone. We would say that this is a feeling state of the kind we have been describing—not directed at anyone in particular, but able to affect many impressions and behavior—seemingly unrelated to the argument, but accompanying the emotional state. Thus feelings and emotions may be associated, even though they are identifiably different.

THE IMPACT OF FEELING STATES ON JUDGMENT AND BEHAVIOR

Now that we have examined what we mean by the term "feeling states," and have explained why we think it important to study them, we may turn to the question of just what their effects on social behavior and judgment have been shown to be. Social psychologists have accumulated evidence indicating that both positive and negative feeling states are important determinants of people's impressions of their world and of their behavior.

According to the evidence, people who are in positive feeling states seem to make judgments and to behave as if they "viewed the world through rose-colored glasses"—everything seems slightly better than usual—and they behave in ways that reflect this and suggest that they are trying to maintain their mood. Likewise, on the other side of the coin, negative feeling states sometimes seem to have the opposite, but parallel, effect on people. People in negative states may tend to see the negative side of things and be more pessimistic than usual, and their behavior may reflect these negative expectations and may serve to keep them in the negative feeling state. People feeling this way may withdraw from social interaction, or they may interact "with a chip on their shoulder." They not only seem to see things in a negative light, and to be irritable, but they often behave in ways that antagonize others and almost ensure the continuation of the negative state. However, in the case of negative feeling states, people sometimes engage in behavior that might reduce the effect of the negative state or even remove it. Clearly, then, the effects of negative feeling states on impressions and behavior are more complex than those of positive states. Sometimes people in negative states behave negatively, in accord with their moods; and sometimes they behave in a prosocial manner, apparently in an attempt to alleviate the negative mood. We will discuss this complexity and suggest a possible interpretation of it later in the chapter. For the time being, let us summarize the evidence.

Positive Feeling States

When Davitz (1970) asked people to report what they felt when they felt happy, they consistently reported such things as, ". . . the world seems basically good and beautiful, men are essentially kind, life is worth living and I keep thinking about how lucky I am." Experimental evidence buttresses these impressions that people in a positive feeling state have a more positive impression of their world than do others. For example, Isen et al. (1978) induced a positive feeling state in some randomly selected people in a shopping mall by giving them a free gift. People who had received the free gift, in contrast to a control group, later reported on an apparently unrelated consumer survey that their cars and television sets performed better and had better service records. Other studies have shown that people in whom a positive feeling state has been induced rate slides of ambiguous scenes as more pleasant than do people who are not in a positive feeling state (Isen & Shalker, 1977; Forest et al., 1979), have lower tachistoscopic thresholds for success-related words (Postman & Brown, 1952), and tend to rate ambiguous facial expressions (a surprise/fear blend, for example) as more positive than do control subjects (Schiffenbauer, 1974). Additionally, studies have found that being in a positive feeling state causes people to express expectations of future success (Feather, 1966) as well as of other kinds of positive events (Masters & Furman, 1975).

Positive feeling states also have been shown to have important effects on social behavior. For example, being in a positive feeling state has been shown to cause people to reward themselves more generously (Mischel, Coates, & Raskoff, 1968), to choose to look at positive rather than negative self-relevant information (Mischel, Ebbesen, & Zeiss, 1973), to help others more (e.g., Aderman, 1972; Batson, Coke, Chard, Smith, & Taliaferro, 1979; Cunningham, Steinberg, & Grev, 1980; Isen, 1970; Isen & Levin, 1972; Isen et al., 1976; Levin & Isen, 1975; Moore, Underwood, & Rosenhan, 1973; Underwood, Froming, & Moore, 1977; Weyant, 1978), to report greater liking for others and more positive conceptions of people (Gouaux, 1971; Griffitt, 1970; Veitch & Griffitt, 1976), to increase willingness to strike up a conversation or to approach strangers for information (Batson et al., 1979; Isen, 1970), and to be more receptive to persuasive communications (Dribbin & Brabender, 1979; Galizio & Hendrick, 1972; Janis, Kaye, & Kirschner, 1965).

Negative Feeling States

The effects of negative feeling states on people's impressions and behavior are more complex than the effects of positive feeling states. While the effects of negative feeling states on *judgments* appear nearly the mirror image of the effects of positive feeling states on judgments, the effects of negative feeling states on *behavior* are more mixed. Sometimes they are the opposite of the effects of positive feeling states, but sometimes negative states produce the same kinds of behavior produced by positive feeling states.

To illustrate this, first consider the effects of negative feeling states on judgments. People in negative feeling states seem to feel that the world is pretty bleak. For instance, Davitz (1970) found that people reported having a sense of being gripped by the situation, let down, and feeling vulnerable and totally helpless when they were in negative moods, as well as feeling less confident, more irritable, and "ready to snap" (Davitz, 1970). In addition, research has shown that people in whom a negative feeling state has been induced rate slides as less pleasant (Isen and Shalker, 1977; Forest et al., 1979) and have lower tachistoscopic thresholds for failure-related words (Postman & Brown, 1952) than do people who are not in a negative feeling state. Being in a negative feeling state decreases attraction towards others and results in more negative conceptions of others (Gouaux, 1971; Griffitt, 1970; Veitch & Griffitt, 1976), and research has also shown that people experiencing negative feelings tend to perceive negative affect in others' facial expressions (Schiffenbauer, 1974).

As far as *behavior* goes, however, it seems that negative feeling states do not as consistently produce antisocial behavior or reduce prosocial behavior. For example, although negative feeling states have sometimes been shown to increase antisocial behavior and aggression (Baron &

Bell, 1976), and have sometimes been shown to decrease prosocial behavior and helping (Moore et al., 1973; Underwood et al., 1977), there are many studies reporting failures to find effects for negative feelings that are opposite to the effects found for positive moods. For example, while Mischel et al. (1973) found that people in positive feeling states did selectively choose to look at positive self-relevant information, people in negative feeling states did not selectively choose to look at negative self-relevant information; while Mischel et al. (1968) found that positive feelings increased self-gratification, they did not find that negative feelings decreased self-gratification; and while Isen (1970) found that positive feelings increased helping, she did not find that negative feelings decreased helping.

In addition, sometimes negative feelings have been shown to *increase* positive behaviors, just as positive feeling states do. For instance, negative feeling states such as guilt or embarrassment, incompetence, anger, and sadness have been shown to increase self-reward or to be associated with increased helping or compliance with a request [e.g., Carlsmith & Gross, 1969; Cialdini, Darby, & Vincent, 1973; Cialdini & Kenrick, 1976 (for older subjects); Donnerstein, Donnerstein, & Munger, 1975; McMillen, 1971; Regan, 1971; Regan, Williams, & Sparling, 1972; Underwood, Moore, & Rosenhan, 1973]. Thus, on the basis of evidence collected so far, we can say that people in positive feeling states are more apt to behave in a prosocial manner than are others, but we cannot make a clear and straightforward prediction for people in negative feeling states.

Finally, there is research that demonstrates additional effects of feeling states on impressions and behavior but cannot easily be categorized as showing effects of either positive or negative feeling states because these studies compared positive and negative states only with each other. Seeman and Schwarz (1974) and Schwarz and Pollack (1977) have shown that children in whom a positive feeling state has been induced are better able to delay gratification than are children in whom a negative feeling state has been induced; and Fry (1975) found that children in a positive feeling state were better able to resist temptation to play with a forbidden toy than were children in a negative feeling state. In addition, Zillmann, Mody, and Cantor (1974, Study II) reported that people's ratings of their own sadness were significantly positively correlated with their ratings of the sadness of an encounter between two people in a film and with their ratings of the sadness of each of those two characters.

We will conclude our presentation of the evidence of the effects of feeling states on judgments and social behavior by saying that it is clear, even given the limited amount of attention paid to feeling states as determinants of social behavior until recently, that these effects are extensive. In fact, the effects of feelings on behavior may be even more pervasive than is apparent from the above list. For example, Weiner has recently speculated that the effects which causal attributions have on expectations for future success or failure may be mediated by feeling states (Weiner, Russell, & Lerman, 1979; Weiner, 1980). Specifically, what Weiner and his colleagues have suggested, on the basis of recent evidence, is that an attribution, say, for a success, may be made to ability, which in turn may lead to positive feelings, which may be what ultimately causes expectations for future success or maintenance of performance.

TOWARD UNDERSTANDING THE PROCESS BY WHICH AFFECT INFLUENCES BEHAVIOR

While the studies described above tell us that feeling states are important determinants of social impressions and behavior, they do not tell us why this is the case. We are left with questions regarding the process by which feeling good results in one's reporting that the world seems basically good, or by which feeling bad sometimes leads to increased helping. There have been attempts to answer these questions before now, some of our own work included; but for the most part, these explanations have not focused on the *process* by which feeling states have their impact on behavior and perception. Berkowitz (1972), for example, has postulated that the reason that someone in a positive feeling state may help another more is that the positive feeling state ". . . affects the potential helper's frustration tolerance or willingness to accept restrictions on his freedom of action. He is more tolerant of the demands the help request imposes upon him than he otherwise would be . . . " (p. 83). This idea is an important one, and other authors have suggested other possible mediating variables that could also fruitfully be pursued. For example, Isen (1970) suggested that people in positive moods might feel more positive toward others and/or more competent, able to cope with the world and events that might occur, and less in need of their resources (Isen, 1970, p. 295). In this chapter we wish to address the question that underlies these variables: by what process might being in a positive feeling state lead to more tolerance? How do positive thoughts lead to other positive thoughts? How do negative thoughts lead to other negative thoughts? How is it that feeling states come to affect behavior and judgments in the ways that they do? These are questions about process, and this chapter proposes a possible set of processes by which these observed relationships may be established and maintained.

The Accessibility Hypothesis

In an earlier paper (Isen, 1975) and article (Isen et al., 1978), Isen and her colleagues described a process suggesting that positive affect plays a role in the organization and utilization of memory. Here we will consider the applicability of that discussion to negative feeling states as well, and will expand on it. In two studies reported by Isen et al. (1978) in which subjects were made to feel good, and were then asked for judgments regarding their possessions (Study 1) or for recall of positive, negative, and neutral trait adjectives learned during one or another of the induced feeling states (Study 2), evidence was found that people in positive feeling states are more likely to retrieve positive material from memory than people who are not in positive feeling states. It was suggested that this occurs because thoughts associated with or responsible for the positive feeling state serve to cue other positive material available in memory, thus making that material more accessible.

Good feeling may cue positive material in much the same way that thinking about category names or words may cue categorically associated material in memory. For instance, Tulving and Pearlstone (1966) demonstrated that the presence of a given retrieval cue (category name) at time of recall served to increase the accessibility of related material (members of the category), resulting in increased recall of that material. Subsequently, other cognitive psychologists found that it takes less time for a subject to identify a letter string as a word if it is preceded by an associated word than if it is preceded by an unrelated word (Meyer & Schvaneveldt, 1971; Posner & Snyder, 1975), to name a word if it is preceded by a related word than if it is preceded by an unrelated word (Jacobson, 1973; Warren, 1977), and to retrieve the name of a category member if the subject has just retrieved a member of the same category rather than of a different category (Loftus, 1973; Loftus & Loftus, 1974) Cognitive psychologists have called this process "priming" (Brown, 1979; Neely, 1976, 1977). Thus it seems that affective state can function like category name or other organizing unit as a cue to prime related cognitive material, and this implies that affective tone may be an important dimension of cognitive organization.

Two studies conducted by Teasdale and Fogarty (1979) provide additional evidence for the position that affective tone may cue related cognitive material and thus may be involved in the organization of memory. Those authors used a paradigm involving latency of recall of positive and negative material and found that, following positive mood induction, pleasant experiences were more quickly recalled than were negative experiences. As in the Isen et al. (1978) study, however, retrieval of negative material was not affected by induced mood state.

Two additional studies supporting the position that feeling states may serve as cues for cognitive material were carried out by Weingartner, Miller, and Murphy (1977) and Bower et al. (1978, Study 3), who found evidence for a state-dependent learning effect as a function of induced "mood." The "state-dependent learning effect" refers to the tendency for material learned when one is in a specific state (say, mania or alcoholic intoxication) to be better recalled when one is again in that same state than at another time (Henry, Weingartner, & Murphy, 1973; Weingartner & Faillace, 1971). This implies, though in a slightly different way, that affective state can serve as a memory cue.

All of these studies, then, provide some support for the hypothesis that feeling states can cue retrieval of material in memory linked to a feeling state. Each study supports this point for positive feeling states, and the Bower et al. (1978) study supports it for negative feeling states as well.

Models of How Increased Accessibility Occurs

In our earlier work we said very little about the way in which a feeling state might "prime" or increase accessibility of similarly toned material in memory. Here we will elaborate upon that earlier work by suggesting two models of the way in which this might occur. One explanation recently proposed by a team of cognitive social psychologists (Wyer & Srull, 1981) uses a "storage bin" conception of memory. The other relies on a conception of "spreading activation." Each position involves assumptions regarding how material is stored in memory and how it is encoded and retrieved, and each has some support in empirical evidence. We will not present this evidence here, nor try to make a case for one or another of these theories. Rather, we simply wish to call these alternative conceptualizations to the reader's attention and illustrate how our ideas fit with some selected current conceptions of memory.

Storage Bin Model. In discussing their model of memory, Wyer and Srull (1981) first make some assumptions regarding how material is stored in memory. In their model, memory is conceived as a " . . . set of content-addressable storage bins" with each bin " . . . tagged in a way that specifically identifies one concept or set of concepts to which its contents refer." Furthermore, information in any one bin may vary in both type and complexity, and any one piece of information may be stored in more than one storage bin.

In addition, Wyer and Srull propose that information is deposited in the bins in the order in which it is transmitted so that the most recently used piece of information is on the top. This is important because, they propose, when a bin containing information that is potentially relevant for the attainment of an immediate processing objective is searched, the most recently deposited material is accessed first. They note that if information is retrieved from any point in a bin for use in processing, it is redeposited on the top of the bin and thus becomes more readily accessible for use.

Information coming in from the environment first passes through a pre-encoder capable of selecting input relevant to the goals of the person at the time. Then the information is passed on to an *Encoder/organizer* whose job it is "to interpret or organize new information by comparing its features with those of previously formed concepts and schemata that exist in Permanent Storage"; and it is assumed that the first concept drawn from a bin will be used, so that further search is unlikely. The information to be encoded may be externally generated information, and/or previously acquired material that is retrieved from memory. Finally, it should be noted that processing goals will determine the selection of the bin from which information is to be drawn.

Using Wyer and Srull's framework, how might feeling states affect judgments and behavior? First of all, the positive or negative mood-inducing event should affect what is on the top of any given bin. This in turn may affect how incoming information is interpreted. For example, imagine what might happen following a positive mood-inducing event. Someone has approached you in a pleasant manner and has just given you a free sample. That may cause "pleasant" to be on top of a storage bin containing "personality traits" and also place your stereotype of kind, concerned, agreeable people at the top of your "types of people" bin. Similarly, it might place "lucky" at the top of your self-descriptive bin and so forth.

This may affect your judgment about how successful you will be in the future, if, in reaching that judgment, you make reference to your "self" bin. Since the first piece of information to be accessed will be "lucky," you'll be likely to predict future good luck or success. Likewise, if you come across someone in need of help, you might wonder what their reaction to being offered help might be, and you might retrieve material from your "people" bin in order to answer that question. Since one of the first bits of information you will retrieve will be that others are agreeable, you might be more likely to go ahead and help than at other times.

Spreading Activation. An alternative way to think about how material is stored in memory, and a way which is increasingly popular among cognitive psychologists, is to think of memory as " . . . a large and permanent collection of nodes (a "node" is a point of intersection in a network) which becomes complex and increasingly interassociated through learning" (Shiffrin & Schneider, 1977; see also Anderson, 1976; Anderson & Bower, 1973; Collins & Loftus, 1975). Next consider the following description of a process of spreading activation (Collins & Quillian, 1972; Collins & Loftus, 1975): They assume that (1) when a concept is processed or attended to, a node is stimulated, and activation spreads out along portions of the network associated with that node, in a decreasing gradient; (2) "the longer a concept is processed (either by seeing or hearing it, or by thinking about it) the longer the activation is released from the node of the concept at a fixed rate"; and (3) "activation is a variable quantity" and intersections or nodes require a threshold for firing (Collins & Loftus, 1975, p. 411).

In order to think about how feelings might be processed in such a system, one has to propose that they are stored in memory, somehow linked to behaviors, objects, and/or situations. This might lead to a rather atomistic picture, but it need not. There are, of course, several forms that such storage might take. For example, it is possible that when material is stored in memory, any associated feeling is also stored in memory linked to that material. Returning to the story at the beginning of our chapter, if Bertha has felt good in the past when her new cook made superb omelettes, then stored in memory along with memories of her cook's omelettes, should be the positive feeling Bertha experienced upon eating the omelettes. Similarly, if one has helped someone in the past, been smiled at and warmly thanked, and felt good as a result, then stored along with helping should be the information that a possible consequence of helping is receiving a smile and an expression of thanks, and linked with that information (one step removed from helping itself) may be the positive feeling tone experienced on the occasions of smiles and thanks. Presumably there are many pieces of information about the world and possible behaviors that are stored in memory and have positive or negative feelings associated with them, and there are presumably many other pieces of information about the world and possible behaviors that do not have any particular feeling tone associated with them.

From these examples it is apparent that material of this kind can be stored either semantically or episodically (Tulving, 1972). For purposes of this chapter we are not distinguishing between kinds of units, although we recognize that such distinctions may be possible and desirable at a later time (Arnold, 1970; Bransford, Franks, Nitsch, & McCarrell, 1977; Jenkins, 1974).

So, in addition to the possibility that feelings are linked to nodes representing individual behaviors or circumstances that occurred in the past, it is also possible that experiences are linked to each other in memory in accord with how they made the person feel. This would imply that some nodes in memory represent feeling tone. Attached to such nodes would be behaviors, objects, situations, or episodes that produced or were associated with a given feeling tone, and memories that are closely associated in this way might be called a category. It is plausible that both positively and negatively toned material is available in memory, probably stored in both of these ways.

Processes Affecting Accessibility of Material in Memory

Having reviewed evidence regarding the effect of positive and negative feeling states on retrieval of material from memory, and having presented two models of how this process may occur, we now propose that a distinction between "automatic" and "controlled" processing, made by Posner and Snyder (1975), will be helpful in understanding the complex effects of feelings on behavior. After introducing first automatic and then controlled processing, we will discuss how these might be influenced by positive and negative feeling states, and then we will propose that controlled and automatic processing operate in concert to produce the varied effects that feeling states have been observed to have on thoughts and behavior.

Automatic Processing

To introduce automatic processing, Posner and Snyder (1975, p. 56) point out that "we are all introspectively familiar with thoughts, ideas or feelings that seem to intrude upon us rather than to occur as a result of our intentions to produce them." Those authors propose that, in contrast with controlled, or conscious, processes and strategies, automatic processes occur (1) without conscious awareness, (2) without intention, and

(3) without producing interference with other ongoing mental activities.[1]

Cognitive psychologists have accumulated good evidence for the existence of such processes (see Posner & Snyder, 1975; Schneider & Shiffrin, 1977; Shiffrin & Schneider, 1977; Hasher & Zacks, 1979), and social psychologists have noted phenomena that may be attributable to them. For example, Schneider, Hastorf, and Ellsworth (1980) discuss "snap judgments" in person perception and suggest that a significant amount of our cognitive activity and some of its resultant social behavior appear to be nonreflective. It may be that such judgments and nonreflective interpersonal behavior are the result of automatic processes, and, in addition, they may be affect-mediated. Further, Zajonc (1968) has shown that mere exposure to a stimulus increases the positivity of judgments about it; and Tesser and his colleagues (e.g. Tesser & Conlee, 1975) have shown that thinking about liked or disliked stimuli increases the polarity of judgments about those stimuli. These and other interpersonally relevant phenomena may result from automatic processes in the following way.

Recall first that in terms of the concept of spreading activation, memory might be considered to be a large, permanent collection of nodes, which becomes increasingly more complex and interconnected through learning, and that stimulation of a node results in activation spreading out along the network toward other nodes. We will further propose that when a node fires, the thought it represents comes to mind. These points imply that the activation threshold of any bit of information in memory can be approached by thinking about material which is associatively related to it (cf. Schneider & Shiffrin, 1977). All of this, of course, happens automatically, without attention or awareness, and without interference with other mental processes.

We have postulated that material may be stored in memory with feeling tone linked to it and/or that there may be "nodes" in memory representing feeling states with examples of objects, behaviors, or situations linked to them that would produce that feeling state. If so, then Tesser and Conlee's finding, that thinking about a positive or negative stimulus results in a more positive (or negative) evaluation being brought to mind, is compatible with the automatic processing formulation. Thinking about a stimulus about which one also feels some affect would be expected to cue or activate other thoughts (almost all of the same affect) about the object and other same-affect-related material. Thus affect should be intensified as additional affect nodes are brought above threshold and fire, that is, as other affect-producing thoughts come to

[1]We should note here that our use of the term "unconscious" does not correspond to the use of the term in the psychoanalytic literature, since we do not relate this unconscious process to "motivated forgetting," "defensive" processes, or any of the host of essentially motivational and derivative concepts and hypotheses that make psychoanalytic theory distinctive. Indeed, our use of the term is almost antithetical to that of psychoanalytic theory, in that in using the term we intend to refer to processes that are effortless and without cost to the cognitive system. (The "mental economy" is presumed to be drained or stressed by the operation of unconscious processes, at least the defense mechanisms, according to the Freudian position.)

mind. Likewise, Zajonc's findings of more positive evaluations following mere exposure to stimuli is understandable as a result of this same process, if one considers that, other things equal, most stimuli would be slightly positive to start with. (This latter point is based on evidence that people usually feel slightly positive, they report most of their experiences to be above a psychological neutral point, and positive material tends to be more accessible (e.g., Bousfield, 1950; Boucher & Osgood, 1969; Fiske, 1980; Matlin & Stang, 1979).

Thus, we are proposing that affect may be subject to automatic processing and are using the automatic processing effect to explain certain social psychological data that involve affect. We suggest, in addition, that there are automatic processes initiated by feeling state-inducing events, both positive and negative, which contribute importantly to many of the effects which feeling states have been shown to have on other impressions and behavior, as well. When, for example, a positive feeling state manipulation, such as the giving of a free gift, takes place, material linked to such acts (including a positive feeling tone and other material associated with that node) should be activated as a result of automatically spreading activation and should either "come to mind," or be brought closer to coming to mind. Thus one may be more likely to think about how kind others are, about how pleasant the day has been, and so on. Once the threshold for activation of positive material is reached, the accessibility of positive material in memory is increased and the person should "be" in a positive feeling state.

This increased accessibility of material related to a person's current affective state may then affect his or her impression of the world and behavior. As an illustration, consider why subjects in positive feeling states in the first study reported by Isen et al. (1978) responded that their cars ran better and had better service records than did others. Receiving an unexpected free gift presumably activated in the person a positive feeling state, with all of its cognitive consequences, as described above. Now, picture our lucky shopper walking along with lowered threshold for the activation of the other information that was stored in memory along with the positive feeling tone (i.e., for positive information), when the shopper encountered the person taking the survey and was asked to rate the performance and overall service record of his or her car. This request activated another set of nodes—those relating to the car. Many different things may be thought of in connection with a person's car, but the person is unlikely to think of them all. The threshold for all of them will be lowered by the question, but these thresholds will not all be crossed nor their associated thoughts about the car brought to mind. The positive ones will have an advantage. In this situation, since the person's feeling state and his/her attempt to think about his/her car intersect at the point where positive things are associated with the car, those positive things should be the aspects of the car most likely to be activated above threshold and to come to mind in response to the surveyor's question. As suggested in another context by Tversky and Kahneman (1973), it is the ones which come to mind first, intrude on the person's consciousness, or, as they put it, are "available," which are likely to affect the answer given on the survey. Thus people in positive moods should "think of" more positive things about their cars and should give better reports on their cars, which is, of course, exactly what Isen et al. (1978) found.

Note that this formulation suggests that the effects of mood on judgment or evaluation are determined by the retrieval process, not by a change in the stored evaluation itself. Thus, in the above example, we would expect that a person who is feeling good should think of more positive aspects of his/her car, assuming that it is an average car, with positives and negatives to be thought of. We would *not* expect a person in a good mood to give a high rating to his old "klunker," about which there simply is not a positive thing to be said. This point also has relevance for the specifications of the situations in which the effect of feelings on automatic processes will be most apparent. (This issue is discussed on pp. 93 –97).

The same kind of analysis of the operation of automatic processes may be applied to explain why being in a positive feeling state increases people's willingness to help others. Returning to our example of helping above, recall that a person may have stored in memory, linked to helping, a number of consequences of helping. A few may be that the helped person may smile and warmly thank the helper (a consequence that is also linked to a positive feeling tone), or that the helper may be inconvenienced, embarrassed, or delayed in his/her own activities (consequences linked to a negative feeling tone), or that the helped person may rather formally thank the helper and leave (a consequence not linked with positive feeling tone). Ordinarily these consequences may be equally accessible. In other words, when a person comes across another in need of help, the chances of various consequences "coming to mind" may be equally likely.[2]

Being in a positive feeling state, however, may alter those probabilities. The positive feeling state should activate associated material, which includes not only events related in time, space, and type, but also in feeling tone. Since feeling tone is conceptualized here as a node in a network, this activation would, in turn, lower the threshold for activation of still other material. In this case the threshold for activation of the node that indicates that one consequence of helping is being appreciated and thanked should be lowered. Note, however, that so far we have said only that the threshold for activation of the "warmly thanked" consequence has been approached, not that it has been crossed. This is not the same as saying that the positive consequence of helping actually comes to mind at this point as a result of the feeling state. Ordinarily it should not, because the person has not yet become aware of the domain or possibility of helping. Most likely, he or she is not even thinking about

[2]It may also be true that they are *not* equally accessible in the neutral state because of differences in their relative frequencies of occurrence in the particular individual's experience. But, for the sake of clarity, we will assume a situation in which they are equal to start out with.

helping at that moment. However, when the person does come across a situation in which help is needed, that situation should activate a helping node. In turn, activation should spread to each possible consequence of helping, and the consequences that receive the most activation should be most likely to "come to mind." Consequences whose thresholds have already been approached by virtue of being associated with a positive feeling state should be more likely than others to receive sufficient activation to bring them to mind. Thus, when one is in a positive feeling state and sees someone in need of help, or when one is asked for help, the probability that positive consequences of helping will come to mind is greater than if one had been in no particular mood; likewise it is helping, rather than some other behavior, that is likely to be facilitated by the positive state.

A similar example that has empirical support can be given for negative moods. If one is in a negative feeling state, possible negative behaviors stored in memory along with negative feelings, such as aggression, may be activated. However, they may not actually "come to mind," and consequently become more probable, until a cue in the environment also activates them. This may be why Berkowitz and LePage (1967) found that negative affect by itself did not enhance aggression, but that negative affect in combination with a cue for aggression (in their study a weapon) did cause aggression to become more likely.

Combining the above ideas with the suggestion of several authors that helping is the result of a decision-making process in which the person making the decision considers the cost–reward matrix associated with helping or not helping; in the particular case at hand (Latané & Darley, 1970; Piliavin, Rodin, & Piliavin, 1969) one can see how the prediction that people in positive feeling states would help more than others is derived (Levin & Isen, 1975). People who are feeling good will be more likely to think of the rewards of helping than would others. Thus they should also be more likely to perceive the rewards of helping to outweigh the costs and be more likely to actually help.

Here it is important to note that we are not proposing that behavior is determined by people stopping and concentrating on retrieving from memory all possible costs and rewards of helping and then calculating which are greater before making a decision about whether or not to help. Indeed, they do not seem to spend enough time or effort making the decision to warrant such a suggestion; nor does this proposal follow from our analysis. Rather, we assume that, as has been demonstrated by Tversky and Kahneman (1973), the "availability heuristic" will be employed, that people's decisions will be affected by the costs and benefits which "come to mind." We are suggesting further that, of the possible list of costs and rewards, only *some*, and in this case most probably a particular subset, that facilitated by the affective state which the person is experiencing, will come to mind.

We have now outlined a process whereby positive feeling states may affect judgments and behavior through automatic processes, and have illustrated the process by explaining how it might account for increases in helping when people are in positive feeling states. The same process may also be used to explain how positive feeling states may affect many other expectations, judgments, and behavior, as noted earlier in the chapter. Such automatic processes may also be applied to some of the effects that negative feeling states have been shown to have on impressions and behavior. To illustrate this, consider the findings that persons who are in negative feeling states find people to be less likable than do persons who are not in negative feeling states (e.g., Gouaux, 1971). Most people have had many experiences, both positive and negative, with strangers. For instance, in the past they have encountered people who have been kind, helpful, and interesting to talk to, as well as some who have been cruel, selfish, and/or boring. Given little information about a stranger in the present, it may be that a person's current feelings will determine which items of that information come to mind when evaluating that stranger. Being in a negative feeling state may make a person more likely to think of others as cruel, selfish, and boring, and consequently less likely to opt for interaction with a stranger.

Specification of the Situations in Which the Effect of Feeling States on Automatic Processing Will Be Most Apparent

What has been said so far might make one think that, through automatic processing, being in a positive feeling state would make most behaviors focused upon more likely because one would be more likely to think of positive things associated with that behavior, and that being in a negative feeling state should make most behaviors less likely because one would be more likely to think of negative things associated with that behavior. After all, if the automatic processing that follows a positive or negative mood induction makes awareness of positive (negative) aspects of behaviors more likely, through the process described above, and thereby influences the decision-making process regarding judgments or choice of behavior, then shouldn't this be true across the board, for all judgments and decisions focused upon? Actually no.[3] We expect behaviors such as helping to be facilitated by a positive affective state, but we do not expect behaviors such as harming to be facilitated by this state in most cases. The mechanisms involved in automatic processing specify to some degree those impressions and behaviors that are likely to be affected by a given feeling state and those that are not.

There are at least three types of cases where the automatic processes triggered by feeling states will not lead to judgment or action consonant with the feeling state (taking positive states as the example): those where the behavior or item under consideration has *no* positive associa-

[3]Even on the basis of what has been said about automatic processing so far, one can think of some behaviors that a positive feeling state might make *less* likely, and some that might become *more* probable as a result of being in a negative feeling state. For instance, if one is in a positive state, one may tend to think of the positive aspects of others and be *less* likely to aggress against them. In contrast, if one is in a negative state, one may tend to think of the negative aspects of others and be *more* likely to aggress against them.

tions for the person, so that there is nothing to be primed; those where the number of negative associations far outweigh the positive, so that, although the positive consequences are more likely to come to mind than they are at another time, they will still be overwhelmed by the negative in the decision-making process; and those where the "strength" of the positive associates relative to other associates is inadequate. The last type requires some elaboration.

Strength of association may be thought of as the likelihood of one bit of information being brought to mind or the speed with which it is brought to mind when cued by an associated piece of information. The idea that strength of associations may vary is implied in notions such as Rosch's (1975), that some members of categories are better exemplars than others. This idea has been explicitly adopted by many theorists and represented in different manners in their models. For instance, the Wyer and Srull (1981) model implies that strength will be most determined by recency of firing; Higgins and King (1981) and Higgins and Chaires (1980) suggest that frequency of firing should be most important; and Collins and Quillian (1972) think of strength in terms of the distance between nodes. In any case, if strengths are established and do vary at the outset of any given event, then behaviors or objects whose negative or non-affect-related associations are stronger, though not more numerous, than their positive associations may not be sufficiently affected by automatic processing of positive feelings to affect the decision under consideration. Positive associations may be primed, but the strength of the negative associations may cause the latter nonetheless to come to mind rather than the positive.

Assuming that negative feeling states have the same cognitive effects as positive feeling states (a proposition about which we are not altogether certain), the limitations described above on the effects that positive feeling states have on impressions and behavior through automatic processes would have counterparts in limiting the effects of negative feeling states. Automatic processes associated with negative feelings should make most behavior, overall, less likely, a prediction that fits with well-established clinical observation of depressed patients, but this should not be the case without exception. For example, behaviors with *no* negative associations should not become less likely; behaviors or impressions of things which have many positive, relative to negative, feelings associated with them should not be affected; and automatic processing should be unlikely to affect behaviors or impressions of things that have positive aspects far more strongly associated with them than negative aspects.

In addition, we should point out that, overall, the effect of automatic processes may be less influential for negative moods and negative material than for positive states and positive material. Matlin and Stang (1979, Chapter 7) reviewed literature on recall of pleasant and unpleasant material and found that in the majority of the studies that they were able to locate, pleasant material was easier to recall than unpleasant material; and Bousfield (1950) reviewed a number of studies that seem to support the idea that pleasant material is represented in greater quantities than unpleasant material in memory and may be more interconnected as well. For instance, White (1936) found that people could give a greater number of associations for pleasantly toned words than for unpleasantly toned words; White and Powell (1936) found evidence that associations for pleasant words were given more quickly than were associations for negative words; and Bousfield (1944) showed that within equal periods of time, subjects were able to write down more pleasant objects, activities, and situations than unpleasant objects, activities, and associations. If, as seems likely, given such evidence, positive material is more abundant and, as suggested by Isen et al. (1978), better interconnected in memory than is negative material, then negative material will tend not to be as efficiently cued through this automatic process as is positive material.

Taking these points together, we can make the general statement, regarding the types of decisions and behavior likely to be influenced by affective state, that the automatic processes proposed here will be constrained by the amount of affectively toned material in memory associated with the item, concept, or decision, and by the number and strength of interconnections among similarly toned material. The more positive or negative items that exist in memory regarding an impression or decision, and the greater the number and strength of interconnections between such items, the greater the impact that positive or negative feelings should have on those impressions and behaviors through automatic processing.

One other aspect of the judgment situation will affect the influence of feelings on judgments and behavior, and that is the clarity of the situation or judgments to be made. This is not unrelated to the issue just discussed. At least two studies indicate that the affective state of the perceiver will influence perception only where the stimuli are to some degree ambiguous. First, in the Schiffenbauer (1974) study mentioned above, while that author found that the affective state of the perceiver did influence the perception of certain emotional expressions, he did not find that the ratings of a "happy" expression were affected. That is, subjects experiencing disgust did not rate "happy" expressions any *less* happy, nor did subjects experiencing humor rate the happy expressions as being any *more* happy, than did subjects in no particular mood. He suggests that happy faces are not open to being influenced by mood state because happy faces are distinctive in their appearance and are not easily confusable with other expressions; they are "unmistakable." We would say that their features do not overlap with those of other expressions, or that they are not well-interconnected with the features of other expressions. Indeed, Schiffenbauer refers to Darwin's (1890) observation of the distinctiveness (from all other faces) of a happy smiling face. Thus, where the evaluation involved a distinctive stimulus, no effect of feeling state was observed, while in the more ambiguous cases, feeling state did influence judgment. Likewise, in a study by Isen and Shalker (1977) in which subjects were presented with positive, ambiguous, and negative slides, only in the case of ambiguous judgments did feeling states influence ratings of the pleasantness of scenes.

In sum, then, our position is not that feeling states greatly distort people's perceptions of the world, but rather that they "tip the balance" of positive and negative information that is utilized in making judgments about the world and decisions about behavior. The impact that they will have through automatic processes is affected by the amount of affectively toned material in memory, by the number and strength of interconnections within such material, and by the clarity of the situation or judgment to be made.

Data Explainable in Terms of Automatic Processes Induced by Feelings

The process that we have described thus far is consistent with the majority of effects positive feeling states have been shown to have; and similarly, but to a lesser extent, it accounts for much of the data on the effects of negative feeling states on impressions and behavior. However, this automatic process does not account for all of the data on either positive or negative feeling states. For example (1) positive feelings have been shown to actually *decrease* the probability of certain types of helping behavior (Isen & Levin, 1972, Study 2; Isen & Simmonds, 1978; Forest et al., 1979); (2) negative feelings have often been shown to increase helping (e.g., Carlsmith & Gross, 1969; Cialdini et al., 1973; Regan et al., 1972) and sometimes have not been found to affect helping (Isen, 1970); (3) children in positive feeling states have been found to be better able to resist temptation than children in negative moods (Fry, 1975; Seeman & Schwarz, 1974; Schwarz & Pollack, 1977),[4] and negative feeling states have sometimes been shown to increase self-reward (Underwood et al., 1973). How are these results to be explained?

Controlled Processing

The automatic processing that we have described is probably not the only means through which feelings influence judgments and social behavior. Rather, as suggested by Posner and Snyder (1975, p. 56), it is likely that "conscious strategies interact with automatic activation processes to determine performance." Recall that Posner and Snyder defined automatic processes as occurring without intention, without conscious awareness, and without producing interference with other ongoing mental activity. They also discussed and presented evidence for controlled, or conscious, processing, involving a mechanism of conscious awareness and intention, one that takes time, requires effort, and

[4]Actually this result can be understood in terms of automatic processing if one argues that the positive mood increases the "attractiveness" of the delay reward, but one must also acknowledge that the mood should increase the attractiveness of the immediate reward as well. Thus the fact that children in positive moods are better able to delay gratification than others is not easily handled by our notions of automatic processing.

is of limited capacity. It ranges in complexity from complicated, planned strategies to the relatively simple "set" to perceive or react (Posner, 1978); but regardless of the degree of complexity of these conscious processes, their distinguishing characteristics are those that drain the limited capacity information processes. We believe that many of the effects of feeling states on behavior cannot be accounted for without suggesting that, in addition to automatic processes, feeling states give rise to certain distinctive controlled processes or strategies.

It may be that a positive feeling state gives rise to a conscious strategy to maintain that state. More specifically, people in positive feeling states may direct their attention to material in memory that will maintain that mood. Thus people in a positive mood might think about behaviors that have produced positive feelings in the past and might be more likely to perform those behaviors in order to maintain their moods. People in negative feeling states may also use controlled strategies, but in that case, in order to change their moods. In other words, they may think of and perform behaviors associated with positive feelings specifically to relieve their negative feeling state.

For example, imagine a man who has just been unexpectedly promoted and who is in a positive feeling state. He may not want simply to go home to his usual routine that night. That seems incompatible with his mood. Instead, he may "feel like" (i.e., think about) going out or having friends over, and actually do so, specifically because such behavior is likely to maintain his positive feeling state.

On the other hand, imagine a man who has just been told that he will not receive an expected promotion and who is in a negative feeling state. He too may find it difficult to go home to his empty house. Therefore he too may "feel like" asking some people to get together with him, and may actually go out, specifically because he knows that such behavior may alleviate his negative feeling state.

The idea that people use controlled processes such as we are proposing is certainly not new. Many others have discussed controlled processes, in general, and there is considerable evidence that people *can* program their attention to receive certain information (see Posner & Snyder, 1975, pp. 69–77).

Even the notion that people use such controlled processes to deal with emotional states is not entirely new. Both folk knowledge and experimental evidence point to the effectiveness of such techniques. "Whistling past the graveyard" is an idiom that refers to a strategy for coping with fear; and the words to two familiar songs, for example, expressly suggest cognitive strategies for dealing with fear and sadness: "Whenever I feel afraid, I hold my head erect and whistle a happy tune, so no one will suspect I'm afraid. . . . Make believe you're brave and the trick will get you far. You may be as brave as you make believe you are." (Rodgers & Hammerstein, 1951, p. 16), and " . . . When the dog bites, when the bee stings, when I'm feeling sad, I simply remember my favorite things and then I don't feel so bad . . ." (Rodgers & Hammerstein, 1959, p. 27).

Experimental evidence confirms that such actions and strategies can influence emotional experience. For example, recent studies have shown that direct manipulation of cognitions can improve mood in both depressed and nondepressed persons (Hale & Strickland, 1976; Raps, Reinhard, & Seligman, 1980; Strickland, Hale, & Anderson, 1975; Teasdale & Bancroft, 1977). Schneider et al. (1980) summarize the literature showing that "putting on a happy face" can make one feel happier (e.g., Laird, 1974; Lanzetta, Cartwright-Smith, & Kleck, 1976; but see also Tourangeau & Ellsworth, 1979; Buck, 1980). In addition, the suggestion of Cialdini et al. (1973) of "negative state relief" as a possible reason that people help when feeling bad seems closely related to this idea of using strategies to improve feeling state; and other authors have pointed to the mood-maintenance effects of behavior such as helping or choosing to look at positive material about oneself when feeling good (Isen & Levin, 1972; Isen & Simmonds, 1978; Mischel et al., 1973). What we are presenting here that *is* new are some of the implications of the differences between automatic and controlled processes and of the fact that automatic and controlled processes act together to produce the observed effects of feelings on behavior.

Distinctions between the two types of processes make for differential predictions regarding behavior in various situations. Conscious strategies, or even "sets," unlike automatic processes, do *not* occur without effort, consciousness, or interference with other ongoing mental activities. They are limited, require effort, take time, cut down on the efficiency with which other material will be processed, and, although they cannot prevent automatic processes, they may serve to reduce the probability that stimuli activated through such processes will come to consciousness (Posner & Snyder, 1975). In addition, since people have limited capacity for effortful activity, control strategies may not always be employed. These differences imply that the cognitive and behavioral consequences of any given emotion or affect-generating situation will depend on whether and how effectively automatic or controlled processes are activated and on specific aspects of the situation related to the factors that influence this (for example, how much effort the person can put forth at the moment, how much other material is demanding attention at the moment, and so forth). Conditions that can attenuate the effectiveness of controlled processes, for example, may play a crucial role in the kind of behavior that will result.

Many of the findings that cannot be explained on the basis of automatic processes can be explained in terms of controlled processes or conscious strategies. Consider first the finding that being in a positive feeling state decreases helping when the helping task is unpleasant and very likely to destroy the subject's mood. In the Isen and Levin study (1972) the type of helping that was decreased involved serving as a confederate who would annoy people. In both the Isen and Simmonds (1978) study and the Forest et al. (1979) study, the helping task involved reading statements that, subjects were told, had been specifically designed to induce negative moods. Assuming that positive affect had given rise to controlled processes compatible with positive mood maintainance, the data from these studies are understandable. Subjects chose not to help in these ways because the act of providing such help might have destroyed their positive feelings. Some subjects in the Isen and Simmonds (1978) study actually verbalized this sentiment.

What about the many studies in which negative feeling states have been shown to increase helping? While they cannot be explained in terms of automatic processing, they can be understood in terms of controlled processes. It seems reasonable to think that most times, when people are in a negative feeling state, they would like to get out of that state, and they will search for activities that might make them feel better. According to the automatic processing component of our model, they should have a relatively hard time thinking of these activities, but according to the controlled process component, under many circumstances they should be likely to perform such an activity that is brought to their attention. Thus, if an experimenter presents the subject with the opportunity to engage in a mood-improving activity, as the experimenter did in the studies mentioned, the subject should be more likely to engage in such behavior than when not feeling "down." Is helping a potentially mood-improving activity? We think so. Our culture values helping, and there is evidence that under most circumstances providing help makes one feel good and/or is compatible with sustaining positive affect (Isen & Simmonds, 1978; Weiss, Buchanan, Alstatt, & Lombardo, 1971). Therefore, when a subject who is in a negative feeling state is given a chance to help in the course of an experiment, one might expect him/her to be likely to do so in order to alleviate that state (Cialdini et al., 1973).

Helping is certainly not the only behavior that might actively be used to alleviate a negative mood. Providing oneself with rewards may also be such a strategy. This may be why Underwood et al. (1973), for example, found that negative feeling states increased children's self-reward, and why both positive and negative states have been shown to have effects on children's ability to delay gratification. Seeman and Schwarz (1974) and Schwarz and Pollack (1977) have shown that children in negative feeling states are more likely to choose a small immediate reward over a larger delayed reward than are children in positive feeling states. Further, a study by Mischel, Ebbesen, and Zeiss (1973) shows that children's feeling states while actually waiting for a large reward affect the length of time that the child will wait. Children in a positive feeling state were able to wait more than twice as long as children in negative feeling states. Finally, Fry (1975) has shown that children in negative feeling states have a more difficult time resisting a temptation to play with a toy than children in a positive feeling state. Clearly, one can see the effects of self-indulgence as a strategy of negative-state relief here, but the findings can best be understood as resulting from a combination of automatic and controlled processing.

As the authors themselves point out, in the Seeman and Schwarz (1974) and in the Schwarz and Pollack (1977) studies, it is possible that the children in the negative-state condition in their studies, faced with a choice between receiving a small benefit now or a large one later, consciously chose the immediate small one in an effort to alleviate their negative feelings. However, this would not explain the difference between conditions in delay behavior, because subjects in positive feeling state conditions should also have been likely to have chosen a small reward right away, in order to maintain their positive feelings. This is where automatic processes may play a role in concert with these controlled processes. That is, *automatic processes* may make the wait for a larger reward seem more aversive to people in a negative feeling state than to people in a positive feeling state, because while waiting the former will have negative thoughts more accessible, while the latter will have better access to positive. Mischel and his colleagues, in a number of studies, have focused on the importance for delay behavior of what the child thinks about, attends to, or imagines while waiting. [See Mischel and Baker (1975) and Mischel and Moore (1973) for a discussion of the role of thought and attention in delay.] Thus the direction of thought and attention provided by the automatic processes which attend affective states may contribute to the eventual delay behavior observed. In addition, Mischel and his colleagues point out the importance of the strategies which the child uses for the purpose of delaying. In the case of affective state, the automatic processes to which we refer may also act to influence delay behavior by affecting the accessibility of various strategies.

In summary, then, the use of controlled strategies or controlled strategies operating in conjunction with automatic processes helps us to understand the observed effects of feeling states on behaviors that were not easily explained in terms of automatic processing alone.

Controlled vs Automatic Processing

So far we have discussed controlled and automatic processing primarily as if they were separable. We have presented one set of results as being interpretable in terms of automatic processes, and we have understood the remaining studies in terms of controlled processes. However, as we saw toward the end of the last section, this separation is artificial. Assuming that both types of processes exist, it is probable that they jointly determine many of the effects that feeling states have on impressions and on behavior, as we suggested, for example, in discussing the effect of feelings on delay of gratification. Sometimes both automatic and controlled processes can be expected to contribute to the same behavior, and sometimes each will contribute to an opposite effect.

The two types of processes we have postulated are most likely to contribute to the same effects in the case of positive feeling states and positive behavior. Both lead to the prediction that a person will think positive thoughts and behave in a positive manner. Recall our earlier example of the person who has just received an unexpected promotion at work. He feels good. The automatic processes we have postulated would suggest that he would be more likely to think of behaviors that have a positive feeling tone linked with them. Since he is in a positive feeling state, and since going out has a positive feeling tone associated with it, the threshold for thinking about going out should be lowered, and the chances of him thinking of going out and actually doing so should be enhanced. Note that we make the same prediction on the basis of controlled processing. If the person feels good and wishes to maintain his mood, he may focus on things which make him feel good, think of going out, and consequently be more likely to do so. Further, we might note that both controlled and automatic processing should be influenced in a similar manner by what is occurring in the person's environment. If a friend calls the man and suggests going bowling, a favorite activity, both automatic and controlled processing would be compatible with the possibility that bowling would become a likely activity for the evening.

It is in the case of negative feeling states that automatic and controlled processes are most likely to lead to differential predictions. For instance, although going out with friends might be a good strategy (control process) for cheering up, this possibility may not occur (automatic process) to the downhearted. Even after the possibility is suggested to a person who is feeling bad, however, he or she may not be as likely to act on it. Consider a man in a negative feeling state who is asked by some friends to go out to see a movie. On the basis of automatic processing we might predict that he will be more likely to think about what a hassle it is to go out, how sometimes his friends are boring, and that movies about which one knows nothing beforehand often turn out to be bad. On this basis, we might suspect that such a person would be less likely to go than would a person in a positive feeling state, even after the possibility is brought to mind for him by someone else. This, then, is the same prediction that would be made on the basis of the automatic process. However, an alternative prediction is also possible: Suppose that the man, seeing no possibility of change if he stays home, intentionally focuses on the ways in which accepting his friend's invitation might make him feel better. He may think about the fact that it's often fun to be with his friends, that the movie just might be good, and that, in any case, it is likely to distract him from his negative feelings. Further, this intentional focus may block material that is being activated through automatic processes from coming to mind. Thus, on the basis of the possibility of such controlled processing, we might predict that a person in a negative feeling state, like one in a positive feeling state, would be *more* likely than others to accept such an invitation. This prediction is opposite to that which one would make on the basis of the automatic process.

This brings us to the problem of how one can predict behavior or impressions in cases where our postulated automatic and controlled processes lead to different predictions. It is in this context that the automatic-process/controlled-process conceptualization may be most useful, since differences between the two types of process may suggest bases for prediction. For example, controlled processes require effort. Thus we might expect that factors that can affect the willingness of a person to put effort into terminating a negative state might be crucial determinants of whether the effects of automatic or controlled processes predominate. Thus fatigue may make a person less likely to employ a strategy in order to overcome the effects of feeling bad.

For another example, it may be that attempts that failed at getting out of a negative mood in the past may make one less likely to attempt to get out of such a state in the present. Thus we might predict that the effects of automatic processes might predominate over the effects of controlled processes for people who have failed in strategic efforts to alleviate their negative feeling states in the past. Seligman and his colleagues (Seligman, 1975) make an argument compatible with this line of reasoning in their "learned helplessness" interpretation of depression. They argue that depressed persons do not "cope" (our analysis would say, "employ a controlled process") with depression because they have come to expect, through learning in the past, that their efforts fail and that they are "helpless."

It may also be that simply being overworked or distracted may reduce the likelihood of controlled processes being invoked. It is especially interesting that Hasher and Zacks (1979) have noted and provided evidence that depression, stress, and old age are all variables that reduce one's capacity for effortful, or what we call controlled, processes, while not interfering with automatic processing. For this reason, we would expect that depression, stress, and old age would reduce the probability that controlled processes will mediate the effects of feeling states on impressions and behavior, and would increase the probability of the effects of automatic processing prevailing. Attempts to work with these persons might attend to the effects of automatic processes, and also specifically try to arm the depressed, the elderly, and those under stress with effective strategies for combating their negative state, as suggested by Beck and his colleagues (1967, 1976).

The same may hold true for those who are very young—they may not have had a chance to develop strategies for alleviating negative states or maintaining positive states. This suggestion is compatible with the findings of Cialdini and Kenrick (1976), that very young children were not as likely as older children or adults to help others when they themselves were in a negative feeling state. Not having well-developed controlled processes or strategies for coping with feeling states, young children may be more at the mercy of the automatic processes triggered by these states, and they may need help in altering them (in settling down, as well as in cheering up). Of course, *automatic* processes associated with feeling states may have less of an impact on young children than on older people, too, since young children may not have had the experiences necessary to build extensive interconnections between similarly toned material in memory.

Thus the cognitive and behavioral effects of feeling states may be less extensive in general for young children. This latter suggestion may help us to understand our informal observation of the ease with which young children, in contrast to adolescents, adults, and even older children, appear to move from one feeling state to another. They can laugh happily one minute, cry bitterly the next, and then be clowning and laughing again, within the space of a few minutes. Most adults do not do this. Indeed, having observed this phenomenon, adults are often heard to wonder aloud how genuine or profound children's affective states are. It may well be that there are other reasons for this situation (distraction, which is related to these notions but not precisely synonymous with them, may play a role in some cases), but one possible aspect of importance may be that children are only in the process of developing, and therefore have relatively underdeveloped cognitive mechanisms for dealing with feelings. This limited cognitive role in feelings may account for both aspects of the apparent paradox: children seem, on the one hand, more vulnerable to feelings, more affected by them or less able to resist them or cope with them, but at the same time, on the other hand, they also seem less profoundly or extensively or long-lastingly affected by them.

Interactions Between Conscious Strategies and Automatic Processes

Not only may automatic and controlled processes act in concert to determine behavior as described above, but they may also influence each other directly. It is easy to see how automatic processes may influence the direction and outcome of the search for strategies or plans for behavior, through priming, in the same way that they influence other items that come to mind.

The case for controlled processing influencing automatic processes may need a bit more explication, however. First, it has already been noted that controlled processes or strategies may prevent material activated by simultaneously occurring automatic processes from "coming to mind" (Posner & Snyder, 1975, p. 65). This too is relatively straightforward. In addition, however, it may also be possible that some conscious strategies (for example, some that may result from a positive feeling state) may *facilitate* automatic processes, helping to cue similarly toned material, and thus enhance positive feelings. That is, over many instances, a conscious strategy to maintain a positive feeling state may have an impact on the extent and strength of interconnections between similarly toned material in memory, and a person may come to associate a greater amount of material with positive feelings. If people in a positive feeling state wish to maintain that state, they may consciously focus on positive material in memory or choose to perform behaviors that have made them feel good in the past. In this way, the positive material focused on, or the positive behavior performed, may become associated with the event that induced the positive feeling state in the first place, and this should result in the establishment of many interconnections of positive material in memory. These extensively developed interconnections should then result in an increased effect when *automatic* processes are later triggered by positive affect; and this enhancement of the automatic processing effect would be attributable to the earlier employment of the controlled process.

Assuming that people do not try to maintain negative feeling states, conscious strategies should not increase interconnections between negative material in memory. Indeed, people experiencing negative feeling states may actively avoid thinking about negative material, instead choosing to focus their attention on things that might alleviate their feeling state. We have reason to expect there to be more and stronger interconnections between positive, relative to negative, material stored in memory, a fact which would account in part for the observation noted earlier of the slight general bias toward the positive found in many cognitive measurements. This fact also holds broader implications for attention and cognition generally and in particular for the effect of positive feeling states on attention and cognition.

SUMMARY

In this chapter we have proposed a framework for understanding the processes through which feeling states affect impressions and behavior. This framework extends ideas set forth earlier by Isen (1975) and expanded in papers by Levin and Isen (1975), Isen et al. (1978), and Isen and Simmonds (1978). Basically, it has been proposed that, taken together, two general types of processes may account for the effects that feeling states have been shown to have on impressions and behavior.

First, automatic processes were proposed. When a person is experiencing a feeling state, thoughts or events associated with or responsible for that feeling state may "automatically," without intention, without awareness, and without interfering with other ongoing processes, cue similarly toned material in memory. We have proposed that this "priming" of compatible material happens in the case of both positive and negative feelings, although not necessarily to an equal extent. In the case of positive feelings, the result is that people seem to view the world through "rose-colored glasses" and to behave in a positive manner. In the case of negative feeling states, in parallel fashion, the resultant tendency is to form negative impressions and to behave in an antisocial manner. However, the effects that negative feelings may have through such automatic processes may be more limited than those that positive feelings have, because the interconnections of negative material in memory may be fewer and weaker.

The second general category of processes through which feeling states may affect behavior are controlled processes. These are more effortful processes such as "sets" or even more elaborate conscious strategies a person intentionally uses to maintain a positive feeling state or to alleviate a negative one. (Although automatic processes may influence the accessibility of various strategies under certain conditions—as when, for example, negative feelings may interfere with the accessibility of effective coping strategies—people may consciously learn or be taught to respond with appropriate strategies by treating undesired states as cues for those strategies.) Thus, while automatic processes may influence thought and action, it is also true that controlled processes may be used to counter, "block," or attenuate the effects of automatic processes.

In most cases, we have seen, controlled and automatic processes would be expected to lead to the same predictions regarding effects of positive feeling states. They would be expected to work against each other, however, in the case of negative feeling states. For instance, whereas a consideration of automatic processes would lead one to predict decreased helping by a person in a negative feeling state, a consideration of conscious processing would lead one to predict increased helping. Thus, too, one would expect that individuals with little experience with conscious strategies or with using conscious strategies to govern automatic processes (say, young children) would be less likely to help when feeling bad. Moreover, consideration of variables affecting the amount of effort a person is able or motivated to invest in controlled strategies and of variables affecting the learning of such strategies may provide answers to questions concerning when negative feeling states will lead to lessened prosocial behavior.

Finally, we have suggested ways in which the automatic process proposed to accompany feeling states can be viewed in the context of the currently popular theory of "spreading activation," or in terms of Wyer and Srull's "storage bin" model of memory, as illustrations of the way in which feelings might affect impressions and behavior.

A Return to the Problem of Definition

"Positive" and "negative" feeling states have been the focus of this chapter. Does this mean that we feel that there are no distinctions to be made within these categories? Of course we recognize that there are distinctions to be made among the so-called "negative" states and among the so-called "positive" states: between anxiety and sadness, between contentment and joy. Furthermore, we think that the differences between such states can be understood within the framework we have set forth in earlier work: their development, differentiation, and cognitive effects will depend on what they make a person think about, what they cue; and their behavioral effects will depend on the combination of this and the strategies that the person has available for enjoying them or coping with them.

We have chosen to speak of positive and negative feeling states, rather than of the more specific states induced or of foci of attention, because we feel that, at least for the present, this may be a useful level of analysis. First, we would agree with those who suggest that there is not yet enough information to allow for more detailed differentiation of emotional states. Scholars in the field of emotion do not agree on even the basis upon which such differentiation should begin; nor are the "emotions" to be included obvious. As Mandler (1975) points out, there is no reason to expect that the common language classification of emotion will serve as an adequate tool for the scientific analysis of emotion. Further, he notes that there is neither logical necessity of, nor evidence for, a single, unified theory of emotion. Thus it may be that for low-intensity feeling states of the kind we have been discussing, general valence may be the appropriate level of representation. Leventhal (1974), in fact, makes just such a suggestion on the basis of data indicating the possibility of innate perceptual mechanisms that are sensitive to specific stimulus features and that give rise to feelings of pleasantness or unpleasantness before more specific expressive reactions based on interpretation are elicited.

In addition, earlier we made what may turn out to be a rather arbitrary distinction between feeling states and emotions. Among other things, we said that emotions disrupt onging behaviors, are tied to specifiable objects and behaviors, and involve arousal, while feeling states do not disrupt ongoing behaviors, influence a great variety of behaviors, and may or may not involve arousal. While these distinctions are more or less valid, and while some authors (e.g., Leventhal, 1974) may eventually want to argue that they *are* different in kind or that they are processed differently, it may not be that feeling states and emotions are completely distinct. The apparent differences may be quantitative rather than qualititive, for example. Nonetheless, the distinction has had heuristic value for purposes of this chapter. It has allowed us to get away from the idea that only emotions have effects on behavior, that feeling states do not. It has also permitted us to consider how feeling states might affect impressions and behavior without our having to appeal to "arousal." On the other hand, there is the possibility that low-level affective states really are different from more intense affect in their information-processing requirements and effects, as suggested above; and our distinction has allowed us to consider this possibility.

We have presented evidence that everyday feelings influence social behavior and cognition, and we have suggested that affective states might profitably be looked at in terms of cognitive processes or their impact on cognitive processes. We hope this will not seem a jarring betrayal of concern with affect or an unorthodox disregard of the time-honored tradition that divides mind or psychological experience into three separate domains—cognitive, conative (motivational/behavioral), and affective. We do not make this proposal because we believe that everything can be reduced to cognitive processes (what some have called "cognitive imperialism"). Rather we make it for its potential utility in suggesting directions for research in understanding affective processes. This reemphasizes the suggestion made elsewhere in this volume (Isen and Hastorf, this volume) that an understanding of affect will not involve only the singling out of affect for study, but also the integration of affect into that which is already known of psychological process. We hope that the kind of analysis that we have made will not be interpreted mechanistically nor as an end-point, but as a suggestion intended to facilitate examination of some new directions and propositions about affect that might otherwise not be apparent.

We would point out that the tripartite division of mind was not intended to segregate aspects of mental events or experience from one another. Rather, the thinkers of the Age of Enlightenment who spoke of that trilogy were concerned with integration of these components, or at least with realization of the ultimate unity of psychological experience or process. (See Isen and Hastorf, this volume.) The psychologists who followed them often simply assumed this integration, although sometimes they described it specifically. McDougall (1923), for example described a sequentially integrated process; we have chosen a different way of integrating these components. We have offered a cognitive interpretation of some of the phenomena attending affect, and we like to think that those earlier scholars would have considered this in keeping with the spirit, if not the form, of their unified approach to psychological experience.

REFERENCES

Aderman, D. Elation, depression and helping behavior. *Journal of Personality and Social Psychology*, 1972, *24*, 91–101.

Anderson, J. R. *Language, memory and thought*. Hillsdale, N.J.: Erlbaum, 1976.

Anderson, J. R., & Bower, G. H. *Human associative memory*. Washington, D.C.: Winston, 1973.

Arnold, M. B. Perennial problems in the field of emotion. In M. B. Arnold (Ed.), *Feelings and Emotion*. New York: Academic, 1970.

Baron, R. A., & Bell, P. A. Aggression and heat: The influence of ambient temperature, negative affect, and a cooling drink on physical aggression. *Journal of Personality and Social Psychology*, 1976, *33*, 245–255.

Batson, C. D., Coke, J. S., Chard, F., Smith, D., & Taliaferro, A. Generality of the "Glow of goodwill": Effects of mood on helping and information acquisition. *Social Psychology Quarterly*, 1979, *42*, 176–179.

Beck, A. T. *Depression: Clinical, experimental and theoretical aspects*. New York: Harper & Row, 1967.

Beck, A. T. *Cognitive therapy and the emotional disorders*. New York: International Universities Press, 1976.

Berkowitz, L. Social norms, feelings, and other factors affecting helping and altruism. In L. Berkowitz (Ed.), *Advances in Experimental Social Psychology*, Vol. 6. New York, Academic, 1972.

Berkowitz, L., & LePage, A. Weapons as aggression-eliciting stimuli. *Journal of Personality and Social Psychology*, 1967, *7*, 202–207.

Boucher, J., & Osgood, C. E. The pollyanna hypothesis. *Journal of Verbal Learning and Verbal Behavior*, 1969, *8*, 1–8.

Bousfield, W. A. An empirical study of the production of affectively toned items. *Journal of General Psychology*, 1944, *30*, 205–215.

Bousfield, W. A. The relationship between mood and the production of affectively toned associates. *The Journal of General Psychology*, 1950, *42*, 67–85.

Bower, G. H., Monteiro, K. P., & Gilligan, S. G. Emotional mood as a context for learning and recall. *Journal of Verbal Learning and Verbal Behavior*, 1978, *17*, 573–585.

Brady, J. V. Emotion: Some conceptual problems and psychophysiological experiments. In M. B. Arnold (Ed.), *Feelings and emotions: The Loyola symposium*. New York; London: Academic, 1970.

Bransford, J. D., Franks, J. J., Nitsch, K. E., & McCarrell, N. S. Toward unexplained memory. In R. Shaw & J. Bransford (Eds.), *Perceiving, acting and knowing: Toward an ecological psychology*. Hillsdale, N.J.: Erlbaum, 1977.

Brown, A. S. Priming effects in semantic memory retrieval process. *Journal of Experimental Psychology: Human Learning and Memory*, 1979, *5*, 65–77.

Buck, R. Nonverbal behavior and the theory of emotion: The facial feedback hypothesis. *Journal of Personality and Social Psychology*, 1980, *38*, 811 –824.

Carlsmith, J. M., & Gross, A. Some effects of guilt on compliance. *Journal of Personality and Social Psychology*, 1969, *11*, 240 –244.

Cialdini, R. B., & Kenrick, D. T. Altruism as hedonism: A social development perspective on the relationship of negative mood state and helping. *Journal of Personality and Social Psychology*, 1976, *34*, 907 –914.

Cialdini, R., Darby, B., & Vincent, J. Transgression and altruism: A case for hedonism. *Journal of Experimental Social Psychology*, 1973, *9*, 502 –516.

Collins, A. M., & Loftus, E. F. A spreading-activation theory of semantic processing. *Psychological Review*, 1975, *82*, 407 –428.

Collins, A. M., & Quillian, M. R. How to make a language user. In E. Tulving & W. Donaldson (Eds.) *Organization of memory*. New York: Academic, 1972.

Cunningham, M. R., Steinberg, J., & Grev, R. Wanting to and having to help: Separate motivations for positive mood and guilt-induced helping. *Journal of Personality and Social Psychology*. 1980, *38*, 181 –192.

Darwin, C. *The expression of the emotion in man and animals*. New York: Appleton, 1890.

Davitz, J. R. A dictionary and grammar of emotion. In B. Arnold, *Feelings and emotions: The Loyola symposium*. New York; London: Academic, 1970.

Donnerstein, E., Donnerstein, M., & Munger, G. Helping behavior as a function of pictorially induced moods. *Journal of Social Psychology*, 1975, *97*, 221 –225.

Dribbin, E., & Brabender, V. The effect of mood inducement upon audience receptiveness. *The Journal of Social Psychology*, 1979, *107*, 135 –136.

Feather, N. T. Effects of prior success and failure on expectations of success and subsequent performance. *Journal of Personality and Social Psychology*, 1966, *3*, 287 –298.

Fiske, S. T. Attention and weight in person perception: The impact of negative and extreme behavior. *Journal of Personality and Social Psychology*, 1980, *38*, 889 –906.

Forest, D., Clark, M. S., Mills, J., & Isen, A. M. Helping as a function of feeling state and nature of the helping behavior. *Motivation and Emotion*, 1979, *3*, 161 –169.

Fry, P. S. Affect and resistance to temptation. *Developmental Psychology*, 1975, *11*, 466 –472.

Galizio, M., & Hendrick, C. Effect of musical accompaniment on attitude: The guitar as a prop for persuasion. *Journal of Applied Social Psychology*, 1972, *2*, 350 –359.

Gouaux, C. Induced affective states and interpersonal attraction. *Journal of Personality and Social Psychology*, 1971, *20*, 37 –43.

Griffitt, W. B. Environmental effects on interpersonal affective behavior: Ambient effective temperature and attraction. *Journal of Personality and Social Psychology*, 1970, *15*, 240 –244.

Hale, W. D., & Strickland, B. R. Induction of mood states and effect on cognitive and social behaviors. *Journal of Consulting and Clinical Psychology*, 1976, *44*, 155.

Hasher, L., & Zacks, R. T. Automatic and effortful processes in memory. *Journal of Experimental Psychology: General*, 1979, *108*, 356 –388.

Henry, C. M., Weingartner, H., & Murphy, D. L. Influence of affective states and psychoactive drugs on verbal learning and memory. *American Journal of Psychiatry*, 1973, *130*, 966 –971.

Higgins, E. T., & Chaires, W. M. Accessibilty of interrelational constructs: Implications for stimulus encoding and creativity. *Journal of Experimental Social Psychology*, 1980, *16*, 348 –361.

Higgins, E. T., & King, G. Accessibility of social constructs: Individual and interpersonal considerations. In N. Cantor & J. F. Kihlstrom (Eds.), *Personality, Cognition and Social Interaction*. Hillsdale, N.J.: Erlbaum, 1981.

Isen, A. M. Success, failure, attention and reactions to others: The warm glow of success. *Journal of Personality and Social Psychology*, 1970, *15*, 294 –301.

Isen, A. M. Positive affect, accessibility of cognitions and helping. In J. Piliavin (Chair), *Current directions in theory on helping behavior*. Symposium presented at the meeting of the Eastern Psychological Association, New York, 1975.

Isen, A. M., & Levin, P. F. The effect of feeling good on helping: Cookies and kindness. *Journal of Personality and Social Psychology*, 1972, *21*, 384 –388.

Isen, A. M., & Shalker, T. E. Do you "Accentuate the positive, eliminate the negative" when you are in a good mood? Unpublished manuscript, University of Maryland, Baltimore County, 1977.

Isen, A. M., & Simmonds, S. F. The effect of feeling good on a helping task that is incompatible with good mood. *Social Psychology*, 1978, *41*, 345 –349.

Isen, A. M., Clark, M., & Schwartz, M. F. Duration of the effect of good mood on helping: "Footprints on the sands of time." *Journal of Personality and Social Psychology*, 1976, *34*, 385 –393.

Isen, A. M., Shalker, T., Clark, M., & Karp, L. Affect, accessibility of material in memory and behavior: A cognitive loop? *Journal of Personality and Social Psychology*, 1978, *36*, 1 –12.

Jacobson, J. Z. Effects of association upon masking and reading latency. *Canadian Journal of Psychology*, 1973, *27*, 58 –69.

Janis, I. L., Kaye, D., & Kirschner, P. Facilitating effects of "Eating while reading" on responsiveness to persuasive communications. *Journal of Personality and Social Psychology*, 1965, *11*, 188 –186.

Jenkins, J. J. Remember that old theory of memory? Well, forget it! *American Psychologist*, 1974, *29*, 785 –795.

Laird, J. Self-attribution of emotion: The effects of expressive behavior on the quality of emotional experience. *Journal of Personality and Social Psychology*, 1974, *29*, 475 –486.

Lanzetta, J. T., Cartwright-Smith, J., & Kleck, R. E. Effects of nonverbal dissimulation on emotional experience and autonomic arousal. *Journal of Personality and Social Psychology*, 1976, *33*, 354 –370.

Latané, B., & Darley, J. M. *The unresponsive bystander: Why doesn't he help?* New York: Appleton-Century-Crofts, 1970.

Leventhal, H. Emotions: A basic problem for social psychology. In C. Nemeth (Ed.), *Social psychology: Classic and contemporary interactions*, New York: Rand McNally, 1974.

Levin, P. F., & Isen, A. M. Something you can still get for a dime: Further studies on the effect of feeling good on helping. *Sociometry*, 1975, *38*, 141 –147.

Loftus, E. F., Activation of semantic memory. *American Journal of Psychology*, 1973, *86*, 331 –337.

Loftus, G. R., & Loftus, E. F. The influence of one memory retrieval on a subsequent memory retrieval. *Memory and Cognition*, 1974, *2*, 467 –471.

Mandler, G. *Mind and emotion.* New York: Wiley, 1975.

Mansfield, K. "Bliss." In K. Mansfield (Ed.), *Bliss and other stories.* New York: Knopf, 1920.

Masters, J. C., & Furman, W. Effects of affect states on noncontingent outcome expectancies and beliefs in internal or external control. *Developmental Psychology*, 1975, *12*, 481 –482.

Matlin, M., & Stang, D. *The pollyanna principle: Selectivity in language, memory and thought.* Cambridge, Mass.: Schenkman, 1979.

McDougall, W. *Outline of psychology.* New York: Scribner, 1923.

McMillen, D. L. Transgression, self-image, and compliant behavior. *Journal of Personality and Social Psychology*, 1971, *20*, 176 –179.

Meyer, D. W., & Schvaneveldt, R. W. Facilitation in recognizing pairs of words: Evidence of a dependence between retrieval operations. *Journal of Experimental Psychology*, 1971, *90*, 227 –234.

Mischel, W. Processes in delay of gratification. In L. Berkowitz (Ed.), *Advances in Experimental Social Psychology*, Vol. 7, New York: Academic Press, 1974.

Mischel, W., & Baker, N. Cognitive appraisals and transformations in delay behavior. *Journal of Personality and Social Psychology*, 1975, *31*, 254 –261.

Mischel, W., & Moore, B. Effects of attention to symbolically presented rewards upon self-control. *Journal of Personality and Social Psychology*, 1973, *28*, 172 –179.

Mischel, W., Coates, B., & Raskoff, A. Effects of success and failure on self-gratification. *Journal of Personality and Social Psychology*, 1968, *10*, 381 – 390.

Mischel, W., Ebbesen, E., & Zeiss, A. Selective attention to the self: Situational and dispositional determinants. *Journal of Personality and Social Psychology*, 1973, *27*, 129 – 142.

Moore, B. S., Underwood, B., & Rosenhan, D. L. Affect and altruism. *Developmental Psychology*, 1973, *8*, 99 – 194.

Neely, J. H. Semantic priming and retrieval for lexical memory: Evidence for facilatory and inhibitory processes. *Memory and Cognition*, 1976, *4*, 648 – 654.

Neely, J. H. Semantic priming and retrieval from lexical memory: Roles of inhibitionless spreading activation and limited-capacity attention. *Journal of Experimental Psychology: General*, 1977, *106*, 226 – 254.

Nowlis, V. Mood: Behavior and experience. In M. B. Arnold (Ed.), *Feelings and emotions: The Loyola symposium*, New York; London: Academic, 1970.

Piliavin, I. M., Rodin, J., & Piliavin, J. A. Good samaritanism: An underground phenomenon? *Journal of Personality and Social Psychology*, 1969, *13*, 289 – 299.

Posner, M. I. *Chronomatic explorations of the mind.* Hillsdale, N.J.: Erlbaum, 1978.

Posner, M. I., & Snyder, C. R. Attention and cognitive control. In R. L. Solso (Ed.), *Information processing and cognition: The Loyola symposium.* Hillsdale, N.J.: Erlbaum, 1975.

Postman, L., & Brown, D. R. Perceptual consequences of success and failure. *Journal of Abnormal and Social Psychology*, 1952, *47*, 213 – 221.

Raps, C. S., Reinhard, K. E., & Seligman, M. E. P. Reversal of cognitive and affective deficits associated with depression and learned helplessness by mood elevation in patients. *Journal of Abnormal Psychology*, 1980, *89*, 342 – 349.

Regan, D. T., Williams, M., & Sparling, S. Voluntary expiation of guilt: A field experiment. *Journal of Personality and Social Psychology*, 1972, *24*, 422 – 445.

Regan, J. W. Guilt, perceived injustice and altruistic behavior. *Journal of Personality and Social Psychology*, 1971, *18*, 124 – 132.

Rodgers, R., & Hammerstein, O. II. *The king and I.* New York: Williamson Music Co., Inc., 1951.

Rodgers, R., & Hammerstein, O. II. *The sound of music.* New York: Williamson Music Co., Inc., 1959.

Rosch, E. Cognitive reference points. *Cognitive Psychology*, 1975, *1*, 532 – 547.

Ryle, G. *The concept of mind.* London: Hutchinson, 1950.

Schachter, S., & Singer, J. Cognitive, social and physiological determinants of emotional state. *Psychological Review*, 1962, *65*, 379 – 399.

Schiffenbauer, A. Effect of observer's emotional state on judgments of the emotional state of others. *Journal of Personality and Social Psychology*, 1974, *30*, 1, 31 – 35.

Schneider, D. J., Hastorf, A. H., & Ellsworth, P. C. *Person perception*, Reading, Mass.: Addison-Wesley, 1980.

Schneider, W., & Shiffrin, R. M. Controlled and automatic human information processing: I. Detection search, and attention. *Psychological Review*, 1977, *84*, 1 – 66.

Schwarz, J. C., & Pollack, P. R. Affect and delay of gratification. *Journal of Research in Personality*, 1977, *11*, 147 – 164.

Seeman, G., & Schwarz, J. C. Affective state and preference for immediate versus delayed reward. *Journal of Research in Personality*, 1974, *7*, 384 – 394.

Seligman, M. E. P. *Helplessness. On depression, development, and death.* San Francisco, Calif.: Freeman, 1975.

Shiffrin, R. M., & Schneider, W. Controlled and automatic human information processing: II. Perceptual learning, automatic attending, and a general theory. *Psychological Review*, 1977, *84*, 127 – 190.

Simon, H. A. Motivational and emotional controls of cognition. *Psychological Review*, 1967, *74*, 29 – 39.

Strickland, B. R., Hale, W. D., & Anderson, L. K. Effect of induced mood states on activity and self-reported affect. *Journal of Consulting and Clinical Psychology*, 1975, *43*, 587.

Teasdale, J. D., & Bancroft, J. Manipulation of thought content as a determinant of mood and corrugator electromyographic activity in depressed patients. *Journal of Abnormal Psychology*, 1977, *86*, 235 –241.

Teasdale, J. D., & Fogarty, S. J. Differential effect of induced mood on retrieval of pleasant and unpleasant events from episodic memory. *Journal of Abnormal Psychology*, 1979, *88*, 248 –257.

Tesser, A., & Conlee, M. C. Some effects of time and thought on attitude polarization. *Journal of Personality and Social Psychology*, 1975, *31*, 262 –270.

Tourangeau, R., & Ellsworth, P. C. The role of facial response in the experience of emotion. *Journal of Personality and Social Psychology*, 1979, *37*, 1519 –1531.

Tulving, E. Episodic and semantic memory. In E. Tulving & W. Donaldson (Eds.), *Organization of memory*. New York: Academic, 1972.

Tulving, E., & Pearlstone, Z. Availability versus accessibility of information in memory for words. *Journal of Verbal Learning and Verbal Behavior*, 1966, *5*, 381 –391.

Tversky, A., & Kahneman, D. Availability: A heuristic for judging frequency and probability. *Cognitive Psychology*, 1973, *5*, 207 –32.

Underwood, B., Moore, B. S., & Rosenhan, D. L. Affect and self-gratification. *Developmental Psychology*, 1973, *8*, 209 –214.

Underwood, B., Froming, W., Moore, B. Mood, attention, and altruism: A search for mediating variables. *Developmental Psychology*, 1977, *13*, 541 –542.

Veitch, R., & Griffitt, W. Good news—bad news: Affective and interpersonal effects. *Journal of Applied Social Psychology*, 1976, *6*, 69 –75.

Warren, R. E. Time and the spread of activation in memory. *Journal of Experimental Psychology: Human Learning and Memory*, 1977, *4*, 458 –466.

Weiner, B. A cognitive (attribution)-emotion-action model of motivated behavior: An analysis of judgment of help-giving. *Journal of Personality and Social Psychology*, 1980, *39*, 186 –200.

Weiner, B., Russell, D., & Lerman, D. The cognition-emotion process in achievement-related contexts. *Journal of Personality and Social Psychology*, 1979, *37*, 1211 –1220.

Weingartner, H., & Faillace, L. A. Alcohol state-dependent learning in man. *Journal of Nervous and Mental Disease*, 1971, *153*, 395 –406.

Weingartner, H., Miller, H., & Murphy, D. L. Mood-state-dependent retrieval of verbal associations. *Journal of Abnormal Psychology*, 1977, *86*, 276 –284.

Weiss, R. F., Buchanan, W., Alstatt, L., & Lombardo, J. P. Altruism is rewarding. *Science*, 1971, *26*, 1262 –1263.

Wessman, A. E., & Ricks, D. F. *Mood and personality*. New York: Holt, Rinehart and Winston, 1966.

Weyant, J. M. Effects of mood states, costs, and benefits of helping. *Journal of Personality and Social Psychology*, 1978, *36*, 1169 –1176.

White, M. M. Some factors influencing the recall of pleasant and unpleasant words. *American Journal of Psychology*, 1936, *48*, 134 –139.

White, M. M., & Powell, M. The differential reaction time for pleasant and unpleasant words. *American Journal of Psychology*, 1936, *48*, 126 –133.

Wyer, R. S. Jr., & Srull, T. K. Category accessibility: Some theoretical and empirical issues concerning the processing of social stimulus information. In E. T. Higgins, C. P. Herman, & M. P. Zanna (Eds.), *Social cognition: The Ontario symposium on personality and social psychology*. Hillsdale, N.J.: Erlbaum, 1981.

Zajonc, R. B. The attitudinal effects of mere exposure. *Journal of Personality and Social Psychology Monograph Supplement*, 1968, *9* (2, pt.2).

Zillmann, D., Mody, B., & Cantor, J. R. Empathic perception of emotional displays in films as a function of hedonic and excitatory state prior to exposure. *Journal of Research in Personality*, 1974, *8*, 335 –349.

ANTHONY G. GREENWALD

EGO TASK ANALYSIS:
AN INTEGRATION OF RESEARCH ON EGO-INVOLVEMENT AND SELF-AWARENESS

This chapter has escaped its original boundaries. In developing an analysis of ego as an organization of knowledge (Greenwald, 1980), I discovered that there was no recent theoretical review of ego-involvement. The editors of this volume kindly provided me license to undertake such a review. In the course of this work I further discovered that ego-involvement was in conceptual disarray. Thus I became involved in the task of providing order for the concept and found that this could be done only by allowing both ego-involvement and myself to be drawn into the company of several other concepts, especially an attractive one of recent vintage, self-awareness.

This history of the writing of this chapter explains the inclusion of a review of the interrupted-task literature that eventuated in the near-demise of the ego-involvement concept. Research on memory for interrupted tasks was voluminous in the two decades from the mid-1930s to the mid-1950s, but subsided about 20 years ago without resolving the problems with which it was concerned. I direct new attention to the interrupted-task problem because it provides needed background for the concept of *task*, which I suggest to be a major unit of personality organization. Tasks are hypothesized to be organized hierarchically. At the highest level are *ego tasks*, which are major enduring aspirations that are hypothesized to vary in *orientation*—ego tasks may be intrapersonally (I-type) or socially (S-type) oriented. Ego task analysis is used to provide an integrated account of both the older ego-involvement literature and the more recent work on self-awareness.

THEORETICAL CONCEPTIONS OF EGO-INVOLVEMENT

The concept of ego-involvement may be so familiar that one is likely to assume that its meaning is well established both in conceptual and operational terms. Surprisingly, neither type of definition is well established. Nevertheless, the phenomena traditionally cited as manifestations of ego-involvement are unarguably important. Their importance is confirmed in an unintended way by the emergence of a variety of newer concepts (which are considered later) that are addressed to the same empirical domain. Our review of ego-involvement starts with the treatments by Allport (1943) and by Sherif and Cantril (1947), which were major early attempts to provide scholarly synthesis to the concept.

Allport's 1943 Analysis

Gordon Allport's article, "The ego in contemporary psychology," may be known best for its enumeration of eight senses of ego, which are summarized here:

1. *Ego as knower* designates the experiencing agent, the implied grammatical subject of predicates of existence, sensation, and action, the "I" that exists, perceives, and behaves in "I am . . . ," "I see . . . ," "I do . . . ".
2. *Ego as object of knowledge* refers to the corporeal aspect of ego, the association of self-ness with the body as a whole or with some location within the body.
3. *Ego as primitive selfishness* defines ego as the antithesis of altruism. It is interesting to note the opposition between this meaning of ego and that of Sherif and Cantril (described below).
4. *Ego as dominance-drive* is closely related to the preceding sense, referring to enhancement of self or self-esteem maintenance.
5. *Ego as passive organization of mental processes* refers to the Freudian psychoanalytic conception of ego as neutral arbitrator among the conflicting forces of id, superego, and environment—ego itself is not a dynamic force. In this sense, ego is the locus of rational mental process—the home of the psychoanalytic reality principle.
6. *Ego as a fighter for ends* contrasts with the previous (passive) sense in having a dynamic character, with ego being the locus of important life goals. [Some neo-Freudian psychoanalytic views, especially Hartmann's (1939), fit better with this category than with the previous one.]
7. *Ego as a behavioral system.* The word "behavioral" may mislead contemporary readers. Allport referred to Gestalt psychological treatments, particularly those of Koffka (1935) and Lewin (1936). This sense of ego corresponds to the "person" in the familiar Lewinian formulation, $B = f(P,E)$, in which behavior (B) is a function of the person (P), and the environment (E), the latter two being the major subsystems of the psychological field.

8. *Ego as the subjective organization of culture* designates a mental organization that is the residue of socialization experience, a definition of ego that Allport associated with the work of Sherif (1936) and Cantril (1941).[1]

The largest section of Allport's 1943 article was devoted to a review of experimental evidence in support of the point that

> ego-involvement, or its absence, makes a critical difference in human behavior. When a person reacts in a neutral, impersonal routine atmosphere, his behavior is one thing. But when he is behaving personally, perhaps excitedly, seriously committed to a task, he behaves quite differently. In the first condition his ego is not engaged; in the second condition it is. And it is my belief that in most of the experiments I shall report one finds that the ego is acting in several, if not all, of the eight capacities I have listed. In other words, *ego-involvement* is, as the phrase implies, a condition of total participation of the self—as knower, as organizer, as observer, as status seeker, and as socialized being. (p. 459)

Although Allport thus identified ego-involvement with all eight of his senses of ego, the passage also makes clear that, in its motivational character ego-involvement is closest to the sixth and seventh senses of ego, which he merged under the label "propriate striving" in his 1955 treatment (see footnote 1). In the 1955 work (p. 48) Allport directly linked the terms "ego-involved" and "propriate."

This capsule review of Allport's 1943 article can be completed by summarizing in Allport's own words his observations of the effects of ego-involvement.

> We have seen that under conditions of ego-involvement the whole personality manifests greater consistency in behavior, reveals not specificity in conduct but generality and congruence. In the field of judgment, we have seen how ego-involvement results in significant distortions of the ordinary psychophysical scales. In memory, we find that retention is characteristically superior (though at times repressions also may be more likely to occur, and rationalizations may creep into ego-involved memory). In intelligence, we note that ego-involvement is indispensable if we would obtain optimum performance. In learning theory, reforms seem indicated to make room for the demonstrable influence of the ego upon the acquisition of skill and knowledge. In motivation, the craving for recognition, status, and personal appreciation turns out to be supreme, so much so that our conceptions of procedure and policy in industrial relations, in education, and in psychotherapy, are profoundly affected. (pp. 472 –473)

[1]Allport provided a new list of eight senses of ego in 1955, although this later work did not receive as much attention as the 1943 article. The main changes in the 1955 chapter were as follows: (a) Three of the usages were relabeled: object of knowledge (#2) became "bodily sense;" passive organization of mental process (#5) became "rational process;" and subjective organization of culture (#8) was relabeled "ego-extension;" (b) primitive selfishness (#3) and dominance-drive (#4) were synthesized under the heading "ego-enhancement;" (c) the motivational senses of ego, as fighter for ends (#6) and behavioral system (#7), were merged under the label "propriate striving;" and (d) two additional usages were identified: "self-identity," referring to the experience of the continuity of personality over time, and "self-image," capturing the notion of an ideal self-concept toward which one aspires.

This was Allport's argument for ego's "admittance to good standing in contemporary psychology" (1943, p. 476). By combining several senses of ego into the definition of ego-involvement, Allport provided a broad concept, but one that was concomitantly imprecise. However, as will be seen, Allport's characterization of the ego-involved person as "seriously committed to a task" (quoted above, 1943, p. 459) fits well with the conclusions reached in the present analysis.

Sherif and Cantril's 1947 Analysis

The other seminal treatment of ego-involvement that is to be considered, by Sherif and Cantril (1947), was based on a definition of ego corresponding to the eighth of Allport's senses of ego—the one he referred to as "subjective organization of culture."

> What is called the "ego" consists, in the last analysis, of a constellation of attitudes which can be designated as ego-attitudes . . . All attitudes that define a person's status or that give him some relative role with respect to other individuals, groups, or institutions are ego-involved. . . . [The] values, goals, standards, or norms which become our attitudes are represented by, set by, or created by group activities and social situations that form the constellation of social realtionships with which we come in contact . . . Ego-striving, then, is the individual's effort to place himself securely in those constellations of human relationships that represent *for him* desirable values, that will make *his* status or position secure. (pp. 92, 96, 114, 115)

Allport had commented on Sherif's (1936) earlier use of a similar definition of ego by saying that it defined ego as "nothing but the social part of man" (1943, p. 458). Although Sherif and Cantril objected to this summary characterization (1947, pp. 150 –152), still it is clear that their view of ego was remarkably social, as was evident also in their interpretation of ego-involvement.

> These contents of the ego, these things, persons, ways of conducting oneself, social norms of various kinds, provide for the individual the standards of judgment or frames of reference which determine to such an important degree his social behavior and reactions. And when any stimulus or situation is consciously or unconsciously related to them by the individual, we can say there is "ego-involvement." (p. 117)

The social character of Sherif and Cantril's conception of ego is made most dramatically apparent in their use of the following example of self-interest:

> We have seen since the end of World War II how the Jews in the United States have taken the initiative in [seeking] help for the tortured and displaced Jews of Europe. . . . In such cases we say that "self-interest" is involved. And we mean by this that individuals identify themselves with different degrees of intensity to various social causes, principles, ideals. (p. 131)

The conceptual coherence of Sherif and Cantril's analysis is an undeniable virtue. The question as to whether its social emphasis is justifiable must be postponed until after consideration of empirical treatments of ego-involvement.

RESEARCH PROCEDURES FOR ESTABLISHING EGO-INVOLVEMENT

It is clear from the published record of two decades of research, from the mid-1930s to the mid-1950s, that laboratory researchers were inspired less by the major conceptual treatments of ego-involvement by Allport and by Sherif and Cantril than they were by an empirical puzzle stemming from Zeigarnik's (1927, 1938) research on memory for interrupted tasks. From the wealth of empirical studies reported in those two decades, one can work backward from the procedures employed to infer the researchers' conceptual definition of ego-involvement. Iverson and Reuder (1956) did just this in a review entitled "Ego involvement as an experimental variable." They concluded that ego-involvement

> appears to be manifest in the situations which threaten the individual's valued self-identity, his feelings of personal importance, or his personal status. . . . Viewed in terms of experimental procedures, then, ego involvement may be defined in terms of a relationship between an individual and a situation which is characterized by the possibility of interference with or deprivation of the need to enhance or to maintain one's feelings of self-esteem. (p. 149)

Threat to self-esteem as the interpretation of ego-involvement is an obvious departure from the Allport (1943) and Sherif and Cantril (1947) analyses. To understand the basis for this development it is necessary to review some details of the extensive ego-involvement research conducted in the interrupted-task paradigm.[2]

Early Research on Ego-Involvement in the Interrupted-Task Paradigm

Many of the 173 studies reviewed by Iverson and Reuder (1956) had employed variants of Zeigarnik's interrupted-task method. In her dissertation research, performed under the supervision of Kurt Lewin in Berlin, Zeigarnik (1927, 1938) found that interrupted tasks were often better recalled than completed ones. Her subjects, who ranged from 13-year-olds to college students, were asked to do a series of about 20 tasks during a session lasting approximately an hour. The tasks were varied, including both manual tasks (making and drawing things) and mental problems (such as verbal puzzles and arithmetic problems). Half the

[2]The following sections on the interrupted-task method and one later in the chapter are intended chiefly for readers who have a teaching or research interest in ego-involvement. These sections attempt to provide some retrospective historical structure for the ego-involvement concept and, in the process, they arrive at conclusions at variance with those of previous reviewers. Readers following the main line of original theoretical development in this chapter should skip at this point to the section entitled Modes of Experimental Involvement and Subject Roles. (p. 117)

tasks were performed to completion, while the remainder were interrupted when the subject appeared to be busily engaged, at which point the subject was asked to start on another task. After completion of the series, subjects were asked unexpectedly to recall the tasks that they had worked at during the session. Results were reported in terms of the ratio of number of recalled interrupted to number of recalled completed tasks. In four versions of the experiment, Zeigarnik found this ratio to be close to 2.0, meaning that interrupted tasks were about twice as likely to be recalled as were the completed ones. Zeigarnik's explanation of this superiority in recall for interrupted tasks, now known as the Zeigarnik effect, was based on Lewin's hypothesis that a task, once started, has a motivational tension associated with it. This tension, which is assumed to persist until the task is completed, is responsible for the enhanced recall of interrupted tasks. This explanation fit well also with Ovsiankina's (1928) subsequent finding that, when provided the opportunity, subjects tended to resume interrupted tasks rather than to repeat completed ones.

Variations in the Effect Among Zeigarnik's Subjects. Zeigarnik was attentive to differences within the subject samples in her experiments and noted the following factors that appeared to be associated with variations in the recall of interrupted tasks: (1) "Ambitious" subjects—those who appeared very much interested in succeeding at the task—showed the highest ratios of recalled interrupted to recalled completed tasks; (2) subjects who interpreted interruption of a specific task as a failure (perhaps because they perceived the task as something that should have been completed in the available time) were less likely to recall that interrupted task than other interrupted ones; (3) children showed the effect of interruption on recall more strongly than adults and also appeared to have a more "natural" approach to the tasks; and (4) adults who "let themselves go" (Zeigarnik, 1938, p. 312) resembled the children just mentioned in showing the effect more strongly than those who were more reserved in their performance.

Effects of "Ego-Involving" Instructions. Several investigators pursued the lead suggested by Zeigarnik's observation of reduced recall of interrupted tasks that were experienced as failures. In a number of experiments subjects were induced to interpret interruptions as failures (and completions correspondingly as successes) by means of instructions that the experimental tasks provided an index of intelligence. Perhaps because a tendency not to recall such failures could be interpreted as an experimental analog of the psychoanalytic ego defense of repression (cf. Rosenzweig, 1943; Zeller, 1950), these instructions came to be referred to widely as ego-involving.[3]

[3]The contrast of ego-involving or intelligence-test instructions with the more relaxed instructions originally used by Zeigarnik has been referred to by various researchers as formal vs informal treatments, stressful vs nonstressful, ego-oriented vs task-oriented, and achievement-oriented vs relaxed. Butterfield (1964) made the reasonable suggestion that these variations should be referred to less interpretively as skill vs nonskill instructions.

The general finding of studies using ego-involving or skill instructions was a reversal of the usual Zeigarnik effect (see reviews by Iverson & Reuder, 1956; Inglis, 1961; Butterfield, 1964; Van Bergen, 1968), that is, more completed than interrupted tasks were recalled. [Marrow's study (1938b) is an important exception to this generalization, which will be taken up later in this chapter.]

The Onset of Confusion: Personality Variables and Recall of Interrupted Tasks

The reversal of the usual Zeigarnik effect by use of skill instructions is not characteristic of all subjects. Subjects who show this pattern have been described in different studies as (1) high on ego strength (Alper, 1948, 1957; Eriksen, 1954); (2) low on need for achievement (Atkinson, 1953; Atkinson & Raphelson, 1956; Caron & Wallach, 1959); (3) high in neurocirculatory efficiency (Abel, 1938); and (4) high in hypnotizability or suggestibility (Sarason & Rosenzwieg, 1942). This collection of findings is most challenging, not to say confusing. How can one construct a commonality that includes low need for achievement, high ego strength, suggestibility, hypnotizability, and the enhanced tendency to recall successes relative to failures?

Complication by Procedural Variations. Any attempt to find the common personality theme among studies of individual differences in recall of interrupted tasks under skill conditions was doomed to defeat as a consequence of variations in procedures used in different studies. For example, all of the studies of the ego-strength dimension used task series consisting of variations of the single task of rearranging scrambled short phrases into whole sentences. This scrambled-sentence task has the virtues of being readily group-administered and easily rendered unsolvable, thereby assuring that it can be interrupted after a certain amount of time without having been completed. Unfortunately, the scrambled-sentence task is of dubious usefulness in comparing memory for completed and interrupted tasks for two reasons. First, unlike Zeigarnik's original tasks, completed (unscrambled) sentences may be more memorable than interrupted (scrambled) ones because they can be encoded more meaningfully. [Think about the relative memorability of AAAMGNR vs ANAGRAM. Caron and Wallach (1959) apparently were the only researchers who were alert to this possibility.] Second, the use of multiple variants of the scrambled sentence task was in direct opposition to Zeigarnik's (1938, p. 313) admonition:

> It is essential for the memorial advantage of unfinished tasks that the tension systems be sufficiently isolated from one another. When the individual tasks lack separate lineaments for the subject, there develops only one large tension system in place of several.

Thus completions of sentences late in a series can make up for earlier failures, perhaps eliminating their persisting tensions. A suggestive analogy is the case of the golfer who hits some good strokes on the 18th hole and promptly forgets about many earlier misses.

Problems in Delineating an Ego-Strength Dimension. The concept of ego strength was linked to the recall of interrupted tasks in the research of Alper (1948, 1957) and Eriksen (1954). Alper (1952) described the strong-ego person as having a high tolerance for failure, defending self-esteem in the stressful (skill instruction) condition by recalling more completed tasks.

> The weak ego S[ubject], on the other hand, needs to defend self-esteem even when the objective situation is not threatening. This he does in the informal [non-ego-involving] session by recalling completed tasks, which are for him in this context dynamically equivalent to successes. When the objective stress is high, however, his defenses no longer operate efficiently. Overwhelmed by the failure experience, he seems to need to admit his failures before others accuse him of failing. (p. 80)

This perhaps plausible link between memory in the interrupted-task paradigm and the concept of ego strength is complicated considerably by examining Alper's description of the basis for classifying subjects as high or low on ego strength. The ego-strength dimension was identified in Alper's research on the basis of intensive clinical testing at the Harvard Psychological Clinic. It was described in the following terms, which can only appear confusing to readers of a subsequent psychological generation:

> The syndrome of personality parameters which characterizes the Strong Egos includes high Ego-Strength, high Conative Conjunctivity, high need for recognition, high need for dominance, low Dejection, Pessimism, and low Ego-Ideal, Intragression. Weak Egos rank high on Dejection, Pessimism, high on Ego-Ideal, Intragression, and low on Narcism, on the need for recognition, the need for defendance, and the need for counteractive achievement. (1946, p. 416)

Eriksen (1954), working in a less conceptually guided tradition, defined ego strength as "the degree to which an individual's behavior is generally in keeping with the realities of the objective situation" and as "the individual's capacity for appraising the reasonable limits in his interpretations and perceptions of his environment" (p. 46). Operationally, subjects were identified as having high ego strength to the extent that their "yes – no responses to suggested interpretations of the Rorschach inkblots are in agreement with norms derived from other individuals of comparable intellectual level and social background" (p. 46). Additionally, Eriksen proposed that this ego-strength dimension was possibly related to the neuroticism and extraversion-introversion dimensions developed in Eysenck's studies of a sample of hospitalized neurotics. The relation to neuroticism was suggested by Eysenck's (1947) finding of a strong (negative) loading on his neuroticism dimension for a measure of "conformity" that was procedurally similar to Eriksen's measure of ego strength. The link to extraversion comes from Eysenck's observation:

> that in level-of-aspiration experiments S[ubjects]s high on the extraversive pole tend to overestimate their performance and are little bothered by failure, while S[ubject]s falling on the introversive pole tend to underestimate their performance and are preoccupied with their failures. (Eriksen, 1954, p. 49).

The ties between Eriksen's and Eysenck's work were developed further in a review of literature by Inglis (1961), and commented on further in another review by Butterfield (1964).

Modes of Experimental Involvement and Subject Roles

An interesting discovery in reading the interrupted-task literature is that some interrupted-task researchers were led to analyses of individual differences that partially anticipated the more recent conception of subject roles (see review by Weber & Cook, 1972). In her initial interrupted-task research Zeigarnik (1938) identified three types of subjects who brought different orientations to their participation in the experiment, as follows.

> The first were those who sought to perform as instructed because they wished to please the experimenter. Another, the ambitious type, strove to excel as if in competition with others. The third type was interested in the task for its own sake and sought to solve each problem in the way the problem itself demanded. (p. 303)[4]

These three types may be recognized, respectively, as Weber and Cook's (1972) *good subject* (Zeigarnik's type who "wished to please the experimenter"), *apprehensive subject* (the type who "strove to excel"), and *faithful subject* (the type who "sought to solve each problem in the way the problem itself demanded").

Alper (1946) developed concepts corresponding to two of these three types, designating them respectively as *ego-involved* and *task-involved*. The ego-involved subject (corresponding to the apprehensive subject role) was one to whom "performance level is important . . . he perceives

[4]This passage continues: "In keeping with these differences the experimenter did not preserve a fixed mien and method with all subjects. Those of the first type were allowed to see the experimenter's pleasure when a task was well done. Work done by the second group was inspected with the air of an examiner, while the third group was allowed to work unmolested, the experimenter in this case remaining passive." This quotation may be read with horror by experimental social psychologists trained in the 1960s and 1970s—experimental treatments are supposed to be fixed, not modified in response to subjects' behavior. However, Zeigarnik's flexibility in response to individual differences may be defensible. The psychological meaning of an experimental treatment may, in the hands of an alert experimenter, be kept more constant across subjects by adapting the treatment to their differences than by ignoring those differences. It is relevant to note that Marrow (1938a) "cleaned up" this and a few other aspects of Zeigarnik's procedure and obtained reliable confirmations of her results.

the situation as threatening to his self-esteem''; in contrast, the task-involved subject (corresponding to the faithful subject role) ''does what he is told to do, and is not concerned as to whether his performance is 'poor' or 'good' '' (p. 236).

A Retrospective Summary of Ego-Involvement Research

Three occasionally intersecting lines of development of the ego-involvement concept can be disentangled from research of the last 40 or so years. By far the major one is that associated with the interpretation of ego-involvement as a threat to self-esteem. This theme was developed in two decades of interrupted-task research. It merged the interest of academic gestalt psychologists in the analysis of task tension systems with clinical psychologists' interest in ego defense. This vigorous line of research subsided in the late 1950s amidst confusion stemming perhaps from nonstandardized task-interruption procedures and strained attempts to account for individual differences. One might be tempted to conclude that the heritage of interrupted-task research is useless and can be ignored, a conclusion offered by Sears (1950) and Van Bergen (1968). Ironically, such a judgment would amount to a collective act of repression, the forgetting of a theoretical task that was never completed. An opposed judgment is supported by the observation that the problems with which interrupted-task researchers were concerned have not gone away—they have only changed their names. In particular, much recent interest in evaluation apprehension and self-esteem is associated with the same experimental procedures used earlier to produce ego-involvement. Perhaps research on the interrupted-task problem declined because researchers did not succeed in sorting out the contribution of person variables, situation variables, and their interaction to the phenomena of memory for interrupted tasks. If so, recent analyses of person-situation interaction (e.g., Magnusson & Endler, 1977) may provide the framework for more successful handling of interrupted-task phenomena.

A second important line of work on ego-involvement developed as part of the strong emphasis by social psychologists on attitudes in the 25 years following World War II. This research on attitudinal ego-involvement has not been reviewed here beyond the attention given to its major background theoretical statement by Sherif and Cantril (1947). Empirically and theoretically, this work is much less problematic than the interrupted-task research. The central finding is that ego-involved attitudes tend to resist change (Sherif, Sherif, & Nebergall, 1965; Ostrom & Brock, 1968). This major finding fits well with the conception of ego as a protective or defensive agency of the personality. The fact that ego-involvement of attitudes was usually established in research by selecting topics that were personally important to audiences gives pause—this procedure has little in common with the establishment of ego-involvement in the interrupted-task research by providing an evaluative climate that threatens self-esteem. This discrepancy will become focal in attempting below to establish a coherent synthesis of ego-involvement conceptions. Research attention to ego-involvement in the attitude domain has subsided in the last decade, apparently a waning of attention to agreed-upon findings and interpretations.[5]

The third line of ego-involvement's history is the not-always-visible wake of Allport's (1943) review. His definition of ego-involvement as "a condition of total participation of the self" (p. 459) has not been translated into research operations but continues to surface in textbook treatments. Few of the empirical phenomena included in Allport's review have received more than occasional research attention in the intervening nearly 40 years.

The following conclusions of this retrospection define the problems that are to be addressed in the next section of this chapter.

1. Ego-involvement is not a unitary empirical concept, being associated with different research operations and conceptual interpretations in the interrupted-task and attitude research domains.
2. The theoretical usefulness of ego-involvement is in doubt, particularly in light of its problems in organizing interrupted-task research.

EGO-INVOLVEMENT: ANALYSIS AND SYNTHESIS

Three different meanings of ego-involvement emerge from its theoretical and empirical tradition. Until a basis for synthesizing them can be provided they will be distinguished by means of subscripts.

Ego-Involvement$_1$ (Concern About Evaluation by Others). This is the sense of ego-involvement that was dominant in the interrupted-task research. Its standard operationalization was to instruct the subject that the tasks to be performed were to be scored to provide a measure of a valued skill, usually intelligence. Ego-involvement$_1$ therefore designates a motivational state, one that is identified elsewhere (e.g., Rosenberg, 1969) as evaluation apprehension.

Ego-Involvement$_2$ (Concern About Self-Evaluation). Perhaps only subtly different from ego-involvement$_1$, ego-involvement$_2$ is better identified with constructs of self-esteem threat and achievement orientation than with evaluation apprehension. The difference between the two is that, in the case of ego-involvement$_2$, the evaluator is oneself rather than an audience. Self-esteem, rather than other-esteem, is at issue. To the extent that many psychologists may regard self-esteem as intimately connected with esteem in the eyes of others, for them the distinction between ego-involvement$_1$ and ego-involvement$_2$ tends to disappear.

[5]In an interesting challenge to these agreed-upon conclusions, Petty and Cacioppo (1979) showed that, with a powerful persuasive message, ego-involvement may be associated with increased attitude change rather than with resistance to change.

Ego-Involvement$_3$ (Personal Importance). This usage has become prominent in the period subsequent to research on the interrupted-task problem, as researchers became interested in attitude change, and particularly in the finding that audiences were more resistant to change on important or controversial topics. This usage is well exemplified in the work of Sherif et al. (1965, which provides a tie to Sherif & Cantril, 1947). Ostrom and Brock (1968), who were also influenced by the earlier Sherif–Cantril formulation, characterized the ego-involvement$_{[3]}$ of a cognition or belief as being a function of the centrality and number of personal values to which it was related, and the strength of those relations. Ego-involvement$_3$ was thus implicated in the resistance to change of important beliefs.

What Do the Three Senses of Ego-Involvement Have in Common?

It should be established first that this question is worth answering, and this requires stirring up a bit more confusion before attempting to restore order. The case for the question's importance can be made by establishing relations of the three senses of ego-involvement to a variety of other constructs that are in current use.

We may start from the opposition of ego-involvement$_1$ (evaluation apprehension) and *task-involvement* that was developed by Alper (1946). This distinction corresponds partially to that between *extrinsic* and *intrinsic motivation* (e.g., Condry, 1977; Deci, 1975; Lepper & Greene, 1978), in designating the contrast between performance motivated by an outcome contingent on performance (approval by others) and that motivated by characteristics of the task itself. But now note that ego-involvement$_3$ (personal importance) is more akin to intrinsic than extrinsic motivation. (This observation suggests not only some incompatibility between ego-involvement$_1$ and ego-involvement$_3$, but also a possible difficulty in the distinction between intrinsic and extrinsic motivation.)

Commitment to a task implies its linkage to important personal values (cf. ego-involvement$_3$). *Importance* and *commitment* are both related to *ego-involvement* also in that all three of these concepts have been proposed—in the analyses of Festinger (1957), Brehm & Cohen (1962), and Aronson (1968), respectively—as essential conditions for arousal of *cognitive dissonance*. Cognitive dissonance is additionally linked (1) to the self-evaluation sense of ego-involvement$_2$ via the suggestion that the motivational state of cognitive dissonance is indistinguishable from motivation to maintain favorable self-evaluation (Deutsch, Krauss, & Rosenau, 1962; Greenwald & Ronis, 1978), and (2) to the evaluation apprehension sense of ego-involvement$_1$ by the competing suggestion that cognitive consistency is an appearance maintained to obtain the favorable evaluation of others, in the *impression management* analysis of Tedeschi, Schlenker, and Bonoma (1971).

The conception of ego-involvement$_2$ as a concern about self-evaluation also provides a link with several theories that incorporate a self-evaluative process. *Social comparison* theory (Festinger, 1954) proposes that self-evaluation is facilitated by the extraction of comparison information from similar others; in *achievement motivation* theory (McClelland, Atkinson, Clark, & Lowell, 1953), self-evaluation is mediated by comparison with internalized standards; in *temporal comparison* theory (Albert, 1977), self-evaluation is based on comparison with past performance; and in *self-awareness* theory (Duval & Wicklund, 1972) the state of self-awareness—which may be elicited by self-focusing devices such as a mirror or camera—has as a consequence the comparison of present behavior with either social or personal standards, whichever may be salient at the moment (Wicklund, 1979).

Only a small portion of the network of concepts that can be connected to the three senses of ego-involvement has been examined in this brief survey. A somewhat deeper view into the ramifications of this network is given in Table 1. The table provides clues to the identification of the shared characteristic of the three senses of ego-involvement.

It may be seen in Table 1 that there has been a great deal of conceptual activity in the domain represented by the three senses of ego-involvement. The recent development of the concept of self-awareness

TABLE 1. Procedural Variables and Psychological Constructs Linked to Ego-Involvement[a]

Procedures	Constructs	
Camera		
Audience	Evaluation apprehension	Ego-involvement$_1$
Skill (intelligence) test	Impression management	
Failure experience	Public self-consciousness	
Personality test	Need for approval	
Social pressure		
Responsibility for aversive consequences	Dissonance arousal	Ego-involvement$_2$
Self-confrontation	Need to maintain self-esteem	
Mirror	Need to evaluate opinions and abilities (social comparison)	
Sound of own voice		
Photograph of self	Private self-consciousness	
Hearing one's name	Need for achievement	
Introspection	Temporal comparison	
Diary writing		
Personal creation		
Decision among valued alternatives	Personal importance	Ego-involvement$_3$
Exposure to controversial message	Commitment	
Linkage of action to basic values		

[a]Note: The three senses of ego-involvement are indicated in groupings with constructs to which they correspond. The linkages between procedures and constructs are not established so unambiguously.

(Duval & Wicklund, 1972; Buss, 1980) accounts for the presence of several research operations (mirror, camera, instructed introspection, etc.) that might not have been included in such a table made a decade ago. The most remarkable fact about Table 1 is that a number of the listed research procedures can be associated with more than one sense of ego-involvement. In particular, the ambiguity about designating certain operations as producing ego-involvement$_1$ or ego-involvement$_2$ is substantial. That is, do procedures such as taking an intelligence test, experiencing failure, or being exposed to disagreeing opinions produce concern about evaluation by others (ego-involvement$_1$) or concern about self-evaluation (ego-involvement$_2$)?

The puzzle represented by the ambiguity of assigning research procedures to the different senses of ego-involvement adds to the puzzle of the existence of divergent senses of ego-involvement. It also suggests part of the solution to the puzzle: *The tendencies to become concerned about evaluation by others and about evaluation by self may be important dimensions along which people vary.* A number of the procedures listed in Table 1 may be difficult to classify because they evoke different kinds of ego-involvement in different people.

The proposal of individual differences in concerns about evaluation by self and by others is only part of the solution that is needed. How is ego-involvement$_3$ to be accounted for? Why do most of the procedures shown in Table 1 elicit concern about evaluation at all? We can proceed further to the needed solution by using the clue contained in the earlier discussion of modes of subject involvement in experiments. A way to summarize that discussion is to note that variations in subjects' involvement in experiments correspond to variations in what they are *trying to do*. Some subjects ("faithful" or "task-involved" subjects) may be trying to follow the experimenter's instructions to the letter; some ("good" subjects) may be trying to help the experimenter in a more personal sense, such as by helping to confirm the experimenter's theory; still others ("apprehensive", "ego-involved", or "ambitious" subjects) may be trying to establish a favorable evaluation of themselves in the experimenter's, or perhaps their own, eyes. Subjects, in other words, can be seen as performing *tasks* in experiments. Some of these tasks, such as those associated with the faithful and good subject roles, may be confined to the laboratory environment, while others, especially the evaluation-relevant ones, certainly exist also outside the laboratory.

The critical notions that emerge from this discussion of subjects' aspirations in experiments are that subjects can be working toward a variety of different goals and some of these may be goals that apply also to situations beyond the immediate laboratory setting. The goal of adhering literally to the specific instructions of the experiment may well be a one-time-only goal. The goal of contributing to the advancement of knowledge may extend across participation in several different experments and surveys. The goal of seeking a favorable evaluation by others may apply to many of one's waking activities for most of one's life.

Ego Tasks: Resolution of the Problem of Multiple Senses of Ego-Involvement

There is no longer a conceptual problem caused by having ego-involvement refer simultaneously to concern about evaluation by others (ego-involvement$_1$), concern for self-evaluation (ego-involvement$_2$), and personal importance (ego-involvement$_3$). These multiple meanings designate activity in the service of different goals that can be important beyond the laboratory setting. Thus an ego-involved$_1$ person is seeking a satisfactory[6] evaluation by others. The ego-involved$_2$ person is seeking a satisfactory self-evaluation. The ego-involved$_3$ person is pursuing the goal of evaluating or reevaluating important social objects, which, interestingly, may themselves be task goals. These three ego-involved tasks can be referred to as *impression management, self-image management,* and *value management,* respectively. When these tasks are pervasive and enduring, they will be referred to as *ego tasks*. This designation suggests appropriately that the tasks operate at an organizationally high level, subsuming various other less-pervasive or short-term tasks.

The meaning of ego-involvement should now be clear. Ego-involvement can occur in an experiment when an otherwise unimportant experimental task, such as responding to a series of self-report items, becomes subordinated to an ego task. This may be achieved rather easily by instructing the subject that the self-report items provide a measure of intelligence or of some other enduringly valued trait.

It is no longer necessary to use subscripts in discussing ego-involvement. Instead, we should be careful to identify the ego task in which the person is involved. Continuation of the subscript usage might also imply, misleadingly, that there are only three ego tasks of any significance. Another likely candidate for ego task status, for example, is memory management. The procedure of asking subjects to judge the self-relevance of various stimuli—a procedure known to have the effect of enhancing memory for the stimuli (e.g., Kuiper & Rogers, 1979)—might have been characterized as producing ego-involvement$_4$.[7]

TASK ANALYSIS: BASIC CONCEPTS

A task is an abstract representation of the manner in which situational and personal factors contribute jointly to performance. The components of tasks are *goals* and *strategies* for achieving the goals. These components are each products of situational and personal factors, as schematized in Figure 1. The Figure 1 representation lends itself readily

[6]The term "satisfactory" is chosen very deliberately as an alternative to, say, "favorable." For certain people, or in some situations, a less-than-favorable evaluation may be satisfactory. This point is to be developed further below.

[7]The important relation between ego and memory processes has been described in several classical treatments (such as Claparède, 1911; Freud, 1901; Koffka, 1935), has been incorporated into my recent analysis of ego's cognitive biases (Greenwald, 1980), and is developed further in a subsequent paper (Greenwald, 1981).

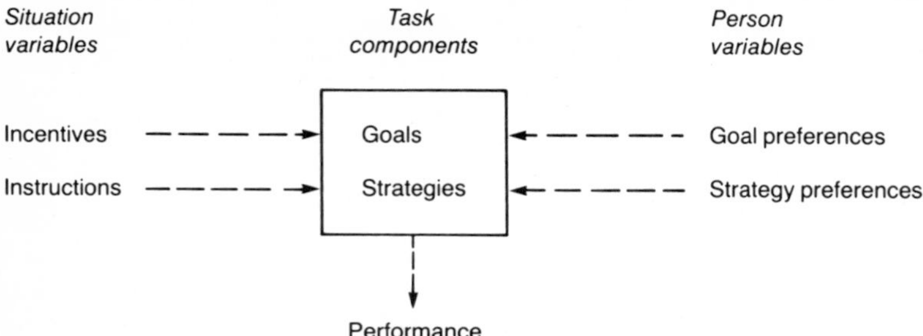

FIGURE 1. Basic concepts of task analysis.

to translation into the well-known Lewinian account of the influence of person and situation factors on behavior. In the Lewinian formula, $B = f(P,E)$ (behavior is a function jointly of the person and the environment). Figure 1 extends the Lewinian account in a manner that can be represented as $B = f(\text{Task}) = f(P,E)$. Thus, *when tasks are operative* the task variables of goals and strategies are assumed to be in a more direct link to performance than are situation or person variables.

An Illustration

The game of golf, or almost any other athletic endeavor, provides ready illustrations of the task concepts in uncomplicated form. The goal of golf is to complete a round while taking as few strokes as possible. Subordinate to this goal is a task that recurs 18 times within the round, getting the golf ball into a 4-inch-diameter cup that is set into the putting surface (the green). Subordinate to each of those 18 tasks are tasks of propelling the ball from one of a few types of places—tee, fairway, rough, or hazard—to (or toward) the green. These three levels of tasks illustrate a common hierarchical aspect of task structures. In the golf illustration, there may be still further subordinate tasks, such as keeping one's eyes on the ball during the stroke, and higher superordinate tasks, such as improving one's scores over a period of time, getting exercise, taking one's mind off other matters, etc. The hierarchical structure of tasks is due to the fact that a strategy can often be decomposed into other goals and strategies.

One attraction of the concept of task is the simplicity of the cognitive structure required to explain "motivated" behavior. The minimum requirements are abilities (1) to initiate or maintain a strategy on detection of goal-not-yet-achieved, and (2) to terminate the strategy upon detection of goal achievement. Thus a golfer can succeed in some minimal sense—and some do little more than that—just by being able to do anything that will propel the ball by means of a golf club, and by being able to judge when the ball has landed in the cup. Of course in the case of golf, as for many other tasks, the availability of suitable strategies will help to achieve goals more rapidly. A task structure with minimal strategic capabilities can achieve remarkable feats when a rapid trial-and-error device is attached to it. It is therefore not surprising that conceptions very much like the present task concept are fundamental to computer-inspired models of complex human performances (e.g., Miller, Galanter, & Pribram, 1960; Newell & Simon, 1972).

Figure 1 indicates that goals are determined jointly by situation variables (incentives) and person variables (goal preferences). In golf, the rules of the game, the layout of the course, the performance levels of competitors, as well as the available prizes provide the incentive aspects of the situation; the golfer's expectations based on past performance and relative concerns about hitting for distance, hitting with good form, and minimizing score constitute personal preferences that determine goals. Strategies are also determined situationally (rules about the use of clubs, instructions from teachers or playing companions) and personally (previous practice, ability to hit various needed strokes).

Limitations of Task Analysis

Task analysis is not intended to be uniformly applicable to all human performances. For example, many reflexive actions and well-practiced habits are executed automatically, mechanically, without cognitive intervention. In golf, the detailed movements that constitute the more rapid portions of various strokes must ordinarily fall outside the scope of a task analysis. Task analysis can also suffer from inaccurate labeling of goals and strategies. For example, a golfer may act in a manner suggesting the presence of a goal of obtaining a high score, in place of a stated goal of minimizing score. The common occurrence of such representational discrepancies by no means invalidates task analysis as a general approach. Rather, a task analysis might be used effectively for therapeutic improvement in the accuracy of symbolic representations of goals and strategies.

Because task goals and strategies are conceived as symbolic representations, the accuracy of any application of task analysis depends on the extent to which (1) observed actions correspond to described strategies, and (2) stopping points of action sequences correspond to described goals. The performer's accuracy in making statements about goals and strategies, just like those of any observer, likely depend on the degree of experience with the task in question, as well as on the possession of generalized skills at symbolically representing performance.

These limitations of task analysis touch on issues at the heart of psychology, including the accuracy of introspection (e.g., Nisbett & Wilson, 1977) and the existence of unconconscious process (e.g., Erdelyi & Goldberg, 1979). I will not venture further into this hornets' nest here, but perhaps I have said enough to indicate that task analysis can provide a context for addressing such issues.

Task Analysis Applied to Experimental Settings

The remainder of this chapter focuses on the ego tasks of self-image management and impression management, which seem particularly rich in potential to account for important individual differences. We start by analyzing two familiar social influence situations, the counterattitudinal role-playing experiment and the conformity experiment, in terms of their self-image management and impression management aspects. Figure 2 presents the task analysis of these experiments.

In Figure 2 it is assumed that a subject is participating in an experiment in association with a psychology course. At the outset, the subject is not ego-involved; rather, the experimental task is subordinated to a task that is three levels below a likely ego task (career development). In the role-playing experiment the subject is induced to give a speech or to write an essay that conflicts with the subject's known (or assumed) prior opinion. When this role playing entails no responsibility for aversive consequences (cf. Collins & Hoyt, 1972; Calder, Ross, & Insko, 1973) the subject remains not ego-involved. However, if the subject is led to perceive responsibility for undesired consequences (such as knowing that the speech may persuade others in undesired fashion), then actions in the experiment may be more directly linked to an ego task. In Figure 2

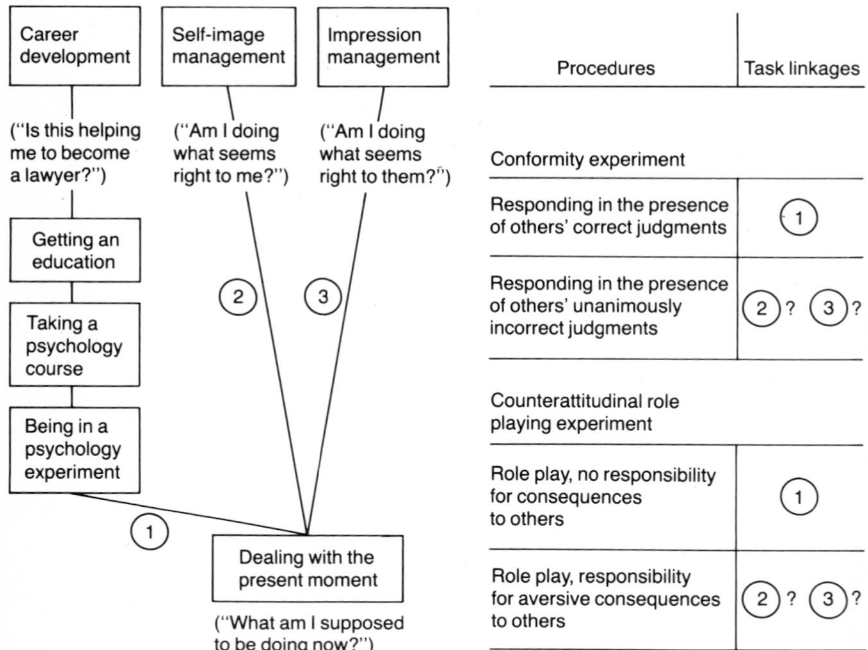

FIGURE 2. Ego task analysis of two experiments.

this ego-task link is shown as being to either a self-image management or an impression management task. Assume, for example, that a self-image management task is invoked by the responsibility-for-aversive-consequences procedure. The subject asks, in effect, "Am I doing what seems right to me?" In order to be able to answer yes to this question (that is, to maintain a favorable self-image), the subject may conclude that the position stated in the speech was not so objectionable after all. Possibly, however, it is an impression management task that will be engaged. This task may have impact on the subject's self-presentation to the experimenter when the (posttest) request for an expression of opinion is made. The subject may, in effect, pretend to have an opinion that is consistent with the role played postion because such a pretense may be expected to produce a favorable evaluation by the experimenter.

These alternative interpretations of the counterattitudinal role-playing experiment in terms of self-image and impression management correspond to the interpretations offered, respectively, by dissonance theorists (e.g., Wicklund & Brehm, 1976) and impression management theorists (Tedeschi et al., 1971). Their debate is not easy to resolve because both positions lead to similar predictions for posttest opinion in the usual role-playing experiment. Further, both explanations can be correct; that is, both processes may occur in the same subject or in different subjects.

The conformity experiment has a similar analysis, with the subject remaining not ego-involved until the occurrence of a critical trial on which a perceptual judgment of a stimulus must be made after observing several others unanimously express a blatantly incorrect judgment to that stimulus. The most compelling aspect of the conformity experiment may well be its capacity to evoke both the tasks of self-image management and impression management, and to put them into conflict with one another. A subject concerned only about doing what seems right personally would unhesitatingly give a judgment in accord with the sensory evidence even though it opposed the majority. Similarly, if concerned only about doing what seems right to others present, the subject would readily join the incorrect majority. The conformity experiment, in effect, obliges the subject to accord relatively greater priority to a self-image management or an impression management task.

This discussion of counterattitudinal role playing and conformity hints at the possibilities of using the analysis of ego tasks to account for important individual differences. It may be recalled from Figure 1 that the explanation of individual differences is incorporated into task analysis via the conceptions of goal preferences and strategy preferences. An impression management task may be used to illustrate these two types of person variables. Consider several women trying to impress the same man. One may maximize physical attractiveness via clothes, grooming, cosmetics; another may express agreement with the man at every opportunity; a third may offer to do him favors or to cook a meal; still another may try to appear very intelligent in his presence. These are strategy differences that might well reflect stable differences in *strategy preferences* for impressing others more generally. But it is also obvious that people vary in *goal preferences* for impression management—people differ in their choice of others upon whom to make a favorable impression. Even more fundamentally, people can vary in their *orientation toward a general goal* of impressing others, that is, people are more or less concerned about the judgments others have of them.

EGO TASK ANALYSIS APPLIED TO PERSON-SITUATION INTERACTIONS

The I – S Distinction in Ego Task Orientations

For the purpose of developing further the application of task analysis to individual differences, it is useful to restrict attention to a manageable range of variations. It would be possible, as just seen in discussing impression management, to consider individual differences in three areas: in strategies used in pursuit of a single goal, in the nature of goals preferred for a given type of task, or in the magnitude of attraction to a general category of goals. An initial focus of the last type, on differences in orientation to goals in the two categories of self-image management and impression management, was suggested by examining Table 1 and considering the behavioral and personality constructs with which the terms in Table 1 are associated. In particular, it was possible to sort a number of these constructs into pairs, with one term in each pair indicating orientation toward a self-image management goal and the other indicating orientation toward an impression management goal. These pairs are given in Table 2. Because it will be cumbersome to use repeatedly the phrases "orientation toward self-image management" and "orientation toward impression management," abbreviated designations, I-type and S-type, are introduced in Table 2. The "I" in I-type indicates the *intrapersonal* orientation of the self-image management ego

TABLE 2. Intrapersonally Oriented (I-type) and Socially Oriented (S-type) Psychological Constructs[a]

I-type	S-type
Independence	Conformity
Isolation	Affiliation
Temporal comparison	Social comparison
Need for achievement	Need for approval
Dissonance reduction	Impression management
Attitude-behavior consistency	Self-presentation consistency
Private self-consciousness	Public self-consciousness
Low self-monitoring (Principled self)[a]	High self-monitoring (Pragmatic self)[a]

[a]The principled self and pragmatic self are developments of the self-monitoring concept by Snyder and Campbell (in press).

task, while the "S" of S-type indicates the *social* orientation of the impression management ego task.

The collection of terms in Table 2 indicates that the contrast between I-type and S-type orientations, in other words between self-image and impression management ego tasks, is deeply ingrained in psychological thought. In addition to the contrasting pairs listed in Table 2, it is tempting to add introversion vs extraversion (Jung, 1921; Eysenck, 1947), inner direction vs other direction (Riesman, Glazer, & Denney, 1950), and internal vs external locus of control (Rotter, 1966). The I−S contrast is evocative also of William James's (1890) distinction between the spiritual (intrapersonal) and social aspects of self. In James's treatment the spiritual self was regarded as a developmentally higher form than the social self, a point that was incorporated in many subsequent analyses of ego development, as will be discussed below.

The terms in Table 2 are a mixture of designations of tasks (*impression management*), motives (*need for approval*), and strategies (*conformity*), and even these distinctions are not fully clear (is *affiliation* a strategy or motive?). This mixture reflects variations among psychologists in theoretical preferences for terms designating hypothesized internal dispositions (motives) vs ones that focus on behavior (strategies). The task analysis attempts to submerge this conflict of theoretical preferences by using a format in which motive and strategy language coexist, as indicated in Figure 1.

The juxtaposition of I-type and S-type constructs in Table 2 should not be interpreted as suggesting that these are necessarily opposing types. Of the terms listed in Table 2, only the self-monitoring pair is measured by a procedure that guarantees a negative correlation between the contrasting terms (Snyder, 1974). In other cases, for which independent measures of the contrasting terms are available, there is no evidence to support the assumption of a negative relationship. For example, Fenigstein, Scheier, and Buss (1975) found that their measures of private and public self-consciousness were significantly (but weakly) *positively* correlated.

Restriction of the Initial Scope of Ego Task Analysis

Even a narrowing of focus to the I-type and S-type ego tasks of self-image management and impression management leaves too broad a domain for initial application. There are compelling reasons, which are not developed in detail here, to suppose that I-type and S-type orientations must eventually be analyzed in terms of a dimension of *level of aspiration*. For self-image management, for example, an individual may be in a growth phase during which there is a strong aspiration to improve self-image; others may be in a more (ego-) defensive mode in which the major aspiration is to protect against deterioration of self-image. Perhaps the majority of people, however, are maintaining a stable self-image that is moderately positive (cf. Myers & Ridl, 1979; Greenwald, 1980). Strategies employed in the interest of self-image management should obviously be expected to differ for such varying levels of aspiration that can be associated with the I-type orientation. For most of the remaining analysis in this chapter, the (presumably) modal level of aspiration for self-image management—that is, maintaining a stable, positive self-image—will be assumed for the I-type orientation.

Similarly, consideration of the S-type orientation will focus on what is assumed to be a modal aspiration of maintaining a stable favorable impression among peers. Higher aspirations are recognized in concepts such as upward mobility or social climbing; lower aspirations are reflected in terms such as social anxiety and insecurity. Analysis of such (presumably) less common levels of aspiration for the I-type and S-type orientations will remain an area for subsequent development of ego task analysis.

A Common Language for Persons, Situations, and Performance

The empirical domain to which ego task analysis is applicable is the broad one of predicting behavior from person and situation information. Bem and Funder (1978) opened their recent methodological contribution to this area of research by commenting:

> The developing consensus that much of the psychologically interesting variance in behavior will be found in the interaction between the person and the situation suggests the need for a common language of description for both persons and situations. (p. 485)

Bem and Funder's technique (see also Bem & Lord, 1979) matches a Q-sort personality *description* of each subject with a Q-sort *template*, which describes a hypothetical person most likely to engage in a given situation-specific behavior. The probability of the subject's engaging in a behavior is expected to be directly proportional to the similarity between the subject's Q-sort description and the behavior's Q-sort template. In contrast, task analysis interprets situation-behavior combinations as task-specific strategies. A person is expected to manifest a given strategy (behavior) to the extent that (1) the situation tends to evoke a task for which the strategy is appropriate, and (2) the person is predisposed to engage in that task.

This is not the place to attempt a detailed comparison of ego task analysis with the template matching technique. It is sufficient to note that ego task analysis also attempts to provide a "common language of description for both persons and situations." Ego task analysis does this by relating situations and persons to a small number of ego tasks. Situations vary in their capacity to evoke different tasks, while persons vary in their propensity to have different tasks engaged. Performance measures are also interpretable in the task language as task-specific strategies. A virtue of the template-matching procedure is its *lack* of commitment to specific personality dimensions; a template for a given behavior can be any one of the very large number of possible configurations of the 100 Q-sort items. By contrast, ego task analysis must depend for its usefulness on the success with which diversity among individuals can be reduced to variations in goal preferences and strategy preferences for a small number of ego tasks, such as self-image and impression management.

The analysis of situations, persons, and performances in terms of the I-type and S-type orientations is summarized in Table 3, which reformats some of the information presented previously in Tables 1 and 2. The most interesting aspect of Table 3 is that a number of important laboratory and nonlaboratory situations are accorded an "ambiguous" classification. In practice, most of the procedures classified as "ambiguous" might be more clearly classed as I-type or S-type, depending on *other* simultaneous procedures. For example, when the subject in an experiment is isolated from others and from the experimenter, or when the subject can self-evaluate performance while others cannot evaluate the subject, many of the ambiguous procedures will, in effect, be I-type. On the other hand, when the experimenter or an audience is present, or

TABLE 3. Situation, Person, and Performance Variations Classified in Terms of I-type and S-type Ego Task Orientations

Situations

I-type	Ambiguous	S-type
Mirror	Skill test	Camera
Person alone	Personality test	Audience present
Evaluation independent of others	Failure experience	Evaluation dependent on others
	Social pressure	
	Symbolic self-confrontation	
	Personal creation	
	Role playing task	
	Decision task	

Person Variables

I-type	S-type
Private self-consciousness	Public self-consciousness
Need for achievement	Need for approval
Principled self (low self-monitor)	Pragmatic self (high self-monitor)

Performance Variables

I-type	S-type
Independence	Conformity
Isolation	Affiliation
Dissonance reduction	Impression management

when evaluation of the subject's performance can be provided only by the experimenter or others, most of the ambiguous procedures would be S-type. The essence of I-type situations is that they focus the subject's attention on evaluation of self in relation to personal standards. In contrast, the essence of S-type settings is that they focus others' attention onto evaluation of the subject.

The constructs listed as person variables in Table 3 are interpreted, in ego task terms, as varying predispositions to have self-image management or impression management tasks engaged. These I-type and S-type orientations may be assessed by Fenigstein et al.'s (1975) recently developed measures of *private* and *public self-consciousness*. (The three highest loading items on their private self-consciousness scale are "I reflect about myself a lot," "I'm generally attentive to my inner feelings," and "I'm always trying to figure myself out." The three highest loading items on their public self-consciousness scale are "I'm concerned about what other people think of me," "I usually worry about making a good impression," and "I'm concerned about the way I present myself.") Another recently developed measure that fits at least partially with the conception of the S-orientation is Snyder's (1974) *self-monitoring* scale, which he described as measuring "the extent to which [people] monitor (observe and control) their expressive behavior and self-presentation" (p. 536).[8] McClelland et al.'s (1953) measure of *need for achievement* was conceived as a measure of motivation to meet or exceed internalized standards, and thus captures an aspect of the I-orientation. It may be contrasted with a *need for approval*, which can be conceived as a motive to meet or exceed others' expectations, corresponding therefore to the S-orientation.

The performance constructs listed in Table 3 are pairs of strategies that are suited, respectively, for self-image management and impression management. It would be inappropriate to view these strategy contrasts as variations in preferred methods for achieving the same goals. Rather, they reflect variations in preferred goals: they are strategies for different ego tasks.

Ego Task Analysis of Interrupted-Task Effects

Research on the interrupted-task paradigm gradually subsided 30 years or so after it was started by Zeigarnik's (1927) dissertation research. The conclusion of the most detailed existing review of this literature (Van Bergen, 1968) was as follows:

> The problem of the selective recall of uncompleted and completed tasks must be regarded as one of those questions which seem to lead nowhere;

[8]Recent factor analyses of the self-monitoring scale (Briggs, Cheek, & Buss, 1980; Leary, Silver, Darby, & Schlenker, 1979) have indicated that its score can be decomposed into three factors, the major one of which is identified by Leary et al. (1979) as public impression management. This factor includes items such as "In different situations and with different people, I often act like very different persons," and "In order to get along and be liked, I tend to be what people expect me to be rather than anything else."

nevertheless one wonders how many thousands more of experimental subjects will yet be needed before the problem, which is essentially a nonproblem, is discarded. (p. 267)

Given Van Bergen's pessimistic conclusion, it is a considerable challenge to attempt retrospectively to make sense of the interrupted-task literature. This attempt, it can be acknowledged in advance, will fall short of being a decisive success. Nevertheless, it is possible to offer a plausible account of the major findings of existing interrupted-task studies, and also to provide a framework within which further clarifying research might be conducted.

The Original Zeigarnik Effect. From the perspective of ego task analysis, the interpretation offered by Zeigarnik (1927, 1938) for her own findings seems satisfactory. In a nonevaluative setting, and using a diverse set of tasks that are moderately interesting in their own right (i.e., nonego tasks), intentions should be established to complete each task. Interruption leaves the intention intact; Zeigarnik characterized this as a persisting *tension*. The surviving intention provides a retrieval aid; hence interrupted tasks are better recalled than completed ones.

Typical Skill-Setting Effects (Successful Tasks Better Remembered). One of the more reliable results in the interrupted-task literature is that evaluative skill-test settings—those typically designated as ego-involving—increase the recall of completed tasks (successes) relative to interrupted ones (failures).[9] This alteration of the usual Zeigarnik effect can be interpreted in either of two ways: (1) The evaluative setting engages one or another ego task, the goal of which is more important than the goals (intentions) of the individual experimental tasks; this undoes the usual tendency for the individual tasks to establish independent persisting intentions; or (2) the evaluative setting may specifically engage a task of self-image maintenance, which can best be served by remembering successes and forgetting failures. The first of these two explanations is the more general, in that engagement of *any* ego task may disrupt the usual Zeigarnik effect. The second explanation applies specifically to treatment-subject combinations that engage the ego task of self-image maintenance; its virtue is that it provides a basis for predicting the occasionally found greater recall of successes than failures, as opposed to equal recall of all tasks.

[9]Van Bergen (1968) concluded from her review of studies that had employed ego-involvement or skill-test procedures that "The most obvious trend which can be discerned in [these studies] is in the non-significance of the results." However, by her count eight of 26 interrupted-task studies that employed skill-test instructions produced greater recall of successes than failures (with none showing a significant opposed result), in contrast to no clear directional pattern for studies she classified as using nonskill instructions. Available techniques of metanalysis (e.g., Smith & Glass, 1977) allow interpretation of this pattern of results as quite reliable evidence for the conclusion that skill-test procedures increase recall of successes relative to failures. Van Bergen's reluctance to base conclusions on effects that were not obtained in the majority of relevant tests is a regrettable flaw in an otherwise very impressive and useful review.

Atkinson's Finding for High Need-Achievement Subjects. In Atkinson's (1953) experiment, subjects low in need for achievement showed the pattern just described as typical for skill settings—greater recall of successes. Subjects high in measured achievement motivation, however, showed greater recall of interrupted (failed) tasks than of successes in the skill-test setting. These findings can make sense in terms of the ego task analysis if it is assumed that high need for achievement scores indicates an atypical I-type orientation, a predisposition to engage a self-image *improvement* ego task, which is best served by eventually succeeding at the initially failed tasks. Thus the intentions to complete failed tasks may persist, leading to their better recall. In connection with this suggested interpretation, it should be noted that Atkinson's skill-test setting was relatively unusual in being I-type (see Table 3); subjects could be aware of their own successes and failures, and there was no obvious evaluative audience.

Marrow's Exceptional Skill-Setting Effect. Marrow's (1938b) Experiment 3 provides an interesting contrast with various later-conducted skill-setting variants of the interrupted-task experiment. Subjects (U. S. college students) were told that the experimenter was interested in comparing performance abilities of American and German student populations. This procedure was used in two replications that varied preliminary information about which of the two populations was better in previous tests and also whether the subjects were given encouragement or discouragement during the experiment. Both variations produced clearly superior recall of failures (interrupted tasks). Note that in Marrow's experiment it was not the subject, but the subject's national group, that was being evaluated. This procedure might have engaged a task that is not common in experimental settings, that is, managing one's group's (rather than one's own) image. Recall of failures may be a strategy in the service of group-image management, but that is a speculation that obviously awaits further test.

As promised, this retrospective interpretation of the interrupted-task paradigm falls short of resolving all of the problems that have caused several previous analysts to express despair. In particular, Alper's (1957) ego strength findings (see earlier discussion) are as troublesome for ego task analysis as they have been for most previous attempts at interpretation. At the same time, ego task analysis holds out the possibility of an eventual resolution being produced by additional data collection in which procedural variations, subject groups, and performance measures are better defined in terms of the I-type and S-type classifications.

EGO TASK ANALYSIS OF SELF-AWARENESS

Parallels Between Ego-Involvement and Self-Awareness

The theoretical analysis of self-awareness by Duval and Wicklund (1972) centered on a contrast between attention focused inward to the self (objective self-awareness) and outward toward the environment (subjective self-awareness). Since then, self-awareness has received much research attention and has undergone a theoretical evolution that recapitulates some of the major themes that emerged in the earlier history of research on ego-involvement. As in the case of ego-involvement, the result of this evolution has been to add interesting complexity to the original concept.

Duval and Wicklund (1972; see also Wicklund, 1975) theorized that self-focusing manipulations would cause awareness of discrepancies between performance and idealized standards, and that these discrepancies would often produce a negative self-evaluation. This aversive self-evaluative aspect of self-awareness resembles the threat-to-self-esteem component of the ego-involvement manipulations that were used in interrupted-task research (cf. Iverson & Reuder, 1956). The contrast between objective and subjective self-awareness (inward vs outward focus) also parallels the contrast between ego-involvement and task-involvement in the formulation of Alper (1946).

Quite recently, Hull and Levy (1979) offered an altered definition of self-awareness, proposing

> that the defining features of self-awareness do not exist in terms of self-focused attention and the operation of a particular kind of self-evaluative process, but rather . . . self-awareness corresponds to the encoding of information in terms of its relevance for self and as such directly entails a greater responsivity to the self-relevant aspects of the environment. (p. 757)

This definition of self-awareness in terms of relevance to self is reminiscent of the personal importance sense of ego-involvement (referred to earlier as ego-involvement$_3$). Although it is possible to view Hull and Levy as being in theoretical opposition to the original Duval and Wicklund (1972) statement, this apparent conflict can be resolved, as a similar one was resolved for the various senses of ego-involvement, by proposing that self-awareness can serve a variety of purposes, or ego tasks.

The most compelling parallel between the self-awareness and ego-involvement concepts is in the extension of self-awareness into the analysis of individual differences, first by Fenigstein et al. (1975) and more recently by Buss (1980). Their conceptions of the contrast between private and public self-consciousness elaborate self-awareness theory in a manner that parallels the present use of self-image and impression management as ego tasks that correspond to the evaluation-by-self and evaluation-by-others senses of ego-involvement. Certainly, the initial successes of the analysis of individual differences by Fenigstein et al. (1975) are partly responsible for the confidence with which the formulation of the I − S distinction in ego tasks could be offered in this chapter. As will be seen, research on private vs public self-consciousness provides some of the strongest confirming evidence for the distinction between ego tasks of self-image management and impression management.

Self-Awareness Research in Support of the I – S Distinction

The general principle that serves to predict the effects of self-focusing manipulations on individuals who differ in private and public self-consciousness can be stated in terms of ego tasks as follows: Procedures that evoke a given ego task should produce effects on performance indices of strategies for that task, and these effects should be most evident for people who have a predisposition toward that task. In generating predictions from this formula, I assume that Fenigstein et al.'s (1975) private and public self-consciousness scales measure I-type and S-type ego task orientations, respectively, and also that procedures and performance measures relate to ego tasks as indicated in Table 3.

Response to Negative Evaluation. Fenigstein (1979) found that women high in public self-consciousness were more sensitive to social rejection, which took the form of being deliberately ignored by two peers holding a conversation, than were women low in public self-consciousness. This relation between the public self-consciousness measure and sensitivity to a social (dis)approval procedure is consistent with the S-type classification of both the procedure and the measure. Also consistent with the ego task analysis, private self-consciousness did not correlate with individual differences in sensitivity to this social rejection. Interestingly, in a second experiment in the same article Fenigstein demonstrated that sensitivity to negative self-relevant information was enhanced by *mirror presence* during the experiment. Fenigstein interpreted the results of the two experiments as supporting a common conclusion about an association between self-consciousness and sensitivity to negative self-relevant information. In terms of ego task analysis, however, the first experiment demonstrated an S-type effect, while the second may have been an I-type effect. The first experiment manipulated negative evaluation by having two peers shun the subject, clearly an S-type procedure, while in the second the negative evaluation was transmitted in an interview in which the experimenter described unfavorable psychological characteristics associated with the subject's birth order. Because the birth-order characteristic is not under subjects' control it is doubtful that this evaluative information would evoke an impression management task, although it might evoke self-image management, which should have been further enhanced by the mirror.

Opinion Moderation in Anticipation of Discussion. Scheier (1980) conducted an experiment in which subjects first recorded their own opinions about the value of punishment as an aid to learning and then wrote an essay on the same topic after learning of an impending discussion of the issue with another subject. The anticipated discussion procedure is known, from previous results (Cialdini, Levy, Herman, & Evenbeck, 1973), to produce a moderation of opinion. In terms of ego task analysis, the anticipated discussion is an S-type procedure and the moderation effect is an S-type strategy; the effect should therefore be strongest for subjects with the S-type predisposition. Scheier found just this, with subjects high in public self-consciousness showing the effect more strongly than those low in public self-consciousness. (The private self-consciousness scale did not predict differences in the moderation effect.) A subsidiary finding demonstrated an I-type effect of greatest consistency between the initially expressed opinion and the one expressed in the later essay for subjects who were simultaneously high in private self-consciousness and low in public self-consciousness.

Mirrors, Audiences, and Cameras. Carver and Scheier (1981) noted six studies "in which individual differences in private self-consciousness have led to effects duplicating those produced by mirror-manipulated self-awareness." Those results are, of course, consistent with the Table 3 classification of both the mirror and the private self-consciousness scale as I-type. Also consistent with Table 3 are the many findings in the social facilitation literature (see Cottrell, 1972), suggesting that the presence of an audience (an S-type procedure) produces evaluation apprehension (that is, engages an impression management task). Despite the consistency of this support for some basic concepts of ego task analysis it would be very desirable to examine, within the context of a single study, a contrast of I-type vs S-type procedures, individual differences and measures. Such a study has recently been reported by Scheier and Carver (1980). In three experiments subjects wrote counterattitudinal essays espousing the position, "Students should have very little or no control over the kinds of courses offered by the University." This counterattitudinal role playing was done sometimes in the presence of a mirror (I-type procedure) or a camera (S-type), subjects were selected both on the basis of private (I-type) and public (S-type) self-consciousness, and a measure of opinion change following essay writing was obtained. In this setting, resistance to opinion change is an I-type result, while opinion change (consistency of self-presentation) is an S-type result. Scheier and Carver found, as expected from ego task analysis, that resistance to opinion change was associated with mirror presence and private self-consciousness, while opinion change was enhanced by camera presence and was associated with high public self-consciousness. The only sense in which this research by Scheier and Carver falls short of thoroughgoing support for the I−S distinction of ego task analysis is in that the mirror or camera procedures were not examined together with the self-consciousness variations in a single experiment. Ego task analysis predicts that, say, the effect of camera presence should be greater for subjects high in public self-consciousness than for ones low in public self-consciousness.

Conformity. I noted earlier that the conformity experiment (Asch, 1951; Crutchfield, 1955) provides a remarkable situation in which self-image and impression management tasks are pitted against one another. The self-image management strategy of resisting group pressure is in opposition to the impression management strategy of conforming. It follows that independence in response to group pressure should be associated with private self-consciousness, while conformity should be associated with public self-consciousness. As this chapter was undergoing final revision for publication, a result confirming this expectation was reported by Froming and Carver (in press). Their experiment used a click-counting task that provided a somewhat more ambiguous perceptual stimulus than the line-judging task initially used by Asch. It will be interesting to see if a similar pattern of findings can be demonstrated with other tasks for which the conformity pressure may violate perceptual experience even more blatantly.

Conclusion: Self-Awareness = Ego-Involvement = Ego Task Engagement

Discovery of the extensive parallels between self-awareness and ego-involvement is in many ways gratifying. The confusions that beset the concept of ego-involvement in its odyssey through the interrupted-task paradigm may now be resolved with the help of the self-awareness findings. Further, one has the feeling of being reunited with an important segment of the intellectual past of personality and social psychology, and of being able to recognize the continuity of theoretical themes from that past work to the present.

There is no need to suggest replacing the term ego-involvement with self-awareness, or vice versa. The two terms represent different historical phases in the development of empirical and theoretical understanding of person-situation interactions. Ego task analysis provides a common language that allows appreciation of the conceptual overlap between ego-involvement and self-awareness. As a brief illustration, consider the contrast between ego-involvement and task-involvement (Alper, 1946) in relation to Duval and Wicklund's (1972) contrast between objective and subjective self-awareness. Ego task analysis can amplify the meaning of these two dichotomies, in addition to revealing their fundamental similarity. In each case, the dichotomy contrasts the engagement of an ego task (i.e., ego-involvement or objective self-awareness) with the operation of a lower-level task (task-involvement or subjective self-awareness). The alternation between inward and outward focus described by Duval and Wicklund (1972) acquires richer psychological meaning when construed as an alternation between cognitive processes that are subordinated to an ego task and cognitive processes subordinated to a lower-level task.

SOME ISSUES YET TO BE DEALT WITH

It is not possible to deal in the present space with all of the theoretically interesting implications of the I-type, S-type distinction and of the proposal that tasks are fundamental units in the organization of personality. However, a few such implications will be noted in order to suggest future directions for ego task analysis.

Ego Development and the I–S Distinction

A number of treatments of ego development have incorporated concepts that can be mapped onto the I–S distinction. Several of these have an antecedent in William James's (1890) distinction between the social self and the spiritual self.

> A man's Social Self is the recognition which he gets from his mates . . . We have an innate propensity to get ourselves noticed, and noticed favorably, by our kind. . . . Properly speaking, a man has as many social selves as there are individuals who recognize him and carry an image of him in their mind. (pp. 293, 294)
>
> By the Spiritual Self, . . . I mean a man's inner or subjective being, his psychic faculties or dispositions. . . . We take a purer self-satisfaction when we think of our ability to argue and discriminate, of our moral sensibility and conscience, or our indomitable will, than when we survey any of our other possessions. (p. 296)
>
> A tolerably unanimous opinion ranges the different selves . . . in an hierarchical scale, with the bodily Self at the bottom, the spiritual Self at top, and the extracorporeal material selves and the various social selves between. (p. 313)

Although James's placement of an intrapersonal orientation (the spiritual self) developmentally above a social orientation agrees with the majority of developmental analyses (see Loevinger, 1976), a few prominent theorists construe the developmental sequence in just the opposite way. In a provocative critique of "self-contained individualism" as a desired or ideal type in contemporary American psychology, Sampson (1977) suggested that a social, or collective, orientation might be more mature than our preferred individualism (see also Hogan, 1975). Similarly, McClelland (1975) placed a socially oriented form of power motivation at a higher developmental level than individualistic forms:

> Many psychologists have had difficulty taking seriously what we are calling the most advanced stage of expressing the power drive in which the self drops out as a source of power and a person sees himself as an instrument of a higher authority which moves him to try to influence or serve others. (p. 20)

The theorists who have proposed that a social orientation of ego represents a maturer perspective have also suggested that this orientation is altruistic or collectivistic in nature. This other-serving characteristic has not been considered in the present formulation of ego task orientations; that is, altruism and collectivism are not readily associated with either I-type or S-type ego tasks. Accordingly, it may prove necessary to propose an additional type of orientation, perhaps designated C-type, with the C standing for communal.

Ego Task Analysis, Collective Tasks, and Deindividuation

An unexpected dividend of ego task analysis is its suggestion of a means of analyzing collective behaviors, which are often the antithesis of ego-involved behaviors. In an instance of collective behavior, whether it be mob violence or organized cheering in a football stadium, military action or congregational prayer in a church, performance is directed by the goals of an organization that exists outside the individual. Collective action is thus in the service of a *group* task, and can be contrasted with individual behavior that is in the service of an ego task.

Although history, current events, and laboratory research provide many instances of collective behavior, understanding of the conditions under which people will become involved effectively in extraindividual tasks remains elusive. People are drawn readily into collective tasks for short periods, such as in audiences at athletic contests, in religious worhsip, and even in ordinary social gatherings. Under rarer conditons, extended participation in a collective task can occur, as in a military campaign or in a philanthropic career. On the other hand, attempts to subordinate individuals to the collective tasks of totalitarian societies have not been notably successful, and have required coercive force by the state for what success they have had.

In some recent experiments, Latané, Williams, and Harkins (1979) have demonstrated a reduced output of effort for collective tasks as compared to individual performances. This slacking occurred under conditions similar to those that have been characterized in other experiments as producing *deindividuation*—subjects are anonymous members of an unacquainted group. Perhaps when the individual, rather than being thus deindividuated, is ego-involved in the collective task—that is, the collective task has become subordinated to an ego task—collective performance would be more effective. This might occur in military units, athletic teams, or entertainment troupes that have high morale and a high level of identification of each member with the group's success.

Task Organization and Memory Organization

Ego task analysis promotes the concept of task to a position of centrality in personality organization. The justification for this central role can be bolstered by showing that tasks occupy a central position in the organization of memory more generally. Among the indications that information in memory is organized in terms of tasks is the superior retention of information when its relation to a persisting task is apparent at the time of acquisition (Nuttin & Greenwald, 1968). Also it is well known that the nature of the orienting task at the time of learning affects the manner of encoding information (see Postman, 1976), and it has been shown recently that ego-relevant information is better retained than non-ego-relevant information (Rogers, Kuiper, & Kirker, 1977). This last point can be taken as indication that ego tasks are especially important in providing the organization of memory. A classic exposition of the interrelationship of ego, tasks, and memory was provided by Koffka (1935) in *Principles of Gestalt Psychology*. A new review is in preparation (Greenwald, 1981).

The usefulness of interpreting task as a unit of cognitive organization is also suggested by examination of many complex computer programs. Programs are most elegant and efficient when they have a clear task organization, for example, with repeated tasks located in subroutines rather than being multiply duplicated through the program. Additionally, it is interesting to note that systems of computer programs typically develop in complexity by adding higher-level tasks on top of existing simpler ones. It is plausible to suppose that this aspect of computer systems development may resemble ego development.

Task Assessment, Cognitive Theory, and Introspective Data

I have proposed that important problems of human motivation can be conceived in terms of ego tasks, but have avoided dealing with a fundamental practical concern of research in motivation, namely, assessment. How is one to identify the task(s) in which a person is engaged at any time? One proposal is simply to ask the person to describe current goals. Aside from the problem that a person might deliberately misrepresent goals, a more fundamental problem with this approach is that the person might not be able to verbalize current goals. One could define this problem away by saying that only tasks that can be verbalized are of interest. However, this limitation seems unwise because the concepts of task analysis may be useful to an observer, such as a psychotherapist, who may impose a construction of goals and strategies on action even when the actor does not. A basically different approach to task assessment is to make use of a goal's property as a stopping (or transition) point of behavior. Although this property is in principle useful, the amount of observation needed to infer tasks from overt behavior (cf. Newtson, Engquist, & Bois, 1977) is certain to be prohibitive of extensive research use.

These assessment considerations mask even more fundamental issues of the relation between verbalizable cognition and behavior. An actor's private verbalizations regarding goals and strategies may be potentially of most interest to task analysis, but for the moment these introspections are given no privileged status in comparison to the person's (possibly different) public verbalizations or an observer's (possibly still different) task interpretations.

CONCLUSIONS

Let us review the answers that have been offered for several questions that could not be answered confidently at the start of this chapter.

First, what is ego-involvement? We can agree with Allport's (1943) characterization of an ego-involved person as behaving "personally, perhaps excitedly, seriously committed to a *task*" (p. 459) and with Sherif and Cantril's (1947) description of ego-involvement as occurring when a situation is related to the person's "standards of judgment or frames of reference" (p. 117), and also with Iverson and Reuder's (1956) conclusion that ego-involvement entails "interference with . . . the need to enhance or to maintain one's feelings of self-esteem" (p. 149). The formulation that accommodates the diversity of these views is built on a definition of ego-involvement as the engagement of an ego task. An ego task consists of a high-order goal (such as self-image maintenance) that subsumes lower-level, more specific goals (such as reading this chapter). Ego-involvement is thus not a narrowly definable phenomenon, and to refer to some behavior or person simply as ego-involved is often not a sufficiently precise characterization to be useful psychologically; it should be necessary also to identify which of a number of possible ego tasks is engaged.

Second, how is ego-involvement produced in experimental situations? Actually, because so many familiar research procedures have the potential to evoke one or another ego task, especially an impression management task, it may be more difficult to suppress than to produce ego-involvement in experimental situations. The interesting question then is, when should one want to induce ego-involvement? Some researchers may avoid ego-involvement just at the time that they should most want to engage an ego task. For example, consider the measure of need for social approval that is obtained from the Marlowe–Crowne (Crowne & Marlowe, 1964) social desirability scale. When this scale is completed under non-ego-involving conditions (that is, with instructions that deemphasize evaluative intent of the tester), the respondent's socially desirable self-presentation may reflect private self-perception rather than a managed public impression. Administration of the scale under conditions that evoke concern about evaluation by others (S-type procedures) may be a more effective way to determine the level of need for social approval.

Third, what are the effects of ego-involvement? Again, the phenomena of ego-involvement are too various to permit a simple listing of effects. Further, any list would be misleading because the manifestation of ego-involvement for one person might be the reverse of that for another. The major hope for reducing this immense potential diversity to manageable proportions is to identify a relatively few widely applicable ego tasks. In particular, the tasks of self-image management and public impression management appear to be important ego tasks for many people. Situations, persons, and performance measures can thus be classified into I-types (for *intrapersonal* orientation) and S-types (for *social* orientation) when they can be associated with the self-image or the impression management task, respectively. These classifications can then be used to generate predictions about person-situation interactions, using the general principles that (1) situations that evoke a certain ego task will have their greatest effects on persons who have a predisposition to engage in that task, and (2) these effects will be most apparent on performance measures that constitute strategies for that task.

Phenomena of ego-involvement overspread the boundaries of personality, cognitive psychology, and social psychology. Task analysis of ego-involvement suggests interrelationships among many concepts that have hitherto led separate conceptual lives in these domains. The compelling basis for these interrelationships is the ease of classifying many existing concepts into I-type or S-type categories as ego task predispositions or strategies. The distinction between I-type and S-type orientations of ego tasks, finally, provides a resolution of the problematic contrast between the conceptions of ego offered by Allport (1943) and Sherif and Cantril (1947). Allport, it will be recalled, emphasized intrapersonal characteristics in his conception of ego, and described the Sherif – Cantril view as "nothing but the social part of man." Could it be that I[ntrapersonal]-type ego tasks were uppermost for Allport, while for Sherif and Cantril S[ocial]-type, if not C[ommunal]-type, tasks were most important?

ACKNOWLEDGMENTS

I am grateful to several colleagues who kindly commented on an earlier version of this chapter: John T. Cacioppo, Michael F. Scheier, Allan Fenigstein, Jay G. Hull, David C. Funder, Deborah Davis, and four students in her graduate seminar, Tom Holtgraves, David Droll, Lynn Kelly, and Claudia Kelly. I hope that other readers will benefit from my attempts to resolve the difficulties that they pointed out. I am additionally grateful to Michael Scheier for providing prepublication information about several of the studies that I have cited. Preparation of the chapter was aided by grants from the National Institute of Mental Health (MH-31762 and MH-32317).

REFERENCES

Abel, T. M. Neuro-circulatory reaction and the recall of unfinished and completed tasks. *Journal of Psychology*, 1938, *6*, 377 – 383.

Albert, S. Temporal comparison theory. *Psychological Review*, 1977, *84*, 585 – 603.

Allport, G. W. The ego in contemporary psychology. *Psychological Review*, 1943, *50*, 451 – 478.

Allport, G. W. *Becoming: Basic considerations for a psychology of personality*. New Haven, Conn.: Yale University Press, 1955.

Alper, T. G. Memory for completed and incompleted tasks as a function of personality: An analysis of group data. *Journal of Abnormal and Social Psychology*, 1946, *41*, 403 – 420.

Alper, T. G. Memory for completed and incompleted tasks as a function of personality: Correlation between experimental and personality data. *Journal of Personality*, 1948, *17*, 104 – 137.

Alper, T. G. The interrupted task method in studies of selective recall: A re-evaluation of some recent experiments. *Psychological Review*, 1952, *59*, 71 – 88.

Alper, T. G. Predicting the direction of selective recall: Its relation to ego strength and n Achievement. *Journal of Abnormal and Social Psychology*, 1957, *55*, 149 – 165.

Aronson, E. Dissonance theory: Progress and problems. In R. P. Abelson, et al. (Eds.), *Theories of cognitive consistency: A sourcebook*. Chicago, Ill.: Rand McNally, 1968.

Asch, S. E. Effects of group pressure on the modification and distortion of judgments. In

H. Guetzkow (Ed.), *Groups, leadership, and men.* Pittsburgh, Pa.: Carnegie Press, 1951.

Atkinson, J. W. The achievement motive and recall of interrupted and completed tasks. *Journal of Experimental Psychology*, 1953, *46*, 381 –390.

Atkinson, J. W., & Raphelson, A. C. Individual differences in motivation and behavior in particular situations. *Journal of Personality*, 1956, *24*, 349 –363.

Bem, D. J., & Funder, D. C. Predicting more of the people more of the time: Assessing the personality of situations. *Psychological Review*, 1978, *85*, 485 –501.

Bem, D. J., & Lord, C. G. Template matching: A proposal for probing the ecological validity of experimental settings in social psychology. *Journal of Personality and Social Psychology*, 1979, *37*, 833 –846.

Brehm, J. W., & Cohen, A. R. *Explorations in cognitive dissonance.* New York: Wiley, 1962.

Briggs, S. R., Cheek, J. M., & Buss, A. H. An analysis of the self-monitoring scale. *Journal of Personality and Social Psychology*, 1980, *38*, 679 –686.

Buss, A. H. *Self-consciousness and social anxiety.* San Francisco, Calif.: Freeman, 1980.

Butterfield, E. C. The interruption of tasks: Methodological, factual and theoretical issues. *Psychological Bulletin*, 1964, *62*, 309 –322.

Calder, B. J., Ross, M., & Insko, C. A. Attitude change and attitude attribution: Effects of incentive, choice, and consequences. *Journal of Personality and Social Psychology*, 1973, *25*, 84 –99.

Cantril, H. *The psychology of social movements.* New York: Wiley, 1941.

Caron, A. J., & Wallach, M. A. Personality determinants of repressive and obsessive reactions to failure-stress. *Journal of Abnormal and Social Psychology*, 1959, *59*, 236 –245.

Carver, C. S., & Scheier, M. F. Self-consciousness and reactance. *Journal of Research in Personality*, 1981, *15*, 16 –29.

Cialdini, R. B., Levy, A., Herman, C. P., & Evenbeck, S. Attitudinal politics: The strategy of moderation. *Journal of Personality and Social Psychology*, 1973, *25*, 100 –108.

Claparède, E. Recognition and "me-ness." In D. Rapaport (Ed.), *Organization and pathology of thought.* New York: Columbia University Press, 1951. (Original French publication, 1911.)

Collins, B. E., & Hoyt, M. F. Personal responsibility-for-consequences: An integration and extension of the "forced compliance" literature. *Journal of Experimental Social Psychology*, 1972, *8*, 558 –593.

Condry, J. Enemies of exploration: Self-initiated versus other-initiated learning. *Journal of Personality and Social Psychology*, 1977, *35*, 459 –477.

Cottrell, N. B. Social facilitation. In C. G. McClintock (Ed.), *Experimental social psychology*. New York: Holt, Rinehart, and Winston, 1972.

Crowne, D. P., & Marlowe, D. *The approval motive: Studies in evaluative dependence.* New York: Wiley, 1964.

Crutchfield, R. S. Conformity and character. *American Psychologist*, 1955, *10*, 191 –198.

Deci, E. L. *Intrinsic motivation.* New York: Plenum, 1975.

Deutsch, M., Krauss, R., & Rosenau, N. Dissonance or defensiveness? *Journal of Personality*, 1962, *30*, 16 –28.

Duval, S., & Wicklund, R. A. *A theory of objective self-awareness.* New York: Academic Press, 1972.

Erdelyi, M. H., & Goldberg, B. Let's not sweep repression under the rug: Toward a cognitive psychology of repression. In J. F. Kihlstrom and F. J. Evans (Eds.), *Functional disorders of memory.* Hillsdale, N.J.: Erlbaum, 1979.

Eriksen, C. W. The case for perceptual defense. *Psychological Review*, 1954, *61*, 175 –182.

Eysenck, H. J. *Dimensions of personality*. London: Routledge and Kegan Paul, 1947.

Fenigstein, A. Self-consciousness, self-attention, and social interaction. *Journal of Personality and Social Psychology*, 1979, *37*, 75 –86.

Fenigstein, A., Scheier, M. F., & Buss, A. H. Public and private self-consciousness: Assessment and theory. *Journal of Consulting and Clinical Psychology*, 1975, *43*, 522 –527.

Festinger, L. A theory of social comparison processes. *Human Relations*, 1954, *7*, 117 –140.

Festinger, L. *A theory of cognitive dissonance.* Evanston, Ill.: Row, Peterson, 1957.

Freud, S. The psychopathology of everyday life. In A. A. Brill (Ed. & Transl.), *The basic writings of Sigmund Freud*. New York: Random House, 1938. (Original German publication, 1901.)

Froming, W. J., & Carver, C. S. Divergent influences of private and public self-consciousness in a compliance paradigm. *Journal of Research in Personality*, in press.

Greenwald, A. G. The totalitarian ego: Fabrication and revision of personal history. *American Psychologist*, 1980, *35*, 603 –618.

Greenwald, A. G. Self and memory. In G. H. Bower (Ed.), *Psychology of learning and motivation* (Vol. 15). New York: Academic Press, 1981.

Greenwald, A. G., & Ronis, D. L. Twenty years of cognitive dissonance: Case study of the evolution of a theory. *Psychological Review*, 1978, *85*, 53 –57.

Hartmann, H. *Ego psychology and the problem of adaptation.* New York: International Universities Press, 1958. (Original German publication, 1939.)

Hogan, R. Theoretical egocentrism and the problem of compliance. *American Psychologist*, 1975, *30*, 533 –540.

Hull, J. G., & Levy, A. S. The organizational functions of the self: An alternative to the Duval and Wicklund model of self-awareness. *Journal of Personality and Social Psychology*, 1979, *37*, 756 –768.

Inglis, J. Abnormalities of motivation and "Ego-functions." In H. J. Eysenck (Ed.), *Handbook of abnormal psychology.* New York: Basic Books, 1961.

Iverson, M. A., & Reuder, M. E. Ego involvement as an experimental variable. *Psychological Reports*, 1956, *2*, 147 –181.

James, W. *Principles of psychology* (Vol. 1). New York: Holt, 1890.

Jung, C. G. Psychological types. In H. Read, M. Fordham, and G. Adler (Eds.), *Collected Works* (Vol. 6). Princeton, N.J.: Princeton University Press, 1961. (First German edition, 1921.)

Koffka, K. *Principles of gestalt psychology*. New York: Harcourt Brace, 1935.

Kuiper, N. A., & Rogers, T. B. Encoding of personal information: Self –other differences. *Journal of Personality and Social Psychology*, 1979, *37*, 499 –512.

Latané, B., Williams, K., & Harkins, S. Many hands make light the work: The causes and consequences of social loafing. *Journal of Personality and Social Psychology*, 1979, *37*, 822 –832.

Leary, M. R., Silver, S. E., Darby, B. W., & Schlenker, B. R. *The multidimensionality of self-monitoring*. Unpublished manuscript, University of Florida, Gainesville, Fla., 1979.

Lepper, M. R., & Greene, D. Overjustification research and beyond: Towards a means –ends analysis of intrinsic and extrinsic motivation. In M. R. Lepper and D. Greene (Eds.), *The hidden costs of reward.* Hillsdale, N.J.: Erlbaum, 1978.

Lewin, K. *Principles of topological psychology.* New York: McGraw-Hill, 1936.

Loevinger, J. *Ego development.* San Francisco, Calif: Jossey-Bass, 1976.

Magnusson, D., & Endler, N. S. (Eds.), *Personality at the crossroads: Current issues in interactional psychology*. Hillsdale, N.J.: Erlbaum, 1977.

Marrow, A. J. Goal tensions and recall: I. *Journal of General Psychology*, 1938, *19*, 3 –35. (a)

Marrow, A. J. Goal tensions and recall: II. *Journal of General Psychology*, 1938, *19*, 37 –64. (b)

McClelland, D. C. *Power: The inner experience.* New York: Irvington, 1975.

McClelland, D. C., Atkinson, J. W., Clark, R. A., & Lowell, E. L. *The achievement motive.* New York: Appleton-Century-Crofts, 1953.

Miller, G. A., Galanter, E., & Pribram, K. H. *Plans and the structure of behavior.* New York: Holt, Rinehart & Winston, 1960.

Myers, D. G., & Ridl, J. R. A better than average insight into pride. *Psychology Today*, August, 1979.

Newell, A., & Simon, H. A. *Human problem solving.* Englewood Cliffs, N.J.: Prentice-Hall, 1972.

Newtson, D., Engquist, G., & Bois, J. The objective basis of behavior units. *Journal of Personality and Social Psychology*, 1977, *35*, 847 –862.

Nisbett, R. E., & Wilson, T. D. Telling more than we can know: Verbal reports on mental processes. *Psychological Review*, 1977, *84*, 231 –259.

Nuttin, J., & Greenwald, A. G. *Reward and punishment in human learning.* New York: Academic Press, 1968.

Ostrom, T. M., & Brock, T. C. Cognitive model of attitudinal involvement. In R. P. Abelson, et al. (Eds.), *Theories of cognitive consistency: A sourcebook.* Chicago, Ill.: Rand McNally, 1968.

Ovsiankina, M. Die Wiederaufnahme unterbrochener Handlungen. *Psychologische Forschung*, 1928, *11*, 302 –379.

Petty, R. E., & Cacioppo, J. T. Issue involvement can increase or decrease persuasion by enhancing message-relevant cognitive responses. *Journal of Personality and Social Psychology*, 1979, *37*, 1915 –1926.

Postman, L. Methodology of human learning. In W. K. Estes (Ed.), *Handbook of learning and cognitive processes* (Vol. 3). New York: Wiley, 1976.

Riesman, D., Glazer, N., & Denney, R. *The lonely crowd: A study of the changing American character.* New Haven, Conn.: Yale University Press, 1950.

Rogers, T. B., Kuiper, N. A., & Kirker, W. S. Self-reference and the encoding of personal information. *Journal of Personality and Social Psychology*, 1977, *35*, 677 –688.

Rosenberg, M. J. The conditions and consequences of evaluation apprehension. In R. Rosenthal and R. L. Rosnow (Eds.), *Artifact in behavioral research.* New York: Academic Press, 1969.

Rosenzweig, S. An experimental study of "repression" with special reference to need-persistive and ego-defensive reactions to frustration. *Journal of Experimental Psychology*, 1943, *32*, 64 –74.

Rotter, J. B. Generalized expectancies of internal versus external control of reinforcement. *Psychological Monographs*, 1966, *80*, (1, Whole No. 609).

Sampson, E. E. Psychology and the American ideal. *Journal of Personality and Social Psychology*, 1977, *35*, 767 –782.

Sarason, S., & Rosenzweig, S. An experimental study of the triadic hypothesis: Reaction to frustration, ego-defense, and hypnotizability. II. Thematic apperception approach. *Character and Personality*, 1942, *11*, 150 –165.

Scheier, M. F. The effects of public and private self-consciousness on the public expression of personal beliefs. *Journal of Personality and Social Psychology*, 1980, *39*, 514 –21.

Scheier, M. F., & Carver, C. S. Private and public self-attention, resistance to change, and dissonance reduction. *Journal of Personality and Social Psychology*, 1980, *39*, 390 –405.

Sears, R. R. Personality. *Annual Review of Psychology*, 1950, *1*, 105 –118.

Sherif, C. W., Sherif, M., & Nebergall, R. E. *Attitude and attitude change: The social judgment-involvement approach.* Philadelphia, Pa.: Saunders, 1965.

Sherif, M. *The psychology of social norms.* New York: Harper, 1936.

Sherif, M., & Cantril, H. *The psychology of ego-involvements: Social attitudes and identifications.* New York: Wiley, 1947.

Smith, M. L., & Glass, G. V. Meta-analysis of psychotherapy outcome studies. *American Psychologist*, 1977, *32*, 752 –760.

Snyder, M. Self-monitoring of expressive behavior. *Journal of Personality and Social Psychology*, 1974, *30*, 526 –537.

Snyder, M., & Campbell, B. H. Self-monitoring: The self in action. In J. Suls (Ed.), *Social psychological perspectives on the self.* Hillsdale, N.J.: Erlbaum, in press.

Tedeschi, J. T., Schlenker, B. R., & Bonoma, T. V. Cognitive dissonance: Private ratiocination or public spectacle. *American Psychologist*, 1971, *26*, 685–695.

Van Bergen, A. *Task interruption.* Amsterdam: North-Holland, 1968.

Weber, S. J., & Cook, T. D. Subject effects in laboratory research: An examination of subject roles, demand characteristics, and valid inference. *Psychological Bulletin*, 1972, *77*, 273–295.

Wicklund, R. A. Objective self-awareness. In L. Berkowitz (Ed.), *Advances in experimental social psychology* (Vol. 8). New York: Academic Press, 1975.

Wicklund, R. A. Group contact and self-focused attention. In P. B. Paulus (Ed.), *Psychology of group influence.* Hillsdale, N.J.: Erlbaum, 1979.

Wicklund, R. A., & Brehm, J. W. *Perspectives on cognitive dissonance.* Hillsdale, N.J.: Erlbaum, 1976.

Zeigarnik, B. Über das Behalten von erledigten und unerledigten Handlungen. *Psychologische Forschung*, 1927, *9*, 1–85.

Zeigarnik, B. On finished and unfinished tasks. In W. D. Ellis (Ed.), *A source book of Gestalt psychology*. New York: Humanities Press, 1938.

Zeller, A. An experimental analogue of repression: I. Historical summary. *Psychological Bulletin*, 1950, *47*, 36–51.

LESLIE ZEBROWITZ McARTHUR

JUDGING A BOOK BY ITS COVER:
A COGNITIVE ANALYSIS OF THE RELATIONSHIP BETWEEN PHYSICAL APPEARANCE AND STEREOTYPING

Generally speaking, victims of stereotyping look different from the perpetrators.[1] Yet, physical appearance has been surprisingly underemphasized in research and theory on the development of stereotypes, which has focused largely upon motivational factors such as economic competition, displacement of aggression, ego-defense, and conformity to social norms. While such motivational bases may certainly play a role in the development of many stereotypes, this chapter will focus on the explanatory power of the stereotyped group's distinctive physical appearance.

There seems to be general agreement among psychologists that a stereotype is a generalization or belief about a particular group of people, most typically the generalization that group members have particular traits (Brigham 1971, p. 30). Stereotypes may be differentiated from other generalizations in a number of ways. They are overgeneralizations in the sense that stereotypes tend to be uniformly applied to all members of a particular group. They tend to be extreme—for example, the attribute "moderately intelligent" or moderately anything else would hardly constitute a stereotype. Also, they tend to be more often negative than positive. These defining characteristics—uniformity, extremity, and negativity—all seem consistent with the argument that stereotypes are the products of faulty thought processes and motiva-

[1]One must acknowledge some exceptions to this general rule. However, even those stereotypes that do not appear to pertain to physically distinctive groups (e.g., occupational group stereotypes) may be fueled by superficial physical differences, such as mode of dress.

tional biases (e.g., Lippmann 1922). However, the present analysis will demonstrate that perceptual-cognitive processes, occasioned by the distinctive physical appearance of stereotyped persons, may also give rise to uniform, extreme, and negative evaluations of these people.

It should be noted that the cognitive analysis of stereotyping developed in this chapter is not meant to deny that stereotypes may have a motivational component. Certainly, many do. However, there are several advantages to the present analysis that argue for its ascendance over more traditional models. One advantage is parsimony. The physical appearance analysis brings together within a single explanatory framework stereotypes about a variety of different groups—e.g., racial minorities, the physically handicapped, the elderly, the obese. Moreover, it links stereotyping to ordinary processes of person perception rather than treating it as reflecting some special type of thought process. A second advantage is that the physical appearance analysis offers a more satisfactory explanation for the specific content of stereotypes than does the "kernel of truth" explanation posited in past analyses. Finally, the physical appearance analysis has the advantage of providing several recommendations for the amelioration of stereotypes, which are more feasible to implement than those suggested by a motivational analysis.

This chapter considers how physical appearance can contribute to the uniformity, negativity, extremity, and specific content of stereotypes. More specifically, it will be argued that (1) the tendency for stereotypes to be *uniformly* generalized to all members of a particular group may derive from assimilation and contrast effects inherent in perceptual categorization on the basis of physical attributes; (2) the tendency for stereotypes to be *extreme* and *negative* may derive from selective attention to physically distinctive persons and to extreme or negative behaviors; and (3) the *specific content* of stereotypes may derive from selective attention to associatively linked actor-behavior pairs.

The first section of this chapter considers how the impact of physical appearance on categorization and selective attention can result in the *formation* of stereotypes about physically distinctive persons. The second section considers the role of these processes in the *perpetuation* of stereotypes, and the last section offers possibilities for the *amelioration* of stereotypes suggested by the present analysis.

THE FORMATION OF STEREOTYPES

Most people form stereotypes about particular groups of people within a cultural context that directly teaches the stereotypes. However, the present discussion of the formation of stereotypes will not focus on how this cultural transmission is accomplished. Rather, it will focus on the question of how stereotypes might have arisen in the culture in the first place. It will be argued that if all stereotypes were somehow erased and if all people were equal in every respect but their physical appearance, then stereotypes could nevertheless reemerge as a result of the basic cognitive processes of categorization and selective attention.

UNIFORMITY

Stereotypes share the feature of "uniformity" in that members of a stereotyped group tend to be viewed as uniformly sharing some attribute (assimilation effect) that is not shared by members of another group (contrast effect). It can be argued that both of these effects are the natural by-products of perceptual processes. More specifically, a tendency to categorize people on the basis of their physical appearance could produce the assimilation and contrast effects characteristic of stereotyping.

According to Bruner (1957), perception is a categorization process in which the "perceptual categorization of an object or event permits one to 'go beyond' the properties of the object or event perceived to a prediction of other properties of the object not yet tested." This analysis implies that the properties perceived in a given stimulus will depend to a great extent upon how that stimulus is categorized. Evidence consistent with this hypothesis was provided in a study by Tajfel and Wilkes (1963), who found that categorizing a line as "long" caused subjects to perceive it as differing more in length from a line categorized as "short" than from another long one of equal discrepancy. Tajfel noted that these findings may represent a simplified example of stereotyping, an essential feature of which is exaggerating some differences between people categorized in a different way and minimizing the same differences within such groups. This suggestion is in keeping with Bruner's (1957) proposition that categorization effects should occur not only for basic perceptual activities, like the judgment of length, but also for more conceptual ones, such as the judgment of personality.

There is considerable evidence that the act of placing people into categories associated with well-known stereotypes does indeed affect the attributes they are perceived to possess. (See below for a discussion of this research.) The question considered in this section is whether it is reasonable to propose that the categorization process can function in the *formation* of stereotypes about physically distinctive people. Two kinds of evidence are pertinent to this question: (1) to what extent are people categorized according to their physical attributes; and (2) to what extent does categorization *in and of itself* yield the assimilation and contrast effects characteristic of stereotyping. [See Hamilton (1979) for a related discussion.]

Categorization on the Basis of Physical Appearance

Although no research has directly examined perceivers' tendency to categorize people on the basis of physical appearance, there is good reason to expect this tendency to be strong. For one thing, visual stimuli have the advantage of primacy, since we usually see people's physical appearance before we experience their other attributes. Before we can learn that someone is "soft-spoken," we have already categorized her as "obese." In addition to the advantage of visual cues in the successive presentation of attributes, considerable research evidence indicates that they dominate subjects' attention when presented simultaneously with other cues in a stimulus array (Posner, Nissen, & Klein, 1976). Finally, differences in peoples' physical appearances tend to be more discriminable than other differences among them. This too should foster categorization on the basis of physical appearance, since it has been found that when perceivers are asked to sort into categories stimuli that vary in a number of attributes, the attribute selected as a basis for categorization is the one with the most discriminable levels in the stimulus array (Imai & Garner, 1965).

In addition to support for the hypothesized dominance of physical appearance cues provided by the foregoing object perception research, considerable person perception research has also documented the potency of such cues. For example, Fiske and Cox (1979) found that whether subjects were asked to describe a familiar person or an unfamiliar person, appearance was typically the first category of description employed. Moreover, the tendency to begin by describing the person in terms of appearance rather than other attributes was observed even when subjects were instructed to describe the person so that someone else would know what it is like to be around him or her. Finally, it should be noted that reliance on the physical appearance category in descriptions of others is present from an early age (Livesley & Bromley, 1973).

Other evidence for the salience of physical appearance in person perception comes from research that has examined perceptions of people as a function of changes in their physical appearance. Mischel (1968) has suggested that the perceiver's tendency to ascribe traits to people may derive, at least in part, from the fact that they always look the same. Consistent with this hypothesis, Kassin (1977) found that perceivers were more likely to ascribe traits to a person whose physical appearance was constant than to one whose appearance noticeably changed. Bowman (1979) found that perceivers were more apt to change their trait ascriptions to a person whose behavior changed when his physical appearance also changed than when his physical appearance remained constant. Both of these studies support the argument that people are categorized on the basis of their physical appearance. When physical appearance remains constant, perceivers find it difficult to recategorize a person on other attributes; changes in physical appearance, on the other hand, facilitate this recategorization.

In addition to the evidence that people are more apt to be categorized in terms of their physical appearance than other attributes, there are some data regarding the question of which physical attributes are most likely to be employed as a basis for categorization. As in object perception research (Lappin, 1967; Williams, 1966), color (i.e., race) seems to be the most salient dimension, followed by sex, age, and facial expression (Milord, 1978). However, one must be wary of concluding that these categorization preferences derive from variations in the intrinsic salience of racial, sexual, age, and expression cues. Particular physical appearance cues are very loaded in our society, that is, they carry with them the assumption of a variety of other attributes, and it may be these correlated attributes, rather than the physical cues per se, that are controlling categorization. It is difficult to construct a pure test of the hypothesis that people are most apt to be categorized on the basis of a particular physical appearance cue simply because that physical cue is inherently most salient. One possibility would be to study very young children who have not yet acquired stereotypes. Alternatively, one could employ appearance cues and other cues that do not really occur in the real world and see which serves as a basis for categorization.

The Impact of Categorization on Stereotyping

As noted above, to support the argument that categorization on the basis of physical appearance plays a role in the development of stereotypes one must demonstrate not only that such categorization occurs before there are any stereotypes but also that such categorization can *in and of itself* produce the assimilation and contrast effects characteristic of stereotypes. An ideal test of the effects of categorization on stereotyping would be to examine perceptions of people who are sorted into different categories on the basis of some physical attribute that has no particular meaning in our culture. Unfortunately, none of the existing research fully meets this criterion, although there are some findings that bear mention.

Secord and his associates (Secord, Dukes, & Bevan, 1954; Secord & Muthard, 1955) found that photographs of people that were clustered together on the basis of similarly rated physiognomic features were also similarly rated with respect to personality, while those photographs placed into different categories on the basis of dissimilar physiognomic ratings were rated disparately on personality traits. In short, people who physically resembled each other were perceived to have similar traits, and people who looked different were perceived to have different traits. It is important to note that the physiognomic features that served as a basis for categorization in this research were relatively meaningless in that they were not associated with a culturally stereotyped group. Thus the results strongly suggest that categorization per se can produce assimilation and contrast effects, although still stronger evidence for the primacy of categorization would be provided by research in which subjects are totally unfamiliar with the physical features prior to the experiment.

Evidence that categorization yields assimilation and contrast also comes from research that has used meaningless nonphysical attributes as a basis for categorization. For example, Gerard and Hoyt (1974) categorized subjects according to their performance on a perceptual judgment task—overestimators and underestimators. Subjects' evaluations of an ingroup member differed significantly from evaluations of an outgroup member, even though there was no objective basis for differentiating among the two. Similarly, a number of studies by Tajfel (1970) have revealed that when subjects are assigned to groups on the basis of some arbitrary criterion, they typically rate the two groups differently on a variety of personal characteristics.

Research by Taylor, Fiske, Etcoff, and Ruderman (1978) has shown that categorizing people in terms of race and sex yields assimilation and contrast effects, some of which cannot be explained in terms of preexisting stereotypes. Subjects in this research listened to a six-person taped discussion while watching slides of each participant as he or she spoke. In one version of the study, there were three black and three white participants, while in another there were three females and three males. Subjects' recall of who had said what was consistent with the hypothesis that they would categorize the stimulus persons in terms of race and sex: intraracial and intrasex errors exceeded the interracial and intersex errors, respectively. This tendency to perceive uniformity in what persons of a given sex or race said cannot easily be attributed to cultural stereotypes, and is best viewed as a consequence of perceptual categorization. Moreover, the finding that physically dissimilar people were perceived as saying different things suggests that perceiving physically dissimilar people as having dissimilar personalities and attitudes (e.g., Stein, Hardyck, & Smith, 1965) may also be a contrast effect deriving from perceptual categorization.

Summary and Implications

It is important to note that a potentially important component of most of the research that has demonstrated stereotyping following categorization of people on some trivial physical attribute has been that those perceiving the categorization were involved in it themselves, either directly or vicariously through their own similarity to one group or the other. Thus, with the possible exception of Secord's work, the process of categorization has produced an ingroup and an outgroup, and this effect may have contributed to the subsequent stereotyping. Further research is needed to determine whether categorization of people will yield stereotyping even when the perceiver is not a member of one or the other category. Such research is important for the argument that the effects of categorization upon stereotyping reflect a perceptual-cognitive effect rather than a motivational one, since self-esteem motives could contribute to a tendency to ascribe different characteristics to members of an outgroup category than to members of an ingroup category.

While the research on categorization effects is not definitive, the existing evidence does suggest that people will tend to be categorized on the basis of their physical appearance, and that such categorization can produce a tendency to view those within a given category as uniformly sharing various attributes (assimilation effect) that are not shared by members of another category (contrast effect). Thus uniformly applied generalizations about the traits of blacks, the elderly, or the handicapped, for example, may derive in large measure from the physical similarities among the people within each group.

EXTREMITY AND NEGATIVITY

While categorizing people on the basis of their physical appearance can account for the tendency to perceive those in a particular category as uniformly sharing some attribute not shared by those in another category, it cannot by itself explain other features of stereotyping. For example, the tendency to attribute extreme and negative characteristics to people categorized together occurs for some categories but not for others. This asymmetry in the impact of categorization upon stereotyping can be understood as a consequence of two other perceptual-cognitive processes: selective attention to novel stimuli (i.e., preferential registration, encoding, and/or recall of such stimuli) and illusory correlation effects.

Selective Attention to Novel Stimuli

Theory and research on selective attention in object-perception have identified several stimulus attributes that draw attention. These include physical properties intrinsic to the stimulus, such as brightness, color, and size; and collative properties, which depend upon comparison or collation of stimulus elements, such as complexity, unit formation, and novelty (Berlyne, 1970). Based upon this evidence, one would expect that categories of people whose physical appearance is novel—i.e., statistically or contextually infrequent—will draw more attention than those whose appearance is more normative. One might also expect that extreme or negative behaviors will draw more attention than moderate or positive ones by virtue either of greater intensity or greater novelty in the real world.

Considerable research evidence reveals that perceivers do indeed attend more to people whose physical appearance is novel and to behaviors that are negative or extreme. Behavioral measures of attention have shown that people look more at pregnant or handicapped or redheaded people than at those whose appearance is more normative (Langer, Taylor, Fiske, & Chanowitz, 1976; Taylor & Langer, 1977; McArthur & Ginsburg, 1981). Also, they look longer at slides depicting negative behaviors or extreme (i.e., intense and atypical) behaviors than at those depicting positive behaviors or normative, moderate ones (Fiske, 1980). Not only do perceivers show preferential registration of both negative and extreme behaviors, but they weight these behaviors more heavily than positive or moderate ones in forming impressions of a stimulus person (e.g., Fiske, 1980; Hamilton & Zanna, 1972; Hodges, 1974; Manis, Gleason, & Dawes, 1966; Podell & Podell, 1963; Rosenberg, Nelson, & Vivekananthan, 1968; Wyer, 1974; Warr, 1974). While this preferential weighting affects impressions of all people, regardless of their physical appearance, the phenomenon of illusory correlation should make the effects most pronounced for impressions of those who are physically distinctive.

Illusory Correlation

Considerable research has demonstrated that when people are exposed to a series of paired events, their perceptions of the correlation between the events tends to weight most heavily those *pairs* that draw attention (e.g., Chapman, 1967; Ward & Jenkins, 1965). These findings have interesting implications for the realm of person perception. When people are exposed to a series of behaviors by members of two different categories, their perceptions of the correlation between category membership and behavior should weight most heavily the pairings of attention-drawing people performing attention-drawing behaviors. Hamilton and Gifford (1976) have tested this hypothesis by showing subjects a series of slides, each of which attributed a positive or negative behavior to a member of some abstract category of persons, A or B. The actual correlation between person category and behavior type was zero. However, perceivers' attention was drawn to one type of behavior and one category of people by making it less frequent within the stimulus materials than the other. As expected, subjects perceived an illusory correlation between being a member of the minority group and performing behaviors that were in the minority. Evaluations of the minority group were more negative than evaluations of the majority when negative behaviors were the infrequent ones, and evaluations of the minority group were more positive than evaluations of the majority when positive behaviors were the infrequent ones. Corresponding with these biased impressions, subjects tended to overrecall instances of infrequent behaviors by minority group members.

The phenomenon of illusory correlation, together with the evidence for selective attention to novel stimuli, provides a cogent explanation for the tendency to form negative, extreme stereotypes about those whose appearance is novel. The person-behavior pairs most salient to a perceiver consist of physically distinctive people performing negative or extreme actions. The preferential weighting of these salient pairs creates the illusion that appearance and behavior are more correlated than they really are, and produces extreme, negative impressions of those with a novel appearance.

Polarized Impressions of Physically Distinctive People

The foregoing argument suggests that the tendency to attribute extreme and negative characteristics to the obese and blacks, for example, but not to the slender and whites may be explained in terms of greater attention to people in the former categories, in general, and to their extreme or negative behaviors, in particular. If this argument is correct, then one would expect more extreme or negative evaluations of people whose physical appearance draws attention for any one of a number of reasons, not just for those whose salient physical appearance is stigmatized in our society. There is considerable evidence for such an effect. More extreme trait ratings have been obtained for stimulus persons who are salient by virtue of (1) having their face rather than their back to the perceiver; (2) being seated in a bright light; (3) movement; (4) a physical attribute that is novel within the situation, e.g., minority race or sex; (5) a physical attribute that is novel in the population at large, e.g., pregnancy, leg brace, red hair. [See McArthur (1981b) and Taylor and Fiske (1978) for more extensive reviews of this literature.]

It should be noted that the tendency to form more evaluatively extreme impressions of a salient than a nonsalient person sometimes takes the form of more positive evaluations and sometimes more negative evaluations. The direction of the effect seems to depend upon the baseline favorability of the impression the person creates. For example, in a study by Taylor, Fiske, Close, Anderson, and Ruderman (1976), which varied the sexual novelty of stimulus persons in a group, one of the actors tended to be perceived negatively, while another tended to be perceived positively. The person who made a generally negative impression was rated even less favorably in a group of opposite-sexed people than in a sexually integrated group. On the other hand, the person who made a generally favorable impression was rated even more positively when standing out in a group of opposite-sexed people than when the group was sexually mixed.

McArthur and Solomon (1978) found that the direction in which salience pushes evaluations varies not only with the general likeability of a stimulus person but also with the specific attributes of that person which are being evaluated. Characters with definite personalities were created in this study in which subjects were exposed to an aggressor and a victim who was basically friendly, passive, and incompetent. When the victim was salient by virtue of either one of two novel physical attributes (red hair or a leg brace) she was rated as more friendly, more passive, and less competent than when her hair color or leg brace were not visible. In sum, it appears that salient stimulus persons receive more *polarized* evaluations: behavior that tends to create a positive impression on a particular attribute will create an even more positive impression when performed by a physically salient person; and behavior that tends to create a negative impression on a particular attribute will create an even more negative impression when performed by someone who is physically salient. Such polarization effects are consistent with the illusory correlation analysis presented above. The direction in which evaluations of a physically salient person will be polarized should depend upon which of that person's behaviors are the most salient, since it is these more attention-drawing behaviors that will enter into the illusory correlation effect.

Summary and Implications

Negative stereotypes of people who belong to some physically distinctive category have typically been attributed to some motivation on the part of the perceiver, be it ego defense, displacement of aggression, or even conformity to social norms. In keeping with this reasoning, Katz and Glass (1979) have argued that *polarized* reactions to certain categories of people, such as blacks and the obese, derive from conflicted feelings toward these groups—hostility and aversion as well as sympathy and compassion. These ambivalent feelings are proposed to create a state of behavioral instability in which either extremely positive or extremely negative responses may occur. However, we have seen that polarized reactions accrue to individuals with a wide variety of attention-drawing attributes, many of which should evoke no particular ambivalence in the perceiver (e.g., a bright light). Thus extreme and/or negative evaluations of people who are salient by virtue of some socially stigmatizing attribute need not presuppose ambivalent feelings based on this stigma. Rather, such stereotypes may derive from perceptual-cognitive processes—the tendency to selectively attend to physically distinctive people and to negative or extreme behaviors coupled with the tendency to perceive an illusory correlation between the salient person-behavior pairs.

While polarization effects do not require ambivalent feelings toward salient people based upon a stigmatizing attribute, they may require that there be some feelings about these people based upon their observed behavior. Physically salient people have reliably elicited polarized reactions whey they have been observed in an affectively toned social interaction—e.g., an interaction involving aggression or humor or personal self-disclosure—but they have often failed to elicit polarized reactions when observed in rather banal, getting-acquainted conversations. [See McArthur (1981b) for a more detailed review of this literature.] These findings suggest that there must be some behaviors that are salient (e.g., extreme, negative) before perceivers will show more polarized evaluations of a salient than a nonsalient person. Such a prerequisite can be understood within the framework of the illusory correlation analysis. If there are no "distinctive actor-distinctive behavior" pairs to be overweighted, impressions of the physically distinctive people cannot be more strongly influenced by extreme behaviors than impressions of those who are not distinctive.

SPECIFICITY

Where Is the Kernel of Truth?

While most stereotypes share the features of uniformity, extremity, and negativity, there are also important differences among stereotypes of various physically distinctive groups which need to be accounted for. For one thing, they do vary in valence: some stereotypes are positive, which indicates that positive behaviors will sometimes draw more attention than negative ones. What is more, they vary in substance. Some stereotypes pertain to the intelligence of a category of people, some pertain to their morality, still others pertain to various specific personality traits. This diversity in the valence and substance of stereotypes is found both between groups (e.g., the stereotypes of blacks, Jews, and the obese are not all the same) and within groups (e.g., the stereotypes of blacks, Jews, the obese, each contain positive elements as well as negative elements and each pertain to a range of psychological attributes).

One possible explanation for the specificity of stereotypes that has frequently been proposed is the kernel of truth hypothesis. For example, Vinacke (1956, p. 285) postulated that "In part wrong, superficial, and limited, they (national stereotypes) nevertheless generalize some actual cultural traits." Brigham (1971, p. 26) concluded from his review of the research that "ethnic stereotypes can have 'kernels of truth', at least in a convergent validity sense, that is, agreement between several groups as to traits that characterize a particular object group." While such convergent validity may sometimes be produced by the actual psychological attributes of the stereotyped group, it may also be produced by the physical attributes of the group. More specifically, particular physical attributes may call to mind particular personality traits, and these shared associative connections could produce widespread agreement as to the attributes of a particular stereotyped group. The plausibility of this assertion is supported by Asch's (1958, p. 86) observation that "when we describe the workings of emotions, ideas, or trends of character, we almost invariably employ terms that also denote properties and processes observable in the world of nature." Asch found that terms that denote both physical *and* psychological properties such as "soft," "hard," "straight," and "crooked" occur in a variety of languages, and it seems reasonable to argue that this linguistic link may work both ways: just as we label someone as "soft" when they literally are "yielding," so may we label someone as "yielding" when they literally are "soft." In short, the "kernel of truth" may often be in the eyes of the beholder. This is not to say that there are not traits characteristic of particular groups. Undoubtedly there are. Rather, it is to suggest that the traits perceived in these groups may frequently be influenced by their physical characteristics rather than by their behavior. Evidence consistent with this argument has been provided by research demonstrating strong links between physiognomic attributes and personality ascriptions.

Associations Between Facial Features and Personality Ascriptions

As noted earlier, studies by Secord et al. (1954) and Secord and Muthard (1955) have found marked agreement among judges on the personality traits attributed to photographed faces, a consensus that could derive only from judges' shared assumptions about the relationship between particular physiognomic features and personality traits. In addition to providing evidence that physiognomic features and personality ratings are related, these studies also addressed the question of which physiognomic features have the strongest influence upon personality ratings. It was found that photographs rated toward the extremes on physiognomic traits were also rated toward the extremes on personality traits.

Thus facial features that one would expect to be most salient, based upon their extremity, yielded the most stereotypic—i.e., extreme—personality ratings. On the other hand, individuals rated average on physiognomic traits also tended to be rated average on personality characteristics.

The answer to the question of which physiognomic traits are associated with which personality traits is a complex one, according to the results of Secord's research. Typically, there was observed an interactive effect of the physiognomic traits such that the impact of a particular facial feature upon personality ratings depended upon the other facial features with which it appeared. However, some marked correspondences between single physiognomic traits and personality ratings have been documented (Secord et al., 1954; Bradshaw, 1969), and it is important to note that these relationships did not simply represent halo effects, i.e., a tendency to attribute good traits to good-looking people. Many faces received high ratings on some unfavorable traits, but not others, and analyses revealed that several general trait clusters were being tapped.

While specific facial features may be linked to both good and bad traits, there does seem to be a halo effect for the constellation of facial features which comprise attractiveness. Considerable research on this topic has revealed that impressions of attractive people are much more positive than impressions of unattractive people on a variety of evaluative dimensions. For example, people who are physically attractive are perceived as more intelligent, more likeable, and less aggressive than those who are unattractive [see Bersheid and Walster (1974) and Adams (1979), for reviews of this literature]. Negative evaluations of unattractive people would follow from the illusory correlation analysis of stereotype negativity if it could be assumed that the appearance of unattractive people is more novel than that of attractive people. If so, then pairings of unattractive people performing negative behaviors would draw more attention than other actor-behavior pairs and yield an illusory correlation between being unattractive and performing negative behaviors. However, it seems reasonable to argue that both a very attractive and a very unattractive appearance would draw attention, since both are statistically infrequent. This suggests that something besides simple shared infrequency is responsible for the tendency to form more negative impressions of unattractive persons. It also suggests that evaluations of both attractive and unattractive people should be more polarized than evaluations of those whose appearance is average. Although I know of no research evidence to support this hypothesis, it is rather difficult to imagine an ugly "man about town," for example, or a beautiful "wallflower," which suggests that we tend to stereotype unattractive people as more introverted than average and attractive people as more extraverted than average, and to have no particular stereotype about the gregariousness of average-looking people.

One important feature of some of the research on facial features is its demonstration that the influence of physical appearance upon trait ascriptions is powerful enough to override objective data more pertinent to the inference. For example, attractive children were rated as more intelligent than unattractive children despite the availability of the children's grades in a variety of subjects throughout the school year (Clifford & Walster, 1973). Similarly, Secord, Bevan, & Dukes (1953) found that ratings of photographs varied with their physiognomic features and were not influenced to any appreciable degree by the placement of occupational labels on the photographs.

Associations Between Other Physical Features and Personality Ascriptions

Facial features are not the only physical attributes shown to be reliably linked with personality ratings. Several studies (Kiker & Miller, 1967; Sleet, 1969; Wells & Siegal, 1961) have found that people could rank, with significant agreement, somatotype photographs on various personality dimensions. These results reflected in large part a halo effect, since the mesomorph physique was ranked highest on all dimensions, and the endomorph was ranked lowest. This rank ordering is in keeping with cultural preferences for a muscular body build and distaste for a fat one. It is also consistent with the illusory correlation analysis of stereotype negativity if it can be assumed that fat people are the least frequent in our culture and muscular people the most frequent.

In addition to general evaluative differences in the ratings of various body types, some differentiated connections between particular body builds and particular traits have been observed. For example, negative ratings of endomorphs were most pronounced on the dimension of laziness, consistent with the cultural stereotype of "fat and lazy." The endomorph also tended to be rated relatively high on the traits talkative, warm-hearted, agreeable, dependent, and trusting. Ectomorphs, on the other hand, tended to be rated most negatively on likeability and adjustment, and not negatively on laziness, consistent with the stereotype of the gangly introvert with lots of nervous energy. The ectomorph was also rated as relatively ambitious, stubborn, pessimistic, and quiet. It should be noted that these stereotypes were obtained from people who had no contact with formal theory of somatotypes, yet they are almost identical to Sheldon's schema (1954).

Hair is another attribute which has been linked with personality ratings. Although stereotypes based upon hair color may be of little social significance, they bear mention because they provide the most unequivocal support for the thesis that physical appearance per se is an important determinant of stereotyping. While the kernel of truth hypothesis provides a feasible explanation for stereotypes about people with particular facial features or body builds, it seems far less plausible to suggest that cultural stereotypes about people with particular hair colors are overgeneralizations from some actual hair-linked traits. And such stereotypes are in fact widely held. Lawson (1971) found that the overall negativity of trait ratings varied linearly with the frequency of a person's hair color in the population. Brunettes received the most favorable ratings, followed by blonds and redheads, a rank ordering which is consistent with the illusory correlation analysis of the negativity of stereotypes. In addition to this overall difference in evaluations of various hair colors, each color tended to be associated with specific traits. Redheads were seen as significantly more cold, tense, and excitable than natural blonds or brunettes; blond women were seen as significantly more delicate, weak-willed, simple, and beautiful than brunettes or redheads; and brunettes were seen as more intelligent, ambitious, sincere, predictable, strong, and dependable than the others. Similar results have been reported by Roll and Verinis (1971).

Origin of Associative Links

The existing research provides strong evidence that the personality traits ascribed to people vary with their physiognomic attributes. The question remains of where these associations come from and how they operate in the creation of stereotypes about physically distinctive groups. In many instances, the associations between particular physical characteristics and particular behaviors are culturally taught. But this explanation does not address the question of how they originated in the culture. Moreover, some incidental findings in the study by Secord et al. (1954) suggest that explicitly learned connections are an unlikely explanation for many of the associative links. Subjects in this study did not perform as if they were recalling rules about what goes with what. Their judgments of personality traits were generally made in a rapid, unhesitating manner, several traits frequently being rated after a single glance at the photograph. These "snap judgments" (Schneider, Hastorf, & Ellsworth, 1979) were made with very high interrater agreement. But, despite their speed and reliability, judges had a hard time stating the basis on which their personality judgments were made, and their judgments of physiognomic traits appeared to be quite labored, suggesting that they were not in the habit of consciously evaluating the thinness of people's lips or the narrowness of their eyes. These findings led Secord et al. (1954) to propose that perceivers are employing well-developed schemata for making trait ascriptions from physiognomic cues. The nature of these schemata is elucidated by Secord's (1958) suggestion that trait ascriptions may derive from strong associations between particular physical characteristics and particular behaviors based upon function, metaphor, or temporal extension.[2]

Functional Associations. A functional association occurs when "the perceiver infers that some aspect of the object person functions in a

[2]These three bases for associative links between physical appearance and personality can be viewed as concrete principles governing the application of the representativeness heuristic (Kahneman & Tversky, 1973; Nisbett & Ross, 1980). The traits that seem to "represent" or "fit" a particular group of people are those that bear a similarity to the group's appearance by virtue of function, metaphor, and/or temporal extension.

particular manner; from this he assumes that the individual possesses an associated attribute." (Secord, 1958, p. 313). For example, the finding that people wearing glasses are perceived as more intelligent than those not wearing glasses (e.g., Thornton, 1943, 1944) may derive from associations to the functional properties of glasses: they function to help one read, and such bookish behavior is associated with intelligence. Functional associations may also account for our surprise at encountering an assertive paraplegic such as played by Jon Voight in the movie *Coming Home*. Legs that cannot "stand up" may be associated with an analogous weakness in personality. Conversely, the functional strength of the mesomorph's muscles may be assumed to be accompanied by strength of personality. Also, the active function of an overweight person's mouth in the realm of food consumption may be generalized to the realm of conversation, yielding the stereotype of the talkative endomorph (e.g., Wells & Siegel, 1961).

Metaphorical Associations. In a metaphorical association, "the perceiver makes an abstract generalization based upon an analogy between some denotable characteristic of the object person and a personality attribute" (Secord, 1958, p. 314). Since the role of semantic similarity in impression formation has been demonstrated for trait to trait inferences (e.g., Ebbesen & Allen, 1979), it seems reasonable to propose that semantic similarity such as that expressed in metaphor or other figurative speech will also play a role in appearance to trait inferences. For example, the stereotype that obese people are warmhearted may reflect the related figures of speech "bighearted" and "softhearted," since the physical appearance of the obese would suggest a big, soft heart. Similarly, the stereotype that the obese are yielding and agreeable may reflect metaphors based upon soft, pliable, fatty tissue. On the other hand, the stubbornness attributed to the ectomorph may reflect the metaphors "rodlike" and "stiff as a poker" inasmuch as poker or rod does characterize the thin person's physical appearance. Metaphor may also be responsible for the energy attributed to thin people, whose appearance suggests that they have "worked their fingers to the bone."

Facial features as well as body build may provide metaphorical associations to particular psychological traits. For example, the tendency to stereotype Chinese people as "sly" (e.g., Karlins, Coffman, & Walters, 1969) may reflect the simile "sly as a fox," since oriental eyes are foxlike. The attribution of pushiness to Jews may reflect the metaphor "nosy," called forth by the stereotypic Jewish nose. The attribution of antisocial, aggressive behavior to the physically unattractive (e.g., Dion, 1972) may reflect the simile "ugly as sin."

In addition to stereotypes based upon metaphorical associations to a person's bodily or facial structure, a variety of stereotypes may be attributed to metaphorical associations to color. For example, the stereotype that people with red hair have an excitable temperament may reflect the metaphor "hotheaded," since the hair on their heads is a fiery color. Likewise, semantic associations to the color black may contribute to stereotypes of black people. For example, Williams (1964) found that the color black is rated as more potent, but less active than white, which coincides with the stereotype that blacks are "strong" but "lazy." [See Gergen (1967) for an extensive review of the literature on associations to the color black.]

Temporal Extension. In addition to functional and metaphorical associations to particular physical attributes, Secord (1958, p. 313) proposed a third basis for inferring personality traits from facial features. This is the process of temporal extension in which "the perceiver regards a momentary characteristic of the person as if it were an enduring attribute." Thus, for example, a perceiver may infer from a temporary, smiling face that the stimulus person has the more permanent traits of friendliness and a good sense of humor. These inferences have in fact been correlated with the wrinkles at the corner of the eye and the degree to which the corners of the mouth were turned up, two cues associated with a smile (Secord, Dukes, & Bevan, 1954). A process related to this type of inference has interesting implications for the genesis of stereotypes about physically distinctive groups of people. It may be that the permanent—i.e. nonexpressive—facial physiognomy of some groups of people resembles certain emotionally expressive states. If so, then the perceiver may infer the "state" from these facial features and go on to infer the "trait."

Considerable research evidence indicates that perceivers show rapid and consensual inferences about the emotional state of a stimulus person from facial cues (e.g., Ekman, Friesen, & Ellsworth, 1972). Moreover, there is evidence that perceivers tend to make undue inferences about a person's traits on the basis of information regarding that person's emotional state (Snyder & Frankel, 1976). Thus it seems reasonable to argue that when a person's static facial features suggest a particular emotion, perceivers may infer a related trait. For example, the finding that thin-lipped people are perceived as conscientious (Secord, Dukes, & Bevan, 1954) may derive from the association of thin lips with a state of concentration in which the set of one's mouth tends to compress the lips. Conversely, thick lips may be associated with laziness, since the slack set of one's mouth in a state of relaxation tends to make the lips fuller. Other plausible examples of temporal extension include perceiving people with a ruddy complexion or protruding eyes as excitable (Secord et al., 1954), since faces do tend to redden and eyes do tend to "bug out" in a state of emotional excitement.

The Impact of Associations on Stereotyping

A variety of examples have been generated in support of the proposition that specific stereotypes may result from associations to physical appearance based upon function, metaphor, or temporal extension. Although the examples are consistent with that proposition, it is important to note that they do not constitute proof of it, and there is need for empirical evidence that such associations do exist. Moreover, to argue that specific stereotypes are a consequence of associations to a person's physical appearance requires more than empirically demonstrating such links. A further understanding of how specific stereotypes may be formed about people with specific physical attributes is provided by the effects of illusory correlation, primacy, halos, and implicit personality theories.

Illusory Correlation. As noted earlier, actor-behavior pairs that draw attention tend to be perceived as more strongly correlated than they really are. The actors who will draw the most attention are, as we have learned, those whose physical appearance is salient for any one of a variety of reasons among which are statistical or contextual novelty. One important determinant of the degree to which a particular behavior will draw attention is its associative connections to the actor. This phenomenon was demonstrated by Chapman and Chapman (1967), who found that both clinicians and naive interpreters of the draw-a-person test tend to overestimate the correlation between particular categories of patients and those drawing behaviors that have strong semantic associations to the patient category. For example, the pairing paranoid patient – atypical eye drawing was perceived to co-occur more often than it really did. By the same token, one would expect that pairings of eyeglasses and intelligent behavior, red hair and hot-tempered behavior, or obesity and yielding behavior would draw more attention than other pairings, yielding an illusory correlation effect in which the salient appearance – behavior pairs are perceived as more strongly related than they really are.

It is important to note that illusory correlation effects should be weaker when a specific behavior is associated with a relatively nonsalient physical attribute, for these appearance – behavior pairings should draw less attention than when the appearance itself is salient. Thus, for example, one would not expect associative connections between thin lips and conscientiousness to yield extreme ratings of thin-lipped people analogous to those one finds for obese people, who are more physically salient. On the other hand, when thick lips become salient by virtue of appearing in a salient black face, the associative connections to thin vs thick lips may indeed contribute to the extreme ratings of blacks on the dimensions of laziness. The argument that associative connections between particular physical attributes and particular psychological attributes should yield strong illusory correlation effects—and hence strong stereotypes—only when the physical attributes are themselves salient is consistent with Secord et al.'s finding that the most extreme personality ratings were found for extreme (i.e., salient) physiognomic traits.

While illusory correlation derived from associative connections between particular physical attributes and particular behaviors may account for certain specific stereotypes about various categories of people, it seems unlikely that such associations can generate the full complement of attributes that typically make up a stereotype. However, illusory correlation resulting from selective attention may be supplemented by other cognitive mechanisms that reinforce and elaborate a particular associative link.

Primacy Effects. Considerable research evidence indicates that there are strong primacy effects in impression formation [see Jones and Goethels (1972) for a review of this literature] such that a person's early behaviors carry much more weight in final impressions than do their later ones. One explanation for this phenomenon is an assimilation effect: the early behaviors guide the perceiver's attention to later behaviors that are consistent with the early ones, while inconsistent behaviors are either unnoticed or discounted. In naturalistic interactions, the behaviors that are first to receive attention may often be those strongly associated with the actor's physical appearance. Once physical appearance has drawn attention to particular behaviors, primacy effects may reinforce the tendency for such behaviors to receive more attention than others.

First impressions may not only guide the perceiver's attention to later behaviors that are consistent with them, but they may also influence the perceiver's memory for a person's behavior. For example, Lingle and Ostrom (1979) had subjects form an impression of a stimulus person on one attribute while exposed to information about the person's behavior. Subjects then made a second judgment about the same person on a different attribute based upon their memory of the behavioral information. These memory-based judgments reflected not the actual behavioral information, but rather subjects' memory for their initial impression combined with a selective memory search for negative stimulus information. Similarly, Lingle, Geva, Ostrom, Leippe, and Baumgardner (1979) have demonstrated that what perceivers infer and remember about a stimulus person tends to be congruent with the theme that was salient when that person's behavior was initially considered. Once a person's physical appearance draws attention to behaviors that yield a particular impression, then this impression may become functionally autonomous, influencing the ascription of other attributes even more than the person's actual behavior. Halo effects and implicit personality theories are likely to govern the inference from attribute to attribute.

Halo Effects. It has been demonstrated in a number of experiments that the valence of perceptions of a stimulus person on one attribute generalizes to other, apparently unrelated, attributes. For example, the finding that people's impressions of attractive people are much more positive than their impressions of unattractive people on a variety of evaluative dimensions (Bersheid & Walster, 1974), may reflect a spreading of affect from the positive attribute "beauty" to other attributes. Similarly one might expect a spreading of negative affect from particular unattractive physical attributes to other, unrelated attributes. One might also expect a spreading of affect from that psychological attribute which is associatively linked to a physical attribute to other psychological attributes. Thus people whose physical appearance is associatively linked to a negative trait may be negatively evaluated on a number of other traits, while people whose physical appearance is associatively linked to a particular positive trait may be positively evaluated on a number of other traits.

Implicit Personality Theories. While halo effects may play a significant role in the elaboration of stereotypes, it must be granted that stereotypes are typically more differentiated than one would expect if such effects completely governed the generalization from one component to others. People who are evaluated negatively on one trait are not evaluated negatively on all others, and implicit personality theories may account for this specificity. Bruner and Tagiuri (1954) introduced the term *naive, implicit personality theories* to describe perceiver's assumptions regarding the relationship among various traits. Each person has a commonsense notion that particular traits go with each other, and it turns out that these naive theories are widely shared. [See Schneider (1973) for a review of the literature on this topic.] Thus most people, knowing that a particular person is, for example, intelligent, would expect the person to also be relatively clever and efficient, while the trait of intelligence may not influence expectancies regarding the person's social behaviors. Evidence for such a specificity has been provided by Zanna and Hamilton (1972), who showed that describing a person as warm or cold influenced inferences about that person's other social traits but had no impact on inferences about the person's intellectual traits. On the other hand, describing a person as industrious or lazy influenced inferences about the person's intellectually relevant traits, but not socially relevant ones. Extrapolating to the realm of stereotypes about physically distinctive people, one would expect that the associative links between eyeglasses and intelligence would produce the stereotype that people who wear glasses are not only intelligent, but also industrious, another intellectual trait, but would not influence inferences about the person's social traits. Research has shown this to be true (Thornton, 1943, 1944), and the particular constellation of traits ascribed to other physically distinctive groups may reflect similar effects of implicit personality theories.

Summary and Implications

Most analyses of stereotyping attribute their specific content to some "kernel of truth," and thus tend to blame the victims of stereotyping for the way they are viewed. The present analysis, on the other hand, suggests that the "kernel of truth" may often be in the eyes of the perceiver. Through function, metaphor, or temporal extension, perceivers may associate a particular physical feature with particular psychological attributes, and these associations together with other cognitive mechanisms can yield full-blown stereotypes. More specifically, *illusory correlation* effects may cause perceivers to overestimate or overweight the behaviors that reflect the associatively linked attribute, particularly for actors whose physical appearance draws attention. *Primacy* effects may both reinforce the perceivers' tendency to selectively attend to behaviors manifesting the associatively linked attribute and also influence perceivers to ascribe other attributes that are suggested more by their first impression than by the actor's actual behavior. *Halo* effects may cause perceivers to ascribe other attributes of the same valence as the associatively linked ones. Finally, *implicit personality theories* may direct these ascriptions toward attributes of a similar meaning.

BLAMING THE VICTIM

As noted above, "kernel of truth" explanations for the specific content of stereotypes blame the victims of stereotyping for the way they are viewed. Stereotyped groups also tend to be held responsible for the discriminatory behaviors directed toward them (e.g., Ryan, 1971). This "blaming the victim" has been explained in terms of the perceiver's needs and motives, such as the need to perceive a just world (Lerner, 1970) or the need to justify one's own behavior (Walster, Berscheid, & Walster, 1970). However, selective attention provides a nonmotivational alternative to these explanations. Considerable research demonstrates that stimuli that are attended are more likely to be perceived as causal than those that are not. This phenomenon was initially observed in the realm of object perception where Koffka (1935, p. 283) argued that "fixation of one of two equivalent objects tends to make it the carrier of motion, whether it moves objectively or not." More recently it has been found that those stimuli that are attended by perceivers of a social interaction also tend to be seen as causal. Since it has been demonstrated that perceivers focus more attention upon those whose appearance is novel, selective attention may thus account for the tendency to blame physically distinctive victims for the discriminatory treatment they receive.

Causal Attribution to Salient Stimuli

Direct evidence for the role of attention in perceptions of social causality was first reported by Storms (1973), who tested Jones and Nisbett's (1972) proposition that actor-observer differences in causal attributions are at least partly due to differences in attentional focus. According to Jones and Nisbett, observers attribute an actor's behavior to his or her own disposition because their attention is focused on the actor, who is salient or "figural" against the ground of the situation. Actors, on the other hand, attribute their own behavior to situational causes because they attend to their environment, which, for them, is salient or figural. Consistent with this argument, Storms found that when observers' attention was focused onto the actor's environment by showing them a videotape of the environment as the actor sees it, the observers attributed the actor's behavior more to situational causes than when their attention was not refocused onto the actor's situation.[3]

Other research has varied the degree to which perceivers attend to an actor vs the actor's environment by manipulating the stimulus characteristics of each rather than by manipulating their physical availability as Storms did. For example, McArthur and Post (1977) conducted a series of five experiments in which the attention-drawing stimuli in an actor's environment consisted of other people. The results revealed that, when an actor's environment—i.e., another actor—drew perceivers' attention, they made more situational attributions for the actor's behavior during a getting-acquainted conversation than when it did not. More specifically, when an actor conversed with someone who was brightly lit, moving, wearing a striped shirt, or who formed a "unit" in Gestalt terms with others present, then the actor's behavior was attributed more to situational causes than when he or she conversed with someone who was dimly lit, stationary, wearing a grey shirt, or who did not form a "unit" with others present.

The impact of unit formation in the foregoing studies has particular relevance for causal attribution to people who are members of some salient category of people. In one study, an actor's behavior was attributed more to situational causes when the "situation" contained three people who formed a perceptual "unit" by virtue of being like-sexed and opposite in sex to the actor than when the situation contained a sexually integrated group. Similarly, a study by Taylor et al. (1976) found a slight tendency for perceivers to make more situational attributions for the behavior of an actor who was a different race from a unit of five others. Evidence that these effects derive from selective attention to people who are members of a salient category rather than from existing racial or sexual stereotypes is provided by a third study, which found the identical effects employing a manipulation of unit formation that has no stereotypic associations. Perceivers attributed an actor's behavior more to situational factors when his situation contained a unit of three people wearing the same color shirt than when it contained people whose shirts varied in color (McArthur & Post, 1977).

Causal Attribution to a Salient Victim

The foregoing evidence reveals that when people interact with someone who draws attention by virtue of clothing, movement, or association with a physically salient group, then their behavior tends to be attributed more to situational causes than when they interact with someone who draws less attention. To extrapolate from this evidence to the phenomenon of blaming the victim requires two assumptions: (1) the increase in situational attribution when actors interact with salient

[3]Although a complementary trend for dispositional attributions was obtained, reflecting somewhat greater dispositional attribution when attention was focused on the actor than when it was focused on the situation, dispositional attributions were not significant in this study or in any of the others reported here. See McArthur (1981b) for a further discussion of this lack of significance.

people is really an increase in attribution to causes in these salient people, and (2) the tendency to perceive salient people as causing an actor's behavior in an innocuous getting-acquainted conversation will generalize to situations in which there is a salient *victim*.

Research by McArthur and Solomon (1978) explicitly tested both of these assumptions. The typical "getting-acquainted" conversation was replaced with a heated discussion about the outcome of a bridge hand between two partners, one of whom emerged as an aggressor and the other as a victim. As noted above, attention to the victim was manipulated by means of a statistically novel attribute: a leg brace or red hair. After watching this interaction, subjects were asked to what extent each of three factors had caused the aggressor's behavior: the aggressor's own personality, the situation, and the behavior and personality of the partner (i.e. the victim). The expectation that the aggressor's domineering, unfriendly, and irritable behavior would be attributed more to causes in the victim when attention was drawn to the victim was confirmed both for the leg brace and for the hair color manipulation of attention. Interestingly, the "partner attribution" measure seems to have usurped any effects of attention on the less specific situational attribution measure for, unlike past research in which there was no partner attribution measure, the situational attribution measure revealed no effect.

It is important to note that the parallel effects for the red hair and the leg brace salience manipulations in the McArthur and Solomon (1978) study rule out certain explanations for the tendency to blame a salient victim of aggression more than a nonsalient one. For example, one might suggest that the need to perceive a just world is particularly violated when perceivers observe a crippled person being victimized, and results in defensive blaming of the crippled victim to restore equity. But it does not seem reasonable to suggest that the need to perceive a just world is more strongly violated when the victim has red hair than when her hair color is not salient. Similarly, the tendency to place more blame upon a salient victim cannot be readily explained in terms of preexisting negative stereotypes about the salient victims. For one thing, it requires quite a stretch of the imagination to generate overlapping stereotypes of crippled people and redheads. More importantly, ratings of the victim's behavior were not significantly correlated with the tendency to attribute the aggressor's behavior to her. This suggests that the tendency to attribute causality to salient people has a different mediation than the tendency to form more polarized impressions of them.

Summary and Implications

The tendency to "blame victims" such as blacks, the aged, and other physically distinctive groups for the discrimination they endure has typically been attributed to the perceiver's needs and motives. However, the evidence reviewed here suggests that this effect may reflect a general tendency to attribute causality to salient stimuli. The finding that blaming of a salient victim can be demonstrated for a novel physical attribute as inconsequential as red hair strengthens the argument for an attentional mediation of this effect. It also suggests that the impact of physical appearance on causal attributions may be very widespread: one would also expect more blaming of victims who deviate from the norm on any number of physical attributes such as height, weight, age, and ethnicity. On the other hand, when such distinctive individuals are the recipients of kind behavior, they should be perceived as more deserving or needy than more physically ordinary people.

There is another possible influence of selective attention upon causal attributions to physically distinctive people that merits investigation. This is associative links between particular events and physical appearance. For example, Heider (1954, p. 7) suggested that "A crime can be blamed on a person because of physical similarity; he looks as if he could have committed this crime." Associations to a person's physical appearance based upon function, metaphor, or temporal extension may each contribute to this type of effect. Thus juries may be more apt to attribute a violent crime to a scarred defendant, by virtue of functional associations between a scar and violent behavior. Or they may be more likely to attribute a violent crime to a red-haired defendant by virtue of metaphorical associations between the color red and volatile behavior. Similarly, they may be less apt to attribute a negligent crime to a thin-lipped defendent by virtue of associations between thin lips and conscientious behavior derived from temporal extension.

MEDIATION OF SELECTIVE ATTENTION EFFECTS

It has been argued that the tendency for physically distinctive people to attract attention together with the tendency for their negative, extreme, and/or associatively linked behaviors to attract attention can account for the extremity, negativity, and specific quality of stereotypes about these groups, as well as for the tendency to blame them for the discrimination they endure. However, to fully understand the role of selective attention in stereotype formation requires some understanding of the mediation of these effects.

As noted earlier, selective attention may be manifested in the preferential registration, encoding, and/or recall of information about salient stimuli. The question to be considered in this section is which of these effects mediates the tendency to form stereotyped impressions of physically salient people and to attribute causality to them. The plausibility of the following specific mediators will be evaluated: (1) more total, available, or relevant *recall* of information about salient than nonsalient stimuli; (2) differential *registration* of information about salient and nonsalient stimuli; (3) more *classically conditioned affect* to salient than nonsalient stimuli (an encoding effect); and (4) more *thinking* about salient than nonsalient stimuli (also an encoding effect). In considering these possibilities it should be borne in mind that the impact of selective attention upon stereotyped impressions, and its impact upon causal attributions may be differently mediated.

Recall

Total Recall. The existing research literature provides little evidence that the effects of selective attention upon impressions or causal attributions are mediated by the total amount of information recalled about salient and nonsalient people. Although there is evidence for greater recall of information about salient persons, there are also a large number of studies in which manipulations of attention have influenced perceivers' impressions and causal attributions without producing any greater recall of the salient person's behaviors. Moreover, measures of total recall have typically been uncorrelated with impressions and causal attributions, even when all are similarly influenced by a salience manipulation. The lack of evidence for total recall as a mediator holds both for measures of verbal recall and for measures of visual recall, although the latter do seem to be more sensitive to the manipulations of visual salience employed in the existing research [see McArthur (1981b), Taylor and Fiske (1978), and Fiske, Kenny, and Taylor (1979) for reviews of this literature].

Available Recall. The failure to find consistent differences in the quantity of information recalled about salient and nonsalient people led Taylor and Fiske (1978) to suggest that it may be greater "availability" of information about a salient actor—i.e., a greater ease of recall (Tversky & Kahneman, 1973)—rather than a greater volume of recall, which mediates the effects of selective attention on social perceptions. However, some recent research by Fiske et al. (1979) has failed to find support for this mediation. Although subjects attributed more causality to a salient than to a nonsalient actor, the amount of visual information they were able to quickly recall (an index of its availability) was nonsignificantly greater for the nonsalient actor. This result renders implausible greater availability of visual information about salient people as a mediator of the causal attribution effects. However, further research is needed before ruling out availability of visual information as a mediator of the impression effects, since these were not examined by Fiske et al. (1979).

While the availability of verbal (as opposed to visual) information about salient and nonsalient people has not been explicitly investigated, this too seems an unlikely mediator of selective attention effects. Taylor, Crocker, Fiske, Sprinzen, and Winkler (1979) conducted a study in which some perceivers were so distracted during their observation of a conversation between two actors that they recalled virtually nothing of the conversation. Yet there was more causal attribution to the salient actor as well as more extreme evaluations of his behavior, effects which could not have been mediated by the differential availability to perceivers of verbal information.

Relevant Recall. In addition to the possibility that differential availability of information about salient people may mediate the impact of selective attention upon impressions and attributions, it has been suggested that a tendency to recall particular information about these people may mediate the effects. For example, McArthur (1981b) suggested that perceivers may show preferential recall of information about salient persons that is *relevant* to the impressions and/or attributions.

Since impressions of physically salient people tend to be overly influenced by their most salient (e.g., extreme, negative, associatively linked) behaviors, a relevant recall mediation would predict that perceivers will show preferential recall of a salient person's salient behaviors. However, the research findings pertinent to this hypothesis are mixed. On the one hand, Hamilton and Gifford (1976) did find recall effects paralleling the impression effects: more of the salient behaviors were attributed to the salient people. However, no intercorrelations between these recall data and the impression data were reported. Moreover, even if there were positive correlations, they would not necessarily reflect an impact of recall upon impressions. The relationship could just as well go the other way with impressions influencing recall, since the recall measure in this study did not tap the degree to which subjects *accurately* recalled a salient person's salient behaviors, but rather tapped the number of salient behaviors attributed to salient people, regardless of accuracy.

Although Hamilton and Gifford's (1976) data do not provide conclusive evidence, they are at least consistent with the hypothesis that greater recall of a salient actor's salient behaviors mediates the tendency for these behaviors to exert a stronger impact upon impressions. Also consistent with this hypothesis are the related findings of Rothbart, Fulero, Jensen, Howard, and Birrell (1978). On the other hand, a series of studies by McArthur and Friedman (1980) found that, while evaluations of salient people were most strongly influenced by their salient behaviors, the number of salient and nonsalient behaviors attributed to these people rarely showed significant effects paralleling the impression data. In addition, the correlations between perceivers' impressions and the number of salient behaviors recalled were typically not significant. A similar independence of impressions and recall of salient behaviors has been reported by other authors (e.g., Chapman & Chapman, 1967; Dreben, Fiske, & Hastie, 1979).

Given the mixed evidence regarding preferential recall of salient behaviors as a mediator of the tendency to form stereotyped impressions of salient people, further research on this topic is needed. Moreover, such research would benefit from the application of the causal modeling approach employed by Fiske et al. (1979) to test the hypothesis that relevant recall mediates the tendency to attribute *causality* to salient people. This research revealed that subjects not only attributed more causality to a salient than to a nonsalient actor, but also that they recalled more visual and verbal information, which they designated as relevant positive evidence for the causal influence of the salient actor. What is more, a structural model employing relevant recall as a mediator fit the causal attribution data better than an unmediated model. While these data are suggestive, preferential recall of information relevant to the causal influence of salient people may be an epiphenomenon rather than a true explanation for the tendency to attribute causality to these people. Relevant recall lacks the quality of a true explanation insofar as the question remains as to why subjects recall more causally relevant information about salient actors. Is it just that they tend to recall more information in general, and it is this subset of recalled information that mediates the causal attribution effects? Or do subjects for some reason focus more attention on evidence for the salient person's causal role?

Registration

The tendency to recall more information relevant to a salient person's causal role may derive from the perceptual organization of the interaction at the time it is registered. In the context of a dynamic social interaction, each person's behavior is typically both cause and effect: Each person reacts to the other, and that reaction causes a reaction in the other. The power of certain stimuli to draw attention may cause the perceiver to organize this interaction chain in terms of the salient person's influence on the nonsalient person, rather than vice versa. For example, in Figure 1 the behavioral exchanges tend to be perceptually organized into units reflecting the causal influence of the salient actor on the nonsalient actor rather than into units reflecting the causal influence of the nonsalient actor on the salient actor, regardless of who actually begins the interaction. As a consequence, the salient actor may be seen as exerting more causal influence than the nonsalient actor even though their actual influence is equal, and this perceptual organization may induce more recall of information relevant to the salient person's causal role.

While attention-drawing stimuli have been shown to affect perceptual organization (e.g., Newtson, 1976; Newtson, Rindner, Miller, & LaCross, 1978), no research has sytematically assessed the perceptual organization of events in a dyadic interaction as a function of the

FIGURE 1. Segmentation of a dyadic interaction into causal influence units as a function of the salience of each member of the dyad. O= = = =o is the causal influence of the salient actor on the nonsalient actor. o – – – –O is the causal influence of the nonsalient actor on the salient actor.

0= = = =o– – – –0= = = =o– – – –0= = = =o– – – –0= = = =o– – – –0

o– – – –0= = = =o– – – –0= = = =o– – – –0= = = =o– – – –0= = = =o physical salience of the actors. However, Watzlawick, Reavin, and Jackson's (1967) discussion of the role of perceptual "punctuation" in interpersonal conflicts does provide some anecdotal evidence that an actor's salience influences both perceptual organization and causal attributions. Their examples suggest, for instance, that in an interaction sequence marked by a lawyer badgering and a witness withdrawing, the lawyer will tend to organize the events as a series of "withdraw – badger" pairs, and perceive his badgering as being caused by the recalcitrant witness. The witness, on the other hand, will organize the same events as a series of "badger – withdraw" pairs and perceive his withdrawal as being caused by the overbearing lawyer. It seems reasonable to suggest that these divergent perceptual organizations derive, at least in part, from the tendency for another person's behavior to be more salient than one's own (see Jones & Nisbett, 1972; Storms, 1973). If this explanation is correct, then one would expect an outside observer of the dyad to organize each interchange as initiated by whichever of the two actors is most salient and thereby to attribute causality to the salient actor. Thus, for example, if the witness is obese, or handicapped, or in some other way physically distinctive, an outside observer would be most apt to organize the interchange as a series of "withdraw – badger" pairs and to attribute causality to the witness. Given the plausibility of this extrapolation from Watzlawick et al.'s (1967) anecdotal data, it would seem worthwhile to conduct more systematic research assessing the hypothesis that salient people are perceived as more causal because their interactions with others are registered in units which capture the impact of the salient person on a nonsalient person rather than vice versa.

Preferential registration of salient stimuli may yield stereotyped impressions of physically distinctive people in addition to yielding causal attributions to such individuals. As noted earlier, perceivers manifest greater visual fixation of salient persons and behaviors than nonsalient ones. This tendency could result in a failure to register information which would counter the stereotype that salient behaviors are representative of salient persons. [See McArthur (1981b) for a more extended discussion.]

Classical Conditioning

In Berlyne's (1970) discussion of selective attention, he argued that responses to a stimulus array may become more strongly associated with salient than nonsalient stimuli. Such a classical conditioning effect provides a plausible mediation for the impact of selective attention upon evaluative impressions. As argued earlier, the most salient stimuli in a social interaction will be the physically distinctive actors' extreme or negative or associatively linked behaviors. If the perceiver's affective responses are most strongly conditioned to these behaviors, then physically salient people will evoke stronger feelings in the perceiver, the nature of which will depend upon the behaviors that have been most salient. If, for example, actors have manifested aggressive behavior, the salient actor should evoke more fear. If they have manifested incompetent behavior, the salient actor should evoke more disdain. If they have manifested altruistic behavior, the salient actor should evoke more admiration. This classically conditioned affect would be expressed in more stereotyped evaluations of the salient actor, that is, evaluations that are more influenced by the extreme, negative, or associatively linked behaviors.

Although a classical conditioning mediation has no direct supporting evidence, research on animal learning has demonstrated stronger conditioning to salient than nonsalient components of a complex stimulus array (e.g., Rescorla & Wagner, 1972). Moreover, the affective conditioning mediation is compatible with several patterns of results in the existing data. For example, it is consistent with the finding that attentional manipulations have more impact upon impressions when perceivers are exposed to affectively toned interactions than when they are exposed to banal getting-acquainted conversations. It is also compatible with the finding that relevant recall about attention-drawing people and behaviors is often independent of evaluative responses, since divergent affective associations could influence perceiver's impressions of stimulus persons independently of their explicit recall of those persons' behavior. Such an effect would be consistent with Zajonc's (1980) distinction between affective and cognitive judgments.

The hypothesis that the impact of selective attention upon evaluative impressions is mediated by classical conditioning would seem to merit an explicit test. One would expect perceivers to manifest more emotional reactivity to the ongoing behavior of a salient actor, as well as a stronger classically conditioned emotional response to the salient actor after the behavior has terminated.

Thinking

While stronger affective reactions to a salient actor's behaviors could result from classical conditioning effects, there is another possible mediation for such reactions. According to Tesser (1978), thought polarizes affect. More specifically, Tesser has supplied considerable evidence to support the argument that thinking about an object causes beliefs about it to be assimilated to the perceivers' relevant schema, and that this produces a more evaluatively consistent set of beliefs, which serves to polarize feelings. It seems reasonable to suggest that perceivers will typically think more about the behavior of those who draw attention than they will about the behavior of those who do not—certainly while the behavior is ongoing, and perhaps afterward as well. If so, then the tendency for selective attention to polarize evaluative impressions could be subsumed by Tesser's analysis of the impact of thought on attitudes. Tesser's analysis may prove capable of accounting not only for more polarized evaluations of physically distinctive people, but also for the direction in which these evaluations become polarized. Tesser's data suggest that the direction of polarization depends upon the particular cognitive schema that perceivers tune in when thinking about a person. Among those factors that can activate a particular schema are the initially salient aspects of the stimulus person's behavior. These, we have seen, may depend upon negativity, extremity, and associative links to the stimulus person's physical appearance.

While more thinking about physically distinctive people seems like a plausible mediator of the tendency to form stereotyped impressions of them, there are some data that may argue against this mediation. The distraction manipulation employed in the earlier mentioned study by Taylor et al. (1979) can be viewed as preventing perceivers from thinking about the social interaction which they are viewing. Consistent with Tesser's theory, distracted perceivers rated both actors less extremely than those who were not distracted. However, the tendency to rate the salient actor more extremely than the nonsalient actor was not significantly reduced among distracted perceivers. Since the distraction manipulation should have prevented perceivers from thinking about either actor, this finding throws into question the viability of the argument that the effects of selective attention are mediated by more thought about salient stimuli. However, they do not provide conclusive counterevidence, since perceivers may have spent more time thinking about the salient actor after the distracting task was over. Although Taylor et al. (1979) did attempt to prevent such thinking by a second manipulation that distracted some subjects while they were rating the actors, this distraction manipulation was not totally successful.

Since it is difficult to devise experimental manipulations that totally foreclose thinking, a simpler test of the hypothesis that more thinking about physically salient people produces more stereotyped evaluations of them would be to increase, rather than to preclude, the thinking of some subjects. Consistent with this approach, another study by Taylor et al. (1979) has compared perceivers' evaluations of salient and nonsalient actors immediately after observing them and after a delay of an hour or a day. While evaluations of the salient actor were more polarized than those of the nonsalient actor, this effect did not increase in the delay conditions, where more thinking about the actors was possible. It is important to note, however, that this research was not designed to test Tesser's hypothesis, and perceivers in the delay conditions were not explicitly instructed to think about the interaction. If they had been so instructed, the delay might have augmented the salience effects. Thus, while these findings do not support Tesser's analysis, neither do they provide conclusive evidence against thought as the mediator of selective attention effects.

Summary and Implications

While the existing data suggest greater recall of information relevant to a salient person's causal role as a possible mediator of the tendency to attribute causality to salient people, further research is needed to determine exactly why perceivers show this pattern of recall. More specifically, it needs to be determined whether it is a by-product of greater recall about salient people in general or whether it derives from the perceptual organization of the interchange between a salient and nonsalient actor.

More recall or registration of salient people's salient behaviors, more thinking about these behaviors, and stronger classical conditioning to these behaviors are all possible mediators of the tendency to form extreme, negative, or specific impressions of those who are physically distinctive. While recall, registration, thinking, and classical conditioning effects are not mutually exclusive, research should be designed to ascertain whether or not one or another is sufficient to produce stereotypic impressions of salient people. For example, it should be determined whether polarized evaluations of salient people will occur even when perceivers are prevented from thinking about them or recalling what they did. Recent research on mere exposure effects suggests that this would indeed occur, since increased exposure to a stimulus polarizes evaluations of it even when the experimental procedure renders subjects unable to recognize the stimuli to which they have been frequently exposed (Moreland & Zajonc, 1979).

THE PERPETUATION OF STEREOTYPES

In the first section of this chapter it has been argued that stereotypes may originate from a number of basic perceptual-cognitive processes, namely, the tendency to categorize people on the basis of their physical appearance, the tendency to pay more attention to people in salient than nonsalient categories, the tendency to pay more attention to negative or extreme behaviors than to positive or moderate ones, and the tendency to pay more attention to behaviors associatively linked to a person's physical appearance than to those not so linked. It is important to bear in mind, however, that stereotypes are often directly taught by the culture—television, books, parents, and peers all provide direct or indirect information about culturally shared stereotypes of particular categories of people. Thus, although perceptual-cognitive processes can account for the formation of stereotypes, they certainly do not stand alone. Interestingly, however, each of these processes can aid in the perpetuation of stereotypes that have been acquired from some cultural source.

CATEGORIZATION

Not only is it true that people may be categorized according to a physical attribute with consequent assimilation and contrast effects when there are no cultural stereotypes pertaining to that attribute, but also placing people into categories that are associated with well-known stereotypes causes perceptions of those people to be assimilated to the stereotype.

For example, Secord, Bevan, and Katz (1956) found that identifying a photograph as a member of the category "Negro" was sufficient to yield the full Negro stereotype even when the photograph was sufficiently ambiguous that if it had been viewed alone it may not even have been recognized as a Negro. More recent research (Taylor et al., 1978; Robinson & McArthur, 1981) has found that categorizing a stimulus person by sex is also sufficient to elicit sexual stereotypes. These studies presented subjects with actual behavior by stimulus persons who, through a methodological ruse, could be categorized either as males or as females. When a stimulus person was categorized as a male, he was rated as more influential, more confident, more analytic, more negative, less warm, and less sensitive than when categorized as a female even though the actual behavior was identical in the two cases. In short, perceptions of the stimulus persons were assimilated to the stereotype of the sex in which they were categorized. Assimilation of behavior to an ethnic stereotype was demonstrated by Tajfel, Sheikh, and Gardner (1964) who had subjects rate the behavior of two Canadians and two Indians after watching each of them participate in an interview. The results revealed that the two Indians were rated more similarly to each other and to other Indians on traits that were part of the Indian stereotype than on traits not included in the stereotype.

Other evidence for the impact of categorization upon behavioral evaluations comes from research in which categorization or labeling is based on a psychological rather than a physical attribute. For example, Langer and Abelson (1974) found that traditional therapists evaluated a person in a tape-recorded interview as more disturbed when he had been categorized as a mental patient than when he had been categorized as a job applicant; that is, perceptions of his behavior were assimilated to the stereotype of a mental patient. Similarly, Cohen (1977) found that people categorized according to their occupation were perceived to possess attributes stereotypically associated with that occupation. Gurwitz and Dodge (1977) found that someone categorized as a sorority member was perceived to possess attributes stereotypically associated with sorority girls, even though her sorority sisters were not described in stereotyped terms. Cantor and Mischel (1977) found that categorizing someone as an introvert or as an extravert increased subjects' confidence that the person had manifested behaviors that were culturally associated with the category into which the person had been placed.

The foregoing research evidence provides strong support for Bruner's (1957) suggestion that the properties perceived in a given stimulus depend upon how that stimulus is categorized. People organize information about others by categorizing them and imputing similar attributes to all of those in a given category. When a category is associated with culturally held stereotypes, perceptions of the people who are placed in it will be assimilated to the stereotype. The question remains as to how categorization produces these effects upon perception. One possibility is that categorization causes perceivers to selectively attend to those behaviors that are consistent with the categorical stereotype. Evidence for such a mediation is provided by research demonstrating the impact of perceivers' expectations upon perception.

SELECTIVE ATTENTION

In the first section of this chapter, it was argued that the inherent or contextual salience of an actor's appearance or behavior influences a perceiver's attentional focus and thereby contributes to the formation of stereotypes. Perceivers' attentional focus may be also influenced by culturally taught expectations. More specifically, perceivers may selectively attend to those behaviors that cultural stereotypes have taught them to expect to be associated with a particular category of people. The consequences of such selective attention for impression formation will be the same as those elaborated earlier in the section on the role of associative connections in stereotype formation. The only difference is that the associative connections considered here are culturally taught and should therefore be viewed as influencing the *perpetuation* of stereotypes rather than their formation.

Expecting is Believing

Considerable research has shown that perceivers' impressions of a stimulus person do move in the direction of what they expect to observe. For example, Kelley (1950) found that students' impressions of a lecturer were much more favorable when they expected him to be "warm" than when they expected him to be "cold." More recently, Snyder and Frankel (1976) found that subjects who expected an interviewee to be upset and uncomfortable because they thought the topic of conversation was sex rated the interviewee as more upset and uncomfortable than those who thought the topic of conversation was politics.

In addition to the evidence that impressions of a stimulus person are assimilated to a perceiver's expectations, there is research that demonstrates that the direction in which impressions become polarized with increased attention to a stimulus person is also influenced by the perceiver's expectations. Such effects were demonstrated for expectations derived from cultural stereotypes about particular categories of people in a series of studies by McArthur and Friedman (1980). These authors tested the generalizability of Hamilton and Gifford's (1976) illusory correlation findings to a situation in which the behaviors that are salient for a salient group of people could be influenced both by culturally derived expectations for a particular demographic group as well as by the behavior's infrequency within the stimulus materials (i.e., novelty).

Consistent with Hamilton and Gifford's (1976) findings, when older people, black people, or females (rated by males) were a distinctive minority, impressions of them moved in the direction of their undesirable behaviors, which were distinctive by virtue of both manipulated infrequency and cultural stereotypes of these groups [see Bennett & Eckman (1973), Brigham (1971), and Broverman, Broverman, Clarkson, Rosenkrantz, and Vogel (1970) for documentation of such stereotypes]. On the other hand, when younger people, white people, or people of the same sex as the subjects were in the minority, impressions of them moved in the direction of their desirable behaviors. Since the desirable behaviors were not infrequent, these latter illusory correlation effects represent a departure from Hamilton and Gifford's shared infrequency effect. More specifically, when a known demographic group is distinctive by virtue of infrequent appearance, impressions are polarized in the direction of those behaviors that are salient by virtue of cultural stereotypes of the group rather than in the direction of those behaviors that are salient by virtue of their infrequency.

The results of a study by Eisen and McArthur (1979) provide further evidence that culturally induced expectations can influence the direction in which evaluations of a salient person will be polarized. Perceivers who expected to watch a videotaped trial and to determine the guilt of the defendant rated him as more responsible for the crime than those who expected to watch a social interaction and to form an impression of someone. Moreover, given a trial set, the more time the defendant appeared on camera, the more negatively he was evaluated, while, given an impression set, the more visibly salient the defendant, the more positively he was evaluated. This differential impact of attention upon impressions of the defendant in the two expectancy conditions may be explained in terms of the information that perceivers were set to process. A trial set predisposed them to focus on criminal responsibility in the defendant's behavior on the night of the crime; the more they saw of him, the more negative information they seem to have discovered, which is consistent with the fact that the trial testimony was designed to produce a guilty verdict. An impression set, on the other hand, predisposed subjects to focus on personality dispositions in the defendant's courtroom behavior; the more they saw of him, the more positive information they seem to have discovered, which is consistent with the fact that the defendant's background and demeanor painted him in a relatively positive light.

Contrast Effects

A paradox, which may have become obvious to the reader, needs to be addressed. The foregoing argument that expected behaviors draw the perceiver's attention conflicts with the earlier argument that novel behaviors do so. After all, one form of novelty is deviation from expectation. The question is, when will the "novel" act draw the perceiver's attention, and when will the "expected" act do so?

Werner (1924) has argued that assimilation effects in object perception appear when the difference between elements is small, contrast when it is great. Similar effects may occur within the realm of person perception. When behaviors are either ambiguous or not too discrepant from expectations, perceivers may show an assimilation effect, noticing what they expect to find and paying less attention to behaviors that do not fit their expectations. But, when an actor's behavior includes some that clearly fall outside of this range of assimilation (Sherif & Hovland, 1961), then perceivers' attention may be drawn more to the highly discrepant "novel" behaviors than to the expected ones. An example of behaviors that clearly fall outside of the range of expected ones is provided in the well known submariner-astronaut study (Jones, Davis, & Gergen, 1961) in which unexpected out-of-role behavior exerted a stronger influence upon impressions than expected in-role behaviors. This "contrast" effect can be attributed to the greater perceptual salience of the unexpected behaviors. However, one would expect it to be replaced with an effect of "assimilation to expectancies" if the behaviors manifested either did not deviate so much from expectancies or were rather ambiguous. Since behaviors in the real world are usually ambiguous, it seems reasonable to argue that impressions manifesting an assimilation to expectancy will be more commonplace than contrast effects. The ascendance of expectancy over novelty effects in the McArthur and Friedman (1980) research is consistent with this argument.

The Mediation of Expectancy Effects

The question of how selective attention to expected behaviors produces the foregoing effects upon impressions admits the same possible answers as those suggested in the earlier discussion of mediation. Preferential attention to expected behaviors may cause these behaviors to be better recalled; it may cause them to be more strongly conditioned to the perceiver's affective responses; it may cause the perceiver to think about them more; and/or it may alter the perceptual organization of a behavioral sequence.

Considerable evidence for greater recall of expected behaviors has been reported. For example, Zadny and Gerard (1974) found that labeling a stimulus person as a "music major" produced more recall of his music-related activities than did labeling him as either a "psychology" or a "chemistry" major, in which case there was more recall of his psychology and chemistry related activities, respectively. In a second study, these authors also found that labeling a social interaction as a "burglary" yielded more recall of the actors' potentially theft-related activities than did labeling it as "two people waiting for friends." Similarly, a series of studies by Hamilton and Rose (1980) demonstrated that traits expected on the basis of stereotypes about particular occupational groups were recalled as describing those groups more often than other types of traits and more often than other groups, even though the actual frequency of descriptions did not differ. Likewise, Rothbart, Evans, and Fulero (1979) found that when a group of people was expected to be intellectual or friendly, there was superior recall and higher frequency estimates for behaviors confirming the stereotype than for those contradictory or irrelevant to it.

Despite the considerable evidence to support the argument that perceivers' expectations influence their recall of information, there is also evidence that indicates that preferential recall of information consistent with expectations is not a necessary mediator of that information's greater impact upon impressions. For example, as noted earlier, although McArthur and Friedman (1980) found that impressions of people from a particular demographic group moved in the direction of the behaviors expected for that group when they were a salient minority, recall of behaviors typically showed no significant salience effects. Also, correlations between the number of positive or negative behaviors recalled and the positivity of impressions were typically not significant. Thus perceivers' impressions seem to weight expected behaviors more heavily than unexpected ones, even when both are equally recalled. This preferential weighting may result from stronger links between expected behaviors and the perceiver's affective responses, from more thinking about the expected behaviors, and/or from a perceptual organization of events in which expected behaviors are perceived as self-initiated causes, while unexpected ones are perceived as reactive effects (e.g., Regan, Straus, & Fazio, 1974).

Whatever the mediation of expectancy effects proves to be, it is worth noting that these effects seem to operate more reliably during the registration or encoding of information than during its recall. Many studies investigating the impact of expectancies upon impressions and recall, when they are given either before or after exposure to a stimulus person, have obtained no significant expectancy effects in the after condition (e.g., Massad, Hubbard, & Newtson, 1979; Snyder & Frankel, 1976; Zadny & Gerard, 1974; Enquist, Newtson, & LaCross, 1978), although there are some exceptions (Snyder & Cantor, 1979; Snyder & Uranowitz, 1978). It should also be noted that the preferential registration or encoding of expected events seems to be a basic perceptual process, and need not be attributed to any motivation to confirm one's expectations. Thus, for example, research on binocular rivalry has demonstrated that people more readily perceive photographic slides whose content is "expected" by virtue of being drawn from their own culture than slides drawn from an unfamiliar culture (Bagby, 1957). Similarly, people more readily perceive violent photographic slides when such scenes have become expected by virtue of police training than when no such training has occurred (Toch & Schulte, 1961), and they more readily perceive a familiar upright face than an inverted face (Engel, 1956; Hastorf & Myro, 1959).

Summary and Implications

The research reviewed in this section reveals that perceivers' expectations about the behavior of another person tend to be self-confirming. Expected behaviors are preferentially registered, recalled, and or weighted in impressions, and the more perceivers attend to a person from whom they expect certain behaviors, the more confirmatory their impressions become. Both of these effects should make self-confirming expectancies most prevalent when expectations concern the behavior of those who are physically distinctive, such as blacks, the elderly, and other culturally stereotyped groups. Because these physically distinctive people are readily categorized, the tendency for perceivers to selectively attend to expected behaviors should be strongest for them: Categorization, and hence the attention-guiding expectations, will occur before any data inconsistent with expectations can be encoded. Furthermore, because the appearance of physically distinctive people draws attention, the tendency for attention to increase the impact of expectations upon impressions will also operate to make self-confirming expectancies most pronounced for these people.

SELF-FULFILLING PROPHECIES

We have seen that associations between a particular physical appearance and particular behaviors can bias impressions. More specifically, behaviors that are salient by virtue of associations based upon function, metaphor, temporal extension, or cultural teachings exert a greater influence on a perceiver's impressions than do nonsalient behaviors. While a stereotype's "kernel of truth" may thus often be in the eyes of the beholder, it must be acknowledged that it is sometimes to be found in the behavior of the stereotyped. However, a "kernel of truth" explanation for stereotypes may be misleading even in these instances. Considerable research evidence indicates that the traits perceivers associate with a particular physical appearance can influence not only the perceiver's impressions, but also the perceiver's behavior toward people with that appearance. In this manner, the perceiver's associations can produce a true self-fulfilling prophecy effect in which perceivers not only see "the kernel of truth" they expect to see but actually create that kernel of truth.

Behavioral Confirmation

Self-fulfilling prophecy effects have been demonstrated in a variety of settings [see Jones (1977) for a comprehensive review of this literature]. For example, Kelley (1950) found that students expecting a lecturer to be warm tended to elicit more warm interactions with him than did students expecting him to be cold. An even more dramatic demonstration of such a self-fulfilling prophecy effect was provided in a study of teacher expectations (Rosenthal & Jacobsen, 1968). Students whose teacher expected them to be "late bloomers," who would do very well during the school year, actually showed greater improvement in IQ scores than controls.

While considerable controversy has centered on the validity and replicability of the Rosenthal and Jacobsen findings (e.g., Elashoff & Snow, 1971), there have been replications (e.g., Meichenbaum, Bowers, & Ross, 1969; Seaver, 1973). One of these is particularly relevant for expectancy effects involving physically distinctive individuals, since it examined the effects of naturally induced teacher expectancies, both positive and negative (Seaver, 1973). More specifically, it was found that pupils taught by teachers who expected them to do well, by virtue of the fact that their older sibling had done well in that teacher's class, performed better than pupils taught by a different teacher from their older, high performing sibling. Similarly, pupils taught by teachers who expected them to do poorly, as their older sibling had, performed worse than pupils taught by a different teacher than their poorly performing older sibling.

Extrapolating to stereotypes about physically distinctive groups, one would expect, for example, that in a society that stereotypes blacks or females as less intelligent than whites or males, respectively, teacher expectations would correspond to some extent with these stereotypes and may produce the same kind of self-fulfilling prophecy along racial or sexual lines as those observed along family lines by Seaver (1973). Evidence consistent with this argument has been provided in a study by Word, Zanna, and Cooper (1974), which demonstrated that white perceivers manifest differences in nonverbal behaviors toward whites and blacks analogous to those manifested toward late bloomers and controls. What is more, a second study by these authors demonstrated that these differences in behavior toward blacks and whites may elicit behaviors that confirm racial stereotypes. In this study a white interviewer was programmed to treat some white applicants as the blacks had spontaneously been treated in the first study, while treating others the way whites had been treated. Those treated like blacks were judged to perform less adequately and to be more nervous in the interview situation than those treated like the whites. Thus the expectation of poor performance by blacks may yield nonverbal behaviors toward members of that racial category, which serve to fulfill the expectations. Other behaviors likely to affect performance have also been shown to vary with a perceiver's expectations (Hastorf, Northcroft, & Picciotto, 1979; Taylor, 1979).

Another striking example of a self-fulfilling prophecy effect involving members of a physically defined category of people has been provided by Snyder, Tanke, and Berscheid (1977). Male perceivers in this study interacted by telephone with a female stimulus person whom they believed to be physically attractive or physically unattractive as a result of being exposed to bogus photographs of her. The results revealed that men with physically attractive partners expected them to be more sociable, poised, humorous, and socially adept than those with unattractive partners. What is more, these expectations initiated a chain of events which served to confirm them. The men who thought they were interacting with attractive women were rated as being more sociable, sexually warm, interesting, humorous, socially adept, attractive, and enjoying the conversation more and liking their partner more. The women responded in kind. Judges rated the women whom the men thought attractive as more confident, more animated, enjoying the conversation more, and liking their partner more. They also rated these women as more sociable, poised, humorous, and socially adept—all the traits the men expected them to have. Similar effects can be anticipated for social interactions with people of other physically distinctive groups for whom there are stereotyped expectations. Thus, for example peoples' interactions with handicapped persons, the aged, racial minorities, or anyone who is readily categorized on the basis of his or her physical appearance may well elicit the very behavior that is expected on the basis of stereotyped preconceptions.

It is important to note that self-fulfilling prophecy effects do not require that the perceiver have strong expectations regarding the behavior of particular people. Merely entertaining the hypothesis that people from a particular category will behave in a particular manner may suffice to set up a self-fulling prophecy effect. This is due to the fact that people test their hypotheses in a biased manner—a manner more likely to confirm them than not. Evidence for such a process has been reported by Snyder and Swann (1978), who gave perceivers hypotheses about the personal attributes of other individuals and had them plan a series of questions to ask of those people in order to test their hypothesis. What perceivers did was to test their hypotheses by treating the person as if the hypothesis were correct. For example, to test the hypothesis that a person was extraverted, perceivers would ask a question such as "what would you do if you wanted to liven things up at a party?" To test the hypothesis that a person was introverted, they would ask a question such as "what factors make it hard for you to really open up to people?" Clearly these questions constrain the information exchanged in a manner that serves to confirm the perceivers' hypothesis. Indeed, the conversational track established by the hypothesis being tested made those people who were being tested for extraversion behave in a sociable and outgoing fashion, while those people who were being tested for introversion behaved in a shy and reserved fashion.[4]

Internalization

Not only can a perceiver's expectations elicit confirmatory behaviors from the stereotyped person, but moreover, these situationally induced behaviors can, in certain circumstances, become internalized into the stereotyped person's self-concept. The result will be an autonomous self-fulfilling prophecy effect—the perceiver's expectations need not be operative for them to be fulfilled, since they operate within the stimulus people themselves. Such effects are anticipated by theories of social

[4]The self-fulfilling prophecy effects discussed thus far involve behaviors that are probably not under the conscious control of the stereotyped person. However, there is another category of self-fulfilling prophecies in which stereotyped people deliberately behave in a manner that will confirm others' expectations because they believe that such behavior will earn approval—e.g., the helpless female. This type of self-fulfilling prophecy effect depends upon the stereotypee's desire to please and/or appease those who expect particular behaviors. Thus, for example, Zanna and Pack (1975) found that the self-presentation of a female subject conformed to the stereotype of an ideal woman held by the man to whom she described herself only when she desired future interaction with that man.

deviance, which propose that once others treat someone as if he were deviant, the person comes to share this definition of himself, and the self-image as a deviant maintains the deviant behavior (e.g., Goffman, 1961, 1963). While these arguments have been applied primarily to deviance derived from institutionalization, research findings reveal that they are equally applicable in less extreme situations.

The study by Snyder and Swann (1978) provides evidence for the foregoing chain of events as well as some insight into the conditions necessary for its occurrence. Stimulus people in this study interacted with perceivers who expected them to be either hostile or nonhostile. Perceivers expecting a hostile person used higher intensity levels of a noise weapon during a competitive task than those expecting a nonhostile person, and, as a consequence of the perceivers' treatment of them, the labeled people soon began to confirm the perceiver's expectations: those people who were expected to be hostile actually delivered higher noise levels than those who were labeled as nonhostile. What is more, people who were led to attribute their own reactive hostility to personal dispositional causes continued to display hostility in a subsequent interaction with a naive perceiver who had no particular expectations for how they would behave. The result was that naive perceivers came to judge these people as hostile, further perpetuating the effect.

In sum it appears that when people are induced to behave in a manner that confirms others' expectations, they will continue to behave in this manner when interacting with different people, provided that they have attributed their original, situationally induced behavior to dispositional causes. Although the research reviewed here does not demonstrate internalization effects for people induced to behave in a certain manner by virtue of their physical appearance, it seems reasonable to expect analogous results. Thus, for example, overweight people who are treated in a manner that elicits the agreeable behavior that is stereotypically expected should come to perceive themselves as compliant, provided that they attribute their reactive behavior to dispositional causes.

Self-Attributions. In the Snyder and Swann study, the experimenters induced certain subjects to make dispositional attributions for their reactive hostility. An important question to raise in generalizing these effects to self-fulfilling prophecies in the real world is under what conditions will people spontaneously attribute their reactive behavior to personal causes? A number of findings in research on the causal attribution process suggest that such attributions should be fairly frequent among those who are physically distinctive. For one thing, there is evidence that behaviors that are highly consistent over time and targets tend to be attributed to dispositional causes more than to situational ones by the actor as well as by observers (e.g., McArthur, 1972; Eisen, 1979). Since members of some physically distinctive group are apt to be repeatedly treated in a like fashion by a variety of people, their reactive behavior will be consistent across time and targets, and they will be more likely to attribute it to their own disposition than to other causes. In addition, evidence has been reviewed in an earlier section indicating that people attribute causality to salient stimuli. If distinctive physical features are salient to those who possess them, then this salience of personal attributes may increase the frequency with which physically distinctive people attribute their own behavior to personal causes, just as it increases the frequency with which outside observers attribute social causality to physically distinctive people (see section on Blaming the Victim).

Evidence that physically distinctive attributes *are* salient to their possessors has been provided in a series of studies by McGuire and his associates (McGuire, McGuire, Child, & Fujloka, 1978; McGuire & Padawer-Singer, 1976; McGuire, McGuire, & Winton, 1979) investigating the spontaneous self-concepts of elementary school age children. They found that when subjects are asked to tell about themselves, they are more likely to mention situationally or statistically novel (e.g., nonmodal) physical attributes than commonplace ones. These effects were obtained for distinctive hair color, eye color, age, weight, sex, and ethnicity. Of course the argument that physically distinctive people are more likely than physically normative people to attribute their own behavior to personal causes requires not only that their physical appearance be a salient component of their self-concept, but also that these physical self-labels influence the processes of causal attribution.

While the research relevant to the role of physical appearance in self-attributions is rather meager, there is some positive evidence. For example, Dion and Earn (1975) found that when subjects had no apparent attribution for negative behavior toward them by others, close to half of them suggested that their opponents may have disliked their personal appearance. Research by Rodin and Slochower (1974) has further revealed that the tendency to attribute events to one's own physical appearance is most pronounced when the appearance is distinctive. Overweight subjects in this study were very prone to attribute a confederate's behavior toward them to their obesity, whether that behavior was nice or nasty, while normal-weight subjects made a variety of different attributions. More recently, Kleck and Strenta (1980) have found that normally nondistinctive people, who were led to believe that they were perceived as either scarred or epileptic in the eyes of an interactant, attributed that interactant's behavior to their own physical characteristics more than those whose perceived characteristics were less distinctive.

The tendency for physically distinctive people to make stronger self-attributions than others is not limited to causal attributions to their physical appearance per se. Duval and Wicklund (1973) have found that people are more apt to blame themselves for negative events and to take personal credit for positive ones when their appearance is salient due to the presence of a mirror than when it is not salient. Similarly, McArthur (1981a) has found that compared with people low in self-reported physical distinctiveness, those who were highly distinctive perceived themselves as more responsible for a variety of interpersonal events.

Given that physically distinctive people are more likely than others to make self-attributions for the behavior of other people, one might argue that distinctive people would also be more likely than others to attribute their own behavior to personal causes, though not necessarily to their personal appearance per se. A distinctive personal appearance may draw attention to aspects of the self that are associatively linked to the physical appearance, and attributions to these associatively linked attributes may be increased rather than attributions to appearance. Thus, for example, the red-haired person who manifests reactive hostility may attribute this behavior not to having red hair, but rather to having particular traits that are associatively linked with red hair.

Self-Concepts. It has been argued that self-fulfilling prophecy effects should be particularly pronounced for physically distinctive people because these individuals are more likely to attribute their reactive behavior to internal causes, an attribution that perpetuates that behavior even when the agent whose expectancies originally elicited it is gone (Snyder & Swann, 1978). In addition to attributing their reactive behavior to internal causes, there are two other ways in which physically distinctive people may come to internalize, and thus confirm, popular stereotypes: (1) physically distinctive people may selectively attend to behavior that confirms the labels others apply to them, thus yielding self-evaluations that are similar to popular stereotypes in their content; and (2) physically distinctive people may manifest more self-focused attention than others do, thus yielding self-evaluations that are similar to popular sterotypes in their polarization.

There is considerable research evidence to indicate that the self-concepts of people who belong to a stereotyped group (defined as "autostereotypes" by Triandis & Vassiliou, 1967) contain many of the stereotypic traits attributed to them by other groups ("heterostereotypes"). [See, for example, Broverman et al. (1970) regarding gender stereotypes; Brigham (1971) regarding ethnic stereotypes; Bennett & Eckman (1973) regarding age stereotypes; Lawson (1971) regarding hair color stereotypes.] While this evidence has sometimes been taken as support for the kernal of truth hypothesis, others have found that, although there seems to be considerable agreement between auto- and heterostereotypes, there may be very little correspondence between these stereotypes and modal group characteristics as measured by a personality inventory (e.g., Abate & Berrien, 1967). This lack of correspondence suggests that the isomorphism in auto- and hetero-stereotypes may reflect isomorphic biases in the processes of self- and other-perception, rather than reflecting any kernel of truth. Considerable evidence supports such an analysis.

Research reviewed in an earlier section has revealed that, when perceivers categorize or label someone, their resultant expectancies about that person's behavior tend to be self-confirming. More specifically, these expectancies produce selective attention to confirmatory behaviors. A similar phenomenon seems to occur for the labeled persons themselves. For example, Ross, Lepper, and Hubbard (1975) gave subjects false feedback, inducing them to perceive themselves as either possessing the ability to discriminate authentic suicide notes from fictitious ones or as not possessing such ability. After this "self-labeling" had been induced, the experimenter completely debriefed the subjects, making clear that the feedback regarding their performance had been bogus. However, when subjects were asked, following this debriefing, to rate their own abilities at suicide note discrimination, there was a significant perseverance effect: those who had initially been led to perceive themselves as able continued to rate themselves as more able than those who had perceived themselves as lacking this ability. To account for this phenomenon, the authors suggested that an initial self perception biases subsequent information processing such that information consistent with the self-perception receives greater attention than information that is inconsistent.

Some evidence consistent with the mediation suggested by Ross et al. (1975) has been provided in a study by Markus (1977). Subjects who categorized themselves as dependent or independent were found to make faster decisions regarding whether or not a trait word pertaining to independence characterized them than subjects who did not label themselves one way or another. What is more, those who labeled themselves more easily retrieved instances of behavior consistent with the label, and assigned higher probabilities to behavior consistent with the label than did nonlabelers. Finally, it was found that those who categorized themselves one way or another were less willing to accept certain information about themselves as valid than nonlabelers were if that information contradicted the self-label.

Although the labels that subjects applied to themselves in Markus' research were self-produced ones, it seems reasonable to expect that externally imposed labels such as in the Ross et al. (1975) research would often have similar effects, that is, fostering greater availability and weighting of information consistent with the label. Such effects should be very likely to occur when a person is "objectively" entertaining the hypothesis that the categorization is apt, since research has shown that, when people use historical knowledge to test a particular hypothesis, they tend to recall information that confirms the hypothesis rather than information that disconfirms it. Snyder and Cantor (1979) gave perceivers a biographical account of the events in the life of a woman named Jane and later asked them to use this knowledge to test a particular hypothesis about her. Those entertaining the hypothesis that Jane might be an extravert retrieved information that confirmed this hypothesis, while those entertaining the hypothesis that she might be an introvert retrieved from the very same biography information that confirmed the introversion hypothesis. One would expect similar information-processing strategies among people who are testing the hypothesis that they themselves have a particular trait, thus yielding selective attention to confirmatory evidence.

The Ross et al. (1975) research reveals that externally imposed labels are internalized, and the Markus (1977) and Snyder and Cantor (1979) research reveals that this internalization may derive from the greater availability and weighting of information consistent with the label. Other research reveals, in addition, that internalized labels influence behavior in a manner that yields a self-fulfilling prophecy effect, the prophecy now being that of the stereotyped person rather than the labeler. For example, Langer and Benevento (1978) found that subjects who had been labeled as "assistants" were subsequently less able to perform a task than those who had been labeled as "boss" even though both groups had performed the task equally well prior to the labeling. Other examples of the impact of labeling upon self-concept and subsequent behavior have been provided in a number of studies (e.g., McArthur, Kiesler, & Cook, 1969; Kraut, 1973; Lepper, 1973; Gurwitz & Topol, 1978).

While the research linking self-labeling to behavior has not employed people who were labeled by virtue of their physical appearance, it seems reasonable to propose that analogous effects would occur. Indeed, if a one-shot label can influence behavior in experimental and real life settings, as it has in the summarized research, then the experience of repeated labeling by significant others should surely produce confirmatory behavior among those to whom trait labels are applied on the basis of their distinctive physical appearance. Research by Gurwitz and Topol (1978) suggests that behavior confirming a label is most likely to occur when the person applying it has supporting evidence and when those to whom the label is applied believe that it also applies to other members of a category to which they belong Such a state of affairs should be commonplace among people labeled on the basis of their physical distinctiveness: the label is presumed to apply to all people possessing that physical attribute, and the person applying the label is often likely to do so on the basis of some sample of behavior, for example, "Oh there you go again, thinking like a woman."

In addition to the ability of selective attention to support the *particular* self-concepts suggested by the labels applied to physically distinctive people, selective attention can also produce more *polarized* self-concepts among the physically distinctive. Research by Wicklund and his associates has demonstrated that when peoples' attention is focused upon themselves by artificial manipulations of their physical salience, such as mirrors, not only do they attribute more causality to themselves, but they tend to rate themselves more extremely on a variety of evaluative dimensions. For example, Ickes, Wicklund, and Ferris (1973) informed some subjects that they had scored low and others that they had scored high on a test of "surgency," an allegedly important and desirable trait. Low scorers who subsequently rated themselves while confronted with a mirror rated themselves lower than those not facing a mirror, while high scorers facing a mirror rated themselves higher. [See Wicklund

(1975) for a more extensive review of this literature.] Thus people's *self*-evaluations become more polarized when they are salient just as people's evaluations of others become more polarized when those others are salient.

In Wicklund's research, the dimensions of self-evaluation that became polarized with self-focused attention depended largely upon what traits had been made salient by the experimental treatment. In situations where peoples' self-focused attention derives from some physical distinctiveness, the dimensions of self-evaluation one would expect to be polarized are those the distinctive attribute makes salient. Evidence for such an effect has been obtained in at least two studies. For example, Dion and Earn (1975) exposed Jewish students to negative treatment by three others. Consistent with McGuire's findings regarding the conditions under which ethnicity will be salient in the spontaneous self-concept, subjects who thought they were the only one in the group who was Jewish were more likely to attribute the treatment they received to their Jewish identity than subjects who did not know the religious identity of the three other participants. What is more, those making an anti-Semitism attribution rated themselves higher on stereotypic Jewish traits than those who did not make such an attribution. Similar effects were reported by Dion (1975) for women's stereotyped self-evaluations in reaction to discrimination based upon sexism. It thus appears that when self-focused attention derives from some distinctive personal attribute, then polarization of self-evaluations occurs for traits which that distinctive attribute makes salient, that is, traits stereotypically associated with the distinctive attribute.[5] Although it was only on positive stereotypic traits that subjects' self-concepts were altered in the foregoing studies, it may be that polarization will occur on negative traits as well under appropriate conditions.

Summary and Implications

Stereotypes about physically distinctive people may begin in the eye of the beholder, but they can often end up a reality. Stereotyped expectations lead people to treat members of a physically distinctive category of people in a manner that elicits the expected behavior. Once elicited, this behavior may be internalized into the self-concept of the stereotyped group members. More specifically, since their distinctive physical appearance is likely to produce self-focused attention, these people may make self-attributions for behaviors that were in reality situationally induced, and they may thus come to expect from themselves what others have expected (and elicited) from them. Direct labeling of physically distinctive people can have the same effect, yielding self-expectations that mirror the stereotyped expectations of others. Whether

[5]It should be noted that Dion and Earn (1975) offered a different explanation for these results, attributing the more stereotyped self-evaluations to stronger feelings of ingroup belongingness and identification in the face of an external threat.

derived from self-attributions for reactive behavior or from selective attention to evidence consistent with externally imposed labels, these stereotyped self-expectations are likely to produce confirmatory behavior that no longer depends upon the presence of a stereotyping beholder.

THE AMELIORATION OF STEREOTYPES

Having identified the role physical appearance can play in the formation and perpetuation of stereotypes, the question remains as to whether or not we have learned anything that might be of value in the attempt to break down existing stereotypes about physically distinctive people. Traditional approaches to the phenomenon of stereotyping suggest that ameliorative measures would require altering the needs that stereotypes serve. However, the present analysis suggests that stereotypes would persist even if their functional utility were removed, since uniform, extreme, negative, and specific evaluations of a group of people may derive merely from the power of their physical appearance to influence perceivers' attention.

While there is not much research on ameliorative measures directly pertinent to the perceptual-cognitive bases of stereotyping, there are some promising ideas to pursue. In particular, it would seem that the breakdown of stereotypes would be facilitated by measures directed toward (1) habituating perceivers to physical attributees that currently draw attention due to their statistical novelty; (2) effecting recategorization of people according to attributes other than their physical appearance; and (3) weakening the associations between physically defined categories of people and particular psychological attributes. Easier said than done, of course, but this section nonetheless considers how one might proceed, with the caveat that the suggested ameliorative measures will be illustrative rather than exhaustive.

HABITUATION

The evidence indicating that physically salient stimuli are evaluated more extremely than less salient ones suggests that reducing the salience of physically distinctive people may succeed in reducing the extremity of stereotypes about such individuals. Since physically distinctive people are salient by virtue of their novelty—i.e., infrequent occurrence—there are two general ways in which one might diminish their salience: (1) integrate them more into various social groups such that they are not so contextually novel; and (2) provide more frequent exposure to them so that they are not so statistically novel.

The ability of true integration to diminish polarized evaluations of people who are distinguished by their physical appearance has been cited earlier (e.g., Taylor et al., 1976). However, this tactic has limited utility in the real world where people with particular physical features are rarer than others. For example, racial integration of the schools will never provide all classrooms with a roughly equal proportion of blacks and whites, because blacks constitute a much smaller proportion of the population. Since token integration yields such polarized evaluations of the minority group, one could argue that it would be better, from the standpoint of stereotyping, to make some schools truly integrated, while leaving others segregated, than to provide token integration in all. Of course, such selective integration may be worse from the standpoint of educational opportunity for minority students and has the further drawback of diminishing stereotypes only among the small proportion of racial majority students who participate in the integrated schools.

While the prospects for reducing the contextual novelty of physically distinctive people is limited by the number of such people available for integration, these constraints do not interfere with the second means for reducing the novelty, and hence the salience, of such people. There is considerable evidence that repeated exposure to a visual stimulus reduces its attention-drawing power as compared with more novel stimuli (see, for example, Berlyne, 1970). This suggests that making physically distinctive people more "visible" in the media and public life would serve to diminish the extremity of evaluations of them. However, it must be noted that exposure has been found to *increase* the polarization of evaluations of a stimulus, at least in the short run. For example, Perlman and Oskamp (1971) found that increased frequency of exposure to photographs of negatively evaluated men—criminals—yielded decreases in attractiveness ratings, while increased frequency of exposure to photographs of positively evaluated men—Who's Who designates—yielded increases in attractiveness ratings. Similar polarization effects have also been found in the realm of object-perception (e.g., Brickman, Redfield, Harrison, & Crandall, 1972).[6]

The tendency for repeated exposure to polarize evaluations of a stimulus is inconsistent with the tendency for repeated exposure to reduce a stimulus' attention-drawing power, since it has been demonstrated that the greater the attention-drawing power of a stimulus, the more polarized evaluations of it will be (see pp. 156 –157). One possible explanation for these apparently contradictory effects concerns the complexity of the stimuli employed in the research demonstrating habituation of attention and those employed in the studies demonstrating polarization of affect. The stimuli employed in the former studies have been less complex than those employed in the latter, and it may be that complex stimuli require more exposure before a satiation or habituation effect will occur. [See Harrison (1977) for a review of the effects of complexity.] If so, one might expect a curvilinear relationship between exposure and the polarization of evaluation in person perception: as exposure increases up to some optimal point, more attention is focused upon a stimulus person, and the polarity of evaluations show a

[6]Other research (Zajonc, Markus, & Wilson, 1974) has shown that these divergent exposure effects require that positive or negative affective associations accompany the repeated exposures. In the absence of such associations, increased exposure (i.e., *mere* exposure) seems to yield *increased* attractiveness, regardless of initial affect. Of course, in the usual contexts of person perception, one would expect initial positive and negative associations to accompany subsequent exposures, thus yielding the polarization effect.

corresponding increase. However, at some point increased exposure will begin to produce decreases in evaluative polarity by virtue of the habituation of attention. The possibility of such an effect suggests that repeatedly exposing people to those whose physical appearance is statistically novel will ultimately reduce the tendency to evaluate these people extremely, but probably not before it increases it. The likelihood that things will get worse before they get better should be borne in mind in implementing visibility campaigns designed to reduce the extremity of evaluations of physically distinctive people. One should also bear in mind that the time frame in which effects occur is likely to be more extended in the real world than in laboratory settings, even if the essential processes are the same.[7]

Some direct evidence that the beneficial effects of exposure to a distinctive group member may require considerable time has been provided by Hamilton and Bishop (1976), who investigated the effects of racial integration upon the attitudes of white suburbanites. Measures of racism at various intervals revealed no ameliorative effects of exposure to a black family until a full year had passed. What is more, those living near a new black family for one or three months tended to endorse more racist attitudes than controls who lived near a new white family for the same time period, an effect that was totally attributable to those respondents who reported actually interacting with the new family, that is, those who were truly exposed to the physically distinctive or nondistinctive people. Although Hamilton and Bishop do not report the statistical significance of these short-term effects, it appears that increased exposure to blacks tended to increase racism before it diminished it.[8]

To summarize, a reduction in the extremity of evaluations of physically distinctive people may be facilitated by (1) fully integrating them with others and/or (2) increasing others' exposure to them. But such measures, even if astoundingly effective, would not serve to obliterate stereotypes. The specific attributes ascribed to physically distinctive people may still differ from those ascribed to others. To alter the content, as well as the extremity, of evaluations of physically distinctive people requires modifications in the tendency to categorize people according to their physical appearance and in the associative links between particular people and particular behaviors.

RECATEGORIZATION

To get people to stop categorizing others is probably an unrealistic aspiration, since categorizations serve a function for the perceiver,

[7]In case it is not obvious to the reader, it should be noted that an ultimate reduction in the polarization of evaluations via increased exposure requires that the contexts in which the exposure occurs not reinforce existing stereotypes.

[8]It should be noted that it may not be the sheer frequency of exposure that produced a curvilinear effect. In real-life settings it is difficult to separate the quantity of exposure from its quality, and either one or both of these factors may have contributed to the curvilinear relationship between the amount of time white families lived near a black family and white racism. [See Amir (1969) for an extensive review of the research on interethnic contact.]

namely, facilitating social prediction. Thus the question becomes how to get people to recategorize on the basis of something other than physical appearance, given that appearance is such a highly discriminable cue. Before considering *how* this might be done, one is faced with the question of *what* categorizations one wants to effect. In pondering this question, one becomes aware that a particular categorization must be evaluated in terms of its aims, not in any absolute sense. The "best" way to categorize people depends upon what variations in behavior one is trying to account for. If one is trying to predict average income, then color is a useful categorization. If one is trying to predict happy-go-luckiness, then color becomes less useful. Thus the appropriate goal of "recategorization" efforts should be to foster more *flexible* categorizations of people rather than to foster some *particular* categorization.

Some insights into how one might foster more flexible categorizations are provided by Tversky (1977), who proposed that the feature of a stimulus object that will be the salient basis of categorization depends upon two types of factors: *intensive* and *diagnostic*. The intensiveness of a feature is something that is difficult to modify, for it is determined by perceptual and cognitive factors that are relatively stable across contexts, for example, color and size. However, the diagnosticity of a feature *is* amenable to change, since it is determined by its classificatory significance, that is, the importance or prevalence of classifications that are based upon it. Thus, if one could somehow make a particular physical feature less diagnostic than some other basis for categorization, than recategorization may occur even though the physical feature remains more intense. One way to do this, according to Tversky (1977), is by adding and/or deleting objects to the set of objects to be categorized.

> When faced with a set of objects, people often sort them into clusters to reduce information load and facilitate further processing. Clusters are typically selected so as to maximize the similarity of objects within a cluster and the dissimilarity of objects from different clusters. Hence, the addition and/or deletion of objects can alter the clustering of the remaining objects. (p. 342)

Consider, for example, Figure 2, adapted from Tversky (1977, Figure 4). Only one of the four faces differs from set 1 to set 2. If the faces a and b are considered by themselves, they are equally similar in set 1 and 2. However, the replacement of p in set 1 by q in set 2 alters the similarity of a and b. Whereas set 1 is most readily partitioned into dark faces vs white faces, set 2 is often partitioned into smiling faces vs nonsmiling ones. From Tversky's data, one would expect a and b to be judged less similar in set 1 than set 2.

Although this example demonstrates how to reduce the ability of skin color to diagnose who is *physically* most similar to whom, it seems reasonable to extrapolate to its ability to diagnose who is *psychologically* most similar to whom. If one brings the faces to life such that we have black and white people whose facial expressions are accompanied by "happy-go-lucky," stern, or neutral behavior, then set 1 (with the help

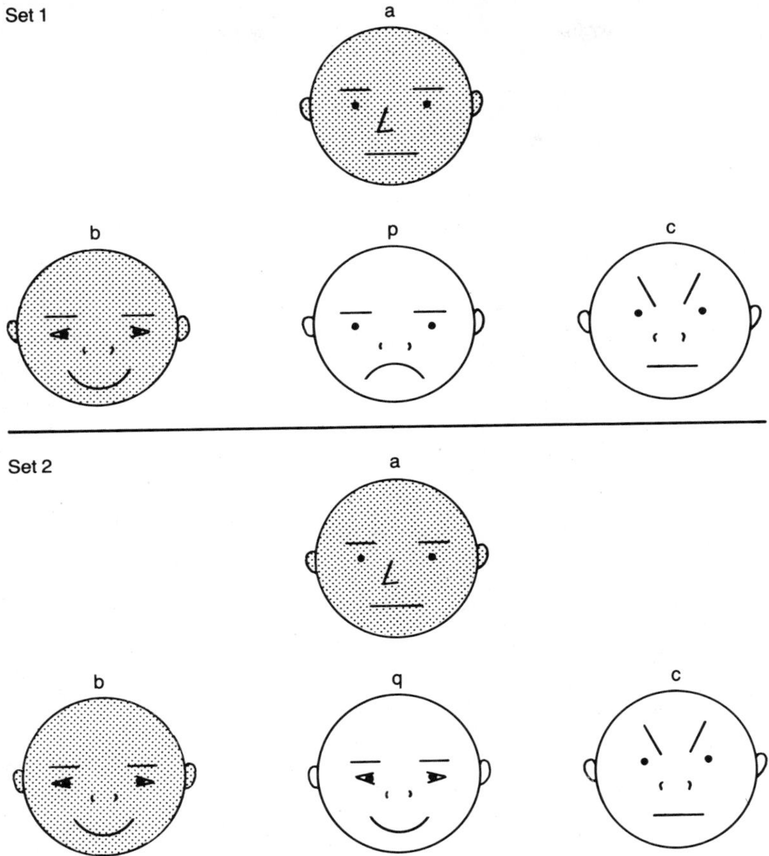

FIGURE 2. Two sets of faces manifesting the operation of diagnosticity principle in person categorization. (After Tversky, 1977.)

of assimilation and contrast effects) will bolster the stereotype that blacks are more happy-go-lucky than whites. Color is diagnostic here in the sense of facilitating classifications, that is, predicting variations in behavior. In set 2, on the other hand, color is not diagnostic of behavior, and this set tends to combat the stereotype that those who are racially similar share psychological similarity as well. It is important to note that dark skin becomes less diagnostic in set 2 as a consequence of changes made in the *white*-faced stimuli. While a standard prescription for reducing stereotypes is to show people that the outgroup members are not really all the same, the present analysis suggests that reducing the similarity of the ingroup can also foster recategorization of the outgroup. Thus focusing peoples' attention upon the variety of expressive styles among whites may do as much, if not more, for breaking down the tendency to categorize people by color as will focusing their attention on expressive styles among blacks that disconfirm the stereotyped expectations.

Research by Weiner and Wright (1973) may be construed as consistent with the argument that attending to the variability of behavior within a physically defined category of people will reduce the diagnosticity of physical cues and thereby the categorization of people on the basis of such cues. In this study, third-grade children were categorized according to an arbitrarily assigned green or orange armband, and their teacher proceeded to discriminate against first one color, then the other. The children who had this experience were subsequently more likely than controls to desire attendance at a picnic with black children and to express unprejudiced beliefs about blacks. The authors interpreted these results as an "empathy effect," since the experimental group could presumably identify more with blacks. But it may also be that experience with categorization on the basis of an arbitrary color feature caused children to notice features more diagnostic of merit than color each time the teacher used this "intense," but "nondiagnostic" feature to determine their outcomes. This increased attention to the variability of "good" behavior within a color category may have contributed to the children's reduced prejudice.

Research by Wilder (1978) did not deal with categorization on the basis of a physical attribute, as Weiner and Wright (1973) did, but it has provided even stronger evidence that increasing people's awareness of the variability in behavior among members of a particular category will weaken the strength of the existing categorization. Subjects in this study were divided into two categories by the experimenter according to the task they were to perform, thus producing an "ingroup" and an "outgroup." Compared with subjects who were given either no information about the behavior of the outgroup or information indicating that the outgroup members all behaved in the same fashion, those who were informed of variability in behavior among the outgroup members showed an increased tendency to see the outgroup as "unrelated individuals" rather than as a "single group." Moreover, along with this reduction in the strength of the outgroup category went a decrease in discrimination toward members of that group.

A corollary to Tversky's diagnosticity principle, the "extension effect," suggests that perceivers' categorizations may be altered not only by increasing the variability among elements within an existing category but also by increasing the size of the stimulus set to be categorized.

> As the stimulus set is enlarged, some features shared by all objects in the original set may no longer be shared by all objects in the extended set. These features then acquire diagnostic value and increase the similarity of the objects that share them. (p. 344)

Consider, for example, the faces depicted in set 3 (see Figure 3). This set is comprised of the faces in set 1 plus four new ones. Whereas ears were

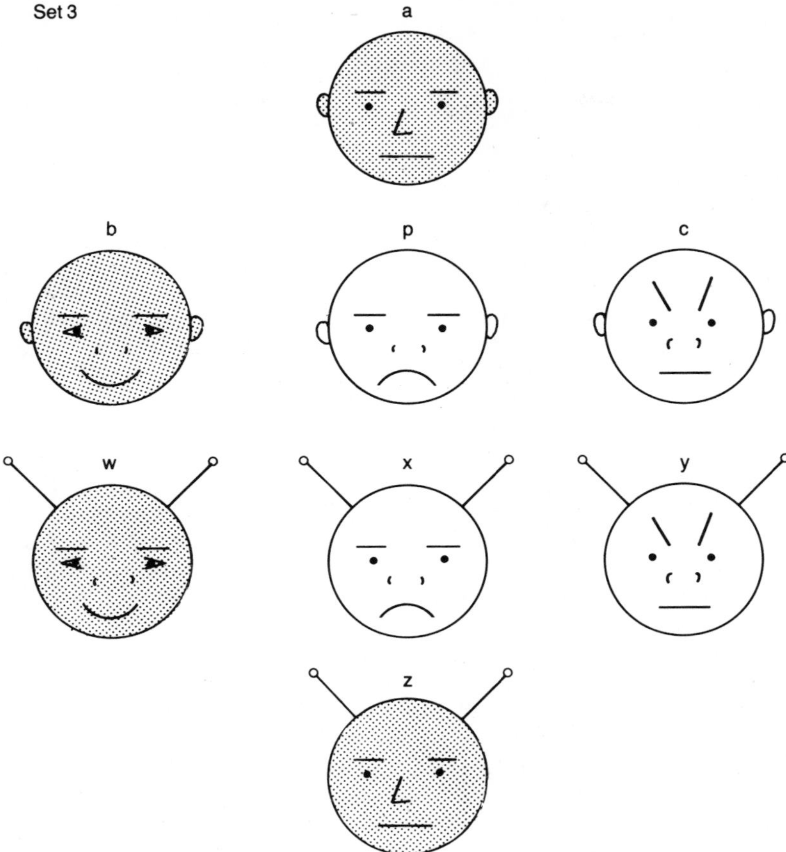

FIGURE 3. A set of faces manifesting the extension effect in person categorization. (After Tversky, 1977.)

not diagnostic features in set 1, they become diagnostic in set 3, where we find that some people have ears and others have antennae—the earthlings are united by the arrival of Martians. On a more realistic plane, the extension effect suggests that the greater variety of people to which a perceiver is exposed, the greater the variety of features which will be found to have "diagnostic" value for categorization. Such an increase in potential classificatory features would seem more likely than not to break down rigid categorizations.

The research reviewed thus far reveals that the tendency to categorize people on the basis of some salient physical feature will be weakened if something else is made more diagnostic of their similarities and differences. The ascendance of other diagnostic attributes seems to be facilitated by exposure to the *variability* of attributes within a physically defined category of people as well as by exposure to a wider *diversity* of attributes upon which people may be categorized.

NEW ASSOCIATIONS

The ease with which one can reduce the tendency to categorize people on the basis of a particular physical attribute will undoubtedly depend upon its *perceived* diagnosticity as well as upon its *actual* diagnosticity. Thus it would seem that efforts on behalf of more flexible categorization must include active attempts to eliminate particular appearance-behavior associations, which may provide an illusion of diagnosticity. However, there are several problems with this latter endeavor. For one thing, while it may be possible to eliminate culturally taught associations, it seems unlikely that this could be effected for those based upon metaphor, function, or temporal extension. The possibility that some of the associations may be veridical presents another problem for attempts to eradicate them. This is also true for the fact that the associative links provide a useful function for people, since, as noted earlier, they simplify behavioral prediction in an informationally complex social world. These problems suggest that rather than simply attempting to invalidate existing associative links, efforts should be directed toward replacing them with more accurate ones.

Now the question becomes, what associations should be taught? As social psychologists, we must admit that we probably do not know many person-behavior associations that have enough validity to warrant propagation. Moreover, we must consider that any such associations may be counterproductive if one's ultimate goal is eradicating stereotypes. As Campbell (1967) argued:

> Remedial education in race relations focused on denying or disproving stereotypes implicitly accepts the prejudiced ingroups' causal conception rather than the social scientists' and is undermined where actual group differences are found. (p. 825)

What Campbell means by the "ingroup's causal conception" is the conception of behavior as being caused by *personal factors*. What Campbell's criticism suggests is that we should educate people not as to what personal attributes do or do not predict behavior, but rather as to what *environmental* factors accurately predict behavior. While the former focus will only serve to create new stereotypes (when it is not undermined by evidence for the predictive utility of the old), the latter focus has the potential for truly weakening existing stereotypes, provided that they are less useful for behavioral prediction than is a situational conception of behavioral causality.

A concrete example will help to support this argument. Assume one wants to diminish stereotyped conceptions of unattractive people as less sociable than attractive individuals. There will be at least two serious obstacles to this effort. First, there may be actual differences in the behavior of attractive and unattractive people. Second, even if physical attractiveness is not an unfailing predictor of behavior, it may still be of some use in reducing the perceiver's social uncertainty. Thus, to diminish this stereotype requires providing the perceiver with another model for predicting behavior, and one which will hopefully allow more accurate prediction than the attractive-unattractive model.

From the Snyder et al. (1977) research, we know that actual behavioral differences between attractive and unattractive people may be predicted from situational causes, namely, the way they are treated. If one could somehow make people more aware of the covariation between environmental influences and behavior, this would hopefully diminish their assumption of a covariation between personal dispositions and behavior. In short, if you want to invalidate a hypothesis, it is better to provide an alternative explanation for the data—and best of all, one which accounts for more variance—than to simply point out the predictive shortcomings of the current hypothesis. Of course the provision of alternative environment-behavior associations need not preclude more direct attempts to change existing person-behavior associations, especially where they are known to be fallacious or at least totally arbitrary. Thus, to counteract the "ugly as sin" association, one might mount a "homely is wholesome" campaign analogous to the rather successful "black is beautiful" association propagated in the last decade.

It is important to note that building new assumptions of covariance may be a difficult task, especially when the new hypothesis is inconsistent with existing assumptions. For example, Dewhirst and Berman (1978) found that people more readily interpreted a spurious association as causal when it was consistent with their a priori expectations and interpreted a true causal association as spurious when it was inconsistent. This occurred even though the subjects were specifically requested to consider two different explanations for a particular set of outcomes. Thus the greater predictive power of an intuitively less plausible explanation probably needs to be explicitly spelled out before that "nonrepresentative" explanation (Kahenman & Tversky, 1973) will be accepted. The reason for this is that people do not make contingency judgments on the basis of statistical theory. They attend to the frequency of "hits"—i.e., expected events—rather than to the probability of events (see, for example, Einhorn & Hogarth, 1978). Thus illusory correlation will diminish only when peoples' attention is explicitly focused upon that evidence that disconfirms their naive hypothesis and supports another. If building new assumptions of covariance is difficult when the new hypothesis is inconsistent with existing assumptions, it is probably even more difficult when the new hypothesis proposes a link between *environmental causes* and behavior to replace the assumed link between *personal causes* and behavior. As Ross (1977) has argued, there is considerable evidence for a "fundamental attribution error" in which behavior is more often attributed to personal than to situational causes.

It has been suggested that reducing the attention-drawing power of physically distinctive people, increasing the flexibility of people's categorization of others, and replacing actor-behavior associative links with environment-behavior links may all serve to ameliorate stereotypes of people whose appearance is distinctive. There are of course many details that would have to be worked out before any of these potentially ameliorative measures could actually be implemented, not the least of which is the possibility that some measures could have adverse effects—at least in the short run.[9]

CONCLUSIONS

Several effects of physical appearance upon stereotyping have been documented in this chapter. Perceivers categorize people according to their physical appearance. This categorization causes the attributes of those within a category to be assimilated to one another and contrasted from those within another category, thus yielding a tendency to view people with a particular appearance as uniformly sharing a particular trait. Perceivers pay more attention to people whose physical appearance is contextually or statistically novel, a response, which in some as yet unspecified manner produces more causal attributions to those people. Perceivers also pay more attention to negative than to positive behaviors and to extreme than to neutral behaviors. This selective attention yields more negative and more extreme evaluations of physically distinctive people through an illusory correlation effect in which for some as yet unknown reason attention-drawing behaviors have the strongest impact upon impressions of attention-drawing people. Finally, perceivers pay more attention to behaviors that are associatively linked to a particular actor. Since specific physical attributes are associated with certain behaviors through function, metaphor, temporal extension, and/or cultural teachings, selective attention to associatively linked behaviors together with illusory correlation can yield specific stereotypes about people with specific physical attributes. In sum, a distinctive physical appearance can produce uniform, extreme, negative, and specific stereotypes about people with that appearance.

It is important to note that the perceptual processes that are set into motion in the perceiver by another person's physical appearance may often operate within a social context in which perceivers' behaviors are influenced by their perceptions, and these behaviors in turn influence the stereotyped persons such that they confirm the perceiver's expectations. Moreover, in confirming the perceivers' expectations, the stereotyped persons may come to stereotype themselves through a process

[9]It should be emphasized that there are many ameliorative measures to be derived from a perceptual-cognitive analysis of stereotyping that have not even been touched on in this section. In particular, consistent with Amir's (1969) observation that most research on contact effects has focused on the impact of intergroup contact on the stereotyp*er*, rather than the stereotyp*ee*, the present analysis has focused on the impact of several interventions upon the stereotyp*er*. One would do well to consider their impact upon the stereotypee as well as other interventions that directly involve the stereotypee.

analogous to that which operates for perceivers. More specifically, physically distinctive people may be more apt than others to see their own behavior as internally caused and may therefore label themselves according to the behaviors they have produced in reaction to a perceiver's expectations. This self-labeling then perpetuates the stereotyped behavior in other settings. Explicit labeling of physically distinctive people by others as well as a tendency for the physically distinctive to manifest more self-focused attention may also foster stereotyped self-evaluations and behavior among these people.

One might wish to argue that the restricted range of social interactions in the experimental research limits the generalizability of these findings to real-world settings. However, it is important to realize that real-life interactions with physically distinctive people are also very restricted. Not only are these people, by definition, in short supply, but people tend to shun those who are around. How many crippled people or obese people or black people does the average reader of this chapter know well? Implementing the ameliorative measures suggested in the last section of the chapter would serve to make the real world less like the experimental settings. By fostering more open-minded exposure to the physically distinctive, these measures would, it is hoped, break the spiral of seeing what is expected, producing what is expected, and transferring the expectancy to the distinctive people themselves.

The impact that a novel physical appearance can have on social stereotypes has two analogues that argue for a perceptual-cognitive interpretation of these effects, as opposed to a motivational one. First, the effects of physical novelty upon social judgments are paralleled by identical effects of other determinants of physical salience that have no particular affective connotations—e.g., bright lights, motion, patterned clothing, instructions to attend to a particular person. Second, the effects of salience manipulations upon social judgments have analogues in the realm of object perception where motivational explanations are implausible. It thus appears that the tendency to stereotype people who "look different" can derive from the attention-drawing qualities of their appearance.

To say that stereotyping can derive from processes of categorization and selective attention is not to deny the possibility that other factors may play a role. Clearly they do. People with particular physical attributes not only draw more attention, but they may also create fear, disdain, repulsion, guilt, or other motivational states in the perceiver. These motivational states undoubtedly play a central role in the development and perpetuation of many stereotypes. For example, McArthur and Solomon (1978) demonstrated that arousal polarizes perceivers' evaluations of stimulus persons in the direction of their most salient behaviors, an effect that is consistent with Easterbrook's (1959) thesis that arousal narrows attention to the most salient cues in a situation. While motivational states may thus exacerbate stereotyping of physically salient people, the point of this chapter is to argue that even if these motivational states were somehow eliminated, the mere physical novelty of particular groups of people would still foster stereotyping. We stereotype people who look different because we look at them differently.

ACKNOWLEDGMENTS

I would like to thank Teresa Amabile, Susan Fiske, and Verne McArthur for their very helpful comments on an earlier draft of this chapter.

REFERENCES

Abate, M., & Berrien, F. K. Validation of stereotypes: Japanese vs. American students. *Journal of Personality and Social Psychology*, 1967, *7*, 435 –438.

Adams, G. R. Social psychology of physical appearance: A dialectic-interactional perspective. Unpublished manuscript. Department of Family and Human Development, Utah State University, Logan, Utah, 1979.

Amir, Y. Contact hypothesis in ethnic relations. *Psychology Bulletin*, 1969, *71*, 319 –341.

Asch, S. E. The metaphor: A psychological inquiry. In R. Tagiuri and L. Petrullo (Eds.), *Person perception and interpersonal behavior*. Stanford, Calif.: Stanford University Press, 1958, pp. 86 –94.

Bagby, J. W. A cross-cultural study of perceptual predominance in binocular rivalry. *Journal of Abnormal and Social Psychology*, 1957, *54*, 331 –334.

Bennett, R., & Eckman, J. Attitudes toward aging: A critical examination of recent literature and implications for future research. In C. Eisendorfer and M. P. Lawton (Eds.), *The psychology of adult development and aging*, Washington, D.C.: American Psychological Association, 1973, pp. 575 –597.

Berlyne, D. E. Attention as a problem in behavior theory. In D. I. Mostofsky (Ed.), *Attention: Contemporary theory and analysis*, 1970, pp. 25 –49.

Berscheid, E., & Walster, E. Physical attractiveness. In L. Berkowitz (Ed.), *Advances in experimental social psychology*, Vol. 7. New York: Academic, 1974, pp. 158 –216.

Bowman, P. C. Physical constancy and trait attribution: Attentuation of the primacy effect. *Personality and Social Psychology Bulletin*, 1979, *5*, 61 –64.

Bradshaw, J. L. The information conveyed by varying the dimensions of features in human outline faces. *Perception and Psychophysics*, 1969, *6*, 5 –9.

Brickman, P., Redfield, J., Harrison, A. A., & Crandall, R. Drive and predisposition as factors in the attitudinal effects of mere exposure. *Journal of Experimental Social Psychology*, 1972, *8*, 31 –44.

Brigham, J. C. Ethnic stereotypes. *Psychology Bulletin*, 1971, *76*, 15 –38.

Broverman, I. K., Broverman, F. E., Clarkson, P. S., Rosenkrantz, P. S., & Vogel, S. R. Sex-role stereotypes and clinical judgments of mental health. *Journal of Consulting and Clinical Psychology*, 1970, *34*, 1 –7.

Bruner, J. S. On perceptual readiness. *Psychological Review*, 1957, *64*, 123 –152.

Bruner, J. S., & Tagiuri, R. The perception of people. In G. Lindzey (Ed.), *Handbook of social psychology*, Vol. 2. Reading, Mass.: Addison-Wesley, 1954.

Campbell, D. T. Stereotypes and the perception of group differences. *American Psychologist*, 1967, *22*, 817 –829.

Cantor, N., & Mischel, W. Traits as prototypes: Effects on recognition memory. *Journal of Personality and Social Psychology*, 1977, *35*, 38 –48.

Carver, C. S., & Scheier, M. F. Self-focusing effects of dispositional self-consciousness, mirror presence and audience presence. *Journal of Personality and Social Psychology*, 1978, *36*, 324 –332.

Chapman, L. J. Illusory correlation in observational report. *Journal of Verbal Learning and Verbal Behavior*, 1967, *6*, 151 –155.

Chapman, L. J., & Chapman, J. P. Genesis of popular but erroneous psychodiagnostic observations. *Journal of Abnormal Psychology*, 1967, *72*, 193–204.

Clifford, M. M., & Walster, E. The effect of physical attractivenes on teacher expectation. *Sociology of Education*, 1973, *46*, 248–258.

Cohen, C. E. Cognitive basis of stereotyping. Paper presented at the meeting of the American Psychological Association, San Francisco, Calif., August, 1977.

Dewhirst, J. R., & Berman, J. S. Social judgments of spurious and causal relations between attributes and outcomes. *Journal of Experimental Social Psychology*, 1978, *14*, 313–325.

Dion, K. K. Physical attractiveness and evaluations of children's transgressions. *Journal of Personality and Social Psychology*, 1972, *24*, 207–213.

Dion, K. L. Women's reactions to discrimination from members of the same or opposite sex. *Journal of Research in Personality*, 1975, *9*, 294–306.

Dion, K. L., & Earn, B. M. The phenomenology of being a target of prejudice. *Journal of Personality and Social Psychology*, 1975, *32*, 944–950.

Dreben, E. K., Fiske, S. T., & Hastie, R. The independence of evaluative and item information: Impression and recall order effects in behavior based impression formation. *Journal of Personality and Social Psychology*, 1979, *37*, 1758–1768.

Duval, S. & Wicklund, R. A. Effects of objective self-awareness on attribution of causality. *Journal of Experimental Social Psychology*, 1973, *9*, 17–31.

Easterbrook, J. A. The effect of emotion on cue utilization and the organization of behavior. *Psychological Review*, 1959, *66*, 183–201.

Ebbesen, E. B., & Allen, R. B. Cognitive processes in implicit personality trait inferences. *Journal of Personality and Social Psychology*, 1979, *37*, 471–488.

Einhorn, H. J., & Hogarth, R. M. Confidence in judgment: Persistence of the illusion of validity. *Psychological Review*, 1978, *85*, 395–416.

Eisen, S. V. Actor-observer differences in information inference and causal attribution. *Journal of Personality and Social Psychology*, 1979, *37*, 261–272.

Eisen, S. V., & McArthur, L. Z. Evaluating and sentencing a defendant as a function of his salience and the perceiver's set. *Personality and Social Psychology Bulletin*, 1979, *5*, 48–52.

Ekman, P., Friesen, W. V., & Ellsworth, P. *Emotion in the human face.* New York: Pergamon, 1972.

Elashoff, J., & Snow, R. E. *Pygmalion reconsidered.* Worthington, Ohio: Charles A. Jones, 1971.

Engel, E. The role of content in binocular resolution. *American Journal of Psychology*, 1956, *69*, 87–91.

Enquist, G., Newtson, D., & LaCross, K. Prior expectations and the perceptual segmentation of ongoing behavior. Unpublished manuscript. University of Virginia, Charlottesville, Va., 1978.

Fiske, S. T. Attention and weight in person perception: The impact of negative and extreme behavior. *Journal of Personality and Social Psychology*, 1980, *38*, 889–908.

Fiske, S. T., & Cox, M. G. Person concepts: The effect of target familiarity and descriptive purpose on the process of describing others. *Journal of Personality*, 1979, *47*, 136–161.

Fiske, S. T., Kenny, D. A., & Taylor, S. E. Structural models for the mediation of salience effects on attribution. Unpublished manuscript, 1979.

Gerard, H. B., & Hoyt, M. F. Distinctiveness of social categorization and attitude toward ingroup members. *Journal of Personality and Social Psychology*, 1974, *29*, 836–842.

Gergen, K. J. The significance of skin color in human relations. *Daedalus*, 1967, *96*, 391–406.

Goffman, E. *Asylums*. Garden City, N.Y.: Doubleday Anchor, 1961.

Goffman, E. *Stigma*. Englewood Cliffs, N.J.: Prentice-Hall, 1963.

Gurwitz, S. B., & Dodge, K. A. Effects of confirmations and disconfirmations on stereotype-based attributions. *Journal of Personality and Social Psychology*, 1977, *35*, 495–500.

Gurwitz, S. B., & Topol, B. Determinants of confirming and disconfirming responses to negative social labels. *Journal of Experimental Social Psychology*, 1978, *14*, 31 –42.

Hamilton, D. L. A cognitive-attributional analysis of stereotyping. In L. Berkowitz (Ed.), *Advances in experimental social psychology*, Vol. 12. New York: Academic, 1979, 53 –84.

Hamilton, D. L., & Bishop, G. D. Integration in the suburbs. *Journal of Social Issues*, 1976, *32*, 47 –67.

Hamilton, D. L., & Gifford, R. K. Illusory correlation in interpersonal perception: A cognitive basis of stereotypic judgments. *Journal of Experimental Social Psychology*, 1976, *12*, 392 –407.

Hamilton, D. L., & Rose, T. L. Illusory correlation and the maintenance of stereotypic beliefs. *Journal of Personality and Social Psychology*, 1980, *39*, 832 –845.

Hamilton, D. L., & Zanna, M. P. Differential weighting of favorable and unfavorable attributes in impressions of personality. *Journal of Experimental Research in Personality*, 1972, *6*, 204 –212.

Harrison, A. A. Mere exposure. In L. Berkowitz (Ed.), *Advances in experimental social psychology*, Vol. 10. New York: Academic, 1977, 39 –83.

Hastorf, A. H., & Myro, G. The effect of meaning on binocular rivalry. *American Journal of Psychology*, 1959, *72*, 393 –400.

Hastorf, A. H., Northcroft, G. B., & Picciotto, S. R. Helping the handicapped: How realistic is the performance feedback received by the physically handicapped. *Personality and Social Psychology Bulletin*, 1979, *5*, 373 –376.

Heider, F. Perceiving the other person. Paper presented at an American Psychological Association symposium on Theory and Research in Interpersonal Perception, 1954. Reprinted in R. Tagiuri and L. Petrullo (Eds.), *Person perception and interpersonal behavior*. Stanford, Calif: Stanford University Press, 1958, 22 –26.

Hodges, B. Effect of valence on relative weighting in impression formation. *Journal of Personality and social Psychology*, 1974, *30*, 378 –381.

Ickes, W. J., Wicklund, R. A., & Ferris, C. B. Objective self-awareness and self-esteem. *Journal of Experimental Social Psychology*, 1973, *9*, 202 –219.

Imai, S., & Garner, W. R. Discriminability and preference for attributes in free and constrained classification. *Journal of Experimental Psychology*, 1965, *69*, 596 –608.

Jones, E. E., & Goethels, G. R. Order effects in impression formation: Attribution context and the nature of the entity. In E. E. Jones, D. E. Kanouse, H. H. Kelley, R. E. Nisbett, S. Valins, and B. Weiner (Eds.), *Attribution: Perceiving the causes of behavior*. Morristown, N.J.: General Learning Press, 1972, 27 –46.

Jones, E. E., & Nisbett, R. E. The actor and the observer: Divergent perceptions of the causes of behavior. In E. E. Jones, D. E. Kanouse, H. H. Kelley, R. E. Nisbett, S. Valins, & B. Weiner (Eds.), *Attribution: Perceiving the causes of behaviors.* Morristown, N.J.: General Learning Press, 1972, pp. 79 –94.

Jones, E. E., Davis, K. E., & Gergen, K. J. Role playing variations and their informational value for person perception. *Journal of Abnormal and Social Psychology*, 1961, *63*, 302 –310.

Jones, R. A. *Self-fulfilling prophecies: Social, psychological, and physiological effects of expectancies*. Hillsdale, N.J.: Erlbaum, 1977.

Kahneman, D., & Tversky, A. On the psychology of prediction. *Psychological Review*, 1973, *80*, 237 –251.

Karlins, M., Coffman, T. L., & Walters, G. Fading of stereotypes in three generations of college students. *Journal of Personality and Social Psychology*, 1969, *13*, 1 –16.

Kassin, S. M. Physical continuity and trait inference: A test of Mischel's hypothesis. *Personality and Social Psychology Bulletin*, 1977, *3*, 637 –640.

Katz, I., & Glass, D. C. An ambivalence-amplification theory of behavior toward the stigmatized. In W. Austin and S. Worchel (Eds.), *The social psychology of intergroup relations*. Belmont, Calif.: Brooks/Cole, 1979.

Kelley, H. H. The warm cold variable in first impressions of persons. *Journal of Personality*, 1950, *18*, 431 –439.

Kiker, V. L., & Miller, A. R. Perceptual judgment of physiques as a factor in social image. *Perceptual and Motor Skills*, 1967, *24*, 1013 –1014.

Kleck, R. E. & Strenta, A. Perceptions of the impact of negatively valued physical characteristics on social interaction. *Journal of Personality and Social Psychology*, 1980, *39*, 861 –873.

Koffka, K. Perceived motion. In *Principles of gestalt psychology*. New York: Harcourt Brace, 1935.

Kraut, R. E. Effects of social labeling on giving to charity. *Journal of Experimental and Social Psychology*, 1973, *9*, 551 –562.

Langer, E. J., & Abelson, R. P. A patient by any other name. . . Clinician group difference in labeling bias. *Journal of Consulting and Clinical Psychology*, 1974, *42*, 4 –9.

Langer, E. J., & Benevento, A. Self-induced dependence. *Journal of Personality and Social Psychology*, 1978, *36*, 886 –893.

Langer, E. J., Taylor, S. E., Fiske, S. T., & Chanowitz, B. Stigma, staring, and discomfort: A novel stimulus hypothesis. *Journal of Experimental Social Psychology*, 1976, *12*, 451 –463.

Lappin, J. S. Attention in the identification of stimuli in complex visual displays. *Journal of Experimental Psychology*, 1967, *75*, 321 –328.

Lawson, E. D. Hair color, personality, and the observer. *Psychological Reports*, 1971, *28*, 311 –322.

Lepper, M. R. Dissonance, self-perception, and honesty in children. *Journal of Personality and Social Psychology*, 1973, *25*, 65 –74.

Lerner, M. J. The desire for justice and reactions to victims. In J. Macaulay & L. Berkowitz (Eds.), *Altruism and helping behavior*. New York: Academic, 1970, pp. 205 –229.

Lingle, J. H., & Ostrom, T. M. Retrieval selectivity in memory-based impression judgments. *Journal of Personality and Social Psychology*, 1979, *37*, 180 –194.

Lingle, J. H., Geva, N., Ostrom, T. M., Leippe, M. R., & Baumgardner, M. H., Thematic effects in person judgments on impression organization. *Journal of Personality and Social Psychology*, 1979, *37*, 674 –687.

Lippmann,, W. *Public opinion*. New York: Harcourt Brace, 1922.

Livesley, W. J., & Bromley, D. B. *Person perception in childhood and adolescence*. London: Wiley, 1973.

Manis, M., Gleason, T. C., & Dawes, R. M. The evaluation of complex social stimuli. *Journal of Personality and Social Psychology*, 1966, *3*, 404 –419.

Markus, H. Self-schemata and processing information about the self. *Journal of Personality and Social Psychology*, 1977, *35*, 63 –78.

Massad, C. M., Hubbard, M., & Newtson, D. Selective perception of events. *Journal of Experimental Social Psychology*, 1979, *15*, 513 –532.

McArthur, L. A. The how and what of why: Some determinants and consequences of causal attribution. *Journal of Personality and Social Psychology*, 1972, *22*, 171 –193.

McArthur, L. A., Kiesler, C. A., & Cook, B. P. Acting on an attitude as a function of self-percept and inequity. *Journal of Personality and Social Psychology*, 1969, *12*, 295 –302.

McArthur, L. Z. Illusory causation and illusory correlation: Two epistemological accounts. *Personality and Social Psychology Bulletin*, 1980, *6*, 507 –519.

McArthur, L. Z. Physical disinctiveness and self-attribution. Unpublished manuscript. Brandeis University. Waltham, Mass., 1981. (a)

McArthur, L. Z. What grabs you: The role of attention on impression formation and causal attribution. In E. T. Higgins, C. P. Herman, and M. P. Zanna (Eds.), *Social cognition: The Ontario symposium*, Vol. 1. Hillsdale, N.J.: Erlbaum, 1981. (b).

McArthur, L. Z., & Friedman, S. Illusory correlation in impression formation: Variations in the shared distinctiveness effect as a function of the distinctive person's age, race, and sex. *Journal of Personality and Social Psychology*, 1980, *39*, 615 –624.

McArthur, L. Z., & Ginsberg, E. Causal attribution to salient stimuli: An investigation of visual fixation mediators. *Personality and Social Psychology Bulletin*, 1981, in press.

McArthur, L. Z., & Post, D. L. Figural emphasis and person perception. *Journal of Experimental Social Psychology*, 1977, *13*, 520 –535.

McArthur, L. Z., & Solomon, L. K. Perceptions of an aggressive encounter as a function of the victim's salience and the perceiver's arousal. *Journal of Personality and Social Psychology*, 1978, *36*, 1278 –1290.

McGuire, W. J., & Padawer-Singer, A. Trait salience in the spontaneous self-concept. *Journal of Personality and Social Psychology*, 1976, *33*, 743 –754.

McGuire, W. J., McGuire, C. V., Child, P., & Fujloka, T. Salience of ethnicity in the spontaneous self-concept as a function on one's ethnic distinctiveness in the social environment. *Journal of Personality and Social Psychology*, 1978, *36*, 511 –521.

McGuire, W. J., McGuire, C. V., & Winton, W. Effects of household sex composition on the salience of one's gender in the spontaneous self-concept. *Journal of Experimental Social Psychology*, 1979, *15*, 77 –90.

Meichenbaum, D. H., Bowers, K. S., & Ross, R. R. A behavioral analysis of teacher expectancy effects. *Journal of Personality and Social Psychology*, 1969, *13*, 306 –316.

Milord, J. T. Aesthetic aspects of faces: A (somewhat) phenomenological analysis using multidimensional scaling methods. *Journal of Personality and Social Psychology*, 1978, *36*, 205 –216.

Mischel, W. *Personality and assessment*. New York: Wiley, 1968.

Moreland, R. L., & Zajonc, R. B. Exposure effects may not depend on stimulus recognition. *Journal of Personality and Social Psychology*, 1979, *37*, 1085 –1089.

Newtson, D. Foundations of attribution: The perception of ongoing behavior. In J. H. Harvey, W. J. Ickes, & R. F. Kidd (Eds.), *New directions in attribution research*, Vol. 1. New York: Wiley, 1976, pp. 223 –248.

Newtson, D., Rindner, R., Miller, R., & LaCross, K. Effects of availability of feature changes on behavior segmentation. *Journal of Experimental Social Psychology*, 1978, *14*, 379 –388.

Nisbett, R. E., & Ross, L. *Human inference: Strategies and shortcomings of social judgment*. Englewood Cliffs, N.J.: Prentice-Hall, 1980.

Perlman, D., & Oskamp, S. The effects of picture content and exposure frequency on evaluations of Negroes and whites. *Journal of Experimental Social Psychology*, 1971, *7*, 503 –514.

Podell, H. A., & Podell, J. E. Quantitative connotation of a concept. *Journal of Abnormal and Social Psychology*, 1963, *67*, 509 –513.

Posner, M. I., Nissen, M. J., Klein, R. M. Visual dominance: An information-processing account of its origins and significance. *Psychological Review*, 1976, *83*, 157 –170.

Regan, D. T., Straus, E., & Fazio, R. Liking and the attribution process. *Journal of Experimental Social Psychology*, 1974, *10*, 385 –397.

Rescorla, R. A., & Wagner, A. R. A theory of Pavlovian conditioning: Variations on the effectiveness of reinforcement and non-reinforcement. In A. H. Black and W. F. Prokasy (Eds.), *Classical conditioning II: Current theory and research*. New York: Appleton-Century-Crofts, 1972.

Robinson, J., & McArthur, L. Z. The impact of salient vocal qualities on causal attribution for a speaker's behavior. Unpublished manuscript. Brandeis University. Waltham, Mass., 1981.

Rodin, J., & Slochower, J. Fat chance for a favor: Obese-normal differences in compliance and incidental learning. *Journal of Personality and Social Psychology*, 1974, *29*, 557 –565.

Roll, S., & Verinis, J. S. Stereotypes of scalp and facial hair as measured by the semantic differential. *Psychological Reports*, 1971, *28*, 975 –980.

Rosenberg, S., Nelson, C., & Vivekananthan, P. S. A multidimensional approach to the structure of personality impressions. *Journal of Personality and Social Psychology*, 1968, *9*, 283 –94.

Rosenthal, R., & Jacobsen, L. F. *Pygmalion in the classroom: Teacher expectation and pupils' intellectual development*. New York: Holt, Rinehart & Winston, 1968.

Ross, L. The intuitive psychologist and his shortcomings: Distortions in the attribution process. In L. Berkowitz (Ed.), *Advances in experimental social psychology*, Vol. 10. New York: Academic, 1977, pp. 174 –221.

Ross, L., Lepper, M. R., & Hubbard, M. Perseverence in self-perception and social perception: Biased attributional process in the debriefing paradigm. *Journal of Personality and Social Psychology*, 1975, *32*, 880 –892.

Rothbart, M., Fulero, S., Jensen, C., Howard, J., & Birrell, P. From individual to group impressions: Availability heuristics in stereotype formation. *Journal of Experimental Social Psychology*, 1978, *14*, 237 –255.

Rothbart, M., Evans, M., & Fulero, S. Recall for confirming events: Memory processes and the maintenance of social stereotypes. *Journal of Experimental Social Psychology*, 1979, *15*, 343 –356.

Ryan, W. *Blaming the victim*. New York: Vintage Books, 1971.

Schneider, D. J. Implicit personality theory. *Psychological Bulletin*, 1973, *79*, 294 –309.

Schneider, D. J., Hastorf, A. H., & Ellsworth, P. C. *Person Perception*. Reading, Mass.: Addison-Wesley, 1979.

Seaver, W. B. Effects of naturally induced teacher expectancies. *Journal of Personality and Social Psychology*, 1973, *28*, 333 –342.

Secord, P. F. Facial features and inference processes in interpersonal perception. In R. Tagiuri and L. Petrullo (Eds.), *Person perception and interpersonal behavior*. Stanford, Calif.: Stanford University Press, 1958, pp. 300 –315.

Secord, P. F., & Muthard, J. E. Personalities in faces: IV. A descriptive analysis of the perception of women's faces and the identification of physiognomic determinants. *Journal of Psychology*, 1953, *39*, 261 –278.

Secord, P. F., Dukes, W. F., & Bevan, W. Personalities in faces: I. An experiment in social perceiving. *Genetic Psychology Monographs*, 1954, *49*, 231 –279.

Secord, P. F., Bevan, W., & Dukes, W. F. Occupational and physiognomic stereotypes in the perception of photographs. *Journal of Social Psychology*, 1953, *37*, 261 –270.

Secord, P. F., Bevan, W., & Katz, B. Perceptual accentuation and the Negro stereotype. *Journal of Abnormal and Social Psychology*, 1956, *53*, 78 –83.

Sheldon, W. H. *Atlas of men*. New York: Gramercy, 1954.

Sherif, M., & Hovland, C. *Social judgment*. New Haven, Conn.: Yale University Press, 1961.

Sleet, D. A. Physique and social image. *Perceptual and Motor Skills*, 1969, *28*, 295 –299.

Snyder, M., & Cantor, N. Testing hypotheses about other people: The use of historical knowledge. *Journal of Experimental Social Psychology*, 1979, *15*, 330 –342.

Snyder, M., & Swann, W. B. Hypothesis-testing processes in social interaction. *Journal of Personality and Social Psychology*, 1978, *36*, 1202 –1212.

Snyder, M., & Uranowitz, S. W. Reconstructing the past: Some cognitive consequences of person perception. *Journal of Personality and Social Psychology*, 1978, *36*, 941 –950.

Snyder, M., Tanke, E. D., & Berscheid, E. Social perception and interpersonal behavior: On the self-fulfilling nature of social stereotypes. *Journal of Personality and Social Psychology*, 1977, *35*, 656 –666.

Snyder, M. L., & Frankel, A. Observer bias: A stringent test of behavior engulfing the field. *Journal of Personality and Social Psychology*, 1976, *34*, 857 –864.

Stein, D. D., Hardyck, J. A., & Smith, M. B. Race and belief: An open and shut case. *Journal of Personality and Social Psychology*, 1965, *1*, 281 –289.

Storms, M. Videotape and the attribution process: Reversing actors' and observers' points of view. *Journal of Personality and Social Psychology*, 1973, *27*, 165 –175.

Tajfel, H. Experiments in intergroup discrimination. *Scientific American*, 1970, *223*, 96 –102.

Tajfel, H., & Wilkes, A. L. Classification and quantitative judgment. *British Journal of Psychology*, 1963, 54, 101 –114.

Tajfel, H., Sheikh, A. A., & Gardner, R. C. Content of stereotypes and the inference of similarity between members of stereotyped groups. *Acta Psychologica*, 1964, *22*, 191 –201.

Taylor, M. C. Race, sex, and the expression of self-fulfilling prophecies in a laboratory teaching situation. *Journal of Personality and Social Psychology*, 1979, *37*, 897 –912.

Taylor, S. E., & Fiske, S. T. Salience, attention, and attribution: Top of the head phenomena. In L. Berkowitz (Ed.), *Advances in experimental social psychology*, Vol. 11. New York: Academic, 1978, pp. 250 –288.

Taylor, S. E., & Langer, E. J. Pregnancy: A social stigma? *Sex Roles*, 1977, *3*, 27 –35.

Taylor, S. E., Fiske, S. T., Close, M., Anderson, C., & Ruderman, A. J. Solo status as a psychological variable: The power of being distinctive. Unpublished manuscript. Harvard Univesity, Cambridge, Mass., 1976.

Taylor, S. E., Fiske, S. T., Etcoff, N. L., & Ruderman, A. J. The categorical and contextual bases of person memory and stereotyping. *Journal of Personality and Social Psychology*, 1978, *36*, 778 –793.

Taylor, S. E., Crocker, J., Fiske, S. T., Sprinzen, M., & Winkler, J. D. The generalizability of salience effects. *Journal of Personality and Social Psychology*, 1979, *37*, 357 –368.

Tesser, A. Self-generated attitude change. In L. Berkowitz (Ed.), *Advances in experimental social psychology*, Vol. 11. New York: Academic, 1978, pp. 289 –338.

Thornton, G. R. The effect upon judgments of personality traits of varying a single factor in a photograph. *The Journal of Social Psychology*, 1943, *18*, 127 –148.

Thornton, G. R. The effect of wearing glasses upon judgments of personality traits. *Journal of Applied Psychology*, 1944, *28*, 203 –207.

Toch, H. H., & Schulte, R. Readiness to perceive violence as a result of police training. *British Journal of Psychology*, 1961, *52*, 389 –393.

Triandis, H. C., & Vassiliou, V. Frequency of contact and stereotyping. *Journal of Personality and Social Psychology*, 1967, *7*, 316 –328.

Tversky, A. Features of similarity. *Psychological Review*, 1977, *84*, 327 –352.

Tversky, A., & Kahneman, D. Availability: A heuristic for judging frequency and probability. *Cognitive Psychology*, 1973, *5*, 207 –232.

Vinacke, W. E. Explorations in the dynamic processes of stereotyping. *Journal of Social Psychology*, 1956, *43*, 105 –132.

Walster, E., Berscheid, E., & Walster, G. W. The exploited: Justice or justification? In J. Macaulay & L. Berkowitz (Eds.), *Altruism and helping behavior*, New York: Academic, 1970, pp. 179 –204.

Ward, W. C., & Jenkins, H. M. The display of information and the judgment of contingency. *Canadian Journal of Psychology*, 1965, *19*, 231 –241.

Warr, P. Inference magnitude, range, and evaluative direction as factors affecting relative importance of cues in impression formation. *Journal of Personality and Social Psychology*, 1974, *30*, 191 –197.

Watzlawick, P., Reavin, J. H., & Jackson, D. D. *Pragmatics of human communication: A study of interactional patterns, pathologies, and paradoxes*. New York: Norton, 1967.

Weiner, M. J., & Wright, F. E. Effects of undergoing arbitrary discrimination upon subsequent attitudes toward a minority group. *Journal of Applied Social Psychology*, 1973, *3*, 94 –102.

Wells, W. D., & Siegal, B. Stereotyped somatotypes. *Psychological Reports*, 1961, *8*, 77 –78.

Werner, H. Ueber Strukturgesetze und deren Auswirkung in den Sog, geometrischoptischen Tauschungen. *Zeitschrift fuer Psychologie*, 1924, *94*, 248 –264, as cited in F. Heider, Social perception and phenomenal causality. *Psychological Review*, 1944, *51*, 358 –374.

Wicklund, R. A. Objective self-awareness. In L. Berkowitz (Ed.), *Advances in experimental social psychology*, Vol. 8. New York: Academic, 1975, pp. 233 –275.

Wilder, D. A. Reduction of intergroup discrimination through individuation of the outgroup. *Journal of Personality and Social Psychology*, 1978, *36*, 1361 –1374.

Williams, J. E. Connotations of color names among Negroes and Caucasians. *Perceptual and Motor Skills*, 1964, *18*, 121 –131.

Williams, L. G. The effect of target specification on objects fixated during visual search. *Perception and Psychophysics*, 1966, *1*, 315 –318.

Word, C. H., Zanna, M. P., & Cooper J. The non-verbal mediation of self-fulfilling prophecies in interracial interaction. *Journal of Experimemtal Social Psychology*, 1974, *10*, 109 –120.

Wyer, R. S. *Cognitive organization and change: An information processing approach*. Hillsdale, N.J.: Erlbaum, 1974.

Zadny, J., & Gerard, H. B. Attributed intentions and informational selectivity. *Journal of Experimental Social Psychology*, 1974, *10*, 34 –52.

Zajonc, R. B. Feeling and thinking: Preferences need no inferences. *American Psychologist*, 1980, *35*, 151 –175.

Zajonc, R. B., Markus, H., & Wilson, W. R. Exposure effects and associative learning. *Journal of Experimental Social Psychology*, 1974, *10*, 248 –263.

Zanna, M. P., & Hamilton, D. L. Attribute dimensions and patterns of trait inferences. *Psychonomic Science*, 1972, *27*, 353 –354.

Zanna, M. P., & Pack, S. J. On the self-fulfilling nature of apparent sex differences in behavior. *Journal of Experimental Social Psychology*, 1975, *11*, 583 –591.

JOHN S. CARROLL RICHARD L. WIENER

COGNITIVE SOCIAL PSYCHOLOGY IN COURT AND BEYOND

Psychologists, legal scholars, and criminologists have a long history of mutual interest. Beginning as early as Munsterberg (1908), psychologists have believed that their understanding of human thought and behavior could be of value in the legal process. Legal scholars have recognized that legal issues of evidence, guilt, responsibility, intention, and punishment are also psychological issues involving our understanding of what the "reasonable man" thinks about and how he behaves. For example, Roscoe Pound (1923) pointed out 60 years ago that in dealing with legal concepts such as foreseeability, "we must rely on the common sense of the common man as to common things" (pp. 951 –952).

The analysis of causal reasoning provides one example of the converging interests of psychologists and legal scholars. At the same time that Heider (1958) provided the foundations for the social psychological study of causal reasoning, Hart and Honoré (1959) provided a legal analysis of causation in which they recognized the importance of understanding lay concepts and judgments about causality. "The assertion often made by the courts, especially in England, that it is the plain man's notions of causation (and not the philosopher's or the scientist's) with which the law is concerned, seems to us to be true" (p. 1).

The purpose of this chapter is to organize and selectively review social psychological research regarding how people think about crime and criminals. Much of this research is directly relevant to the exercise of discretion by actors in the legal system, such as judges and jurors (cf. Shaver, Gilbert, & Williams, 1975; Abt & Stuart, 1979). This research is also useful for understanding how people react to criminals and to crime in our society, and even for considering "expert" theories of crime and proposals for dealing with criminals.

The chapter is organized around selected research topics that have characterized cognitive social psychological approaches to the perception of crime and criminals. We have left out a variety of topics social psychologists have investigated that do not strongly imply a theory about how perceptions and cognitions mediate the relationship between events and behavior (e.g., the jury as a small group). For a more general view of social psychology and legal issues, the reader might consult Abt and Stuart (1979) and Saks and Hastie (1978). We have also focused almost entirely upon research that requires subjects to function in a legal context—to evaluate criminals, act as mock jurors, and so forth. Research that has implications for our discussion, but is not placed in the legal context, is only reviewed if it is very important. The astute reader will no doubt realize that some very well-established research areas (e.g., eyewitness identification) are not represented. We selected those topics that create a single conceptual path of growing complexity in the way social psychologists have represented the judgments and behaviors of persons evaluating crime and criminals. We tried to create a presentation that builds toward the newest and most complex approaches.

The first section of this chapter reviews research focusing on the task of evaluating a criminal defendant and applying sanctions. The assignment of punishment is seen as similar to an evaluative judgment: the more negative characteristics the defender possesses, and the fewer positive ones, the more harsh the punishment. Drawing from the attraction literature, research in this paradigm also investigates the similarity of defendant and evaluator. Equity theory adds the idea that the sanction could be used to restore equity among criminal, victim, other criminals, and society as a whole.

The second section of the chapter reviews attribution research, exploring the idea that sanctions should depend upon the defendant's degree of responsibility. Although much attribution research defines responsibility as either internal to the defendant or external, other research follows Heider's (1958) qualitatively different levels of responsibility that parallel legal analyses of culpability. This introduces the complexity of judging what the defendant intended and knew, as well as what the "reasonable person" should have known or done.

As social psychologists studied the legal system, they became more sophisticated about how the system works. Besides using sanctions such as prison sentences for punishment and retribution, the legal system also deals with crime by attempting to deter potential criminals with the threat of punishment, to incapacitate criminals in prison where they cannot victimize society, and to rehabilitate criminals through programs inside and outside prison and by diversion from the legal system into treatment programs (out of the criminal justice frying pan into the mental health fire). The third section reviews social psychological research regarding how actors in the legal system integrate these multiple goals and how the goals are differentially important in different tasks and for different individuals. Attribution researchers responded to this complexity by adapting and developing dimensional models of causal attributions that relate different dimensions to different goals.

Most recently, along with the growing momentum of applied social psychology, researchers studying the legal system are relying in greater measure on actors within the legal system making actual judgments as part of their job, rather than college students doing semirealistic laboratory analogues. One result has been to make more evident the importance of the specific content of real-world tasks and the vast knowledge possessed by actors within the legal system. Some social psychologists are addressing the contextual material by carefully observing naturalistic behavior and describing the empirically derived relationship between information available to an actor and the actor's decisions (e.g., Ebbesen & Konečni, 1975). Others have begun developing models of such decisions that attempt to represent the characteristics of the task and the knowledge possessed by the decision-makers.

The development of schema theories of knowledge organization and use in cognitive psychology and cognitive social psychology (e.g., Taylor & Crocker, 1981) provides a way to characterize the complex knowledge people have about natural situations. Because the applied social psychology movement has taken us out of the laboratory where subjects are "naive," we are confronting the failure of our theories to explain the knowledgeable behavior of subjects in their natural setting. Cognitive social psychology, our newest theoretical endeavor, contains the means for understanding our newest applied directions. In the final section of the chapter we attempt to reorganize some of the confusing results and implications of earlier theoretical approaches and put forward a new model of judgments about crime and criminals that is also a reformulation of attribution theory based on the schema models.

SANCTIONING

Social psychologists have been giving subjects the task of evaluating evidence in a criminal case, deciding guilt, and assigning punishment for several decades (Gerbasi, Zuckerman, & Reis, 1977). A great deal of mock jury or mock juror research has involved the role of demographic and personality characteristics of the jurors in determining verdicts. Other studies have investigated the effects of judges' instructions, size of jury, decision rule, and format or order of evidence (Davis, Bray, & Holt, 1977; Gerbasi et al., 1977). Although these studies present a number of interesting concepts, we will focus on the major theoretical themes that link together a number of studies: impression formation and distributive justice (equity).

Impression Formation

Beginning with Landy and Aronson (1969), many social psychologists have approached the evaluation of criminal cases as an impression formation situation. If the mock juror likes the defendant, the defendant is considered less guilty and treated more leniently; if the defendant is disliked, the reverse occurs. Factors such as the personality, attitudes, background, and appearance of defendants have been used to make them likeable or not. In general, these factors are not legally relevant, but do have validity in the experiences of trial lawyers. As Clarence Darrow said, "Jurymen seldom convict a person they like or acquit one they dislike. . .facts regarding the case are relatively unimportant" (Sutherland & Cressey, 1966, p. 442).

Landy and Aronson (1969) had mock jurors read a negligent homicide case in which a drunk driver goes through a red light and kills a pedestrian. Three descriptions of the defendant were included: a well-liked and stable insurance adjustor (attractive), a divorced janitor with a criminal record (unattractive), and an employee from nearby (neutral). Attractive and neutral defendants received shorter sentences than unattractive defendants. Although the descriptions used in this study confounded attractiveness with age and the defendant's own injury in the act, later studies have confirmed these results (Reynolds & Sanders, 1973; Sigall & Landy, 1973). Studies have found that very simple changes in a few trait labels can markedly change sentences, such as describing the defendant as "loving and warm" or "cold and unapproachable" (Kaplan & Kemmerick, 1974; Sigall & Landy, 1973). However, this general support should be qualified by a few studies indicating a reverse effect or no effect, and some studies showing that attractiveness effects disappear when juries deliberate (Davis et al., 1977).

Efran (1974) had students role-play jurors on a student-faculty court who judged the guilt of a hypothetical student caught cheating on an examination. Written case descriptions were accompanied by photographs of the defendant varying in physical attractiveness. Attractive defendants were rated less guilty and as deserving milder punishment. Solomon and Schopler (1978) also found that attractive defendants received milder punishment in a fraud case than average or unattractive defendants.

Sigall and Ostrove (1975) reasoned that attractive defendants are expected to have more success and status and therefore be less likely to commit future crimes. This may be the reason why they are treated leniently. To test this, they created stimulus materials crossing three levels of physical attractiveness from photographs of women with two different crimes—a burglary and a swindle each of $2200. Subjects should view the attractive swindler as having a higher risk of recidivism than the unattractive swindler, since attractiveness is an asset for confidence swindles, but attractiveness should operate oppositely for burglary. The results showed that the attractive swindler was given a longer sentence than the unattractive swindler, while no differences were found among levels of attractiveness in the burglary condition. Of course, there are alternative explanations for these results. For example, using one's appearance to con people may be seen as more reprehensible than just fast-talking them, or there may even be a "beautiful but bad" stereotype of women.

Another limitation on the effects of physical attractiveness seems to be the severity of the crime. Piehl (1977) found that physical appearance affected sentencing judgments about hypothetical traffic offenders when the accidents were minor (attractive defendants were punished less), but attractiveness had no effect when the accident was severe—resulting in the death of another driver.

A few studies have manipulated the attractiveness of the victim rather than or along with that of the defendant. Landy and Aronson (1969) described unattractive victims who were notorious criminals and attractive victims who were pillars of the community. The results were only marginally significant in the direction of longer sentences for crimes against more attractive victims, and much weaker than the effects of defendant attractiveness.

Kerr (1978) manipulated the physical attractiveness of an auto theft victim and also her responsibility for the theft (whether she locked the car and removed her keys). Results indicated that when the victim was blameless, the more attractive victim produced a willingness to convict the defendant on less evidence of guilt, but no relationship of attractiveness and willingness to convict was apparent when the victim was careless.

Research has also revealed the similarity –attraction effect in criminal cases. Mock jurors whose attitudes had been previously measured evaluated a hypothetical defendant whose case history included material indicating similarity to the juror or dissimilarity on attitude topics. High authoritarian subjects recommended more punishment and were more certain of the defendant's guilt when the defendant was more dissimilar (Mitchell & Byrne, 1973). Good and Good (1977) also found similarity-leniency using descriptions tailored to premeasured attitudes of subjects. Griffitt and Jackson (1973) used the Landy and Aronson case materials but replaced the attractiveness manipulation with a statement indicating the defendant's conservative attitudes toward God, Country, and sex roles. Subjects who agreed with these attitudes were more lenient toward the defendant. Lussier, Perlman, and Breen (1977) found that psychiatric nurses recommended less punishment for hypothetical drug offenders when they indicated more positive attitudes toward marijuana or more personal drug usage.

Distributive Justice

Beginning with Homans' (1961) classic statement on distributive justice, social psychologists have argued that people expect that rewards will be distributed equitably—those who contribute more positive inputs should receive more positive outcomes (Adams, 1965; Walster, Berscheid, & Walster, 1973). This principle translates readily into increasing punishment for more severe criminal acts.

However, balancing suffering against the crime does not always translate into a matching of crime and years in prison. Austin and Utne (1977) proposed that if the defendant has already suffered as a result of committing the crime (i.e., was injured), then mock jurors should be more lenient. Subjects were indeed less punitive in recommending sentences when defendants had suffered more, but a uniform decrease in penalty with increasing suffering was evidenced only for the mild crime of simple robbery. Only "excessive suffering" (i.e., paralysis) reduced the recommended penalty for the more serious crimes of assault and rape. Interestingly, the effect of defendant suffering on punishment did not depend on whether the offender had suffered during the commission of the crime or incidental to it while out on bail. Similarly, in civil cases juries consider the financial situation of the defendant in assigning penalties. They seem to seek individualized justice rather than the strict application of legal rules (Erlanger, 1970). In a misdemeanor shoplifting case, Fontaine and Emily (1978, p. 329) observe a judge dispense individualized justice: "At your age, the humiliation at having been arrested and coming to Court would be sufficient."

Equity does not only reflect the suffering of victim and defendant, but could also be part of comparisons among criminals. Jurors are sometimes unwilling to punish defendants for crimes that others commit without punishment, yet sometimes jurors are apparently punishing the unlucky scapegoat for the crimes of many uncaptured people. DeJong, Morris, and Hastorf (1976) found that a defendant was punished less when his accomplice escaped, apparently as a way of making the treatment of all the defendants equitable.

If these actions are generalizable to actual juries, it is obvious that the layperson's idea of distributive justice is not fully compatible with the legal concept of justice. The jury has an accepted role of deciding that community standards demand the law not be applied. In cases where the defendant has suffered or has endured hardship, the jury will be lenient. In cases where the law demands a punishment more severe than the jury feels proper, they will often fail to convict (Brooks & Doob, 1975; Vidmar, 1972). Historically, juries have responded to the imposition of mandatory death penalties by acquitting more people. However, the discretionary domain of the jury would certainly not extend to considering escaped accomplices nor to the physical or attitudinal attractiveness of the defendant.

Summary

This section presents research in which social psychologists extended familiar paradigms into the domain of crime. Subjects were asked, in effect, to evaluate criminals on a good–bad dimension, reflecting a desire to punish or a certainty of guilt. On the whole, the impression formation and distributive justice models direct our attention to certain inferences that determine how much punishment (and in some cases guilt) will be assigned, such as a liking for the defendant and equity judgments. These inferences are based on identifiable cues. Physical and personality characteristics of the defendant and the similarity of defendant to evaluator influence liking. The defendant's suffering and the outcomes for other criminals affect equity judgments.

Even within these simple paradigms, complex results are evident. The attractiveness of the defendant has opposite effects if the crime is attractiveness-based; one plausible explanation suggests that sentencing involves risk judgments as well as evaluations. This prefigures our discussion later in the chapter. Also, the attractiveness of the victim has no simple effect on sentencing.

The next section of this chapter expands the model of what inferences a sanctioner makes by introducing the psychological and legal concept of responsibility.

ATTRIBUTING RESPONSIBILITY

The development of attribution theory in the past two decades provides the most active research area in social psychology and a framework for analyzing a wide variety of social behaviors. The application of the attributional paradigm to crime, criminals, and the law was initially easy because attribution theory and legal thought focus on the same issues. Yet difficulties arose because people are not so "naive" about the law, and attribution theory must integrate itself with existing legal scholarship.

As attribution theory developed within social psychology, it readily became apparent that the relationships among intent, responsibility, and causality would be of central interest. In his seminal statement analyzing naive judgment, Heider (1958, pp. 112, 113) points to the crucial role of intention: "People are held responsible for their intentions and exertions but not so strictly for their abilities." Further, the contribution of environmental factors is considered by the perceiver: "in general, the more they are felt to influence the action, the less the person is held responsible."

In these statements, Heider refers to two issues that have guided much of subsequent attribution research. First, the central distinction in attribution theory has been between events attributed to the actor and those attributed to the environment, which we will call causal locus. Guided by Heider and even more by Kelley (1967) many attribution theorists have conceptualized causality and responsibility in terms of causal locus. Second, in contrast, other attribution researchers have drawn upon Heider's distinction between intended and unintended events, which also find expression in the theoretical work of Jones and Davis (1965) and Weiner (1974).

The result has been a high degree of confusion in attribution research regarding what is conceptualized as responsibility—either causal locus or intent. Further, for a few social psychologists familiar with philosophical and legal analyses of responsibility, there is the problem that responsibility has other meanings beyond causation and intention. The law in general holds a person culpable for his or her acts when the criminal act (*actus reus*) is accompanied by a criminal state of mind (*mens rea*). The determination of what constitutes a "criminal state of mind" in type and degree is a central problem for a large legal literature (e.g., Hart

& Honoré, 1959). Responsibility typically refers to accountability, which is a product of social norms and moral principles that draws upon perceptions of causality and intention but is not synonymous with them [see Fincham & Jaspars (1980) for an excellent discussion of these issues].

Although we have mentioned some of the complexities of responsibility attribution, our discussion will reflect the empirical research that has investigated how crime is attributed to criminals and the effects of these attributions. Essentially, the underlying model is that sanctions will be applied to criminals depending upon their perceived responsibility for the crime. The dependent measures for this research have been judgments of guilt, suggested sentence, and/or attribution questions regarding the responsibility of the criminal. Attribution research into perceived responsibility has used two very loose definitions of responsibility as either causal locus or degree of intent. The third and final topic we will review is the attributed responsibility of the crime victim.

Causal Locus

Attribution researchers rarely make a direct manipulation of causal locus but allow subjects to infer or attribute locus from other manipulated cues. This serves the dual purpose of validating theories regarding how causal locus is attributed and also confirming that guilt judgments or sanctioning are affected in parallel. For example, Lussier et al. (1977) tested a prediction drawn from Kelley (1967) that criminals who have committed similar crimes in the past will have the crime attributed to them more than will criminals lacking such consistency. They found that subjects attributed drug offenses more strongly to the person and recommended more severe punishment than they did to first offenders (cf. Hans & Doob, 1976).

Another hypothesis from Kelley's (1967) work is that the more people who behave in a similar fashion in a given situation, the more observers will attribute causality to the situation and less to the people involved. Feldman and Rosen (1978) asked college students to act as judges in a robbery case involving the defendant alone or with an accomplice. Subjects rated the lone defendant as far more responsible for the crime, but did not recommend a longer sentence, nor did sentence correlate with responsibility. However, an archival study of a sample of 140 actual theft cases revealed that the 70 single perpetrators received significantly longer sentences than did the 70 multiple perpetrators. This effect remained after controlling for value of goods taken and age of defendant. This effect can also be interpreted as an instance of discounting (Kelley, 1967) or adding more noncommon effects of the crime (Jones & Davis, 1965). Since one offender of a pair may have committed the crime either for criminal outcomes *or* to please the partner, the presence of two plausible causes reduces attribution to the offender.

Kelley's later work (Kelley, 1973; Cunningham & Kelley, 1975) put forth the idea that acts with more severe outcomes produce greater attribution to the actor. Rosen and Jerdee (1974) had business students evaluate infractions of company rules that resulted in mild or severe consequences. Severe consequences produced greater attributions of personal responsibility and recommendations for more severe disciplinary action.

Intent

Despite the predominant focus of attribution research on causal locus, a substantial amount of theory and research have followed Heider (1958) and Jones and Davis (1965) to examine the degree of intent of the actor rather than causal locus. Hendrick and Shaffer (1975) found that a murderer who had mutiliated the victim after death was considered to have been more intentional and received longer recommended sentences from simulated jurors than a murderer who had not. Sosis (1974) had high school students act as mock jurors in a motor vehicle crime taken from Landy and Aronson (1969). She found that Internals on Rotter's (1966) Internal – External Locus of Control Scale rated the offender more responsible for his acts and recommended more severe punishment than did Externals. Sosis interprets this as a projection of the Internal's belief that events are generally controllable and people are therefore responsible for what outcomes occur.

One of the most promising linkages between attribution research and legal concepts comes from a categorical classification of types of responsibility that offers a more detailed understanding than a quantitative scale and reproduces some distinctions present in legal analyses of responsibility. Heider (1958) identified five levels of responsibility attribution which he considered as "forms" or "stages" ranging from primitive to sophisticated. The levels have been named by Sulzer (1971):

1. Association—the person is responsible for anything associated with him, e.g., a family is driven out of town because one member of the family committed a crime.
2. Causality—the person is responsible for anything he or she caused, even unintentional or accidental events. Piaget (1932) calls this objective responsibility.
3. Foreseeability—the person is responsible for anything that could have been foreseen or predicted, even if unintentional.
4. Intentionality—the person is responsible for only those events that were intended, what Heider (1958) calls personal causality and Piaget (1932) labels subjective responsibility.
5. Justifiability—the person is responsible for intentional acts only when these acts were not provoked by the environment, e.g., self-defense and mercy killings. Responsibility is lessened if "anybody would have felt and acted as he did under the circumstances" (Heider, 1958, p. 114).

These levels of responsibility reproduce many of the critical distinctions in legal culpability that determine degree of punishment. The law generally recognizes four levels of culpability for voluntary acts (*Model Penal Code*, 1962):

1. Purposely—the person intended the act and wished to cause the effects.
2. Knowingly—the person was aware of his acts and it was "practically certain" that the effect would occur.
3. Recklessly—the person "consciously disregards a substantial and unjustifiable risk" that a law-abiding person would observe in the actor's situation.
4. Negligently—the person fails to perceive a substantial and unjustifiable risk that a law abiding person would have observed in this situation.

In addition, the law distinguishes involuntary acts such as reflexes or hypnotic suggestions for which the person is not criminally liable. Other legal defenses that reduce responsibility include factors justifying the act, such as public duty, self-defense, or protecting others, factors involving diminished responsibility, such as mental disease, youth, and intoxication, and situational circumstances such as coercion or force that "a person of reasonable firmness in his situation would have been unable to resist" (*Model Penal Code*, 1962). Finally, there are some crimes that do not require a proof of responsibility or *mens rea*, such as parking violations. These offenses have "absolute liability" for reasons including the difficulty of establishing mental state after the fact and the importance to the community of regulating these behaviors.

Comparing the legal distinctions to Heider's levels, we find the association level to be unused in modern law, although "guilt by association" may indeed have a psychological reality. The causality level corresponds to absolute liability in the law. Foreseeability encompasses acts committed negligently, recklessly, and knowingly, wherein degree of foreseeability rises from "should be aware" through "conscious disregard" to "practical certainty." The intentionality level is equivalent to the purposive level of legal culpability. Finally, Heider's justifiability relates to legal defenses of a justificatory or situational nature.

Not surprisingly, attribution research reveals that responsibility ratings increase from situations presented at an association level to those at an intentionality level, and then decrease with justifiability. Shaw and his associates (Shaw & Sulzer, 1964; Shaw & Reitan, 1969) presented subjects, including children, lawyers, and policemen, with descriptions of acts varying in the presence of Heider's levels. Not only did responsibility ratings follow the above pattern, but punishment for criminal acts followed this same pattern. These distinctions are paralleled in the courtroom where, for example, a person who fires a gun and kills someone by accident will not be punished. However, if the death could have been foreseen (playing with a loaded gun, target practice in a back alley at night), the person could be guilty of negligent homicide, manslaughter (reckless), or even murder (knowingly), depending on the inputed foreknowledge. The presence of an intent to kill generally establishes first-degree murder, but responsibility can be erased or lessened in cases of self-defense, mental illness, drunkenesses, and so forth.

It should be noted that the law makes more distinctions among kinds and degrees of responsibility than does attribution theory. In fact, the factors summarized above only touch the surface of legal scholarship that makes even more and different kinds of distinctions in civil domains as well as criminal. Fincham and Jaspars (1980) and Hart and Honoré (1959) offer insightful analyses that cannot be meaningfully reproduced here. A major issue for attribution theory is to separate legal and commonsense ideas about responsibility. It may be that attribution theory is simply weak in analyzing how people think about responsibility and could profit from centuries of legal thought. On the other hand, it could be that legal principles become applied by jurors and other actors in the legal system in ways that transform them into commonsense judgments of a simpler nature more closely related to the concepts of attribution theory. Attribution researchers at least have the tools for gathering evidence relevant to this issue (McGillis, 1978).

The Responsibility of the Victim

Probably the most heavily researched area of responsibility attribution in the legal system is that of apportioning responsibility between offender and victim. Approached from Kelley's (1967) attribution theory, the victim is an external factor who, if attributed some causality, would lead to discounting or lessened causality for the offender. In terms of Heider's levels, the victim's actions may offer a justification for the offender's behavior. There is a third viewpoint as well that argues for the observer attributing responsibility to offender and victim in such a way as to feel more comfortable about his or her own future.

Jones and Aronson (1973) presented a rape case to mock jurors and varied the respectability of the victim as a virgin, a married woman, or a divorcee. Subjects gave longer sentences to a defendant if he raped a virgin rather than a divorcee, yet the victim was rated more responsible for the rape when described as a virgin or married woman than when described as a divorcee. A possible explanation is that raping a virgin is a more serious crime than raping a divorcee, thus defendants are punished more. A second explanation is that the more serious event tends to be explained with multiple necessary causes (Kelley, 1972), that is, more than one cause must have been present; both defendant *and* victim must be responsible. The first part of this explanation is consistent with a study by Thornton (1977), in which greater physical attractiveness of a rape victim increased the sentences recommended (by males only), but did not affect responsibility or guilt judgments. The author suggests that the rape of an attractive woman is more serious and elicits more retribution than the rape of an unattractive victim.

However, the Jones and Aronson results have also been explained as defensive attributions, that subjects reduce threat when they attribute responsibility to respectable females. In essence, to maintain a belief that the world is a just place where good people prosper and bad ones suffer, it is necessary to find fault with the more respectable female (Lerner & Miller, 1978). People expect respectable females to be safe *unless* they do something to precipitate trouble.

Smith, Keating, Hester, and Mitchell (1976) found that greater responsibility was ascribed to a victim who was unacquainted with her assailant than to one who knew him. This could also be a defensive attribution in that the random assault is more threatening to subjects. This fear is alleviated by attributing responsibility to the otherwise innocent victim. Interestingly, Smith et al. found that a more respectable victim (a social worker or nun) was considered *less* responsible for a rape than a less respectable victim. Feldman-Summers and Lindner (1976) also found less responsibility attributed to a more respectable victim. Thus the relationship between respectability and responsibility is by no means clear-cut and may depend on the details of the crime and the specific types of respectability.

Other defensive attribution results are equally confusing. Gold, Landerman, and Bullock (1977) found that subjects who believed they had a high probability of becoming a rape or mugging victim derogated the victim more for a completed than an uncompleted crime. Subjects who did not identify with the victim were more sympathetic toward the more severely victimized victim. In contrast, Kaplan and Miller (1978) found that parents of females were harsher in verdicts and sentences than parents of males, but only when the rape occurred in a situation their daughter could readily encounter.

The confusing pattern of results extends to physical attractiveness as well. Thornton (1977) found that sentences were harsher when the defendant had raped a more attractive victim, but Seligman, Brickman, and Koulack (1977) found victim attractiveness had no effect on sentence nor blame for rape, mugging, and robbery crimes. Attractive women were considered more likely rape victims, and unattractive rape victims were thought more likely to have provoked the assault.

Krulewitz and Nash (1979) found that rape victims were considered more responsible for a completed than an attempted rape. Subjects believed that the rapist's behavior depended on how the victim reacted, espectially when the attempt was not completed. This belief that rape victims have some control over the incidents may reflect a defensive attribution. Males considered the victim less at fault if she physically resisted the attack, while females considered the victim more at fault when she resisted. Men assigned more punishment to the rapist if the victim resisted, while females assigned more if the victim did not resist. Clearly, the meaning of physical force and implied victim consent differs between the sexes.

Borgida and White (1978) manipulated a set of cues in rape cases indicative of victim consent (relationship of victim and defendant, use of force, resistance, location of rape) and amount of evidence regarding the victim's prior sexual history. Evidence of victim consent or active sexual history produced more not guilty verdicts, higher ratings of victim consent and responsibility, lower ratings of victim credibility, and a reverse pattern for the defendant. Interestingly, verdicts were more strongly related to judgments about the victim than about the defendant.

The responsibility of crime victims is certainly strongly related to judgments made about a case. However, research about how responsibility affects verdicts and sentences, and how responsibility judgments are made, has produced a complex field of results. Simple theories have not fared well, and results seem to depend on the exact nature of dependent variables [responsibility, fault, guilt, blame, and cause are not synonymous (Fincham & Jaspars, 1980)] and the details of crime, evidence, and setting. Luginbuhl and Frederick (1978) point out that subjects have sometimes been asked to act as "naive observers" and at other times to act as "jurors." The confusion of role may be compounded by subjects being asked to assign a sentence without first determining guilt and by the order in which guilt and impression measures are taken.

Summary

There has been substantial support accumulated for the idea that attributing a crime to the offender produces more punishment. Most of the research has again conceived of a quantitative scale where offenders are more or less responsible, and this maps onto quantitative guilt or punishment scales.

However, major difficulties have emerged in understanding the specifics of responsibility and its relationships to other variables. Some researchers argue that responsibility is causal locus, others that it is degree of intent; some argue that responsibility comes in types but that the types are orderable, and still other researchers use terms like fault, intent, guilt, responsibility, and accountability in different ways.

It would seem that attribution theorists headed off in the right direction but quickly ran out of maps. Little systematic analysis exists of the different terms people use or the different meanings of the same word (responsibility, intent, cause, and reason have multiple usages). Critical issues confronting both attribution theory and the law can be addressed once this groundwork is laid. At present, the recent paper by Fincham and Jaspars (1980) offers the most illuminating discussion of these problems in attribution theory.

THE CAUSES OF CRIME

Most of the research about crime we have reviewed gave subjects the task of determining guilt and punishment. In a typical study, college students would be asked to imagine that they were jurors evaluating a criminal case. They were asked to respond with a length of sentence representing degree of sanction and sometimes guilt, and often asked to attribute cause on a scale from internal to external (relative to the defendant), or degree of responsibility of the defendant.

However, as Jones and Thibaut (1958) have noted, a perceiver can have multiple goals or "sets" that affect which inferences are made about another person. Applying a social sanction is but one goal, the one most closely tied to our previous discussion of blame. Jones and Thibaut call this a situation-matching set. A perceiver may also be concerned with diagnosing the criminal to determine why he or she exhibited criminal behavior, what Jones and Thibaut label a causal-genetic set. A third goal is to manage one's own behavior as it is affected by crime, a value-maintenance set. In short, there is every reason to believe that perceivers who are engaged in different tasks may engage different goals and therefore different inference processes. Further, different perceivers may view the same task in different ways and therefore engage in functionally different tasks. For example, asking a member of a jury pool, a psychiatrist, and a close friend of the criminal to evaluate a criminal case could link the evaluation process to three different goals carried by these individuals: situation-matching, causal-genetic, and value-maintenance, respectively.

This section of the chapter focuses on the goals beyond sanctioning and includes work combining multiple goals in a single task. We first examine instances where people are asked to figure out why people commit crimes, the problem of crime causation. We then examine some ideas about crime prevention, which represent how the public deals with the threat of crime by adjusting their own behavior.

Crime Causation

Public opinion polls have inquired into the causes of crime for over a decade. Gallup (1970) asked which was more to blame for crime, society or the individual criminal. The majority of respondents believed society was more to blame. When asked to name specific causes of crime, polls in the past decade have mentioned a complex set of factors, including the following (Erskine, 1974):

1. Parental upbringing and the breakdown of family life
2. Bad environment
3. Leniency in the laws and enforcement of justice
4. Drugs
5. Mental illness
6. Permissiveness in society
7. Poverty and unemployment

Public opinion has definitely not developed a consensus on crime causation. Miller (1973) provides a useful analysis of how sociopolitical ideologies provide different ideas about crime drawn from markedly different viewpoints on society and individuals. The conservative political right proposes that the bulk of serious crime is produced by people who have had defective upbringing, inadequate moral and religious training, bad neighborhoods, and lack of positive role models. As a result, they lack self-control and care little about society or other people. The criminal propensities of these people are encouraged by counterculture elements who support the violation of legal and moral rules and by the leniency and ineffectiveness of the criminal justice system. In contrast, the liberal political left proposes that inequities in wealth, power, and privilege lead the victims of society to commit crimes out of need or frustration. These same people are further victimized by the system that directs its attention to them while ignoring or diverting the crimes of the affluent and powerful. Those individuals who commit crimes without adequate justification are usually disturbed or sick people who need help rather than punishment.

Expert opinions regarding crime causation are as variable as lay opinions. The list of criminogenic conditions and predisposing factors uncovered by various disciplines is truly awesome. There are psychiatric viewpoints proposing that crime is a symptom of underlying conflict (e.g., Abrahamsen, 1960), and there are sociological viewpoints focusing on subcultural values (e.g., Miller, 1958). There are personality theories, body physique theories, chromosome theories, family theories, demographic theories, theories proposing that crime is a rational choice, social disorganization theories, role-model theories, learning theories, theories that society produces criminals by labeling certain persons as criminal, and so forth (Nettler, 1978; Schrag, 1971). There are also typological theories that classify criminals into types, each of which is associated with different behavior patterns and underlying reasons for crime (e.g., Clinard & Quinney, 1973).

In a highly naturalistic study of expert attributions, Carroll (1978, 1979) studied five parole board members who filled out a questionnaire immediately following 272 actual parole hearings. One board member heard each case. Two items on the questionnaire measured attributions in an unstructured way: "Opinion on underlying cause for offense committed" and "Opinion on reason for criminal record/history." The 557 attributional statements that were given by the board members were grouped by similarity into 25 categories and an uncodable group (4% of all statements). The most frequent causes and their frequencies for the questions are shown in the following table.

Cause	Offense	History	Cause	Offense	History
(a) Drug abuse problem	15	23	(g) Immaturity	2	6
(b) Alcohol abuse problem	12	19	(h) Easily influenced	3	4
(c) Influence of associates	6	11	(i) Victim precipitated	7	1
(d) Long-term greed for money	9	7	(j) Mental problems	4	3
(e) Sudden desire for money	7	2	(k) Drunkenness	7	0
(f) Lack of control	4	5	(l) Aimlessness	1	4
			(m) Domestic problems	4	1
			(n) Environment	2	2

Examining the five board members separately, it is evident that they tended to give different causal attributions. For example, on attribution for the cause of the offense, one board member made 30% of attributions to alcohol abuse, whereas the others made only 4 –7% (excluding one who made too few decisions for analysis). A second board member made 40% of attributions to money, compared to figures of 6%, 3%, and 18% for others. A third board member made 15% of attributions to victim precipitation, whereas only 3 –5% of other board members' attributions were in this category.

It is interesting to note that one attributional category showed uniformity across board members. The proportion of attributions made to drugs varied from 15 to 19% of each board member's cases. This may be indicative of what is the clearest or most consensual attribution for crime.

Although cases are not assigned to board members in a completely random fashion, it is difficult to detect or imagine any selection biases capable of producing the large effects in attributions. Instead, it seems clear that individual board members indeed focus upon different aspects of the case material when answering these attributional questions.

These studies of causal attributions for crime reveal a complex set of causes. It seems fair to say that people perceive crime as multiply determined, and that different crimes are produced by different causes. But if we change the attributor's goal, and make them personally involved by introducing the context of crime in our neighborhood, we change the resultant attributions.

Crime Prevention

Kidder and Cohn (1979) have written a unique and provocative analysis of public views regarding crime prevention. They point out that

> when people talk about crime as a social problem, they attribute it to social conditions, such as poverty, unemployment, neglect of children, and other social factors that appear to be linked with high crime rates. However, when they choose to do something in response to their own *fears*, they act to reduce their personal risk of victimization. . .by staying in at night, installing locks, or joining neighborhood patrols. (p. 261)

This precisely exemplifies the distinction between the goal of understanding or finding causes for crime and the goal of behaving adaptively in response to crime.

Kidder and Cohn (1979) sent a large team of researchers into the field to attend neighborhood crime-prevention meetings and to interview community organizers, community leaders, merchants, and residents in three cities. In this context of crime prevention and personal reactions to crime, the field notes reveal a combination of traditional crime causes and a new set of causes focused on the crime victim. These causes have direct implications for reducing the chance of victimization and have weak if any implications for reducing crime rates. Examples include: (1) "I think they (victims) are careless as a rule. They leave their lights on. They don't lock their doors"; (2) "It is an unfortunate fact of life that senior citizens are an easy target"; (3) "You come in dressed up and looking affluent, and you become a target"; and (4) "The most important facet of crime prevention is neighborhood awareness. Unfortunately, people don't want to get involved if a crime happens. . ." (p. 247).

It would be important to relate attributions regarding crime made by victims and neighboring nonvictims to the actions taken by these people to reduce their chances of victimization. Do people change their behavior as a result of these attributional processes? Very few data exist that bear on this issue. Rosenbaum (1980) measured attributions of responsibility to self, offender, and chance for crime victims, and correlated this with precautions taken following victimization. Nonvictims were asked these questions regarding crimes as a whole and new precautions taken in the past two years. Victim precautions were related to greater self-blame in one study but not a second, and to greater attributions to chance in one of two studies. Nonvictims were more likely to report additional precautions if they attributed victimizations to chance.

These results are difficult to interpret for any attributional model. A major problem is certainly that the terms "responsibility" and "chance" are very vague. The actual phrasing was "To what extent do you hold yourself responsible for what happened?", a similar question for the offender, and "Do you see this incident as a chance event that could have happened to anyone?" The chance question seems to request risk information—how likely is any random person around here to be victimized? Specific questions phrased toward specific attributions could be more useful.

Multiple Goals and Dimensional Models

Attempting to determine the causes of behavior or to adjust one's own behavior are not really goals in the sense of desired end-states. Rather, these are subgoals or means to other ends. The real goals or desired end-states are such things as justice, reduction in crime rates, cost effectiveness, rehabilitation of offenders, personal recognition, moral retribution, freedom from fear, and so forth. Such goals are a function of the task people are asked to do and the values they bring with them. Some of these goals involve selecting sanctions, some involve making attributions, and others involve a variety of judgmental processes.

Carroll and Payne (1976) reviewed literature suggesting that the parole decision consists of two goals: punishing offenders for their criminal acts and protecting society by incapacitating predicted recidivists. They further proposed a dimensional model of causal attributions drawn from Weiner's (1974) theory of attributions in achievement settings. This model proposed that parole decision-makers respond not simply to the criminal facts of a case, but they also make causal attributions regarding why the offender committed crimes. To the extent that crime is attributed to factors inside the offender, particularly intentional factors, there will be a resultant increase in blame and a desire to punish the offender. To the extent that crime is attributed to stable and enduring factors, there will be a resultant increase in predictions of recidivism and a desire to incapacitate the offender. This dimensional model looks like the following:

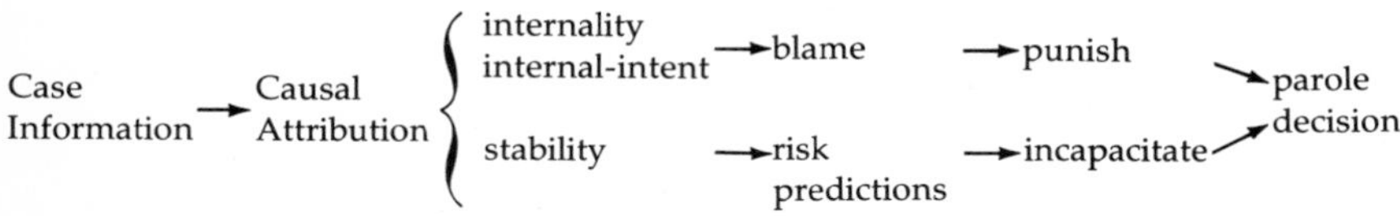

Support for this model was immediately forthcoming. Carroll and Payne (1977a,b) gave college students brief crime reports in which they systematically varied the description of the crime and some background information suggestive of a causal attribution. An example of one crime report containing a murder and an external–stable–unintentional cause was the following:

> Mr. Green is a 25-year-old male convicted of second-degree murder. He was in a bar having a drink and talking to the victim when they began to argue, push, and punch each other. He pulled out a gun and shot the victim several times; the victim was pronounced dead on arrival at the hospital. Mr. Green surrendered himself to police called by the bartender. He has no previous record of convictions. Interviews indicated that he could not find a good job because his skill had been replaced by mechanization. The circumstances around the crime had been acting on him for some time.

Students responded to more internal causes of crime by rating the crime more severe, the criminal more responsible, their desire to put the criminal in prison for punishment more intense, and suggesting a longer prison term. Internal –intentional causes were judged the highest on responsibility. The more stable, long-term causes of crime produced higher expectations for recidivism, a greater desire to put the criminal in prison for incapacitation, and longer prison terms. Prison term was assigned on the basis of both punishment and incapacitation, and was an additive sum of internal –external judgments and stable –unstable judgments. Crimes with internal –stable causes were given an average prison term of 9.1 years, compared to 6.6 years for internal –unstable, 5.2 years for external-stable, and 3.7 years for external –unstable causes.

However, the same study conducted with expert parole decision-makers did not produce the same results. The impact of the attributional information was much less. Further, internal –stable causes were treated as different from all others, producing higher judgments of responsibility, criminality, and risk of recidivism. These differences between experts and students seem partly due to a failure to make the task adequately represent the parole decision. First, parole decision-makers in Pennsylvania did not make sentencing decisions; they made release/withhold release decisions. Research on parole boards across the country indicates that those boards making sentencinglike decisions differ markedly from those making in/out decisions (Gottfredson, Cosgrove, Wilkins, Wallerstein, & Rauh, 1978). Second, comments from the experts showed that they felt uncomfortable making decisions based on so little information about each case. This may have reduced their reliance upon the more subjective causal information.

In order to provide a more naturalistic study of expert parole decisions, Carroll (1978) had experts fill out a questionnaire following actual parole hearings in Pennsylvania. A description of what types of attribution are made was presented earlier in this chapter. The questionnaire also tapped a great deal of information about each case relevant to the goals of the decision-maker, inferences made about each case, and some key facts about each case. Analyses have been made of a total of over 1000 cases, the first 272 of which were reported in Carroll (1978) and contained attribution assessments.

These analyses (Carroll, 1978; Carroll & Coates, 1980; Carroll, Wiener, Coates, & Alibrio, 1980) have shown that the goals of the parole decision in Pennsylvania are *not* punishment and incapacitation. The parole board considers that the minimum sentence assigned by the judge (which offenders must serve before becoming eligible for parole) is the punitive component of incarceration. If an offender is to remain in prison beyond the minimum sentence, it is not generally for punishment of past crimes. Instead, what is important is risk of future crime, chance for rehabilitation, and maintaining order in prison. For each of these goals, behavior in prison is considered more important than criminal behavior outside prison. Conduct in prison is a major determinant of judgments about risk and rehabilitative potential, as well as important in its own right.

No wonder, then, that Carroll (1978) found that attributions about the causes of criminal behavior had relatively weak effects on parole decisions.

Had we asked why the offender had conducted himself in prison as he did, or why he said what he said in the parole hearing, such attributional judgments might have revealed even stronger effects on parole decisions. Even though attributions about crimes are less important to parole decisions than other features of the cases, their theoretical importance is evident. Essentially, crimes attributed to more stable causes led to higher predictions of recidivism risk and less likelihood of parole. This does indeed confirm half the attributional model of Carroll and Payne (1976). The portion of the model dealing with punishment is missing in Pennsylvania because it is not part of the decision task in that state.

Even among expert decision-makers who interact with each other continually, there are bound to be strong individual differences in what goals are most important for a task. Carroll (1979) found that five board members differed in the degree to which they adhered to incapacitation, rehabilitation, or prison stability goals. Such results are quite common in criminal justice research. Hogarth (1971) found that judges' sentences were related to the perceived purposes of incarceration in the specific case, particularly incapacitation and punishment. Analyses based on how the individual judge perceived and understood the "facts" of the case were several times more predictive than analyses based on facts in the case files coded "objectively" by the researcher. He concluded that "one can explain more about sentencing by knowing a few things about the judge than by knowing a great deal about the facts of the case" (p. 350).

In an experiment manipulating the goals of a sentencing decision, McFatter (1978) assigned subjects to follow retribution, rehabilitation, or deterrence goals. He found that these goals led to clear differences in sentencing strategies. For example, rehabilitators incarcerated minor criminals longer than did retributors, but this effect reversed for major criminals. Presumably, rehabilitators wanted to put people in prison to change them, not to match penalty with offense. Such change takes more time than retribution in minor cases, but less time in major cases.

Summary

In this section we have observed that people who evaluate crime and criminals can have any of multiple goals, including sanctioning, self-protection, diagnosis, and public safety. In the process of seeking these goals, people make causal attributions about why crime occurs. We have shown that a large number of causes are potentially given for crime and that these causes do influence subsequent judgments and decisions. Which attributions are given for a particular crime depends not only upon the nature of the crime and the criminal, but also upon the specific goals and knowledge of the attributor.

COGNITIVE PROCESSES: TOWARD A SCHEMA THEORY

In previous sections of this chapter we have discussed how an attributional framework is useful for understanding judgments and decisions about crime and criminals. We can certainly document that attributions are made during such tasks, and that they are not artifacts of research itself. For example, Carroll and Payne (1977a) and Fontaine and Emily (1978) have observed spontaneous spoken attributions by actual parole board members and judges. These attributions were not prompted by attributional questions nor instructions to make "psychological" evaluations.

Problems with the Attribution Process

What has not been explicated is how these attributions are made. Existing models of the attribution process generally propose that the attributor assembles information in order to make a dimensional or gross attribution such as internal vs external. For example, Shaver (1975, p. 32) presents a model where the attributor first decides whether an action was intended. If it was intended, the attributor considers any possible coercion. The results of these dimensional considerations (intentional vs unintentional and coerced vs free) is an attributional category such as "personal disposition," which is translated into a specific attribution ("hostility") by unspecified processes.

Kelley's (1967, 1971) early work with the Covariation Principle exhibits a similar structure. Utilizing information about the past history of the actor with this and similar stimulus objects, and the past history of other people, an attribution is made to the actor, the stimulus, or the situation. Although this description is seemingly straightforward, it actually conceals much of the attribution process. Consider the prototypical test of Kelley's theory conducted by McArthur (1972). She presented subjects with events such as "Sue is afraid of the dog" and the information hypothesized to be of use to attributors: "Sue is not afraid of other dogs, Sue has been afraid of this dog before, and other people are afraid of this dog." Subjects are asked to report why Sue was afraid of the dog by checking something about Sue, the dog, the situation, or a combination of things.

The problem with this study is that it is confirmatory: the subject's thoughts are channeled by the task into following the hypothesized tracks. Subjects are told how to encode the information, the information is selected, and the goals are set by the questions asked. In contrast, consider the task we examined previously of a parole board evaluating a parole applicant. Imagine a board member examining the case materials of a robber. According to Kelley, it is appropriate to use the Covariation Principle because we have information about the prior history of the robber. We have his criminal record, as well as his family background, job history, education, and so forth.

If the crime is "Mr. A robbed Mr. B," the attributor needs to know the following information: (1) distinctiveness—has Mr. A robbed other people? (2) consistency—has Mr. A robbed Mr. B before? and (3) consensus—have other people robbed Mr. B? As you can see immediately, only one of these questions makes great sense for a parole board to ask. Yet even this question is not as productive as questions such as "Has Mr. A committed other crimes, how many and of what type?", "What were the details of the crime?", "What were Mr. A's motives?", and "What kind of person is Mr. A?" There is a structure to the behavior, which is understood by parole boards (and most other people to some degree) in their attempts to uncover a pattern of criminal behaviors such that a particular crime is one of a category of crimes, and a particular criminal is one of a class of criminals. The information about the case is evaluated in terms of the organized knowledge of the parole board member regarding crime and criminals.

Support for this interpretation of the "McArthur Study" comes from Garland, Hardy, and Stephenson (1975). They presented subjects with the same event descriptions, but had subjects request information in order to make a specific attribution either to the person ("What further information would you require in order to say that Sue is afraid of dogs?") or to the stimulus ("What further information would you require in order to say that this is a frightening dog?"). Only a small proportion of requests could be coded as consistency, distinctiveness, or consensus. Most centered on finding out more about the actor or more about the stimulus, suggesting that subjects were trying to identify what kinds of persons and things were involved in the event. In the case of Mr. A robbing Mr. B, people would be interested in hearing about Mr. A's personality, his drug and alcohol use, his economic situation, and his family life, rather than about who else Mr. A has robbed and who has robbed Mr. B.

Why do people seek to know what kind of person Mr. A is and what circumstances exist in his life? It is simply that these are what people mean by *cause*. If we find out that Mr. A has a drug habit, it suggests that he committed the crime to get money for drugs. If we find out that Mr. A is unemployed, it suggests that he committed the crime to provide money on which to live. If we find out that Mr. A is a psychopath, it suggests that he does not know right from wrong and committed the crime on impulse or for greed and had no moral qualms. Again, these potential causes arise from people's knowledge of crime and criminals, not from a logical (Sherlock Holmes) analysis of the information in the case history.

Recognize, as we noted before, that the attribution processes of someone living in Mr. B's neighborhood would be quite different. Their attributions about why Mr. A robbed Mr. B would include more about how Mr. B became a victim (Kidder & Cohn, 1979), and they would undoubtedly seek more information about Mr. B. It is important to know whether Mr. B was careless, or stupid, or had a lot of money, or whether the neighborhood is poorly lit, or unpatrolled, or filled with junkies. When attributing cause, people will ask these specific questions and find them more informative than how many other times Mr. B has been robbed.

Other attribution theories are equally unilluminating when examined in detail. The Jones and Davis (1965) theory of Correspondent Inference (see also Jones & McGillis, 1976) is focused upon voluntary purposive acts. A robbery is a good solid example. Yet, again, the proposed attributional analysis does not bear fruit. Jones and Davis propose that we list the effects of the action, and then examine the effects of plausible alternative actions that were not taken. The effects of the robbery are such things as obtaining money, spending the money, scaring a victim, the victim losing money, some thrill value, and various risks of getting caught and processed by the criminal justice system. Plausible alternatives would include robbing somebody else, committing a different type of crime (e.g., burglary, assault), or doing something noncriminal like getting a job, collecting welfare, or going out on a date. Each of these alternatives has its associated effects. The sheer volume of noncommon effects of criminal acts is potentially limitless, which the theory would suggest makes correspondent inference ambiguous. However, people do readily blame criminals for their acts (Carroll, 1979).

The theory specifies how a subject would reason about a structured set of alternatives and effects. Yet, how does this structure arise if not provided in the research task? In the above robbery example, how do you decide what alternatives are plausible and what the effects are? Even if we simplify it, and make lots of assumptions, the results are still ambiguous. Let us say that there is one alternative to robbery, and that is getting a job. The effects of robbery are money, thrill, and capture by police. The effects of getting a job are money, boredom, and security. Now any reasonable person views this as a decision with uncertain alternatives and many trade-offs. We do not know how *likely* capture is perceived to be, how much money each alternative is expected to yield, how to trade thrills against security, and so forth. If someone managed to work through this, it is possible to see the robber characterized as a "rational" entrepreneur who is maximizing his money, a thrill-seeking sickie, or a guilt-ridden neurotic seeking punishment. In any case, it is the attributor's general knowledge of events that allows him or her to wade through this. Thus it is the hidden process of deciding what is relevant and what implications exist that is the basis of the attributional process, not the overly general "theory."

Note also that this crime has more hedonic relevance for a neighbor of Mr. B's than for a neutral observer. The neighbor should therefore find more correspondence, that is, identify some intent and disposition of Mr. A as a cause of the crime (Jones & Davis, 1965). Instead, attributors focusing on neighborhood crime pay relatively more attention to the role of the victim and the setting in creating crime opportunities.

A New Model of the Attribution Process

We would like to propose, instead, a different model of the attribution process consistent with the new thrust of theory development in cognitive social psychology. This model draws directly and explicitly on the knowledge of the attributor, rather than indirectly and obliquely.

The model consists of three phases. In the first phase, the attributor establishes the goal of making an attribution. The attribution may be sought because an attributional question was asked (Why did Mr. A rob Mr. B?) or because some other task requires attribution as a subtask (Is Mr. A guilty? How long a sentence? Will he rob again? Should I buy new locks or move out of this neighborhood?). The issue of why an attribution is sought is not trivial, and the attributions considered to be satisfactory probably depend upon what initiated this phase of the attribution process.

In the second phase, consideration of knowledge about the situation and persons involved leads to the rapid generation of one or more attributional hypotheses. For example, a robbery offense, past property offenses (auto theft, shoplifting, burglary), no job, and history of drug abuse suggests an addict supporting a habit via crime. If we did not have evidence of a drug habit around which to organize the impression, we might have several possibilities—an undisclosed drug habit, an unskilled petty criminal with no ties to "straight" society, and so forth.

These attributional hypotheses are not gross dimensions nor categories such as "internal" or "external," but are specific causes. We believe they can best be considered as part of *schemas*. Hypotheses are produced when a schema is evoked. For example, in parole decisions, the causes given by the experts were drugs, alcohol, desire for money, influence of associates, lack of control, and so forth. If there were a "drug" schema, it would probably contain information (suppositions) about the personality of the criminal, the kinds of crimes likely to be in the record, reasons why these crimes are committed, reasons why the criminal got involved with drugs, prognosis for treatment, social history, and so forth. When evaluating a case, case information may evoke the "drug offender" schema, which provides a way of organizing what is known about the case, filling gaps, suggesting new information, and suggesting the causes for crime and the potential for cure. Thus knowledge organized in schemas structures the examination of case information, so the decision-maker talks about "cases like these" and appears to know more about the case than has been read.

The causal attributions that are associated with these schemas are specific causes such as "supporting a drug habit" rather than general causes such as "internal to the criminal." Yet these causes can be said to have attributes such as the degree to which they are internal to the actor or stable over time. But a cause is given at a conventional level of meaningfulness arising from our understanding of the events that occurred and the people in them. Ultimately, any stated cause is one element in a causal chain (Brickman, Ryan, & Wortman, 1975; Schneider, Hastorf, & Ellsworth, 1979) and often is one cause among contributing causes. The cause that is stated is the one that is most informative (cf. Jones & McGillis, 1976) or conventionally meaningful. This is analogous to object-naming: we call a chair a chair rather than a piece of furniture because "chair" is its conventional level of meaningfulness and utility. This level seems to be the most inclusive level at which instances share common attributes, are used in similar ways, and are easiest to code in images or words (Rosch, Mervis, Gray, Johnson, & Boyes-Braem, 1976).

In the third phase of the attributional process, the attributor evaluates the attributional hypotheses by seeking additional information consistent with one or another of these hypotheses. In the case of a parole board evaluating a parole applicant, hypotheses drawn from the early information guide the search for and interpretation of later information. We also propose that this information-processing tends to be confirmation-biased. Carroll and Payne (1976, 1977a) found that information search was guided by the typical hypotheses subjects have about crime: Internals who typically attribute crime to criminals (Sosis, 1974) tend to ask for information about the criminal earlier than Externals, who tend to ask earlier for information regarding the environment around the criminal. This is consistent with confirmatory biases found by Snyder and his associates (Snyder & Swann, 1978; Snyder & Cantor, 1979). It is also consistent with studies of expert decision-making in other domains such as medical diagnosis (Elstein, Shulman, & Sprafka, 1978).

The above model is quite closely related to proposals put forth by Kruglanski, Hamel, Maides, and Schwartz, (1978). They propose that the attributional process begins with the formulation of a question or a desire for increased knowledge, such as "Why was my fiance with that blonde in the cafe?" The next step is the generation of one or more pertinent answers, or hypotheses. The answers are then checked against what is known by deducing various implications from each answer and examining their consistency with pertinent evidence. If several hypotheses are assessed simultaneously, it is particularly important to examine conflicting implications of the hypotheses (critical tests). The attribution process stops when an "adequate" answer is found, one that is consistent with available knowledge and more consistent than alternative answers.

Support for the Model

The most apparent implication in our model (and Kruglanski's) is *specificity*. In contrast with attributional models positing a small set of general attributional categories (e.g., person, stimulus, circumstances), a small set of attributional cues (e.g., consistency, distinctiveness, consensus), and an exhaustive, logical processing of these cues, this model proposes a large set of specific attributions, a large set of potentially relevant cues, and a hypothesis-driven, confirmation-biased, selective attributional process based on local consistency (consistency among what the attributor thinks of at any one time). The attribution process thus draws upon the enormous store of knowledge each person possesses about social situations and people.

Support for the specificity of attributional knowledge is readily available. Research on achievement attributions is one major area demonstrating specificity. Weiner's early work (e.g., Frieze & Weiner, 1971) focused on four attributions—ability, effort, task difficulty, and luck—organized on two dimensions—internal vs external and stable vs unstable. Later work has gradually added both dimensions and specific attributions within dimensions. There are now five or six dimensions or qualities of attributions that are of theoretical interest (Weiner, 1979) and in any particular domain or task, there are a dozen or more specific attributions people use to describe events (e.g., Frieze, 1976). One characteristic of the approach taken by Weiner, Frieze, and their colleagues is to elicit specific attributions from subjects and code these into categories for each domain of research interest. Thus numerous specific attributions have been identified for attributions about loneliness (Peplau, Russell, & Heim, 1979), crime (Carroll, 1979), behavior of alcoholics (McHugh, Beckman, & Frieze, 1979), wife battering (Frieze, 1979), and others.

These specific attributions have typically been analyzed in terms of their dimensional characteristics. However, Weiner, Russell, and Lerman (1979) found that specific self-attributions are associated with specific emotions. For example, success attributed to intense effort generates delight and exhilaration; success attributed to ability produces surprise and wonder. Similarly, failure can produce feelings of inadequacy, shame, fear, depression, apathy, or horror depending upon whether it is attributed to lack of ability, lack of effort, lack of interest, bad luck, and so forth.

Research has also shown that specific attributions are triggered by specific cues, rather than by an exhaustive analysis of information. Frieze (1976) summarizes some of these relationships in achievement stiuations. For example, performance changes associated with incentives is a cue for effort attributions. In an interesting reconceptualization of the Kelley (1967) consistency–distinctiveness–consensus analysis, Orvis, Cunningham, and Kelley (1975) showed that one cue was sufficient to evoke an attribution, and did so as strongly as the complete three-cue combination from the Kelley "Cube." Low consensus produces an attribution to the person, high distinctiveness produces an attribution to the stimulus, and low consistency produces an attribution to circumstances.

Kruglanski et al. (1978) report several studies in which variations in the goals and structure of an attributional task change the type of attributions that are relevant. In one study they gave subjects one of two goals, e.g., "decide whether to invite John to a party" vs "decide whether to buy tickets to movie X" and the event "John plans to see movie X on Saturday night." Subjects were asked whether they would rather know that the event was due to person vs stimulus (something about John or something about the movie) *or* know that the event was due to means vs ends (John goes to the movie to watch the movie or for some other purpose). Person vs stimulus categories were opposed by either means vs ends, ability vs effort, or intentional vs unintentional categories, whichever seemed most relevant for the specific event. When the goal was relevant to the person vs stimulus category, subjects preferred knowing these attributional categories. To decide about purchasing tickets to the movie, knowing that John bought tickets because of something about the movie rather than something about John is clearly relevant. However, when the goal was to decide whether to invite John to a party on the night of the movie, subjects wanted to know why John was planning to go to the movie (means vs ends).

In a second study, subjects were asked to make attributions either in the traditional personal vs stimulus alternatives, or in a different set of categories (means −ends, ability −effort, or intentional −unintentional). Subjects were asked to choose between two sets of information to make this attribution: consensus, distinctiveness, and consistency, or information pertaining to the alternative causal categories (such as means −ends). When asked to attribute to person or situation, subjects preferred the traditional Kelley cues. However, when the alternate causal cateories were being assessed, the alternate information was preferred. In short, this study demonstrates that different information is perceived as relevant to different types of attributional categories. It should be noted that the Garland et al. (1975) study suggests that attributors find consensus – distinctiveness – consistency less important even for determining causal locus than information about the nature of the people and stimuli in the situation.

Further evidence for the specificity of attributional categories comes from an unpublished thesis by Fisher (1976). She presented subjects with one of three situations: an *achievement* situation in which an insurance salesman sells some number of insurance policies, a *social* situation in which a student receives some number of "well-liked" ratings from other students in a small group communications course, and a *sanctioning* situation in which a judge sentences a criminal to a number of years in prison. Subjects were given an appropriate role (boss, teacher, or parole board member) and one of two goals: to make an attribution or to make a decision regarding the actor (promote the salesman, give a letter of recommendation to the student for a public relations job, grant parole to the criminal). Finally, one third of the subjects were given information indicating that the actor had been relatively successful (sold more policies, was liked by more people, or received a lesser sentence than average), and one third was given information indicating a relative failure. Subjects were asked to tell what information they would like to have in order to complete the task.

The information requests from all subjects across all conditions were coded into categories by coders blind to the conditions that produced the requests. Again, consistency, consensus, and distinctiveness were infrequent compared to requests for more information about the actor's conduct, actor's characteristics, details of the situation, and the presence of specific attributions. More interesting, however, was that the 18 conditions (3 situations × 2 tasks each × 3 levels of success – failure information) could be compared for how similar they were in information requests by correlating each pair of conditions across the proportion of information requests in each category (arc sine transformation was used on the proportions). The results showed that the conditions strongly grouped themselves by situation. Each situation called forth different kinds of information. In the achievement situation, information requests were similar across the two goals, but different information was requested for success, failure, and no information. This is consistent with the nature of achievement situations and research on them (Weiner, 1979; Frieze, 1976). In the social situation, all conditions of goals and successfulness were similar. In the sanctioning situation, successfulness information did not change information requests, but subjects requested different information to make a causal attribution than to grant parole.

Taken together, the Kruglanski et al. (1978), Garland et al. (1975), and Fisher (1976) studies strongly support the idea of specificity in the attribution process. Specific situations and goals generate differential information search and different attributional categories are considered to be relevant responses. In terms of our schema theory, we propose that a specific event activates certain schemas that contain a rich set of suppositions, including attributions. Individuals who have different goals, or who have different knowledge about events such as this, may activate different schemas or the content of these schemas may vary across people. The schemas guide the search for further information by suggesting what would confirm or be consistent with the schema.

Support for the Model from Parole Decision Research

Further evidence drawn from research on parole boards also supports the arguments we have presented. Carroll and Payne (1977a) collected verbal protocols from expert parole decision-makers examining actual case materials (in one third of these protocols the decision-maker performed his actual job with real cases and real consequences while speaking his thoughts out loud into a tape recorder). Consider the examination of case information illustrated by one set of excerpts from a verbal protocol. The subject begins, "All right, well, the first thing I usually do is see if what he's here on. Since it's a, you know, the guy's been convicted of burglary. Plead guilty to it." The initial focus is on the crime for which the parole applicant was incarcerated. More details of the crime follow: "Now this is not too bad. He broke a window and entered a food market. He left a credit card box uh, left with the credit card box containing uh, 37, —oh, a cardboard box containing 37 cartons of assorted cigarettes totaling so much money. So, he stole a bunch of cigarettes. And he did this with uh—one other person. So, that's really not too bad."

These early characterizations of the crime as relatively mild have immediate implications: "I really don't have to delve too much into—into what he actually did in terms of uh, that might indicate psychological motivations for the crime." This expert's desire to understand the causes of the crime is tempered by the idea that mild crimes either do not have to be understood as fully or they do not have "deep" motives behind them.

However, the crime must be put in the context of the criminal's past record, "so well, I wanna look at prior records to see if the present offense is along with other types of behavior." The pattern of criminal behavior is quite important to parole decision-makers, both in terms of crime types (property crime, violent crimes, sex crimes) and trends (increasing seriousness, longest time between crimes, recency of past crimes). In this case, the expert finds that "both reports indicate that he hasn't been in trouble since '64 till '75."

Having established the criminal history, the expert turns to look at the characteristics of the criminal that are interpreted diagnostically as predictors of future behavior and causally as postdictors of past crimes. "So then, I start reading social history on him. I look for things like supports. . . uh—how skilled he is, his intelligence level, his potential, that way. Uh—and the things going against him, drug abuse, alcohol abuse, uh, psycho—extreme psychological problems, uh, family problems, interpersonal kin—uh, behavior problems."

The above list of problems seemed to act as an agenda for examining the information in the case, as if they were a set of possible causes for the offender's behavior. The expert first considered family relationships and spontaneously expressed and then rejected a "spoiled kid schema": "Sometimes, uh—the parents are overprotective and they've always covered him for everything he's ever done. And if that's indicated here, that would certainly be a, you know, somethin' that I would look at as—as a reason for the way he is now and also somethin' that would you know—add—detract from him bein' able to make it when he hits the street. Nothing like that is indicated here."

After considering several other possibilities, the expert finds that "he indicated he was intoxicated at the time of the crime," which could indicate that during the years he was not arrested (1964 to 1975) that he might have been "in and out of trouble. . .(and) awfully lucky that he didn't get caught." Later, more information turns up: "he—he also indicated to the counselor that when he found himself out of work that he started hitting the bottle. Which is, you know, that's his, you know, reason for—for doin' it, for goin' to the alcohol, as to why—why there would be some alcohol abuse."

Gradually, the focus of interest shifts back along the causal chain (Brickman et al., 1975) to the alcohol problem. The expert concludes, "the difficulties that the guy had in the past—the records would show that it was due to alcoholism, you know. . .the guy has the ability to be stable out there. . .what he did was so—was done so impulsively, man. He was out—he had been drinking with this cat—and uh,—they were drunk. . .and they needed cigarettes. And he went into the place and he got the cigarettes. . .The alcohol is probably uh—an escape to dealin' with uh—uh—depressions or whatever. . .You know, with superior intelligence and he's not usin' it. And that's this man's case. So—I would seek—I would seek therapy also in the areas of trying to uh—get him to realize you know, his capabilities."

Although we do not have enough data in the protocols to substantiate the schema proposal in more than an anecdotal way, there are clear demonstrations that hypothetical crime causes and criminal types are readily available to parole experts and that case information is scanned for information consistent with these hypotheses. Attributions seem to arise within these protocols from a process of referring specific cases to existing categories of crime and criminals, and not by logical covariation principles nor analysis of alternative behaviors available to criminals. A second, briefer, example illustrates the rapidity with which hypotheses are generated. The first three statements in one protocol were as follows: "Ah, ok, this summarization sheet says 22-year-old single man. Young, perhaps an immature kind of individual." The next statement is "ah, charge?" indicating that a potential cause, immaturity, arose before the crime was even known!

The potential causes that we have mentioned in these sample

protocols—alcohol, drugs, loss of job, family problems, immaturity—are all included on the list of 25 attributional categories developed by Carroll (1978, 1979) in coding attributions made by parole board members about actual cases. The commensurability of data obtained by different methods strengthens the thrust of the arguments we have presented.

Analyses of the antecedents of attributions in expert parole decisions bring into doubt the adequacy of traditional attributional principles. Attribution theorists propose that a criminal record (high consistency) produces internal attributions, and generally propose that more serious crimes would also produce internal attributions (multiple necessary schema). There is research supporting both hypotheses regarding crime (Lussier et al., 1977; Rosen & Jerdee, 1974). However, analyses of our parole cases indicate that most indices of crime and record are unrelated to attributions. Crime *type* was related to internal attributions, but not the *severity* of the crime. For example, murder, the most serious crime, was considered the most external and unstable of crimes. Drug crimes were considered the most internal, followed by burglaries. Apparently, once again, it is the specifics of crimes and criminals that trigger attributions such as drugs, alcohol, money, poor associates, personality problems, victim precipitation, environmental stress, and so forth.

One final argument comes from the study of simulated parole judgments made by students and experts where crime descriptions were paired with different causes for different subjects (Carroll & Payne, 1977a,b). Some of the causes produced different patterns of judgments in students vs experts. In some instances, the crime report read that the criminal's wife had just left him for another man. Students treated this as a justification for crime (wife leaves → emotional turmoil → crime). In contrast, experts rated the criminal even worse, suggesting they saw this marital problem as part of a pattern of social instability (he is messed up in lots of ways). Even more interesting, there was an interaction among crimes and causes for the experts. A murderer who had been put out of his job by technology was seen as least responsible among the different murderers. However, the technological unemployment produced very high responsibility ratings for the crime of selling heroin. Thus unemployment mitigates murder but exacerbates heroin sale because (we conjecture) it becomes reinterpreted as part of a "drug habit" schema.

In summary, we have tried to point a new direction for attribution theory in this section of the chapter. Problems with the existing theoretical statements have been pointed out, and a proposal put forth identifying several important characteristics of the attribution process that are ignored or treated differently in the traditional theoretical statements: (1) the goals of the attribution process, (2) specificity of attributions and knowledge connecting cues to attributions, (3) attributional knowledge comprising part of schemas that contain much other knowledge, (4) the evocation of schemas or attributional hypotheses early in a task, and (5) the search for information to confirm the hypotheses that are under consideration. Support for these ideas was presented in recent research and reinterpretation of past research. Our final evidence for the schema hypothesis is a pilot study specifically designed to measure schemas in expert parole decision-makers.

Pilot Study

Social psychologists employing the schema concept for understanding representations of people have generally assumed the existence of consensual schemas, measured certain aspects of them, and tested schema effects on memory and ease of processing (Taylor & Crocker, 1981). For example, Cantor and Mischel (1977) used the schemas "extravert" and "introvert," which were intuited and shown to exist. Cantor, Smith, French, and Mezzich (1980) took existing categories from psychiatric diagnostic manuals. Cohen (1977) used "waitress" and "librarian" occupational categories.

In contrast, we face the problem in studying expert legal decision-makers that we do not know what are the consensual schemas, if they exist. Little research has been done evoking previously unknown schemas. Fiske, Kinder, Destefano, and Larter (1979) got subjects to sort photographs of Congressmen into piles by similarity and then to label the piles. This procedure netted three categories used by over half the subjects: "conservative," "crook," and "honest Abe." It should be noted that the direct procedure of asking subjects to name types of politicians produced only idiosyncratic labels.

In order to elicit schemas about criminals, we sought to develop a procedure with high face validity. In a practical sense, parole experts *might* scoff at us if asked to sort and label photographs. In a theoretical sense, we felt the content of the task had to be rich enough to evoke schemas (although an "empty" task had worked for Fiske et al.).

Accordingly, we developed the idea of taking pieces of information from actual cases, mixing them up in a big pile, and letting subjects sort the pile into cases. We reasoned that schemas would emerge as the organizing principle for constructing at least some of the cases. There was also the intriguing possibility that expert subjects might be quite accurate at reproducing the actual cases (and more accurate than college students).

As we worked with this idea, we began modifying the procedure. In order to keep the task manageable, only a small number of cases and a small number of variables per case could be used. Although there are few practical limits on the number of college students available, the number of parole experts and their time is strictly limited. With ten cases, we felt the chances of uncovering schematic cases might be poor. Instead, we decided to use information abstracted from cases rather than actual cases. We picked out 16 important variables from our knowledge of parole decision-making in Pennsylvania and Wisconsin and previous studies of information search in parole (Gottfredson, Wilkins, & Hoffman, 1978). We then looked at the distribution of values for each variable in our own data from 1000 parole cases (Carroll et al., 1980) and selected values at the deciles. These values were then written as prose statements using the style and examples of real parole cases on hand.

We now had ten instances of 16 case variables, or 160 items for subjects to sort. These items were typed out on small cards. To observe the sorting and keep the task under control, we used a pegboard with hooks in ten columns of 16 rows on which subjects hang the cards. Pilot testing with undergraduates rapidly suggested procedural changes. To shorten the task, items were set in 16 piles by variable rather than all collapsed together. This shortens search time and time familiarizing oneself with the stimuli. Further, subjects were asked to put up to only eight items in each case, based on our reasoning that schemas would be evoked early, and therefore later items would be unimportant to the schema or even randomly placed in order to fill up the available places.

The task was presented individually to four members of the Wisconsin Parole Board as an investigation of attitudes and beliefs concerning inmates and the parole process. Subjects were asked to create a description of up to ten realistic inmates using the 16 information categories. Each "inmate" is complete when eight cards fill the column on the board. They were asked to select any piece of information in any order they desire, and told they could change any cards as they went along. They were given 40 minutes to complete as many meaningful descriptions as they could. Subjects were interviewed afterward regarding their inmate characterizations and their reactions to the task.

The four subjects treated the task as meaningful and reported that it called upon many of the facets of the parole task. They generally felt the information presented on cards was valid, of the type they typically see. Their approach to the task was orderly, but two different strategies emerged. Two subjects composed cases one at a time, placing up to eight items for one inmate and then proceeding to the next inmate. The other two composed cases by distributing some or all ten items from one category across inmates and proceeding to the next category. It is possible that the former strategy is more schematic, although we have no evidence at this point. Clearly, task features regarding the organization of information presented to subjects or instructions could influence these task strategies.

The use of information appeared orderly even for only four subjects. Table 1 summarizes some statistics on the usage of information. Most "inmates" were constructed beginning with current offense, and then adding criminal record and sentence. Of 40 "inmates," offense was used first on 90%, and these three categories appeared immediately in 58%. At this point, there seem to be dual goals in operation. First, parole can be evaluated only when certain information is known. Hence discipline and parole plan are usually utilized. The fixed nature of this goal is evident because parole plan is usually made part of a case but only at the very end. Second, the inmate is being characterized or constructed using items that appear moderately often immediately after the first three: alcohol abuse, drug abuse, vocational report, and psychological report.

We should note that use of these categories is *underestimated* because

TABLE 1. Information Use in the Pilot Study

Information	Percent Usage [a]	Median Order of Use [b]	Earliest Use [c]	Characterization
Current offense	98	1	1	Always, and first
Prison sentence	92	3	2	Often, and early
Criminal record	90	2	2	
Institutional discipline	85	5	4	Often, and in the middle
Parole plan	82	8	7	Often, and late
Type of institution	60	5	4	Moderately often, and in the middle
Alcohol abuse	55	5	4	
Drug abuse	40	4	4	
Vocational report	40	6	4	
Psychological report	38	4	4	
Others (6 categories)	18	5	4	Rarely, and in the middle

[a]Percentage of 40 "inmates" in which this item appeared.
[b]Median order of use in "inmates" for whom this item appeared.
[c]Earliest use on ten cases by second subject. One subject used record first on one case but no other subject did, and another subject used it second on at least one case, thus the score is 2.

items presenting the *absence* of a characteristic (no drug abuse, no alcohol abuse, average work, normal personality) were often left out of the description. This is both a clever way for subjects to make eight-item descriptions maximally informative, and perhaps reflective of our psychological impressions of people—the expected or normative is not explicitly made part of our impression because it is implied by default.

After constructing the ten inmates, subjects were asked to describe the inmates, beginning with the one for whom they have the best image, and including only those for whom they have a "good understanding." They were also asked if they would parole the inmate, why they believe the crime occurred, and what strategy they used in the test.

It was obvious that subjects treated these inmates as highly realistic. One subject said, "I could attach names to all these people," and another said, "we've seen some of these people." In all, subjects described 31 of the 40 inmates they constructed. Among these descriptions some similar characterizations could be subjectively detected. These may be consensual schemas, although the data are much too provisional at this point.

The four subjects each produced a description that might be labeled the "impulsive auto thief." These descriptions included the crime of auto theft, no prior record for three of the four subjects, and descriptions of an impulsive, situational crime and an impulsive personality. The crime is described as "goofy. . .for no damn reason," "situational," and "crime of convenience." The criminal is described as "irresponsible and impulsive," "limited controls," "wayward. . .lack of focus," and "not very bright." Two subjects include alcohol abuse in their descriptions, the other two do not. All four recommend parole; for three of the subjects the auto thief had served 12 months of a 24-month sentence, for the other he had served 18 months of a 4-year sentence.

Somewhat less clear descriptions were each produced by three of the four subjects regarding four case types: (1) an "armed robber" who is a drug abuser, has an extensive criminal record, "criminal values" or "greed . . . desire to live at the expense of others." He has a long sentence, has served considerable time already, has poor institutional discipline, and is denied parole; (2) a drug dealer who sells drugs for the money, yet has some talents. He is described as "good intellect and potential," "has better abilities," and "reasonable education." The descriptions differ regarding drug use: "not a drug user," "uses some," and a full drug habit; (3) the "crime of passion," a convicted murderer whose crime is due to "emotional reactivity. . .passion," "passion offender. . .no pathology," or "low threshold of frustration. . .easily ticked." There is no prior record, good adjustment, and low risk after release. Two of the three subjects recommended parole. It is interesting how different this murderer is to the fourth subject's murderer, who is hostile and violent, has problems with drinking, problems adjusting to the institution, and is denied parole; and (4) a "manipulator" who was convicted of credit-card fraud. He is described as "psychopathic," "criminal values. . .disregard for others" and "tries to outsmart the system." He is not a drug or alcohol abuser and has a short sentence.

In summary, the pilot study has fulfilled our basic goal of providing a rich task that experts treat as interesting and valid for exploring their knowledge of crime and criminals. The descriptions of criminals exhibit suggestive overlaps that may reflect schemas. However, these schemas are certainly not uniform categories like "chair" but appear to consist of overlapping features and "fuzzy" similarity reminiscent of the psychodiagnostic categories investigated by Cantor et al. (1980). It is hoped that the extension of this task to a larger number of subjects may produce a firmer set of schemas from which to launch future research on parole decisions and related topics.

CONCLUSIONS

Social psychological research into crime and the legal system is both old and new. Although the first studies were performed 50 or more years ago, the current explosion of research began with a trickle of studies in the 1960s that became a torrent in the 1970s. These ten years or so of research have established theoretical and applied directions for social psychology in the 1980s.

Theoretical Directions

Research on legal processes began with a very loose conceptualization of a single evaluative dimension encompassing guilt, responsibility, punishment, liking, attractiveness, deservingness, and so forth. It has taken several years of confusing results to bring about the recognition that the various concepts and terms are neither synonymous nor uniformly related to the evaluative dimension. Instead, each concept carries its own connotations as well as meanings shared with some other concepts. Although social psychologists are now attending to these different concepts, it will be some time before a general framework arises that is related to social psychological theory and legal processes.

The complexity in terminology both leads and accompanies a growing complexity in theoretical models used to understand legal processes. Impression formation or attraction models posit a simple set of inferences regarding the positiveness or attractiveness of characteristics of a criminal. Attributional models increase complexity by proposing that the observer examines not only the qualities of the criminal, but also the characteristics of the victim and the environment in which behavior occurs. Inferences are made regarding causality that mediate evaluations. These inferences require mental gymnastics such as inferring what a criminal knew and how others would have behaved in such circumstances.

The growing sophistication of cognitive social psychologists has served to embed the attribution process within the larger task subjects are given. Thus attributions are made in the service of other goals elicited by the task and subjects' own values. Subjects seek not only to evaluate people, but to predict future events, adjust their own behavior, pursue personal goals, and so forth. Early attribution research in the laboratory presented subjects with impoverished tasks that lack any important goals other than generalized problem solving (answer the questions), yet were highly structured in the cues they provide, the responses they require, and the absence of contextual cues.

Attribution researchers have begun to investigate behavior in tasks with their own goals and structure, such as naturalistically valid juridic, judicial, or parole decisions, sometimes including expert subjects. This is part of the general movement toward applied foci in social psychology. It has become evident that theories must deal with the knowledgeable behavior of subjects in a rich context with meaningful goals. Theories are beginning to incorporate context, knowledge, goals, and task structure into the attribution process and behavior in legal settings. In essence, the applied focus on behavior in naturalistically rich settings is complemented by the development of content-rich theories in cognitive social psychology. Thus in this chapter we have proposed a schema-based attribution theory that is closely tied to the tasks and issues in the legal system. We believe this is a sound direction for the future development of theory.

Applied Directions

In some ways this chapter is an effort at application because it assembles social psychological research on crime and criminals. These attempts at application have directly fostered the development of theory by introducing task variables, goals, and context. However, in what ways has this research actually produced an impact upon the legal system or provided future promise?

Our review points out that social psychologists have generally been naive about the law and the functioning of the criminal justice system. Much research fails to produce applications because it extends social psychology to the researcher's *idea* of the legal system rather than to the *reality* of it. Along with suitable chastening (e.g., Davis et al., 1977), social psychologists are becoming more sophisticated about the context they are researching. In many ways legal scholars and practitioners are far ahead of us in analyzing the legal process. Unless we develop respect for their observations, we should hardly be surprised at their reaction to our observations. Legal scholarship represents a description of the task and context without which social psychologists too often produce solipsistic research.

The key point of connection between theory and application is that the people who do the legal tasks and make the decisions transform the formal legal structure of the tasks into an informal psychological structure. The law may recognize dozens of distinctions among types of responsibility, but if jurors (and judges) understand responsibility differently, then it is the psychological reality that determines behavior. As illustrated by the quotations with which we began this chapter, the "Law" itself is a theory of what *ought* to be, but it is applied by people each day to determine what *is*. That process of application, what is often called discretion, is certainly the province of psychological research. However, we must recognize that the "Law" will utilize psychological research not to determine what *is*, but to produce the social values and goals that *ought* to be.

ACKNOWLEDGMENTS

Support for the writing of this proposal and much of our research described here was provided by National Institute of Mental Health Grant #MH32855. We gratefully acknowledge the cooperation of the Pennsylvania Board of Probation and Parole and the Wisconsin Parole Board.

REFERENCES

Abrahamsen, D. *The psychology of crime.* New York: Columbia University Press, 1960.

Abt, L. E. & Stuart, I. R. (Eds.),*Social psychology and discretionary law.* New York: Van Nostrand-Reinhold, 1979.

Adams, J. S. Inequity in social exchange. In L. Berkowitz (Ed.), *Advances in Experimental Social Psychology*, Vol. 2. New York: Academic, 1965.

Austin, W. & Utne, M. K. Sentencing: Discretion and justice in judicial decision-making. In B. D. Sales (Ed.), *Psychology in the legal process.* New York: Spectrum, 1977.

Borgida, E. & White, P. Social perception of rape victims: The impact of legal reform. *Law and Human Behavior*, 1978, *2*, 339 –352.

Brickman, P., Ryan, K., & Wortman, C. B. Causal chains: Attribution of responsibility as a function of immediate and prior causes. *Journal of Personality and Social Psychology*, 1975, *32*, 1060 –1067.

Brooks, W. M., & Doob, A. N. Justice and the jury. *Journal of Social Issues*, 1975, *31*, 171 –182.

Cantor, N., & Mischel, W. Traits as prototypes: Effects on recognition memory. *Journal of Personality and Social Psychology*,1977, *35*, 38 –48.

Cantor, N., Smith, E. E., French, R. S., & Mezzich, J. Psychiatric diagnosis as prototype categorization. *Journal of Abnormal Psychology*, 1980, *89*, 181 –193.

Carroll, J. S. Causal attributions in expert parole decisions. *Journal of Personality and Social Psychology*,1978, *36*, 1501 –1511.

Carroll, J. S. Judgments made by parole boards. In I. H. Frieze, D. Bar-Tal, & J. S. Carroll (Eds.), *New approaches to social problems: Applications of attribution theory*. San Francisco, Calif.: Jossey-Bass, 1979.

Carroll, J. S., & Coates, D. Parole decisions: Social psychological research in applied settings. In L. B. Bickman (Ed.), *Applied social psychology annual*, Vol. 1. Beverly Hills, Calif.: Sage, 1980.

Carroll, J. S., & Payne, J. W. The psychology of the parole decision process: A joint application of attribution theory and information-processing psychology. In J. S. Carroll & J. W. Payne (Eds.), *Cognition and social behavior*. Hillsdale, N.J.: Erlbaum, 1976.

Carroll, J. S., & Payne, J. W. Judgments about crime and the criminal: A model and a method for investigating parole decisions. In B. D. Sales (Ed.), *Perspectives in law and psychology*, Vol. 1: *Criminal justice system*. New York: Plenum, 1977. (a)

Carroll, J. S., & Payne, J. W. Crime seriousness, recidivism risk, and causal attributions in judgments of prison term by students and experts. *Journal of Applied Psychology*, 1977, *62*, 595 –602. (b)

Carroll, J. S., Wiener, R., Coates, D., & Alibrio, J. J. A multistage model of parole decisionmaking. Unpublished manuscript, Loyola University of Chicago, 1980.

Clinard, M. B., & Quinney, R. *Criminal behavior systems: A typology*, 2nd ed. New York: Holt, Rinehart & Winston, 1973.

Cohen, C. E. Cognitive basis of stereotyping. Paper presented at the meeting of The American Psychological Association, San Francisco, August, 1977.

Cunningham, J. D., & Kelley, H. H. Causal attributions for interpersonal events of varying magnitude. *Journal of Personality*, 1975, *43*, 74 –93.

Davis, J. H., Bray, R. M. & Holt, R. W. The empirical study of decision processes in juries: A critical review. In J. L. Tapp & F. J. Levine (Eds.), *Law, justice, and the individual in society: Psychological and legal issues*. New York: Holt, Rinehart & Winston, 1977.

DeJong, W., Morris, W. N., & Hastorf, A. H. Effect of an escaped accomplice on the punishment assigned to a criminal defendant. *Journal of Personality and Social Psychology*, 1976, *33*, 192 –198.

Ebbesen, E. B., & Konečni, V. J. Decision making and information integration in the courts: The setting of bail. *Journal of Personality and Social Psychology*, 1975, *32*, 805 –821.

Efran, M. G. The effect of physical attractiveness on the judgment of guilt, interpersonal attraction, and severity of recommended punishment in a simulated jury task. *Journal of Research in Personality*, 1974, *8*, 45 –54.

Elstein, A. S., Shulman, L. S., & Sprafka, S. A. *Medical problem solving: An analysis of clinical reasoning*. Cambridge, Mass.: Harvard University Press, 1978.

Erlanger, H. S. Jury research in America: Its past and future. *Law and Society Review*, 1970, *4*, 345 –370.

Erskine, H. The polls: Causes of crime. *Public Opinion Quarterly*, 1974, *38*, 288 –298.

Feldman, R., & Rosen, F. Diffusion of responsibility in crime, punishment, and other adversity. *Law and Human Behavior*, 1978, *2*, 313 –322.

Feldman-Summers, S., & Lindner, K. Perceptions of victims and defendants in criminal assault cases. *Criminal Justice and Behavior*, 1976, *3*, 135 –150.

Fincham, F. D., & Jaspars, J. M. Attribution of responsibility: From man the scientist to man as lawyer. In L. Berkowitz (Ed.), *Advances in experimental social psychology*, New York: Academic, 1980.

Fisher, J. E. Information requests for attributions and judgments. Unpublished Master of Arts thesis, University of Pittsburgh, Pittsburgh, Pa., 1976.

Fiske, S. T., Kinder, D. R., Destefano, T., & Larter, W. M. Schematic approaches to understanding political leaders. In "Cognitive Approaches to Politics." Symposium presented at the meeting of The American Psychological Association, New York City, September, 1979.

Fontaine, G., & Emily, C. Causal attribution and judicial discretion: A look at the verbal behavior of municipal court judges. *Law and Human Behavior*, 1978, *2*, 323 –338.

Frieze, I. H. The role of information processing in making causal attributions for success and failure. In J. S. Carroll and J. W. Payne (Eds.), *Cognition and Social Behavior*. Hillsdale, N.J.: Erlbaum, 1976.

Frieze, I. H. Perceptions of battered wives. In I. H. Frieze, D. Bar-Tal, & J. S. Carroll, (Eds.), *New approaches to social problems: Applications of attribution theory*. San Francisco, Calif.: Jossey-Bass, 1979.

Frieze, I. H., & Weiner, B. Cue utilization and attributional judgments for success and failure. *Journal of Personality*, 1971, *39*, 591 –606.

Gallup, G. Society more to blame for crime than individual. Gallup Poll, October, 1970.

Garland, H., Hardy, A., & Stephenson, L. Information search as affected by attribution type and response category. *Personality and Social Psychology Bulletin*, 1975, *1*, 612 –615.

Gerbasi, K. C., Zuckerman, M., & Reis, H. T. Justice needs a new blindfold: A review of mock jury research. *Psychological Bulletin*, 1977,*84*, 323 –345.

Gold, A. R., Landerman, P. G., & Bullock, K. W. Reactions to victims of crime: Sympathy, defensive attribution, and the just world. *Social Behavior and Personality*, 1977, *5*, 295 –304.

Good, L. R., & Good, K. C. Influence of attitude similarity on parole recommendation. *Journal of Social Psychology*, 1977, *101*, 135 –137.

Gottfredson, D. M., Cosgrove, C. A., Wilkins, L. T., Wallerstein, J., & Rauh, C. *Classification for parole decision policy*. Washington, D.C.: National Institute of Law Enforcement and Criminal Justice, 1978.

Gottfredson, D. M., Wilkins, L. T., & Hoffman, P. B. *Guidelines for parole and sentencing*. Lexington, Mass.: Lexington, 1978.

Griffitt, W., & Jackson, T. Simulated jury decisions: The influence of jury-defendant attitude similarity-dissimilarity. *Social Behavior and Personality*, 1973, *1*, 1 –7.

Hans, V., & Doob, A. M. Section 12 of the Canada Evidence Act and the deliberations of simulated jurors. *Criminal Law Quarterly*, 1976, *11*, 235 –253.

Hart, H. L. A., & Honoré, A. M. *Causation in the law*. Oxford: Clarendon Press, 1959.

Heider, F. *The psychology of interpersonal relations*. New York: Wiley, 1958.

Hendrick, C., & Shaffer, D. Murder: Effects of number of killers and victim mutilations on simulated jurors' judgments. *Bulletin of the Psychonomic Society*, 1975, *6*, 313 –316.

Hogarth, J. *Sentencing as a human process*. Toronto: University of Toronto Press, 1971.

Homans, G. C. *Social behavior: Its elementary forms*. New York: Harcourt, Brace, & World, 1961.

Jones, C, & Aronson, E. Attribution of fault to a rape victim as a function of respectability of the victim. *Journal of Personality and Social Psychology*, 1973, *26*, 413 –419.

Jones, E. E., & Davis, K. E. From acts to dispositions. In L. Berkowitz (Ed.), *Advances in Experimental Social Psychology*, Vol. 2. New York: Academic, 1965.

Jones, E. E., & McGillis, D. Correspondent inferences and the attribution cube: A comparative reappraisal. In J. Harvey, W. Ickes, & R. F. Kidd (Eds.), *New directions in attribution research*, Vol. 1. Hillsdale, N.J.: Erlbaum, 1976.

Jones, E. E., & Thibaut, J. W. Interaction goals as bases of interpersonal perception. In R. Tagiuri & L. Petrullo (Eds.), *Person perception and interpersonal behavior*. Stanford, Calif.: Stanford University Press, 1958.

Kaplan, M., & Kemmerick, G. Juror judgment as information integration: Combining evidential and nonevidential information. *Journal of Personality and Social Psychology*, 1974, *30*, 493–499.

Kaplan, M. F., & Miller, L. E. Effects of jurors' identification with the victim depend on likelihood of victimization. *Law and Human Behavior*, 1978, *2*, 353–362.

Kelley, H. H. Attribution theory in social psychology. In D. Levine (Ed.), *Nebraska symposium on motivation*. Lincoln, Neb.: University of Nebraska Press, 1967.

Kelley, H. H. *Attribution in social interaction*. Morristown, N.J.: General Learning Press, 1971.

Kelley, H. H. *Causal schemata and the attribution process*. Morristown, N.J.: General Learning Press, 1972.

Kelley, H. H. The processes of causal attribution. *American Psychologist*, 1973, *28*, 107–128.

Kerr, N. L. Beautiful and blameless: Effects of victim attractiveness and responsibility on mock jurors' verdicts. *Personality and Social Psychology Bulletin*, 1978, *4*, 479–482.

Kidder, L. H., & Cohn, E. S. Public views of crime and crime prevention. In I. H. Frieze, D. Bar-Tal, & J. S. Carroll (Eds.), *New approaches to social problems: Applications of attribution theory*. San Francisco, Calif.: Jossey-Bass, 1979.

Kruglanski, A. W., Hamel, I. Z., Maides, S. A., & Schwartz, J. M. Attribution theory as a special case of lay epistemology. In J. H. Harvey, W. Ickes, & R. F. Kidd (Eds.), *New directions in attribution research*, Vol. 2. Hillsdale, N.J.: Erlbaum, 1978.

Krulewitz, J. E., & Nash, J. E. Effects of rape victim resistance, assault outcome, and sex of observer on attributions about rape. *Journal of Personality*, 1979, 557–574.

Landy, D., & Aronson, E. The influence of the character of the criminal and his victim on the decisions of simulated jurors. *Journal of Experimental Social Psychology*, 1969, *5*, 141–152.

Lerner, M. J., & Miller, D. T. Just world research and the attribution process: Looking back and ahead. *Psychological Bulletin*, 1978, *85*, 1030–1051.

Luginbuhl, J., & Frederick, J. T. Experimental research on social perceptions of rape victims: A review and critique. Paper presented at the meeting of the American Psychological Association, Toronto, August, 1978.

Lussier, R., Perlman, D., & Breen, L. Causal attributions, attitude similarity, and the punishment of drug offenders. *British Journal of Addiction*, 1977, *72*, 357–364.

McArthur, L. The how and what of why: Some determinants and consequences of causal attribution. *Journal of Personality and Social Psychology*, 1972, *22*, 171–193.

McFatter, R. M. Sentencing strategies and justice: Effects of punishment philosophy on sentencing decisions. *Journal of Personality and Social Psychology*, 1978, *36*, 1490–1500.

McGillis, D. Attribution and the law: Convergence between legal and psychological concepts. *Law and Human Behavior*, 1978, *2*, 289–300.

McHugh, M., Beckman, L., & Frieze, I. H. Analyzing alcoholism. In I. H. Frieze, D. Bar-Tal, & J. S. Carroll (Eds.), *New approaches to social problems: Applications of attribution theory*. San Francisco, Calif.: Jossey-Bass, 1979.

Miller, W. B. Lower class culture as a generating milieu of gang delinquency. *Journal of Social Issues*, 1958, *14*, 5–19.

Miller, W. B. Ideology and criminal justice policy: Some current issues. *Journal of Criminal Law and Criminology*, 1973, *64*, 141–162.

Mitchell, H., & Byrne, D. The defendant's dilemma: Effects of jurors' attitude and authoritarianism on judicial decisions. *Journal of Personality and Social Psychology*, 1973, *25*, 123–129.

Model Penal Code. (American Law Institute, 4025 Chestnut Street, Philadelphia, Pa., 19104), 1962.

Munsterberg, H. *On the witness stand: Essays on psychology and crime.* New York: Clark, Boardmen, 1908.

Nettler, G. *Explaining crime*, 2nd ed. New York: McGraw-Hill, 1978.

Orvis, B. R., Cunningham, J. D., & Kelley, H. H. A closer examination of causal inference: The role of consensus, distinctiveness and consistency information. *Journal of Personality and Social Psychology*, 1975, *32*, 605 –616.

Peplau, L. T., Russell, D., & Heim, M. The experience of loneliness. In I. H. Frieze, D. Bar-Tal, & J. S. Carroll (Eds.), *New approaches to social problems: Applications of attribution theory.* San Francisco, Calif.: Josey-Bass, 1979.

Piaget, J. *The moral judgment of the child.* London: Routledge & Kegan Paul, 1932.

Piehl, J. Integration of information in the "Courts:" Influence of physical attractiveness on amount of punishment for a traffic offender. *Psychological Reports*, 1977, *41*, 551 –556.

Pound, R. The theory of judicial decision. *Harvard Law Review*, 1923, *36*, 940 –962.

Reynolds, D. E., & Sanders, M. S. The effects of defendant attractiveness, age, and injury severity on sentence given by simulated jurors. Paper presented at the meeting of the Western Psychological Association, Anaheim, April, 1973.

Rosch, E., Mervis, C. B., Gray, W. D., Johnson, D. M., & Boyes-Braem, P. Basic objects in natural categories. *Cognitive Psychology*, 1976, *8*, 382 –439.

Rosen, B., & Jerdee, J. H. Factors influencing disciplinary judgments. *Journal of Applied Psychology*, 1974, *59*, 327 –331.

Rosenbaum, D. P. Victim blame as a strategy for coping with criminal victimization: An analysis of victim, community, and police reactions. Unpublished doctoral dissertation, Loyola University of Chicago, 1980.

Rotter, J. B. Generalized expectancies for internal versus external control of reinforcement. *Psychology Monographs*, 1966, *80* (1, Whole No. 609).

Saks, M. J., & Hastie, R. *Social psychology in court.* New York: Van Nostrand-Reinhold, 1978.

Schneider, D. J., Hastorf, A. H., & Ellsworth, P. *Person perception*, 2nd ed. Reading, Mass.: Addison-Wesley, 1979.

Schrag, C. *Crime and justice: American style.* Rockville, Md.: National Institute of Mental Health, 1971.

Seligman, C., Brickman, J., & Koulack, D. Rape and physical attractiveness: Assigning responsibility to victims. *Journal of Personality*, 1977, *45*, 554 –563.

Shaver, K. G. *An introduction to attribution processes.* Cambridge, Mass.: Winthrop, 1975.

Shaver, K. G., Gilbert, M. A., & Williams, M. C. Social psychology, criminal justice, and the principle of discretion: A selective review. *Personality and Social Psychology Bulletin*, 1975, *1*, 471 –484.

Shaw, M. E., & Reitan, H. T. Attribution of responsibility as a basis for sanctioning behavior. *British Journal of Social and Clinical Psychology*, 1969, *8*, 217 –226.

Shaw, M. E., & Sulzer, J. L. An empirical test of Heider's levels of attribution of responsibility. *Journal of Abnormal and Social Psychology*, 1964, *69*, 39 –46.

Sigall, H., & Landy, D. Radiating beauty: Effects of having a physically attractive partner on person perception. *Journal of Personality and Social Psychology*, 1973, *28*, 218 –224

Sigall, H., & Ostrove, N. Beautiful but dangerous: Effects of offender attractiveness and nature of crime on juridic judgment. *Journal of Personality and Social Psychology*, 1975, *31*, 410 –414.

Smith, R. E., Keating, J. P., Hester, R. K., & Mitchell, H. E. Role and justice considerations in the attribution of responsibility to a rape victim. *Journal of Research in Personality*, 1976, *10*, 346 –357.

Snyder, M., & Cantor, N. Testing hypotheses about other people: The use of historical knowledge. *Journal of Experimental Social Psychology*, 1979, *15*, 330 –342.

Snyder, M., & Swann, W. B., Jr. Hypothesis testing processes in social interaction. *Journal of Personality and Social Psychology*, 1978, *36*, 1202 –1212.

Solomon, M. R., & Schopler, J. The relationship of physical attractiveness and punitiveness: Is the linearity assumption out of line. *Personality and Social Psychology Bulletin*, 1978, *4*, 483 –486.

Sosis, R. Internal –external control and the perception of responsibility for an accident. *Journal of Personality and Social Psychology*, 1974, *30*, 393 –399.

Sulzer, J. Heider's "levels model" of responsibility attribution. Paper presented at the Symposium on Attribution of Responsibility Research, Williamsburg, Va., July, 1971.

Sutherland, E. H., & Cressey, D. *Principles of criminology*. Philadelphia, Pa., Lippincott, 1966.

Taylor, S. E., & Crocker, J. Schematic bases of social information processing. In E. T. Higgins, P. Hermann, & M. P. Zanna (Eds.), *The Ontario symposium on personality and social psychology*, Vol. 1. Hillside, N.J.: Erlbaum, 1981

Thornton, B. Effect of rape victim's attractiveness on a jury simulation. *Personality and Social Psychology Bulletin*, 1977, *3*, 666 –669.

Vidmar, N. Effects of decision alternatives on the verdicts and social perceptions of simulated jurors. *Journal of Personality and Social Psychology*, 1972, *22*, 211 –218.

Walster, E., Berscheid, E., & Walster, G. W. New directions in equity research. *Journal of Personality and Social Psychology*, 1973, *25*, 151 –176.

Weiner, B. Achievement motivation as conceptualized by an attribution theorist. In B. Weiner (Ed.), *Achievement motivation and attribution theory*. Morristown, N.J.: General Learning Press, 1974.

Weiner, B. A theory of motivation for some classroom experiences. *Journal of Educational Psychology*, 1979, *71*, 3 –25.

Weiner, B., Russell, D., & Lerman, D. The cognition-emotion process in achievement-related contexts. *Journal of Personality and Social Psychology*, 1979, *37*, 1121 –1220.

JOANNE MARTIN

STORIES AND SCRIPTS IN ORGANIZATIONAL SETTINGS

People in organizations tell stories. These stories recount incidents that appear to be drawn accurately from an oral history of the organization's past. The central characters of these stories are members of the organization. For example, IBM (International Business Machines) employees tell a story about a 90-pound security supervisor who dared to challenge Thomas Watson, Sr., the intimidating Chairman of the Board of the corporation. She was

> . . . a twenty-two-year-old bride weighing ninety pounds whose husband had been sent overseas and who, in consequence, had been given a job until his return. Every wife of a serviceman received a week's pay each month during these absences, and they were a super-loyal contingent of employees. The young woman, Lucille Burger, was obliged to make certain that people entering security areas wore the correct clearance identification.
>
> Surrounded by his usual entourage of white-shirted men, Watson approached the doorway to an area where she was on guard, wearing an orange badge acceptable elsewhere in the plant, but not a green badge, which alone permitted entrance at her door.
>
> "I was trembling in my uniform, which was far too big," she recalled. "It hid my shakes but not my voice. 'I'm sorry,' I said to him. I knew who he was all right. 'You cannot enter. Your admittance is not recognized,' That's what we were supposed to say."
>
> The men accompanying Watson were stricken; the moment held unpredictable possibilities. "Don't you know who he is?" someone hissed. Watson raised his hand for silence, while one of the party strode off and returned with the appropriate badge. (Rudgers, 1969, pp. 153 –154).

Organizational stories often have a point, that is, a moral. The content of the moral may vary, depending on who is listening to the story, why that particular story is being told, and who is telling it. For example, a security supervisor might conclude that she or he is to enforce the company security rules, no matter what the status of the person who is breaking the rule, i.e., "the rule of law not of men" is supreme at IBM. An executive, hearing the same story, might conclude that lower-level employees are to be supported when they adhere to IBM rules, even if this adherence should be personally inconvenient for a high-ranking executive, i.e., "pulling rank" is not condoned at IBM.

One cannot work in an organization without hearing stories like this one. Such stories, when repeatedly told, gain the status of myths or legends. A collection of such stories creates an organizational folklore. This folklore is the topic of many company-related, casual conversations. Such stories are told to new employees—informally during breaks and formally in training programs and speeches—to explain "how things are done around here." Such stories are the topic of cocktail and mealtime conversations, as long-time employees tell anecdotes about each other, past employees, and, particularly, the top management of the organization.

Although such storytelling is a pervasive phenomenon in organizational settings, several issues are not well understood. Why do these stories have particular types of content? Why are similar stories told in very different organizational contexts? What functions do these stories serve? This chapter examines the organizational and psychological research relevant to these issues, including the results of several experiments my colleagues and I have conducted. Because the organizational and psychological researchers have somewhat different points of view, this chapter offers a critical examination and empirical extension of both types of research, beginning below with the organizational point of view.

GENERATING ORGANIZATIONAL COMMITMENT THROUGH IMPLICIT FORMS OF COMMUNICATION

Organizational researchers have various perspectives on stories, depending on their approach to organizational theory. Two perspectives are particularly relevant here. The first emphasizes the rational structure of organizations, including formal job definitions and status hierarchies. The second conceptualizes organizations as systems composed of ideas. Each of these perspectives is discussed below.

The first approach to the study of organizations, labeled rational, emphasizes observable, measurable social facts. Thus one representative body of literature examines the observable, formal structure of organizations, that is, the hierarchy of job descriptions, the number of subordinates supervised by each manager, and the distinction between the responsibilities of line and staff personnel (cf. Scott, 1961). Studies of decision-making, representative of this conventional, normative rational approach, describe a sequential process, whereby a single problem is defined and alternative solutions generated and evaluated, thus leading to a thoughtfully considered selection of the best solution to the problem (e.g., Thompson & Tuden, 1959).

A second approach to organizational theory conceptualizes organizations as idea systems, the meaning of which must be managed. Thus organizations are not merely systems of observable, measurable social facts. According to this second approach, study of the formal structure of an organization may be misleading, in that the formal structure and official pronouncements of organizational representatives may bear little direct relationship to the actual ways employees get work done. For example, a school official may talk about classroom facilities and teacher certification procedures, but such formal communication may be only loosely coupled with the actual work of the school—educating children (Weick, 1976). Studies of decision-making, representative of this second approach, are typified by a model that conceptualizes an opportunity to make a decision as a garbage can. Into this garbage can are dumped problems, "issues, and feelings looking for decision situations in which they might be aired, solutions looking for issues to which they might be the answer, and decision-makers looking for work" (Cohen, March, & Olsen, 1972, p. 2).

The theoretical differences in emphasis between these two approaches to the study of organizations are reflected in the types of communication which each approach emphasizes. The approach labeled rational, with its emphasis on observable, measurable social facts, stresses predominantly explicit forms of communication. An explicit message is characterized by full, clear expression, so that there is no room for ambiguity or reason for difficulty or individual differences in interpretation. Examples of explicit forms of communication include quantitative figures, rules and procedures, and abstract policy statements. The second approach to the study of organizations stresses the management of the meaning of ideas and emphasizes implicit, symbolic forms of communication (Pfeffer, 1981). Such implicit messages allow for ambiguity and individual differences in interpretation. In implicit communications, the point of the message is often left unstated, the conclusion to be drawn by the information receiver. Stories are one of the many forms of implicit communication used in organizational contexts. Thus the conceptual focus of this chapter, on stories, fits within the second of these approaches to the study of organizations.

It is interesting to note that in organizations some types of information are communicated easily using explicit terms, while other types of information are communicated most effectively using implicit means. This argument is developed below.

Organizational representatives prefer to use explicit, unambiguous means of communication, whenever this is possible, so that misunderstandings and differences in interpretation will not occur. In organizational contexts quantitative forms of explicit communication are preferred. Perhaps because of the power of the almighty dollar in both the private and public sectors, financial figures are used most frequently. Thus corporations refer to profits, price-earnings ratios, and return on investment. When dollar figures are inappropriate, quantitative representation is still preferred, for example, in specifying the number of grievance procedures initiated by union members or the percentage of blue-collar employees laid off. Less easily quantifiable information, such as morale, often is expressed as a mean on a seven-point scale.

Occasionally managers have to communicate information that does not easily lend itself to quantification. Even though quantification may not be possible, they still prefer explicit, rather than implicit, forms of communication. For example, when the large automotive companies wished to combat the alienation expressed by their assembly-line workers, they articulated their concern in explicit terms, phrased as an abstractly worded corporate objective, "to improve the quality of the working life of our employees."

The problem with this emphasis on explicit forms of communication is that there are many types of information that are extremely important in organizational settings and that do not easily lend themselves to such explicit forms of expression. For example, managers find it difficult, if not impossible, to communicate explicitly information concerning (1) the culture of their organization, (2) beliefs about why a particular process is the most appropriate means of accomplishing a given task, (3) management philosophy, and (4) the rationale for a policy that is difficult to justify in financial terms. Below, an explanation is offered for why these four types of information are particularly important in organizational settings. Subsequently, an illustration of the difficulty of expressing these types of information in explicit terms is presented.

Organizational Culture

Organizations have cultures, that is, environments that are distinctive because of assumptions about "how things are done around here" (cf. Ouchi & Johnson, 1978). Such assumptions are seldom stated explicitly in rule books or procedure memos. As a result, new employees at an organization often find themselves exhausted and discouraged after their first few days at work; they come home with the feeling that they have constantly been doing something wrong, although they are not quite sure what it was. In fact, they are tired because they are struggling to learn the unspoken rules of the organization's culture.

Beliefs About Process

One of the most important aspects of an organization's culture consists of the employees' beliefs about the process that is appropriate for achieving a given task (e.g., Staw & Ross, 1979). Task objectives are often quite explicit, for example, to decide the theme of a Christmas sales promotion. The appropriate process for achieving a task, however, is often never stated explicitly. Thus, in a film of Japanese department store executives, a young man is seen presenting his superior with his ideas about the Christmas sales campaign for his division of the department store. Rather than complimenting the young man on his initiative or commenting on the quality of his ideas, the ranking executive simply observes quietly that the young man "would learn." In Japan, sales campaigns are not planned without extensive consultation with divisional employees. The young man had broken one of the company's unspoken rules about process. In order to "save face" his boss did not confront him directly with his mistake. Such unspoken rules, about the appropriate process for a given task, are also common outside of Japan.

Management Philosophy

It is a central tenet of organizational theory that it is extremely useful to have a well-articulated philosophy of management (cf. Ouchi & Price, 1978). For example, one classic book of advice for would-be administrators states that the key task of the manager is to state clearly those purposes or philosophy that make the organization distinctive and can unite the organization's members (Selznick, 1957).

In the public sector, the need for a coherent management philosophy surfaces in part, as a need for a sense of "mission." For example, the U.S. Government Energy Department is plagued by poor communication, administrative inefficiencies, and considerable general confusion. One reason for this, in addition to the usual "shakedown" problems experienced by new bureaucracies, is the fact that the agency is composed of warring factions, with different histories and conflicting objectives. The Atomic Energy Commission, the regulators of the oil industry, the conservation experts, the environmentalists, and the energy development specialists do not have a well-articulated common mission. Without such a mission, these bureaucrats often work at cross-purposes, and the effectiveness of the agency as a whole is severely hampered. As this example illustrates, organizations function more effectively when their top-level employees articulate a coherent philosophy of management.

Organizational Policies

A manager has to communicate the organization's policies and their rationale in a manner that generates commitment (e.g., Selznick, 1957). When a policy has obvious positive effects, the policy can be communicated straightforwardly, in explicit terms. Its rationale can also be stated explicitly, for example, in terms of financial benefits.

However, explicit forms of communication are less useful if a policy has few obvious positive benefits or even some negative consequences, for example, being extremely costly in terms of time and/or money. The rationale for such policies usually emphasizes interpersonal rather than financial factors, such as humanism ("we care about our employees"), or a desire to maximize an organization's control over its employees ("to increase their ties to the company"). The policy of improving the quality of the working life of assembly-line employees, discussed above, is an example of a policy that is often defended primarily with such nonfinancial rationales. In cases such as these, it is particularly important and difficult for top management to communicate the policy effectively.

The Problem: A Lack of Credibility

As the discussion above indicates, it is important for the management of an organization to (1) create and maintain a distinctive organizational culture; (2) establish and transmit beliefs about process; (3) communicate management philosophies in a credible manner; and (4) generate commitment to organizational policies that have primarily nonfinancial rationales. Management is not the only group interested in the communication of these four types of information. Lower-level employees—the targets of management's efforts at communication—also have a vested interest. They need to know if a philosophy or a policy is designed to make the organization look good, while having few positive (or perhaps some hidden negative) effects on employees. In effect, employees give management statements credibility ratings, reacting as sceptics to corporate propaganda or as "true believers" to policies or procedures that will apparently benefit them. Thus both management and lower-level employees need to know which methods of communicating these types of information will be most likely to cause a true believer reaction. Top management is interested in eliciting such a reaction and employees want to avoid being credulous of corporate propaganda.

In attempting to communicate information about organizational culture, beliefs about process, management philosophy, and some organizational policies, organizational representatives often find explicit forms of communication ineffective. An example of ineffective, explicit communication of an organizational policy illustrates this problem dramatically. IBM has a famous open-door policy, whereby employees dissatisfied with their supervisor's decisions can appeal those decisions upward through the organizational hierarchy, all the way to the president's office if they so desire. Tom Watson, Jr., son of the founder of the corporation, has stated the policy using the abstract terms of a corporate objective:

> If a man was not getting along or if he thought he was being treated unfairly by his manager, he was told to go to the plant or branch manager. If that did not work, he was then invited to come and lay his case before my father. (T. Watson, Jr., 1963, p. 19)

People who are unfamiliar with the open-door policy find this explicit and abstract policy statement neither memorable nor believable. They wonder if a busy man, whose time is so financially valuable, would really take the time to talk to all the employees who wanted access to him. The open-door policy lacks an obvious financial rationale. Explicit descriptions of such policies, such as the abstract statement above, run the risk of being forgotten or dismissed as corporate propaganda. Explicit communication of information concerning organizational culture, beliefs about process, and management philosophy is likely to be equally ineffective.

Solution: Implicit Forms of Communication

Organizational representatives usually resolve this problem by relying on implicit, often symbolic, forms of communication. For example, companies invent rituals, like Christmas parties, and rites of passage, such as training programs for new employees (Meyer & Rowan, 1978). They often develop special jargon and elaborate metaphors. Thus, for example, members of Boards of Directors use a western metaphor to describe mergers and acquisitions (Hirsch, 1980). Tender offers are referred to as "ambushes," resistance as a "shoot out," and the investment houses representing each corporate participant as "hired guns." The most common form of implicit communication, however, is the story. Organizational members tell anecdotes to illustrate the points they want to communicate. In time, these stories, if they are widely shared, come to have the status of organizational myths or legends.

Each of these forms of implicit communication serves to transmit what Polanyi (1967) has called "tacit knowledge." Polanyi draws the analogy of a blind man, who has only indirect knowledge of the sidewalk, gained by tapping the sidewalk with his cane. Likewise, organizational participants often learn the culture, beliefs about process, management philosophy, and some policies of an organization through implicit forms of communication, such as rituals, ceremonies, jargon, metaphors, and—most commonly—stories. This chapter will focus on this latter form of implicit communication.

In summary, this first section of the chapter has attempted to put the topic of organizational stories into a larger context, by discussing two approaches to the study of organizations, one which emphasizes explicit, and the other implicit, forms of communication. Two forms of explicit communication were discussed: quantitative, used primarily to make employees aware of financial objectives and accomplishments, and abstract statements, used to communicate rules, procedures, corporate policies and objectives. Such explicit forms should be used when it is possible and desirable to avoid misinterpretation or individual differences in interpretation. It was argued that explicit forms of communication are often not memorable or credible. Thus explicit forms should be used when memorability and credibility are not of primary importance, as when financial figures and rules can be looked up, if they have been forgotten, and when adherence to policies and procedures can be obtained without generating ideological commitment on the part of employees.

Several forms of implicit communication were also discussed, including rituals, special language, and stories. Such implicit forms should be used when differences in the interpretation of a message are either impossible to avoid or advantageous, as for example when communicating nuances in management philosophy or local variations in an organization's culture. It was argued that implicit forms of communication transmit these types of information in a memorable and credible manner. Thus they should be used when memorability and credibility are particularly important. For example, new employees face information overload while they are learning the ropes of their new position, a time when fellow employees and official training programs emphasize implicit and easily memorable forms of communication—stories and rituals. Some policies and philosophies of management require powerful and extensive employee commitment for their effective implementation, and so should be transmitted through implicit forms of communication, such as stories or special language.

Thus it is argued that implicit and explicit forms of communication are used to communicate different types of information, thus serving different types of organizational purposes. In the next section of this chapter, the organizational research that supports these arguments is presented.

ORGANIZATIONAL MYTHS, LEGENDS, SAGAS, AND STORIES

Organizational research on the content and functions of stories draws primarily on three bodies of research (Wilkins, 1978; Wilkins & Martin, 1979): anthropological myths, organizational sagas, and organizational stories. Highlights of the research from each of these areas are presented below.

Anthropological Myths and the Legitimation of Community Beliefs

Anthropologists have produced one of the most detailed bodies of research relevant to this topic, although very little of this work has focused on stories or myths from contemporary organizational contexts. Instead, anthropologists have used isolated communities and tribal societies as the settings for their research. They have relied on traditional anthropological field methods of conducting research, including interviewing community members and recording different versions of various myths. In addition, many anthropologists have taken this raw data and performed casual and/or formal content analyses and structural analyses of the myth content. Almost without exception, the research methodology is qualitative, rather than quantitative.

Anthropologists who study myths focus on a subset of the anecdotes and stories told by community members. In one representative definition of an anthropological myth, the type of story of interest to the researcher is defined as sacred; at least some components of the myth must be of dubious historical validity, and the content is restricted to origins or transformations of the beliefs and values of the community (Cohen, 1969, p. 339). When anthropologists discuss the functions that such myths serve in tribal societies, the organizational relevance of this research becomes clear. Myths serve to maintain and express solidarity among members of a community, legitimate the power structure of the community's institutions, and validate the rituals of the tribe (e.g., Cohen, 1969).

In the first section of the chapter, when an example of an ineffective explicit statement of an organizational policy was needed, an abstract statement of the open-door policy was quoted. That example was chosen because the open-door policy has also been stated using different forms of implicit communication. Indeed, there is a story told at IBM about the origins of this policy that fits many aspects of the definition of an anthropological myth:

> The Open Door grew out of T. J. Watson's close and frequent association with individuals in the plant and field offices. It became a natural thing for them to bring their problems to him and in time this was established as a regular procedure. My father encouraged this in his visits. He spoke of it in his telephone broadcasts to offices and plants. (T. Watson, Jr., 1963, p. 19)

As in an anthropological myth, the content of this story clearly concerns origins—in this case, how the founder of the company originated the open-door policy. The story was told by the founder's son at a series of lectures he gave at Columbia Business School. His purpose in telling the story was to legitimate the policy and, perhaps, the powerful position of the Watsons. The story is apparently told with some sentiment, although it is probably going too far to refer to it as sacred. Finally, the story is mythlike in that it represents an embellishment of history. In fact, the founder's door was not always open to disgruntled employees. All too often, employees attempting to appeal a decision to Watson, Sr., were denied access to him, either through broken appointments or unconscionably long delays. Those who did gain access were often disappointed to find he later reneged on promises he had made (Rodgers, 1969, p. 152 –153). Thus this particular story has many of the characteristics of an anthropological myth.

Organizational Sagas and Commitment to Unique Institutional Values

A body of research more directly relevant to organizations is Clark's (1970) research on organizational sagas. Clark studied contemporary liberal arts colleges, rather than tribal societies. His methodology, like that of the anthropologists, was qualitative. He interviewed past and present organizational members. In addition, he drew on the archives of these institutions: school publications, memoranda, and speech transcripts. After sifting through this mass of interview and archival data, Clark selected those pieces of information which, he argued, composed the organization's saga. Thus, as is the case with other qualitative methodologies, this approach has the advantages of providing rich and detailed data and the disadvantages of potential biases in the researcher's attention, perception, and interpretation of that data.

Clark defines a saga as a collection of stories about an organization's past. A saga reads as if it were a history of the organization, rooted in fact. Clark found commonalities in the content of the sagas of each of the liberal arts colleges he studied. The sagas began at either the founding of the institutions or critical turning points in their development. The central characters in the sagas were the institutions' founders or the architects of their transformations, such as the presidents of the colleges. The sagas generally read as if they had been authorized by the institution, as in fact many parts of them had been. Thus the sagas described the organizations' histories in the most favorable light possible. Perhaps most interestingly, each saga stressed a unique accomplishment of the institution. The stories, of which the saga was composed, illustrated an educational philosophy, some aspect of the culture or atmosphere of the college, a belief about the process of educating students, or an unusual policy that distinguished this college from other liberal arts colleges of comparable size and location.

Clark argued that such sagas served a variety of functions for the colleges. The saga described the unique qualities of the institution to its members—its employees (staff and faculty), its clients (the students), and the general public (including alumni/ae and potential donors). The favorable impression created by the saga helped these people justify their commitment of years, even a lifetime, of time and effort to that particular organization. Thus a collection of stories, ostensibly based on the history of the institution, served to generate commitment to an organization's culture, philosophy, beliefs and/or its policies.

To extrapolate from Clark's research on liberal arts colleges to organizations in the private sector is not difficult. In fact, many large corporations' histories—in Clark's sense, their sagas—are told in authorized company "biographies." For example, the story quoted above, concerning the origins of the open-door policy by Watson, Sr., is one small component of the long saga of IBM (e.g., Belden & Belden, 1962). Given that sagas are by definition favorable to an organization, IBM's saga does not include details about the extent to which the open-door policy is empty rhetoric, rather than an accurate description of fact.

Organizational Stories and the Legitimation of a Management Philosophy

Wilkins' (1978) research on stories is, of all the organizational research on this topic, the most relevant to the conceptual focus of this chapter. Wilkins investigated the relationship between organizational story telling and commitment. His research methodology involved a combination of qualitative and quantitative approaches. He conducted both open-ended interviews and a series of close-ended surveys in two organizational settings. The organizations were in the same industry, were of comparable sizes, and had similar profit levels. The organizations differed in terms of employee morale. One of these organizations had high levels of employee commitment while in the other corporation commitment was quite low (Ouchi & Johnson, 1978). Wilkins found an association between the number and type of stories told in the interviews and levels of employee commitment; a larger number of stories and more stories favorable to the organization were told by employees of the highly committed organization. Wilkins concluded that organizational stories, like myths and sagas, were used as a commitment-generating mechanism.

Wilkins drew on the research on anthropological myths and sagas to develop a series of hypotheses about the content of organizational stories. In accord with those hypotheses, Wilkins found that most stories concerned the culture of the organization, generally shared beliefs about the appropriate process for getting work done, or specific policies, as illustrations of the management's general philosophy. Like myths, these stories usually concerned the origins and transformation of these policies and practices. Like sagas, these stories generally were assumed by the story teller to be historically true and often referred to an unique accomplishment of the organization. Unlike a saga, however, these organizational stories referred to a single episode, rather than to a large segment of the history of the organization.

IBM employees tell a story that fits these aspects of the definition of an organizational story. It describes how the open-door policy was used to register a complaint about the behavior of Dick Watson, brother of Thomas, Jr.

> . . . Dick flew to Britain to review the activities of the little UK company, which was not doing as well as its continental counterparts. He went along on a sales visit to an ITT company and was dissatisfied with the way the account was handled. He then called the entire sales force together and tore them to pieces for their inept, un-IBM-like behavior and results. This was an unfair tongue lashing at best, and particularly demoralizing to a sales team which was trying to compete with a firmly entrenched UK computer industry, including IBM's former agents who had been given more than 30 years head-start by the Old Man. One of the indignant salesmen wrote a letter complaining about Dick's own un-IBM-like behavior. Tom Hudson, who headed IBM UK at that time, risked Dick's enmity by letting the letter go through. Within ten days Dick was back, apologizing to the assembled salesmen and characteristically turning the meeting into an educational session. (N. Foy, 1975, p. 47)

Whereas Watson, Jr.'s statement of the origins of the policy, cited above as an example of a corporate myth, is not a wholly accurate description of fact, even people critical of IBM have told this story about Dick Watson as if it were true (Foy, 1975). Authors of "biographies" of IBM draw several conclusions or morals from the Dick Watson story. One moral of the stories is that the open-door policy is commonly used at IBM, even by employees with complaints about the behavior of members of the Watson family itself. The story also illustrates some positive benefits of the policy, in this case, that even top executives will apologize for making undeservedly harsh criticisms of employees. As these morals indicate, the story should generate commitment to the open-door policy and, more generally, to IBM's philosophy of management.

Likewise, in Wilkins' research, when the organizational employees completed telling a story, they almost always could say what the moral or morals of the story were. These morals generally made specific reference to an aspect of the organization's culture, an organizational policy or practice, and/or the management's philosophy. Particularly in the corporation where commitment was high, the morals drawn from organizational stories were favorable to the organization. Later sections of this chapter explore the theoretical implications of these morals.

Shortcomings of the Organizational Research on Stories

Each of these bodies of research emphasizes the attitudinal functions served by myths, sagas, and organizational stories. In particular, these narratives are said to generate commitment to organizational policies and management philosophy. There are several questions which this research has left unanswered, in part because of its reliance on qualitative methodology, such as case histories and open-ended interviews.

The first set of questions concerns causality. Do stories cause commitment? Does the presence of strong organizational commitment facilitate story telling? Is there a feedback cycle? Or, is the observed association between stories and commitment a spurious relationship?

The second set of questions focuses on the absence of comparison data and control groups in the organizational research. If stories do cause commitment, do they cause more commitment than other means of communicating the same information? Do stories have more impact on attitudes than more explicit forms of communication?

The third set of questions, which the organizational researchers have left unanswered, is concerned with the content of organizational stories. If stories have a stronger impact on attitudes such as commitment, why is this so? What is it about the content of a story that maximizes (or minimizes) its effects on attitudes? If we could provide answers to these sets of questions, we would address important shortcomings of the organizational research on stories.

In summary, these first two sections of the chapter have presented the organizational perspective. We have elaborated the reasons why organizational researchers have a strong interest in implicit forms of communication. The organizational research on one particular form of implicit communication—stories—has been highlighted. Stories were shown to be frequently used to transmit information about organizational culture, process beliefs, management philosophy, and organizational policies. This research has demonstrated an association between story telling and commitment, but it has left unanswered questions about causality, comparison data, and the content of stories. As the next sections of the chapter demonstrate, psychological research can provide some of the answers to these questions.

"FOR EXAMPLE IS NO PROOF," BUT NEVERTHELESS, STORIES HAVE A POWERFUL IMPACT

In this section the first two sets of questions, left unanswered by the organizational researchers, are addressed from the perspective of cognitive social psychology. The first set of questions, concerning causality, has a methodological rather than a theoretical answer. Issues of causality are resolved more effectively with experimental methodology than with the qualitative methods used in the organizational research on stories. Most of the organizational researchers take the position that stories cause commitment, rather than the reverse. This form of the causality hypothesis, then, is most congruent with previous research. In addition, it has the most interesting implications for action, in that generating commitment is probably of more practical importance than increasing the frequency of story telling. For these reasons, then, the hypothesis that *stories cause commitment* was tested in experimental settings, using stories (and other forms of communicating information) as independent variables and using attitudes, such as commitment, as dependent variables.

The second set of questions concerns the fact that the organizational research does not compare the impact of stories with the impact of other ways of communicating the same information. To address this issue, we need to know what alternative forms of communication are most likely to be used. One way to formulate these alternatives is to draw on personal experience.

A Lecture on Milgram and a Nazi Refugee

Lecturers can use various methods of communicating a point. Like most teachers of introductory psychology, I have lectured on Milgram's (1974) famous obedience experiments. These experiments demonstrate that approximately two thirds of a heterogeneous adult subject sample were willing, in obedience to an experimenter's instructions, to administer shocks to another person, at a voltage level clearly labeled as dangerous to life. The first time I presented this experiment I used abstract language like that above to describe the procedure and summarize the results. When I asked my students to indicate anonymously on paper how they thought they would behave in this situation, only one or two thought the experiment had relevance for their own behavior.

The next year I taught the Milgram experiments I supplemented the abstract summary of the procedure and findings with some statistical data, a table breaking down the results by the demographic characteristics of the subjects. Again, the students found the results to have little relevance for their own behavior.

The third year, admitting defeat, I asked my teaching assistant to give the Milgram lecture. She supplemented the abstract summary of the procedure and results by reading a transcript of a postexperimental interview with one of Milgram's subjects, a German woman who had come to the United States after the rise of Hitler. During the Second World War this woman had not understood how her family and friends in Germany could have participated in the genocide. Referring to her experience in the Milgram experiment, she tearfully said, "Now I understand." This dramatic description of the reactions of a single subject convinced many of the students of the potential personal relevance of these experimental results, in a way which the abstract summaries and the statistics had not. This example, however, is misleading if it suggests that a reliance on explicit forms of communication, such as abstractions and/or statistics, is primarily an academic phenomenon. Similar issues arise in organizational contexts.

The "Quality of Working Life" Policy and a Man Named John

Some organizations rely on explicit forms of communication when they present policies to their employees or the public. For example, the "quality of working life" policy is often stated in abstract terminology, as a corporate objective: "Our goal is to improve the quality of the working life of employees." Companies sometimes supplement this abstract policy statement with supporting information. That information, however, is usually quantitative in nature. For example, annual reports issued by corporations using this policy sometimes contain figures indicating the percentage of the budget invested in various quality of working life programs, such as providing on-site recreational facilities for employees. Sometimes data about improved employee morale are included, but these, too, are expressed quantitatively, as means on questionnaire scales.

I once got a chance to talk with the Chairman of the Board of one of the corporations claiming to use this policy. When I asked him about it, he did not describe the policy in abstractions, or regale me with financial figures about the company's investment. Instead, he told me a story about how the quality of working life program had changed the life of a man named John, an assembly-line worker. This organizational representative knew the persuasive impact of a corporate "war story."

Differing Forms of Communicating Information

The lecture and the policy example are conceptually very similar. In each example, three forms of communicating a message were used. The first is an abstract statement. Thus, the results of the Milgram experiments were summarized in abstract sentences and the quality of working life policy was described in the abstract language of a corporate objective. The second form of communication, like the first, is explicit. It consists of quantitative figures, such as a statistical table from the Milgram experiment or financial and morale data from the annual reports. The third form of communication, in contrast to the first two, is implicit; it is a story, focusing on the reaction of a single experimental subject or employee. These characteristics of the three forms of communication are summarized in Table 1.

The impact of these three forms of communication can be contrasted, thus addressing the second set of questions left unanswered by the organizational research. That research suggests, but provides no evidence, that *a story should have a stronger impact on attitudes, such as commitment, than explicit forms of communication, such as abstract statements or statistics*.

This hypothesis contradicts a basic statistical principle concerning sample size. A story or a case example is based on a sample size of one. Data, on the other hand, are based on multiple observations and so should be statistically more reliable than a case example. Although abstract statements contain no explicit references to sample size, the abstraction is presumably based on generalizations from multiple observations. If one considers sample size, a story should be much less convincing than data or abstract statements. As the old Yiddish saying puts this point of view, "for example is no proof."

The hypothesis based on the organizational research, then, suggests that people do not consider sample size issues. Before presenting research findings relevant to this hypothesis, it is interesting to note that this and other related hypotheses concerning "failures" in human inference processes generate considerable emotional reaction, particularly among academics. Some of the reactions focus on the recipients of communication, claiming that it would be unfortunate, indeed a sign of ignorance, if people did not consider sample size issues when making judgments. Other reactions are more blasé, saying that support for the hypothesis would not be surprising since even statisticians have to learn about sample size considerations.

TABLE 1. Different Forms of Communicating Information

Form of Communication	Academic	Organizational	Sample Size
		EXPLICIT	
Abstract statement (words)	Summary of results	Corporate objective	Not specified, multiple observations implied
Quantitative data (numbers)	Statistics	Financial and other numerical figures	Multiple observations
		IMPLICIT	
Story (words)	Description of reaction of single subject	Individual case history	Single observation

There is also the possibility, less frequently discussed, that sample size issues may be ignored, not for reasons of ignorance, but because these issues have been temporarily forgotten or even deliberately overlooked. Under some conditions people may have very good reasons for placing more weight on a case example, rather than on abstract or statistical information. In some settings, particularly academic ones, any information given can be assumed to be correct. In other settings, this may not be so.

For example, the credibility of the communicator of the information may be suspect. Thus the recipient of the communication may dismiss the communicator's abstraction as being a misleading statement of opinion, rather than an accurate summary based on multiple observations. Likewise, statistics may be dismissed as lies. When a communicator's credibility is suspect, a case example full of concrete details may be, or may give the impression of being, the most truthful form of communication—after all, who would make up all those details? Although it is logically possible that all those concrete details may be fabrications, it may seem unlikely. Thus, when the credibility of the communicator is suspect, a recipient of communication may deliberately decide that a case example, in contrast to abstractions or statistics, is more likely to be undistorted by the communicator. As indicated by the alternatives of ignorance, temporary memory lapse, and deliberate oversight, one area of controversy has focused on the reasons why a recipient of communication might not consider sample size issues.

A second type of dispute focuses on the dilemma of the communicator who must decide whether or not to use a story or case example, if this would increase the persuasive impact of the message. There are at least three points of view on this issue: double standard, rational, and playful. Each is discussed below.

The double-standard point of view stresses the validity of the statistical principles concerning sample size. This point of view affirms that, in order to convince an academic audience that something is true, intellectual integrity requires careful and explicit abstractions, based wherever possible on quantitative data from large samples. Such information should be convincing to most academics whose training has emphasized the processing of information on an abstract level and the skills necessary to assess the validity of quantitative data.

However, according to this first point of view, it is an error to assume that because these types of information convince academics they will also convince nonacademic people. Abelson (1976) refers to this assumption that abstract and quantitative forms of communication are persuasive to nonacademics as the "academicians' error." Some people find a double standard implicit in this label: the implication is that abstractions and quantitative data are the preferable mode of communication among academics, but a different standard should be used with a lay audience. For a lay audience, it may be more effective to use an appeal to emotion, through the use of dramatic case examples, such as the transcript of the German woman who participated in Milgram's experiment. This double-standard point of view also implies that, unless academics are willing to avoid exclusive reliance on abstractions and statistics, they run the risk of creating a science whose findings are doomed to be forgotten or disbelieved.

A second perspective, labeled rational, takes issue with the double-standard pont of view. The rationalists assert that academics are not making a mistake by relying on potentially unpersuasive abstractions and statistics. Instead, these academics are deliberately taking a moral stance, preferring to appeal to reason rather than to emotions. According to this rationalist point of view, academics are not fools. Academics are teaching themselves and others to use data to make intelligent decisions, and to avoid being convinced unthinkingly by propaganda or other emotional appeals. Thus, according to the rational point of view, it is a good thing, not an error, if academics avoid the use of case examples and stories.

The third point of view emphasizes the fun and creative inspiration that comes from suspending conventional rationality, enjoying foolishness, and being playful. Vivid case examples and dramatic stories are fun. Both the communicator and the recipient of communication can, in their imaginations, put themselves into the positions of the various protagonists in a story, perhaps having insights they might otherwise miss. Thus, according to this third point of view, the avoidance of stories is a bad idea, since all parties to the act of communication miss the fun and insights which may come from suspending conventional ideas of rationality.

Choosing among the double-standard, rational, and playful points of view requires value judgments. For example, should academics persuade lay people that certain scientific findings are true; teach nonscientists the skills to decide the validity of those scientific conclusions for themselves; or give lay audiences an opportunity to have playful, creative insights, perhaps beyond those academics themselves intend to communicate? These value-laden controversies will have to be addressed if academics decide they want to try to change the attitudes and/or behavior of communicators or recipients of communication. There is, however, a prior question.

Each of the points of view in these controversies is based on assumptions concerning differences in the persuasive impact of stories, abstractions, and statistics. The first step in resolving these controversies, then, is to determine whether, or under what conditions, the hypothesis concerning the stronger impact of stories is correct. In the next sections of this chapter, two types of psychological research relevant to this hypothesis are presented.

Baserate and Consensus Information: Underutilized if Not Ignored

Both baserate research and consensus information research are concerned with the impact of distributional information, about multiple instances of a phenomenon, as opposed to the impact of a case example concerning a single instance of a phenomenon. Baserate research focuses on a particular kind of distributional information, labeled baserate statistics. The experimental design generally used in this research has two conditions. In the first, the people are given baserate information by itself. In the second condition, referred to below as the combination condition, the baserate statistics are supplemented by information about a single case example. In these studies, dependent measures are cognitive. For example, people are asked to make predictions or judgments about category membership (Kahneman & Tversky, 1973; Tversky & Kahneman, 1973). In a well-known representative problem, subjects are given baserate statistics about the average frequency of repairs required for Volvos. In the combination condition, the baserate statistics are supplemented with information about a single Volvo, a "lemon" which frequently breaks down. The subjects are then asked to estimate the probability that a Volvo will require repairs. When they have received only the baserate statistics, people rely heavily on these figures when they make their predictions. When the baserate information is supplemented by the case information about the "lemon," however, the baserate statistics are underutilized, and the case example has a strong impact on the judgments made.

In a second type of psychological research, evidence of a similar phenomenon has been found. This research investigates the impact of a different kind of distributional information, labeled consensus information, which describes how a number of people behave in a given situation. Several different experimental designs are used. Most commonly, the impact of consensus information is contrasted to the impact of no information (e.g., Nisbett, Borgida, Crandall, & Reed, 1976). Another design contrasts the effects of a combination condition (consensus information plus information about a target individual) to the effects of a condition where only the target individual information is available (Nisbett & Borgida, 1975). Finally, one study contrasts the impact of the consensus information with the impact of the information about a target individual (Borgida & Nisbett, 1977). The dependent variables in these studies are almost always cognitive. This research has found that consensus information is underutilized (Nisbett & Ross, 1980).

Of these studies, the work by Borgida and Nisbett (1977) is the most relevant to our interests. This is the only experimental design where the impact of case information by itself is contrasted with the impact of consensus information by itself. In this study, subjects are students who are deciding what courses to take. They are given information about the opinions of students who have previously taken these courses. That information is presented either quantitatively, as means on evaluation forms, or in the form of face-to-face interviews with individual students. The dependent variable is a measure of commitment, that is, whether or not the study participants actually registered to take the courses. The results of this study are representative of the results of the other experiments cited above. The quantitative consensus information had little impact on commitment, while the individual interviews had considerable impact. Since the consensus information was based on the behavior of a number of individuals, whereas the interviews concerned the behavior of only a single target individual, sample size was not the major factor in influencing these people's judgments.

More recently, psychological researchers have attempted to explore the boundary conditions of this phenomenon (Azjen, 1977; Feldman, Higgins, Karlovac, & Ruble, 1976; Hansen & Donoghue, 1977; Wells & Harvey, 1977). The finding has proven to be quite robust. Although neither type of distributional information is completely ignored, the case example information consistently has a strong impact.

The baserate and consensus information results are congruent with, but do not directly support, the proposition, based on the organizational research, that organizational stories are a more effective means of generating commitment than explicit forms of communication, such as statistics or abstract statements. There are three reasons why the psychological research does not provide direct support for this hypothesis. First, in the psychological research all three of these forms of communicating information are not contrasted within a single experiment. Second, commitment, with the exception of Borgida and Nisbett (1977), is not used as a dependent variable. Instead, the dependent measures have been cognitive—measures of recall, predictions of category membership, or causal attributions. The final and most important limitation of the psychological studies is that, given the cognitive nature of the tasks the subjects are given, there is no reason for subjects to question the truthfulness of the source of the information they are given. In organizational contexts, in contrast, recipients of communication are often sceptical about the credibility of the communicator, who may be expressing empty rhetoric or corporate propaganda.

Facilitating the True Believer Reaction: California Wine as Fine as French Chablis

Melanie Powers and I (Martin & Powers, 1979) conducted an experiment designed to test the hypothesis based on the organizational research, while avoiding the limitations of the psychological research discussed above. The independent variable was the form of communication; an abstract statement was supported by a story, data, or a combination of data plus story. Four types of dependent variables were used, including willingness to make predictions, accuracy in a recognition task, belief, and persuasiveness. We predicted that, when the abstract statement was supported by a story, it would be the most memorable, most likely to be used as a basis for predictions, most believable, and most likely to be considered persuasive.

To provide a conservative test of this proposition we selected a subject sample that was well aware of the truth of the old Yiddish saying, "for example is no proof." The subjects in this experiment were M.B.A. students at the Graduate School of Business at Stanford University. This degree program emphasizes quantitative training, so these subjects, in contrast to the general population, should be more likely to utilize statistical information.

Given our interest in organizations, we developed stimulus materials that concerned an organizational policy, in this instance an advertisement that communicated a policy to people outside of the organization; the experimental subjects were asked to evaluate the effectiveness of an advertisement for white wine from a new California winery. The text of the advertisment contained a one-paragraph policy statement, which was given to all subjects. This policy stated in abstract language that the winery, unlike most other California wineries, would attempt to duplicate the quality-enhancing wine-making procedures used in the Chablis region of France.

Subjects were randomly assigned to one of four conditions. In the control condition, the advertisement text contained only the abstract policy statement. Subjects in the remaining conditions received information which supported the policy statement, concerning the frequency with which certain wine-making procedures were actually used by the new California winery, and by most wineries in California and in Chablis. In the story condition, this information was presented in the context of a story about the wine-making procedures used by the founder of the winery. In the data condition, the same information about procedures was presented using numbers presented in tabular form. Subjects in the combination condition received both the story and the data.

The four types of dependent measures required subjects to make predictions about the winery's use of particular wine-making procedures, recognize the exact wording of the policy statement they had all read, rate the extent to which they believed the content of that policy statement, and, finally, rate the persuasiveness of the entire advertisement text.

The following pattern of results was predicted for each of the types of dependent measures: story > combination (data plus story) > data > control. Specifically, the story information was predicted to have a greater impact than the distributional information on both cognitions and attitudes. This is a particularly demanding prediction, since it requires that the statistical information be not only underutilized, but also utilized *less* than the story information. Thus, even the combination of story and distributional information is predicted to have less impact than the story by itself.

An alternative hypothesis, consistent with statistical principles concerning sample size, is that the distributional information would have a greater impact than the story information. This alternative hypothesis was tested for each of the dependent measures, as follows: data > combination > story > control. The first prediction will be referred to below as the story hypothesis and the second as the data hypothesis.

The data were analyzed using one-way analysis of variance, with planned contrasts testing the two alternative hypotheses. Of the four types of dependent measures, only the prediction results were nonsignificant. Subjects in all four conditions were equally willing to make predictions consistent with the policy statement. The effect of the story information was equally as strong as the effect of the statistical information. These results are congruent with most of the previous baseline and consensus information research, where the distributional information was underutilized, but not completely ignored.

The second type of dependent variable concerned errors in recognition of the content of the policy statement. Subjects in the story condition, in contrast to subjects in the data and combination conditions, were significantly more likely to make recognition errors; that is, subjects exposed to the story by itself were most likely to distort their memories of the original policy statement, remembering it as even more favorable to the winery than the original advertisement had been. The subjects in the data and combination conditions remembered the policy statement quite accurately, perhaps because the exposure to data in both of these conditions stimulated objective, accurate encoding of the information presented in the advertisement.

The third type of dependent measure concerned belief in the content of the policy statement. As predicted, the planned contrast testing the story hypothesis was significant for five out of six measures of belief. For example, subjects in the story condition, in contrast to the other conditions, were significantly less likely to doubt the truthfulness of the policy statement. The story, then, had a stronger impact on beliefs than the other forms of communicating information.

The fourth type of dependent measure asked subjects to rate the persuasiveness of the entire text of the advertisement they had read. On these measures, contrary to predictions, the planned contrast testing the data hypothesis was significant. If the advertisement text contained data, subjects were significantly more likely, for example, to recommend that the advertisement actually be used by the winery. These quantitatively trained M.B.A.s thought that the advertisement containing statistical information would be most persuasive.

In summary, this first experiment provides strong evidence that stories have a powerful impact on both cognition and attitudes. The story had as strong an impact as the data on people's willingness to make predictions. The story had a significantly stronger impact than the data on belief. People exposed to the story were significantly more likely to distort their memories of a policy statement in a direction favorable to the organization. In spite of this evidence of the power of a story, people were significantly more likely to rate the data as persuasive. Apparently, these people were unaware that the story was most likely to cause a true believer reaction.

Detecting Corporate Propaganda: No Mass Layoffs

The generalizability of the results of this first experiment would be more firmly established if that design were replicated using different story content, different statistical information, and a different type of policy.

In addition, the first study is limited in that it focuses exclusively on information which supports the policy statement. Would the same pattern of results be found if the story and data information indicated that the policy was corporate propaganda rather than an accurate description of the organization's behavior?

In a second experiment (Martin & Powers, 1980) we addressed this question and conceptually replicated the first study. The designs of the two experiments were similar. Three forms of communicating information were used (story, data, or a combination of data plus story). In an extension of the previous study, a second independent variable, type of information, was added; thus, the information either supported or disconfirmed the policy statement. Four types of dependent variables were used, including both cognitive and attitudinal measures.

As in the first experiment, both the story hypothesis (story > combination > data) and the data hypothesis (data > combination > story) were tested separately for the supporting and disconfirming information. In the conditions where the information supported the policy, we predicted that, in accord with the story hypothesis, the results of the winery study would be replicated. Thus, for example, the policy-supporting story would produce the most belief, etc. We reasoned that if the information supports the policy, neither the story nor the data can be assumed to be accurate, since the organization would have a reason to falsify information so that it would support a policy. Under these conditions, we predicted that concern with the issue of sample size would be minimal, and the story should have a greater impact than the data.

In the conditions where the information disconfirmed the policy, we also predicted that the story hypothesis would be supported. Thus, for example, the policy-disconfirming story should produce the most disbelief, etc. This pattern of results would extend the findings of the first experiment to include stories that both support and disconfirm a policy.

We also tested an alternative hypothesis, that when information disconfirms a policy statement, data should have a greater impact than story information, producing a pattern of results in accord with the data hypothesis. We reasoned that, if information disconfirms a policy, this puts the organization and/or the policy in an unfavorable light. It is possible that the policy is empty rhetoric or corporate propaganda. An organization has no reason to distort information so that it does *not* support a policy. Thus there is no reason to suspect the validity of either the story or the data under these conditions, and so the data, because they are based on a larger sample size, should have a greater impact than the story. After all, a single case example which contradicts a policy statement can be dismissed as an exception to the policy rule. Although we tested this data hypothesis, we predicted it would not be supported.

M.B.A. students were again used as subjects. All subjects read a policy statement (based on an actual policy statement by a corporate representative) concerning a firm's commitment to avoid mass layoffs. In times of economic difficulty, according to the policy statement, all members of the organization would take a temporary cut in pay and employees would be guaranteed that they would keep their own, or a similar, job.

Subjects were randomly assigned to conditions, thus determining what form of information (story, data, or combination) they would receive and whether that information would support or disconfirm the policy. The story information concerned a single company employee named Phil. The product sold by his division was discontinued. Phil was either dismayed to learn he was fired or relieved to learn that he would keep a job with the company, with a temporary cut in pay. The data information concerned the (high or low) frequency of turnover and pay cuts for company employees, before and after the product was discontinued.

The data were analyzed using a two (type of information) by three (form of communication) analysis of variance for each of the dependent measures. Planned contrasts were used to determine whether the story had a greater impact than the other forms of communicating information.

For virtually all the dependent measures the type of information (supporting or disconfirming) had a significant main effect. For example, subjects exposed to the supporting information were significantly more likely than subjects exposed to the disconfirming information to believe the policy statement. These results are not discussed further, as the primary focus of theoretical interest is the effect of the form of communication. These latter results, for each of the four types of dependent variables, are discussed below.

The dependent measures of prediction asked subjects to estimate the likelihood that the company would order mass layoffs and require temporary cuts in pay. The form of the communication (story, combination, or data) had a significant main effect on the first of these prediction measures, concerning the frequency of mass layoffs. When the information supported the policy, subjects exposed to the story were significantly more likely than subjects exposed to the combination, and equally likely as subjects exposed to the data, to predict that mass layoffs would be avoided. In all the conditions where the information disconfirmed the policy, subjects predicted that mass layoffs would occur. Thus, in these latter conditions no significant differences due to form of communication were found. The second prediction measure, concerning the predicted frequency of pay cuts, was not affected by the form of the communication. Subjects in all conditions thought pay cuts likely.

The second type of dependent variable was cognitive—a measure of accuracy of recognition of phrases from the policy statement. No significant differences in recognition were found, as the policy statement was recalled quite accurately by subjects in all conditions.

Several measures of subjects' belief in the policy statement were used. The form of communication had a marginally significant main effect on responses to the first of these items, concerning the truthfulness of the policy statement. As predicted, when the information supported the policy, subjects exposed to the story were significantly more likely than subjects in the data condition, and equally as likely as subjects in the combination condition, to consider that statement truthful. When the information disconfirmed the policy, no significant differences due to form of communication were found. On the remaining measures of belief, no significant differences among any of the conditions were found.

Commitment to the policy was measured in a variety of ways. Perhaps the most sensitive measure, since it did not use a nine-point scale, was an item asking the subjects to measure their commitment in dollars by estimating how much of a salary increase they would require before they would leave the "no mass layoffs" organization for a comparable job elsewhere. When the information supported the policy, subjects exposed to the story were significantly more likely, in contrast to subjects in the data and the combination conditions, to require a larger salary increase. When the information disconfirmed the story, on this dependent measure only, the form of communication made a significant difference; the story had significantly *weaker* effect than the combination, equal to that of the data. The remaining commitment measures, concerning endorsement of various aspects of the policy, were unaffected by the form of the communication.

The results of this second experiment replicated those of the first for each of the dependent variables that yielded significantly differences among the conditions. When the information supported the policy, subjects exposed to the story, in contrast to the data or the combination of data plus story, were at least *as* likely, often significantly *more* likely to predict the policy would be implemented, to believe it, and to be committed to it. This pattern of results supports the story hypothesis. However, unlike the first experiment, no recognition differences were detected. (The implications of the absence of significant effects on recognition is discussed at the conclusion of the chapter.)

In an extension of the first experiment, disconfirming information was also studied. When the information disconfirmed the policy, the form in which that information was communicated had no impact. The story, the data, and the combination had equally strong effects. Whenever disconfirming information was available, the policy statement was dismissed as corporate propaganda. It was less likely to be used to predict organizational behavior, to be believed, or to generate commitment.

One exception to this pattern was found. When the information disconfirmed the policy, the story, in contrast to the other forms of communication, had a significantly *weaker* effect on subjects' estimates of the salary they would require before they would quit for a comparable job elsewhere. For most of the other dependent measures, when the information disconfirmed the policy, there was a similar nonsignificant trend for the story to have a weaker impact than the data or the combination, in support of the data hypothesis. Two-tailed t-tests were used in the planned contrasts for disconfirming information, because both the story and the data hypotheses were tested. Had one-tailed t-tests been performed, this tendency, for the story to have the weakest impact when the story disconfirmed the policy, would have been significant for many of the dependent measures. This opens the possibility that disconfirming information may reverse—not just eliminate—the advantages of presenting information in story form.

Whether or not further research provides evidence of such a reversal, these first two experiments extend the baserate and consensus research by including, within a single experimental design, a larger number of forms of communicating information. The range of dependent variables is also expanded to include, in addition to the usual cognitive variables such as recognition, attitudinal variables such as belief and commitment. When the information supported the policy, the story had an equal or significantly greater impact than other forms of communicating information. Sample size considerations were consistently underutilized and often completely ignored by the subjects. Thus the first two experiments provide an unusually dramatic demonstration of the powerful impact a story can have.

When the information disconfirmed the policy, the story format lost its advantage. However, sample size considerations were still not given their due, in that the impact of a story was equal to that of data. This latter pattern of results is congruent with the results of much recent research (e.g., Wells & Harvey, 1977), in that the distributional information was not ignored, but it was underutilized. Thus, even when the impact of the story was not significantly different from that of the other forms of communication, it still had a strong impact on attitudes and cognition—stronger than it should have if sample size had been taken into account.

Before introducing the next section, it is useful to note how these two experiments provide answers to the causality and comparison data questions left unanswered by the organizational researchers. A causal connection between stories and commitment has been demonstrated, in that stories have been shown to cause belief in and commitment to organizational policies. In addition, comparison data have been provided, contrasting the effects of stories with the effects of other forms of communication. As the organizational researchers predicted, stories were found to have a powerful effect on commitment to organizational policies—at least as, and often more, powerful than communicating a policy in an abstractly worded statement or supporting a policy with quantitative data. Thus these two studies represent extensions of both the organizational and psychological research discussed in the introduction to this section.

MAXIMIZING THE IMPACT OF STORIES

The first two of the questions left unanswered by the organizational research, concerning causality and comparison data, have been addressed. The third question, concerning the content of the stories, has so far not been answered. If stories have such a strong impact on attitudes and cognition, why is this so? What changes in the content of a story would maximize (or minimize) its impact?

One answer to this set of questions is that stories may simply be more memorable than other forms of communicating the same information. Two bodies of research, concerning memory for concrete language and concerning knowledge structures, such as scripts, suggest why this might be so. Each is discussed below.

Memory for Concrete Language

The first of these two bodies of research demonstrates that concrete as opposed to abstract language (1) is easier to remember and (2) has a greater impact on attitudes. Considerable evidence has been amassed in support of the first part of this proposition. Abstract words were found to be more difficult to learn than concrete words (Paivio, 1969). Sentences composed of abstract words were more difficult both to recall (Beggs & Paivio, 1969) and to recognize (Holmes & Langford, 1976) than sentences of concrete words. Yuille and Paivio (1969) manipulated the level of abstraction of paragraphs of "connected discourse." The least abstract paragraphs proved to be the easiest to recall. In terms of relevance to the topic of stories, it should be noted that "connected discourse" does not imply that the paragraph had the structure of a story or, indeed, that it made much sense. Nevertheless, these results suggest the hypothesis that concrete, as opposed to more abstract, stories should be easier to recall and recognize. Such results would be congruent with the results of the research discussed in the preceding section, since both abstract policy statements and the various types of distributive information are more abstract than the detail-filled case examples and organizational stories used in these studies.

Concrete information also has been shown to have a greater impact than abstract information on attitudes. For example, Reyes, Thompson, and Bower, (1980) added "irrelevant" details to the testimony of an eyewitness in a court trial. They found that, when the detail was vivid and concrete, as opposed to abstract and pallid, it made the eyewitness testimony more believable and, therefore, that testimony had a greater influence on judgments of guilt. These results suggest that presence of concrete details may make a story more believable than abstract forms of presenting the same information.

Two explanations of these findings are commonly offered. The first, favored by researchers of cognition such as Paivio, is based on the premise that concrete words are more memorable because it is easier to form a mental image of a concrete word. The second explanation is based on the premise that concrete information is simply more interesting: "Almost by its nature, baserate or consensus information is remote, pallid, and abstract. In contrast, target case information is vivid, salient, and concrete" (Nisbett et al., 1976, p. 24). Because the vivid information is more interesting it attracts more attention and is more thoroughly processed. Therefore, according to this second explanation, it is easier to remember.

To date, it is unclear whether both, neither, or one of these explanations is true. For our purposes, both lead to the same hypothesis, that concrete stories will have a greater impact than abstract stories on both cognition and attitudes.

The Difference Between a String of Connected Sentences and a Story: A Script

Clearly, the research on concrete language addresses only a subset of the reasons why stories have such an impact. Stories are more than strings of concrete words or paragraphs of connected discourse. Bower (1976) defines what distinguishes a story from other forms of narrative, such as paragraphs of connected discourse. Stories have settings, central characters, plots—with crises and resolutions—and, often, a moral.

Unfortunately, for our purposes, the stories studied in this type of cognitive research are artificial. For example, the central characters are often barnyard animals and the settings are often imaginary, such as a nonexistent island kingdom. Nevertheless, organizational stories have many of the same distinguishing characteristics that are present in the artificial stories. Organizational stories by definition have organizational settings and central characters, that is, organizational members. Such stories have plots, in the sense that an episode, consisting of a sequence of events, is described. Finally, Wilkins' (1978) research indicated that most organizational stories have morals. A theoretical framework that gives further insight into why stories have such a strong impact on attitudes and cognition should deal with these characteristics of stories which make them more than simply strings of concrete words or paragraphs of connected discourse. Such a theory should include concepts related to such story characteristics as settings, central characters, plots, and perhaps morals.

The fact that stories often have morals suggests a second criterion for such a theoretical framework. A moral is a general rule, an abstract inference drawn from a narrative description of a single incident or series of incidents. The fact that people can often draw morals from stories suggests an explanation for why stories might be remembered so accurately and have a strong impact on attitudes. People may use stories, even a single story, to build a theory inductively. If people did not reason in this rather sloppy, inductive manner, they would have a very limited ability to learn, personally from their own experience or vicariously, from the experiences of others, transmitted, for example, through stories. Thus, stories should be remembered and believed because they are used to develop general rules, or morals, concerning what will happen, should an incident, similar to that described in the story, occur in the future. Although it is possible that people do not use stories to develop inductive theories, this proposition is consistent with the data on the morals of organizational stories and would offer a cogent explanation for the cognitive and attitudinal impact of stories.

For these reasons, a conceptual framework, which met two criteria, was sought. First, it should deal with those characteristics, such as setting and plot, which distinguish stories from other streams of language. Second, it should present an explanation of how knowledge structures are developed inductively, that is, how people build a theory based on a story.

There are numerous theories about knowledge structures, many of which meet this second criteria by making explicit reference to the process whereby such structures develop (see, for example, Minsky, 1975; Neisser, 1976; Rumelhart & Ortony, 1977). Much of the recent research on knowledge structures has focused on a particular type of structure, labeled a schema. A schema is a theory about a stimulus domain, a conceptual structure which organizes information gathered through personal or vicarious experience. Thus, people can have schemas about personality, such as introverts (Cantor & Mischel, 1979); impressions of strangers (Hamilton, 1980); and characteristics of the self (Markus, 1977). A review of this research states that one of the primary functions of a schema is to answer the question, "What is it?" that is, "What are the attributes of a particular stimulus domain?" (Taylor & Crocker, 1979).

A more critical approach to this work on knowledge structures, such as schemas, would raise a similar question about the central concept itself: "What is it?" Or, more to the point, "What isn't a schema?" The definitions of knowledge structures, such as schemas, are often so vague and general that it is not clear what, if anything, they exclude. In an apt summary of this problem, one student has asked, "How is a schema different from a sponge?"

One type of knowledge structure avoids this problem by specifying in some detail the content and attributes of a particular type of knowledge structure. This type of knowledge structure has been labeled a script (Schank & Abelson, 1977). It is particularly useful, for the purpose of studying stories, because its content and attributes have striking similarities to the characteristics of a story found by Bower (1976): setting, central characters, and plot. Thus scripts meet the first criterion, presented above, for a useful theory for examining the impact of stories.

In addition, like other approaches to knowledge structures, the concept of scripts addresses the question of how people build theories inductively—the second criterion discussed above. However, unlike many of the other knowledge structure theories, scripts provide a detailed model and considerable research (e.g., Nelson, 1979; Nelson & Gruendel, 1979) concerning how complex knowledge structures change as they become more abstract, that is, how people move from a single incident, perhaps described in a story, to a more abstract theory about this type of incident. For these reasons, the concept of a script meets the two criteria for a useful framework for exploring the cognitive and attitudinal impact of stories. Scripts, and their relationship to stories, are discussed in detail below.

A script is defined by Abelson (1976, p. 34) as . . . "a coherent sequence of events expected by the individual." The events are sequenced in this order because the occurrence of one event results in conditions that enable the next to occur (Schank & Abelson, 1977), much like the plot of a story. In addition to such sequences of events, scripts contain roles, settings, and props—much like their namesake, the dramatic script. Scripts also have entry conditions or "headers," the prerequisites necessary to activate the script, and branches, which contain optional event sequences. Most importantly perhaps, scripts contain slots, that is, abstract concepts which can be filled with various concrete instantiations of the concept.

Previous research has used the term script to refer only to the mundane event sequences we encounter frequently, such as waiting in a doctor's office or going to a restaurant. The example most often cited is the restaurant script. It has roles, such as waiter or waitress, customer, etc. It has a setting, a restaurant, and props, such as tables, forks, and plates. The entry conditions for the restaurant script include a customer who has money and who is hungry. The sequence of expected events includes entering the restaurant, ordering food, eating it, paying, and leaving. Optional branches might include sending a meal back to the kitchen if it was not cooked to specifications. Finally, roles, such as the customer, and some props, such as the type of food ordered, are slots, which can be filled by a variety of specific individuals and particular types of foods.

The previous research on scripts focuses on the cognitive functions of scripts such as the restaurant script. Scripts are said to reduce the information processing requirements made of peoples' limited-capacity minds. People are bombarded with an overwhelming amount of information. Activating a script is somewhat like a pilot putting a plane on automatic control. There is no need to monitor every incoming piece of information and no need to employ full intellectual powers in trying to understand what is happening. People know what to expect and unless something unexpected occurs, it is safe to place much of their intellectual attention elsewhere, to use their limited resources to understand what is novel rather than what they already know. For example, scripts help people to remember things they might otherwise forget. Scripts also permit people to fill gaps in their knowledge, guessing what they cannot recall (Bower, Black, & Turner, 1979).

The Relationship Between Scripts and Organizational Stories: Blueprints for the Future

At first glance, scripts and organizational stories seem dramatically different. As the example of the restaurant script indicates, previous use of scriptal concepts has examined scripts that are excrutiatingly boring because such scripts represent familiar, frequently repeated event sequences. This point can be restated by saying that scripts are a way of conceptualizing situations one finds boring or, in stronger terms, a way of transforming an interesting situation into a boring one. A script reduces an incident to the commonalities it shares with other similar incidents; the uniqueness is removed.

In contrast to such scripts, an organizational story is often interesting. Such a story deals with events perceived as special and which probably have occurred, at least in this particular form, only once. Moreover, one reason the story is interesting is that it is filled with unique and vivid details.

This discussion of the difference between scripts and organizational stories is an accurate representation of how previous researchers have used these concepts. The use of these concepts in this chapter represents an extension of this previous usage. The key to understanding the relationship between these two concepts, as used in this chapter, is to stress the fact that these differences are maintained. A script is *not* the conceptual equivalent of a story. Instead, an organizational story has a script embedded in it. A script is the essential core, that is, the skeleton that makes an organizational story more than just a string of unique details. That essential core contains a setting, the organizational context; a sequence of events, the plot; and roles, that is, the central characters. Thus, the key to understanding the relationship between scripts and organizational stories is that a script is the essential core which remains, after the details specific to a given incident are stripped away.

This relationship between scripts and stories can be clarified by analyzing some examples. In the paragraph below an organizational story is recounted. This story is told by employees of a large electronics firm. The central characters are an assembly-line worker and the president (founder) of the firm. The story, as it is told by a plant supervisor, goes as follows: "I started on a plant tour with him (the president), having planned the route we would take through the plant. He, however, took me wherever he wanted to go—in this case, the production line. He leaned over one of the assembly-line workers and asked her how things were going. She interrupted him abruptly and said firmly, 'I'm sorry, but you can't come in this area without your safety glasses.' He apologized, red with embarrassment, went back to get his safety glasses, and then came back and complimented her on her guts. They chatted for quite some time. He was very impressed that she had challenged his behavior without being intimidated" (paraphrased from transcript of interview, Wilkins, 1978).

Employees at IBM tell a different version of the same story. This second version, the story of the 90-pound security supervisory who challenged the Chairman of the Board, was quoted in the introduction to this chapter.

It is possible, without much dispute over details, to construct a script which captures the essential elements of both these stories. This organizational script has two roles, a lower-level subordinate and a top executive. Interestingly, in all versions of this story that I have heard, the low-level employee is female and the top executive male. The entry condition, which triggers the beginning of the script, is that the executive breaks a regulation. The following sequence of events then occurs: the subordinate notices that the regulation has been broken, she challenges the executive, and he then complies with the regulation. There is a branch, in that in some of these stories the executive apologizes, while in others, such as the IBM version, he does not. There are also several slots. For example, the type of regulation can vary. In these two examples, one regulation concerned safety glasses and the other, a badge.

It is interesting to note the implications of the fact that two stories about executives breaking regulations come from different organizations. In our research, we have been reading corporate histories, biographies of organizational founders, and transcripts of open-ended interviews from organizational field settings (Wilkins, 1978; Wilkins & Martin, 1979; Martin, 1980). We have been struck by the similarity of the types of scripts which underlie organizational stories which are told in radically different organizational contexts. In spite of differences in story details, there seem to be some scripts which are shared by a large number of organizations. For example,

1. "No Mass Layoffs" script about an organization's refusal to fire employees when economic times get tough
2. "Horatio Alger" script about the employee who starts at the bottom and climbs to the top
3. "Great Man is Human" script, where the founder or president of a company makes a personal gesture toward a lower-level employee, for example, buying a present for a new baby
4. "We Appreciate and/or Tolerate Deviance" script, where a top executive goes out of his way to respond well to a complaint or challenge from a subordinate

As these examples indicate, the content of scripts is often common to a wide variety of organizational contexts. The functions served by such scripts should also be common to a wide variety of organizational settings. When an employee encounters a new situation, he or she can try to recall a script that matches this situation, using role requirements and entry conditions to see if the script and the new situation are similar. For example, the employee can ask if an executive broke a regulation and if the new situation involved a lower-level female employee. If the entry condition is met and these requisite roles are filled, the employee can then see if the scriptal sequence of events has occurred: Has the subordinate noticed the regulation has been broken? Did she challenge the executive? Thus, this script contains all the essentials of this type of situation, once the details specific to any one particular incident are stripped away. In other words, the script that is embedded in a story about a single incident contains the essential elements of that story that would be present also in accounts of other similar situations.

Three things are gained by using scriptal concepts in this way to understand organizational stories. First, the scriptal perspective offers an explanation for why stories may be more memorable than other means of communicating information. Second, scripts also offer an explanation for why organizational stories may have a strong impact on attitudes, such as organizational commitment. Finally, the script perspective offers a model of how people build abstract theories inductively from concrete stories about single incidents. Each of these points is explained below.

It was suggested at the beginning of this section of the chapter that stories may have a stronger cognitive impact than other forms of communicating information. The research on the memorability of concrete, as opposed to abstract, language suggests one explanation for this strong cognitive impact; stories may be more memorable because they are filled with concrete details. It is the vivid, interesting, and unique details about people, props, settings, and events that grasp people's attention and stick in their memories perhaps because such details are easily imaginable. Script theory offers an additional explanation for the cognitive impact of organizational stories. Not only are the concrete and unique details in a story memorable, the setting, roles, and sequences of events are also memorable—precisely because these latter elements are not unique; they are common to any situation that fits the script. Thus the research on concrete language suggests that the details in organizational stories may be particularly memorable. The research on scripts suggests that the setting, roles, and sequence of events in an organizational story may also be particularly memorable. Both types of research support the hypothesis that stories should have a stronger cognitive impact than other forms of communicating information.

The script perspective also offers an explanation for the finding by organizational researchers that organizational stories have a strong impact on attitudes such as commitment and belief. People may remember organizational stories because such stories contain a script about how the organization will behave in the future. Suppose an employee experiences a situation or learns of a situation vicariously through a story. The employee can then see if this new situation fits any script, that is, determine if the new situation meets the entry condition and includes the requisite roles. If so, that script can be used to fill in gaps in the employee's knowledge and/or to predict what will happen next. Thus, for example, if an executive breaks a regulation, and a subordinate notices, an employee familiar with this particular script can predict that the executive will be reprimanded by the subordinate and will voluntarily comply with the regulation.

In addition to filling gaps in knowledge and enabling an employee to predict what other employees will do, scripts can be used to help an employee make personal decisions about his or her own behavior. If an employee encounters a situation similar to the situation described in the script, the employee can place him- or herself in either the executive or the subordinate role, whichever is appropriate, and can draw conclusions about how he or she should behave in situations of this type. These conclusions about behavior are guided by the morals implicit in the story. Morals can be conceptualized as descriptions of appropriate behavior for various employee roles. The moral to the regulation-breaking story indicates that it is appropriate for subordinates to challenge top executives who break regulations. An executive learns that such challenges have apparently occurred in the past. He or she may conclude that, if challenged by a subordinate, compliance is in order.

An organizational story, then, does more than tell how a single incident was resolved; it gives a preview of what may happen if a similar incident should occur again. A story contains a blueprint that can be used to predict future organizational behavior—one's own behavior as well as the behavior of other employees. If the presence of a script increases a person's willingness to predict what will happen in a given type of situation, this willingness to make predictions reflects belief in the accuracy of the script and, hence, the truthfulness of the organizational story. This line of reasoning implies that, to the extent that an organizational story is perceived to contain a script useful for predicting behavior, that story should be believed and should generate commitment. Thus the script perspective offers an explanation for the attitudinal, as well as the cognitive, functions served by organizational stories.

This use of the script perspective to illuminate the content and functions of organizational stories has extended previous use of scriptal concepts. The previous use of scripts has been restricted to explaining how people structure knowledge about boring, routine events. Scripts have been used above to explain part of the cognitive impact of organizational stories, which are interesting, rather than boring, and unique, rather than routine. In addition, the script perspective has been expanded, beyond its previous focus on the structure of knowledge, to support hypotheses concerning the attitudinal, as well as cognitive, functions served by organizational stories.

This extension of the script framework is justified by how it extends understanding of organizational stories. Scripts, as discussed above, offer an explanation for why organizational stories may have a strong impact on both cognitions, such as memory, and attitudes, such as willingness to make script-consistent predictions, belief, and commitment. Another advantage, gained by using a script approach to understanding the impact of organizational stories, is that scripts provide a model of how we build abstract theories from personal or vicarious experience of single incidents. The next section is devoted to a discussion of the implications of this complex idea. Before continuing, however, a review of the content of this section can be used to support a hypothesis that is related to the issue of theory building.

This section has presented two lines of argument drawn from recent cognitive research. By reviewing and combining these two lines of argument, a hypothesis is developed which neither line of argument has yet systematically addressed. The first line of research focuses on the effects of concrete language, with stimulus materials consisting of isolated words or phrases, details "irrelevant" to the main points of eyewitness testimony, and paragraphs of "connected discourse." These studies demonstrate that concrete language has a greater impact than abstract language on both attitudes and cognition. Unfortunately, for our purposes, this research is not sensitive to those characteristics that make a story more than a collection of connected words and sentences.

The second line of research, concerning scripts, addresses precisely this problem. A story is a story, in part, because it has central characters, a setting, and a plot. Like a story, a script has roles, a setting, and a sequence of events. It is argued that organizational stories contain scripts, and thus those scripts may have effects on attitudes as well as cognition.

These two lines of argument, concerning concrete language and scripts, can be combined. As language can vary from concrete to abstract, so scripts and organizational stories can vary from the concrete—based on a single incident and full of vivid details—to the abstract—based on multiple incidents with few, if any, details. This supports the hypothesis that *organizational stories and scripts that are concrete should have a stronger impact on attitudes and cognition than organizational stories and scripts that are presented at a higher level of abstraction*. The next section explores this hypothesis.

THE IMPOTENCY OF ABSTRACT SCRIPTS AND STORIES

The hypothesis above can be tested with an experimental design, where the independent variable is the level of abstraction of an organizational script or story, and where the dependent variables include cognitive measures, such as recall or recognition, and attitudinal measures, such as willingness to make predictions about, believe in, and make commitment to the content of a script or story.

The problem of how to operationalize the independent variable raises some fascinating issues. It is easy to imagine how to construct a concrete story, making it full of specific details about a single incident and a central character. However, it is not immediately obvious how to construct an abstract story. The underlying question is an old one: How do we learn from, that is, how do we generalize from the personal and/or vicarious experience of single incidents? How do we abstract from the concrete? Our research addresses this question only indirectly, insofar as learning is expressed in language. Rather than attempting to explore the complex relationship between knowledge and language, we restrict attention to the abstraction process as it is reflected in language.

One type of research relevant to this question is the Yuille and Paivio (1969) study cited above. In this study the paragraphs of connected discourse were constructed at three levels of abstraction, necessitating changes in the types and numbers of nouns, verb forms, adjectives, and conjunctions. The most concrete paragraphs were found to be the most memorable.[1]

[1]Another type of cognitive research has addressed the issue of level of abstraction. Prototype researchers have varied three levels of abstraction of nouns (e.g., Rosch, Mervis, Gray, Johnson, & Boyes-Braem, 1976; Smith & Medin, 1979), comparing, for example, armchairs, chairs, and furniture. Others have also varied the level of abstraction of personality constructs comparing, for example, a donor to a repertory theater, a patron of the arts, and a cultured person (Cantor & Mischel, 1979). In a

It is important to note a limitation in the usefulness of the research on concrete language. Stories and scripts are even more complex than the paragraphs of connected discourse. A theory of abstraction that pertains to scripts and stories must address the issue of how such complex stimuli change as they become more abstract. How does the content of a script or story based on a single incident differ from the content of a script or story based on multiple similar incidents?

As discussed in the previous section, script research is relevant to this question, as it picks up where the rest of the cognitive literature leaves off. Abelson (1976) has directly addressed the question of how scripts change as they become more abstract, although he does not present a systematic theory. Thus, the best way to examine the implications of these ideas is to discuss the examples he presents.

In these examples, Abelson varies the level of abstraction of a transgression and punishment script. The lowest level of abstraction is labeled episodic. A single incident is stored in memory as a script containing, as all scripts do, such elements as roles and a sequence of events. Thus a child might store a simple episodic script having two events: "the time I stole a cookie" and "boy did I get spanked."

If the child has multiple experiences of this type, she/he may develop a script at the intermediate level of abstraction, labeled categorical. Abelson's example of the categorical transgression and punishment script consists of two parts: doing forbidden things (under which various transgression episodes, such as stealing a cookie, are collected) and getting punished (under which various punishment episodes are gathered). According to Abelson, then, a categorical script takes the form of a series of general statements, at least some of which are followed by examples of the general concept. These examples are drawn from more than one incident, thus melding material from multiple similar incidents into a single script.

The third and highest level of abstraction is labeled hypothetical. The hypothetical version of the transgression and punishment script has a complex causal structure:

> Me doing bad things could lead to my getting punished if my parents found out (unless I could make it look like my brother did it), but if it weren't too serious or they were in a good mood, or if I could sweet-talk my mother and she could get around my father, then maybe I'd just get a mild scolding (Abelson, 1976, p. 35).

Thus, according to Abelson, a hypothetical script consists of a string of conditional clauses. Each is stated in general terms without illustrative

---

(footnote continued)

variety of cognitive tasks, the prototype researchers found an intermediate level of abstraction to be most efficient. The intermediate level apparently serves the function of conveying a more useful amount of information than the most concrete and most abstract levels. This finding does not agree with the results of the cognitive research, which has found the most concrete language to be the most memorable. One explanation for this disparity is that the function of conveying information may be different from the pure recall and recognition tasks used by the cognitive researchers such as Yuille and Paivio.

examples of either "bad things" or types of punishment, with the exception of the concrete reference to getting a mild scolding.

In some ways the hypothetical script is similar to the moral of a story. The moral of Abelson's episodic version of the transgression and punishment script might be: "if you get caught doing something wrong, you will get punished." A moral, then, takes the form of a short abstract rule. In contrast, a hypothetical script is longer and more complex than a moral. It includes and may expand the sequence of events present in an episodic script. Using words like "if" and "then," it specifies the causal relationship among these events. Words such as "unless" are used to explain the conditional nature of some of these relationships among the events. Thus a hypothetical script can be thought of as an elaborated version of the moral of a story. It is more elaborate because it includes the essential elements of a script (roles, setting, sequence of events) and because of its complex causal structure. A hypothetical script, then, is more like a hypothesis or mini-theory than it is like a simple rule or moral.

It is important to note that Abelson implicitly is presenting a developmental model of the process of abstraction. An individual first experiences or learns vicariously about a situation. That situation is then remembered at an episodic level of abstraction. As other similar incidents occur, the internal structure of knowledge, that is the script, becomes more abstract, first in categorical, then in hypothetical form. The research presented in this section of the chapter does not share this developmental focus. Rather than studying scripts that originate in the mind of the experimental subject, we are studying the effects of scripts created by the experimenter. This implies that scripts are used not only within the individual, to comprehend, but also between individuals, to communicate a sequence of ideas.

In our research (Martin, Patterson, & Price, 1979; Martin, Patterson, Harrod, & Siehl, 1980), we have attempted to rationalize Abelson's levels of script abstraction. In the process of doing so we have developed some more systematic ideas, outlined in Table 2, concerning how the process of abstraction is reflected in language. Each of the three levels of abstraction is discussed below.

In the episodic script, a single incident is described in the past tense. The central characters are individuals with individuating characteristics, such as a proper name. The logical structure of the episodic script is represented by words like "and," "that," and "while." The episodic script contains more details than the more abstract scripts. It does not include words like "usually" to indicate the frequency with which events are expected to occur. Such frequency words are unnecessary because a single incident happens only once.

In the categorical script, several incidents are combined into a single script. The central characters are referred to by their role, as indicated by a job title or a word like "employee," rather than by individuating characteristics, such as a proper name. The sentences in a categorical script consist of general statements that describe the script events in the

TABLE 2. Characteristics of Scripts at Varying Levels of Abstraction

Characteristics	Episodic Most Concrete	Categorical Intermediate	Hypothetical Most Abstract
Raw material	Single incident	At least two incidents	At least two, probably more incidents
Form	Description of single incident	Series of general statements, illustrated with specific examples	Series of general statements with few, if any, specific examples
Central character(s)	Person(s) with individualizing characteristics, i.e., a proper name	Roles, i.e., a job title or "employee"	Roles, i.e., a job title or "individuals"
Verb tense	Past	General statements in "eternal present," with examples in present or past	Future or "eternal present," with some use of conditional and/or subjunctive
Logical words and phrases	i.e., "and," "that," and "while"	i.e., "and," "or," "such as," and "for example"	i.e., "if," "then," and "unless"
Frequency indicators	None	i.e., "usually," "frequently," "some," and "most"	i.e., "usually," "frequently," "some," and "most"
Number of details	Many	A moderate number	Very few, if any

"eternal present" tense, followed by illustrative examples from various incidents, phrased in either the present or the past tense. The words indicating this logical structure include "and," "or," "such as," and "for example." The categorical script contains an intermediate level of detail and an intermediate number of words indicating frequency, like "usually" and "some."

In the hypothetical script, Abelson uses a complex inferential structure and subjunctive and conditional verb tenses. We have found it useful to simplify Abelson's ideas. Pretests of our experimental subjects have indicated that the complexity of Abelson's highest level of abstraction does not accurately represent most people's logical processes or grammatical habits. Like Abelson, in our hypothetical script we merge several similar incidents into a single abstract statement which contains few, if any, examples. Central characters are referred to as "individuals" or by reference to their job titles. The verb tense is predominantly future or "eternal present," with some conditional or subjunctive tenses when these seem natural, rather than too formal. The logical structure is conditional, as indicated by words like "if," and "then." Many frequency words like "usually" are used to indicate the probabilistic nature of the conditional clauses. A minimal number of details is included.

So far, these descriptions of how we vary the level of abstraction of scripts are quite abstract and therefore, if our hypothesis is correct, these descriptions should be neither memorable nor persuasive to the reader. Therefore, some concrete examples of this research are presented below.

A Military Transgression and Punishment Script

The subjects in this experiment (Martin, Patterson, & Price, 1979) were Coast Guard recruits in their last week of bootcamp training. This subject sample was selected because the transgression and punishment script would be relevant. Bootcamp training is designed to teach recruits, among other things, that those who break regulations, however petty, will be punished. As part of a larger ongoing evaluation of the bootcamp experience, these subjects periodically completed questionnaires. The stimulus materials in this experiment consisted of a paragraph embedded in one of these periodic questionnaires. The paragraph concerned a new Coast Guard recruit who had just finished bootcamp [called a Seaman Apprentice (S.A.)], and his executive officer. Each version of the paragraph contained six events as follows: (1) a new S.A. reports late for duty, thus breaking a Coast Guard regulation; (2) a personal excuse is offered; (3) the executive officer refuses to accept the excuse; (4) the incident is referred to mast (a nonjudicial disciplinary review); (5) the new recruit is found guilty; and (6) is sentenced with a variety of punishments. This script illustrates an organizational policy, that those who break regulations will be punished, even if they offer serious excuses for their behavior.

Subjects were randomly assigned to read one of three versions of this paragraph. The independent variable, level of abstraction, was manipulated by rewriting this transgression and punishment sequence three times, as an episodic, categorical, and hypothetical script. To illustrate how the content of the paragraph changed at the different levels of abstraction, one sentence from each is quoted below:

> *Episodic*: His excuse for being late was that his father had become seriously ill while he was visiting home.
>
> *Categorical*: Most new S.A.'s give serious personal excuses, such as family illness or problems with a girlfriend.
>
> *Hypothetical*: If he gives serious personal excuses for what he did, then . . .

The number and average length of words and sentences in each of the paragraphs were virtually identical.

After reading the paragraph, the subjects were asked to answer a number of questions about its content, without referring back to it. These questions were the dependent measures of recall, willingness to make script-consistent predictions, and belief in and commitment to the policy implied by the script. This study tested the hypothesis that the level of abstraction of the paragraph would have a monotonic effect on recognition and attitudes, so that the most concrete, episodic script would be recalled the most accurately and would generate the greatest willingness to make predictions, to believe in the policy, and to be committed to it.

Although subjects in all conditions accurately remembered the scriptal sequence of events, level of abstraction did have the predicted effect on accuracy of recall. The most concrete (episodic) script was recalled most accurately. The few errors were confined to paraphrases or omissions of details, not essential to understanding the meaning of the script. The moderately abstract (categorical) script was recalled with moderate accuracy. The errors did not reflect substantive misunderstanding of the script. The most abstract (hypothetical) script was recalled least accurately. The types of recall errors suggest the possibility of distortion, since words indicating qualifications, frequency, and logical connections (i.e., "if," and "then") were omitted. The omission of such words in the hypothetical script simplifies the probabilistic, conditional causal structure. Such simplification is consistent with Bartlett's (1932) finding of simplification and omission in memory tasks. In accord with our pretest data, actual hypothetical scripts may be more simplified than the hypothetical scripts constructed by Abelson.

Contrary to predictions, the dependent measures of predictions yielded no significant differences among conditions. Irrespective of who broke the regulation or the seriousness of the offense, subjects predicted that the sequence of events described in the script would occur.

The dependent measures of belief and commitment tended also to produce no significant differences among the conditions. Some of the measures did show a significant or marginally significant trend in the predicted direction, with the episodic (most concrete) condition producing the most belief in the policy statement. Significant results, however, were scarce because subjects in all conditions tended to believe the policy statement and be committed to it.

In retrospect, it is surprising that even these weak attitudinal effects were found. The Coast Guard subjects were about to complete a grueling bootcamp experience designed to teach them that if they disobeyed any regulation, they would be punished. Consequently, these subjects were already familiar with a transgression and punishment script. Reading a one-paragraph script was therefore unlikely to change their attitudes about this script or their commitment to the Coast Guard.

The lack of significant attitudinal effects could be due to one of three reasons. First, the level of abstraction could have no effect on attitudes, even if people have no firmly set opinions prior to reading the script. Second, a stronger manipulation could produce the predicted effect.

Third, the predicted effect could occur only if people have no firm, preconceived opinions about the issue at hand. The latter finding would have interesting implications. It is possible that, if a person has a well-developed theory or a strong, preconceived opinion, both concrete and abstract information will have no effect on that attitude. The third explanation of the results of the Coast Guard experiment would provide an important limitation to the powerful impact of stories. That impact should occur only when people do not have firm preconceived ideas.

The Open-Door Policy Revisited

To explore these three alternatives, a second levels-of-abstraction experiment was conducted (Martin, Patterson, Harrod, & Siehl, 1980). This experiment had three objectives: (1) to replicate the cognitive results of the first experiment; (2) to test the attitudinal hypotheses a second time, with a subject sample of people who had no strong feelings about the policy; and (3) to use stimulus materials which concerned a different policy and which contained more elaboration, thus being more like an organizational story rather than like a script.

The stimulus materials in this second study of levels of abstraction focused on the open-door policy described in the beginning of this chapter. The stimulus materials consisted of an organizational story concerning the implementation of this policy. The same script was embedded in each story. The script included several roles: an employee who tries out the policy, two supervisors, a regional representative, and the company president. Each story contained the same sequence of events: (1) the employee makes a request which he feels is legitimate; (2) that request is denied; (3) the employee decides to use the open-door policy; (4) his appeal is passed up to his supervisor's boss, who hears and denies it; (5) the employee takes the complaint to the company president; (6) the president delegates a regional director to hear the appeal, collect information, and make a recommendation; (7) the president reviews the regional director's findings, and if the appeal is reasonable, the president grants the request.

As in the previous study, multiple sets of stimulus materials were prepared, varying the level of abstraction of this script. To illustrate how changes in the level of abstraction affect the content of these organizational stories, extracts are presented below:

> *Episodic:* . . . about a guy named Jim Bingham who had a disagreement with his supervisor and decided to try out the open-door policy. Bingham was a salesman who had requested a transfer to New York City. His supervisor, a sales manager named Fred Drake, knew that Bingham's performance had been rated as terrific, and that requests of this kind from top performers were supposed to be given priority. In spite of this, Drake refused to allow the transfer, saying Bingham was, in his opinion, "locally irreplaceable." Bingham disagreed with Drake's decision . . . .

> *Categorical:* . . . about some employees who had disagreements with their supervisors and had decided to try out the open-door policy. One was a

> salesman who had requested a transfer, knowing that his performance had been rated as terrific and that requests of this kind from top performers were supposed to be given top priority. Another was an engineer who had requested that a letter of reprimand be removed from his file, because it concerned a problem which he felt was out of his control. Both requests were refused by the supervisors, on the grounds that the salesman was locally irreplaceable and the engineer was theoretically responsible . . . .
>
> *Hypothetical:* . . . about some individuals who try out the open-door policy. Two conditions determine whether individuals decide to try out the policy. The first condition is that they have a disagreement with their supervisor. That is, they make a request of their supervisor which is supported by a reason which they believe legitimates it, and that request is denied by the supervisor . . . .

The number and average length of the words, sentences, and paragraphs in these stories were virtually identical.

In this second study of levels of abstraction, the subjects were M.B.A. students. This causes two important differences between this study and the Coast Guard study. First, M.B.A students are unlikely to have strong beliefs about or commitment to, this particular policy. As a result, it should be easier for the manipulation of level of abstraction to have an effect on these subjects' attitudes as well as their cognition. Second, since the M.B.A.s are better educated than the Coast Guard recruits, the stimulus materials can be more complex. The additional complexity permits the hypothetical script to take on a conditional inferential structure, more like that of Abelson's hypothetical script. Thus we can see if these highly educated subjects, like the Coast Guard recruits, simplify this hypothetical structure when they recall the abstract narrative.

The data in this second study of levels of abstraction have just been collected, using a procedure identical to that of the previous study. Preliminary results indicate that both the attitudinal and cognitive effects will be strong and that simplifying errors in recalling the abstract materials will be made, thus replicating the cognitive and strengthening the attitudinal results of the first study.

SUMMARY

These studies of the effects of the level of abstraction have implications for both organizational theory and cognitive social psychology. The organizational perspective will be discussed first. These studies address the third set of questions left unanswered in the organizational research: what is it about an organizational story that makes it such an effective tool for communicating a policy? How can a story's impact be maximized? The Coast Guard study produced strong evidence that the more concrete scripts were recalled significantly more accurately, and were slightly more believable. The second study varied the level of abstraction of an organizational story rather than a script. Preliminary results indicate that the concrete story will be found to be significantly more memorable and believable.

These results suggest that organizational stories have such a strong cognitive impact because they are usually concrete. They usually contain a description of a single incident, full of vivid details. The results of our research and the research on concrete language are in agreement that the more concrete the story, the more memorable it should be.

The data concerning the attitudinal effects of the concrete story are weak in the Coast Guard study, although it appears that these effects will be stronger in the second levels of abstraction study. We expect that the concrete story will be found to be more believable for the following reasons. In a concrete story, the storyteller is not making any generalizations, so the veracity of the story content is not particularly questionable. On the other hand, in an abstract story, the storyteller is, by definition, making generalizations about several similar or related incidents. These generalizations are, in effect, opinions that the story audience may find questionable. For these reasons, concrete scripts and stories should be more believable, as well as more memorable, than more abstract scripts and stories.

To answer the last part of the question left unanswered by the organizational researchers, these results have implications for the person who wants to maximize or minimize the impact of a story. If a manager wants to maximize the impact of a story, she or he should make that story as concrete as possible. If an employee wants to determine if a policy statement is corporate propaganda, she or he should be particularly wary of a tendency to be swayed by a vivid, concrete story.

These two studies are relevant to script theory, as well as to the organizational research. Three contributions have been made. First, Abelson's ideas concerning the level of abstraction of scripts have been systematically extended and developed. Table 2, for example, outlines how the content and/or language of a script changes as it becomes more abstract. The recall results from the Coast Guard study suggest, in addition, that one component of Abelson's conceptualization requires revising. The complex conditional structure of his hypothetical script may need to be simplified, if it is to represent natural thought processes accurately.

The second contribution of this research is that it suggests a limitation to the previous research (e.g., Bower et al., 1979) that demonstrated the facilitative, gap-filling, effects of scripts on memory. Those facilitative effects may be limited to episodic scripts, as more abstract scripts may be less memorable, and therefore less likely to impact performance on memory-related tasks.

The third way this research differs from previous reseach is that both attitudinal and cognitive functions of scripts have been studied. Previous research has focused exclusively on cognitive functions of scripts, primarily episodic scripts. We have studied a second type of script function—the attitudinal functions of increasing willingness to make script-consistent predictions, to believe that the script is an accurate representation of reality, and to become committed to its content. Thus this research contributes in several ways to the psychological research on scripts, as well as to the organizational research on stories.

Before leaving the topic of levels of abstraction, there is one observation that raises some intriguing questions. In these two studies, the level of abstraction was manipulated by the experimenter. Scripts, however, are generally conceptualized as structures of knowledge which develop internally. Thus, people experience incidents or learn of stories which then are used as raw material for developing scripts. It would be interesting to see if Abelson's ideas correctly anticipate changes in the content of those internal scripts as they become more abstract. One approach would be to use a repeated measures design—presenting subjects with descriptions of several similar incidents and asking them to write or modify a script after reading each description. The text of those scripts could then be content-analyzed to see how stories about similar incidents cause changes in the content of a story-relevant script.

There is a second type of idea that could be tested with such a design. If the process of abstraction is performed by the subject, rather than being done by the experimenter, then the higher level of abstraction would be based on the subjects' personal experience of a large number of similar incidents. Therefore, the *higher* levels of abstraction should be associated with *greater* accuracy of recall of the script elements, *more* willingness to predict script-consistent events, and *stronger* script-relevant beliefs. The pattern of effects in a study of internal script development should be the opposite of the pattern found in the two studies discussed above, where the level of abstraction was manipulated externally by the experimenter. Our future research will focus on the internal development of knowledge structures such as scripts.

FROM BARNYARD ANIMALS AND RESTAURANTS TO ORGANIZATIONAL POLICIES: THE TRANSITION FROM THE COGNITIVE PERSPECTIVE

Because of our interest in organizational issues, we have designed stimulus materials dealing with organizational policies and philosophies of management. Unlike the commonly used example of the restaurant script, these materials emphasize the unique accomplishments of various organizations, rather than mundane or boring routine events. Unlike the fantasy stories about barnyard animals and imaginary islands favored by cognitive researchers, these materials are based on fact. The open-door policy, the military transgression and punishment script, the no mass layoffs policy, and the California winery that wanted to duplicate the quality of European wines—these are actual organizations and real policies.

Insofar as these scripts and stories accurately represent how the organization will behave in the future, they have real consequences for people's behavior. Therefore, these stimulus materials can affect feelings and beliefs. Cognitive researchers, naturally enough, generally restrict their attention to cognitive dependent measures. The vividness and the lack of artificiality of our stimulus materials expands the range of relevant dependent measures to include attitudes as well as cognition.

There are a number of difficulties in this transition from the cognitive perspective. These difficulties are not unique to our research. At least two of these difficulties are shared, in various situations, by many social psychological researchers: problems of experimental control and a lack of clarity concerning the relationship among dependent variables. Each is discussed in turn below.

In the transition from cognitive to social psychological and/or organizational concerns, it gets more difficult to design a well-controlled experiment. An example highlights some of the difficulties of maintaining experimental control. The control problem of particular relevance to our research is the issue of informational equivalence. Although this problem is germane to all the experiments discussed above, consider it in the context of the Coast Guard study. As stories or scripts become more abstract, the content of the text changes. Some of these changes in language have been discussed above. Inevitably, a concrete paragraph will contain more details than an abstract paragraph. By necessity, an episodic script, concerning a single incident that happened once, will have no need for words indicating frequency. Just as inevitably, changes in language bring changes in the type of information communicated. These stimulus materials aim to represent the effects of changes in level of abstraction as these changes normally occur. To the extent that this objective of realism is accomplished, the stimulus materials cannot contain precisely equivalent information at different levels of abstraction. As our stimulus materials become more vivid, with a greater potential impact on attitudes and emotions, they also become more complex. Thus it is more difficult, as the methodology textbooks point out, to design a well-controlled experiment, and, at the same time, maximize realism. The cognitive researcher's barnyard animals and restaurants have clear advantages in terms of experimental control.

The second problem caused by the transition from the purely cognitive perspective is a lack of clarity about the relationship between our cognitive and attitudinal dependent measures. In the experiments discussed above that I have conducted with my colleagues, the relationship between these two classes of dependent measures is not consistent. Our first two experiments compared the impact of a story with the impact of other forms of communicating information. In the first of these experiments, cognitions and attitudes were positively correlated, in that distortions in recognition were congruent with attitudes. In the second experiment, although attitudinal effects were found, no significant differences on the recognition measures occurred. Thus no evidence of a correlation between the cognitive and attitudinal measures was provided. In the third experiment, the Coast Guard study, the recall differences were striking, while the attitudinal effects were only marginally significant. Thus in this third experiment there was a modest positive association between cognition and attitudes. Overall, the results of these studies do not provide consistent evidence concerning the relationship between the two classes of dependent measures.

Because the relationship among the dependent variables is inconsistent, it is difficult to develop an explanation for why stories have this cognitive impact, on recall and recognition, and this affective impact, on attitudes such as belief. Several alternate explanations for the impact of stories, which concern the relationship between cognitive and affective reactions, are discussed below.

The simplest explanation attributes the impact of stories to the fact that stories consist generally of concrete language. For example, the story about the security supervisor included numerous concrete details, such as the fact that she was a recent bride weighing 90 pounds. As discussed above, such concrete language is more memorable than abstract language (e.g., Yuille & Paivio, 1969). Further, the research of Bower and his colleagues (e.g., Reyes et al., 1980) suggests that the easier recall of vivid, concrete details influences attitudinal judgments at a later point in time. Thus, according to this first explanation, stories have such an impact because the presence of concrete language makes them memorable, and then what is remembered influences attitudes. This concrete language explanation is congruent with the fact that organizational stories are frequently told to new employees. Because new employees are threatened with information overload, the easy memorability of stories should be particularly valuable at this time. This first explanation suggests that all widely shared stories should be full of vivid, concrete details.

There are at least two problems with this first explanation. It does not easily explain the results of Martin and Powers (1980), where attitudinal differences were not caused by differential recall, since no significant differences in recall were found. In addition, a story is more than a paragraph of connected discourse or a string of concrete language. A story contains central characters, a setting, and a plot (Bower, 1976) and these elements of a story, as well as its concrete details, are memorable. For example, people remembered the abstractly worded sequence of events in the military transgression and punishment script, whether or not those events were accompanied by concrete details (Martin et al., 1979).

Script theory suggests that organizational stories have scripts embedded in them. Scripts contain the elements that distinguish a story from a string of connected discourse, such as a sequence of events. Thus the script framework suggests a second explanation for the impact of stories. Stories are memorable because they contain a script. That script not only describes the most important facts concerning a past sequence of events, it also can be used to predict how the organization will, and how an employee should, behave in the future. If the script is used in this way as a basis for predictions, then such predictions indicate belief in the predictive validity of the script and hence the story from which the script came. Thus, according to this second explanation, stories are memorable and impact attitudes because stories have scripts embedded in them.

This second explanation has several practical implications. Organizational stories should concern types of event sequences that are expected to recur. Such stories should be told to warn new employees of types of situations which may happen to them. Long-time employees should use such stories to point out similarities between past and current events. According to this second point of view, then, the most widely shared stories should concern only those types of event sequences which have some relevance for the future.

The problem with both these explanations is that they emphasize primarily the cognitive advantages of stories. However, as discussed above, stories are often told to appeal to emotion, rather than reason. Such stories are usually told with some sentiment (Clark, 1970) and are recounted in order to engender an emotional reaction in the audience. Thus, a new security supervisor, reluctant to confront high-ranking executives, may find it easy to identify with the timid and nervous bride in the IBM story. By encouraging such emotional identification, organizational stories may arouse affect. Affect is a detailed system in the memory, so that affect may drive memory, by serving as a cue for remembering the content of material (Isen, Shalker, Clark, & Karp, 1978).

This emphasis on the primacy of affective reaction is also congruent with the research of Posner and Snyder (1975). These authors draw a distinction between automatic and conscious processing. Automatic processing is solely the result of past learning, occurring without intention. Conscious processing, on the other hand, is under current control. People have a limited capacity for conscious processing, since such processing interferes with other mental activity. If stories trigger a primarily affective reaction, this affect may serve as a cue for automatic processing (Clark & Isen, this volume). According to this point of view, the seeming ease of remembering a story may not be due to any effortful cognitive activity. Rather, if the story arouses emotion, it may be processed automatically.

The interesting implication of both these affective points of view is that this explanation for the impact of stories allows for instances where recall is not correlated with attitudes, as in Martin and Powers (1980). The reasoning underlying this statement is as follows. If what makes a story memorable is its ability to arouse affect, that affect may be either positive or negative. Thus, an affectively arousing story may be accurately remembered and either believed, if the affect is positive, or disbelieved, if the affect is negative.

A fourth explanation for the impact of stories is derived from the work of Zajonc (1979). Zajonc takes the position that affective reaction, when it occurs, can directly follow sensation. For our purposes, the sensation would be the hearing or reading (seeing) the story. This initial affective reaction, according to Zajonc, may or may not dominate subsequent cognitive processing, depending on the salience and strength of the affective reactions. Thus Zajonc's perspective is congruent with Clark and Isen's position that affect is subject to automatic processing, while later cognitive processing may be under more conscious control. What is distinctive about Zajonc's point of view is the immediacy and primacy of the initial affective reaction.

Clore and Kerber (1980) offer a fifth point of view. They take the position that both cognitive reactions, such as recall for descriptive features (like the components of a story) and attitudinal reactions (such as attitudes or evaluations) must be present before a person can make an "evaluation cognition," that is, before a person will make an attribution or construct a script to be used for prediction. This process, however, is cyclical. The evaluative cognition, such as the script, can then be used as a hypothesis, in order to recognize and categorize aspects of a new situation. In this stage of the process, then, these cognitive processes, such as recognition, would precede the formation of attitudes about the new situation. There are other models of the relationship between cognition and affect (e.g., Greenwald, 1968; Fiske, 1980), but for our purposes, it is not useful to distinguish further among these variations.

Taken as a group, these explanations for the impact of stories suggest that a story may have a strong, immediate and perhaps automatic affective impact, which then can, but does not necessarily have to, impact the conscious processing of both cognitive reactions (such as memory for the concrete details and scriptal elements of the story) and attitudinal reactions (such as willingness to believe the story or make script-consistent predictions).

The data are not currently available that would permit the conclusion that this explanation is correct or that another explanation is empirically superior. As the diversity of explanations suggests, the relationship between affect and cognition is an issue that is currently generating considerable controversy and is, as yet, unresolved. It would be useful, in future research on stories, to address this issue directly. In the meantime, the question about why stories have such impact cannot be answered definitively.

The lack of clarity about the relationship between the cognitive and attitudinal effects of stories and the problems of experimental control are serious issues. They are evidence that the transition from the cognitive to the social psychological and/or organizational perspective is fraught with difficulties. Clearly, cognitive theories and methodologies cannot be swallowed whole, without important changes (Zajonc, 1980). However, this difficult process of transition and transformation is worth the effort. It can provide results that extend cognitive theories in new ways, as well as provide answers sought by noncognitive researchers.

Our research provides an example of the advantages of attempting this transition. The organizational research on stories has relied on qualitative methods and focused on the attitudinal effects of stories. In our research we have used experimental methods and have expanded the field of interest in a direction rare for organizational research—we have studied the cognitive effects of stories. We have answered questions of interest to, but so far unanswered by, the organizational researchers. We examined the causal relationship between story telling and commitment to an organization's policies and its philosophy of management. We have demonstrated that stories did indeed cause attitudinal reactions, such as belief and commitment. We compared the impact of stories to the impact of other means of communicating information about a policy, such as abstract statements of corporate objectives and quantitative data. We demonstrated that stories were more memorable, and more believable than these other, more explicit forms of communication. Finally, we varied the content of a story, in an attempt to maximize and minimize its impact. We found that more concrete narratives were definitely more memorable and slightly more believable.

These results provide empirical support for many of the ideas suggested by the organizational research. As predicted, an implicit form of communication, in this case a concrete organizational story about a single incident, was more effective than any of the other forms of communication studied. Polanyi's blind man, relying on his cane for indirect knowledge, may know more about sidewalks than those of us who can see. When an organization wants to communicate information about its culture, its beliefs about process, its philosophy of management, or its policies which lack an obvious financial rationale, then indirect and implicit forms of communication, such as a concrete organizational story, are more likely to be memorable and believable, and are less likely to be dismissed as corporate propaganda.

In the process of addressing these organizational questions, our research has also elaborated cognitive and social cognitive theories in a number of different ways. Taylor (1980) observed that when cognitive theories are used in the less artificial and more complex settings favored by social psychologists, what had been a main effect in the cognitive research often becomes an interaction in the social psychological research. This phenomenon has occurred in our research. For example, when information supported a policy, a story often had a greater impact than other forms of communicating information. When information disconfirmed a policy, the impact of the story was weakened, so that it became equally or even less impactful than other forms of communicating the information. Also, as Taylor (1980) suggested, the transition from the cognitive into the social realm can necessitate the elaboration of a theory. For example, in our script research, Abelson's levels of script abstraction were systematically explored and, in the case of the hypothetical script, revisions were suggested. Perhaps most importantly, the range of dependent measures has been extended to include attitudes, as well as cognitions.

Our research is not unusual in this elaboration of the cognitive and social psychological theories. As the other chapters in this book illustrate, many social psychological researchers, in the process of making a transition from the cognitive perspective, have found interactions rather than simple main effects, discovered limitations of previous research, and extended theories in directions often unanticipated by their originators. Thus it is worth the trouble to undertake the difficulties of the transition, from restaurants and barnyard animals to the less artificial settings which are the traditional domains of social psychologists and organizational researchers.

ACKNOWLEDGMENTS

My colleagues on the work presented in this chapter include Melanie E. Powers, Raymond Price, Kerry Patterson, Caren Siehl, (doctoral candidates in the Graduate School of Business, Stanford University), and Wendy Harrod, currently on the faculty in the Department of Sociology, Iowa State University. In addition to their contributions, I am grateful for the helpful comments of Alice Isen, Al Hastorf, and Jerry Clore.

REFERENCES

Abelson, R. P. Script processing in attitude formation and decision making. In J. S. Carroll & J. W. Payne (Eds.), *Cognition and social behavior*. Hillsdale, N.J.: Erlbaum, 1976.

Azjen, I. Intuitive theories of events and the effects of base-rate information on prediction. *Journal of Personality and Social Psychology*, 1977, *35*, 303 –314.

Bartlett, F. C. *Remembering*. London: Cambridge University Press, 1932.

Beggs, I., & Paivio, A. Concreteness and imagery in sentence meaning. *Journal of Verbal Learning and Verbal Behavior*, 1969, *8*, 821 –827.

Belden, T. G., & Belden, M. R. *The lengthening shadow: The life of Thomas J. Watson*. Boston, Mass.: Little Brown, 1962.

Borgida, E., & Nisbett, R. E. The differential impact of abstract vs. concrete information on decisions. *Journal of Applied Social Psychology*, 1977, *7*, 3, 258 –271.

Bower, G. H. Experiments on story understanding and recall. *Quarterly Journal of Experimental Psychology*, 1976, *28*, 511 –534.

Bower, G. H., Black, J. B., & Turner, T. J. Scripts in memory of text. *Cognitive Psychology*, 1979, *11*, 177 –220.

Cantor, N., & Mischel, W. Categorization processes in the perception of people. In L. Berkowitz (Ed.), *Advances in experimental social psychology*, Vol. 12. New York: Academic, 1979.

Clark, B. *The distinctive college: Antioch, Reed and Swarthmore.* Chicago, Ill.: Aldine, 1970.

Clore, G., & Kerber, R. Affective schemata in the person perception cycle. Unpublished manuscript, University of Illinois, 1980.

Cohen, M. D., March, J. G., & Olsen, J. P. A garbage can model of organizational choice. *Administrative Science Quarterly*,, 1972, *17*, 1, 1 –25.

Cohen, P. S. Theories of myth. *Man*, 1969, *4*, 337 –353.

Feldman, N. S., Higgins, E. T., Karlovac, M., & Ruble, D. N. Use of consensus information in causal attributions as a function of temporal presentation and availability of direct information. *Journal of Personality and Social Psychology*, 1976, *34*, 694 –698.

Fiske, S. Social cognition and affect. In J. H. Harvey (Ed.), *Cognition, social behavior and the environment*. Hillsdale, N.J.: Erlbaum, 1980.

Foy, N. *The sun never sets on IBM.* New York: Morrow, 1975.

Greenwald, A. G. Cognitive learning, cognitive response to persuasion, and attitude change. In A. G. Greenwald, T. C. Brock, & T. M. Ostrom (Eds.), *Psychological foundations of attitudes.* New York: Academic, 1968.

Hamilton, D. L. Cognitive representations of persons. In E. T. Higgins, C. P. Herman, & M. P. Zanna (Eds.), *Social cognition: The Ontario symposium on personality and social psychology*. Hillsdale, N.J.: Erlbaum, 1980.

Hansen, R. D., & Donoghue, J. M. The power of consensus: Information derived from one's own and others' behavior. *Journal of Personality and Social Psychology*, 1977, *35*, 294 –302.

Hirsch, P. *Ambushes, shootouts, and knights of the roundtable: The language of corporate takeovers*. Paper presented at the meetings of the Academy of Management, Detroit, Mich., August 1980.

Holmes, V. M., & Langford, J. Comprehension and recall of abstract and concrete sentences. *Journal of Verbal Learning and Verbal Behavior*, 1976, *15*, 559 –566.

Isen, A. M., Shalker, T. E., Clark, M., & Karp, L. Affect, accessibility of material in memory and behavior: A cognitive loop? *Journal of Personality and Social Psychology*, 1978, *36*, 1 –12.

Kahneman, D., & Tversky, A. On the psychology of prediction. *Psychological Review*, 1973, *80*, 237 –251.

Markus, H. Self-schemata and processing information about the self. *Journal of Personality and Social Psychology*, 1977, *35*, 63 –78.

Martin, J. The credibility of policy statements: IBM's open door policy. Unpublished manuscript, Stanford University, Stanford, Calif., 1980.

Martin, J., & Powers, M. If case examples provide no proof, why underutilize statistical information? Paper presented at the meetings of the American Psychological Association, New York, September 1979.

Martin, J., & Powers, M. Scepticism and the true believer: The effects of case and/or base rate information on belief and commitment. Paper presented at the meetings of the Western Psychological Association, Honolulu, May 1980.

Martin, J., Patterson, K., & Price, R. The effects of level of abstraction of a script on accuracy of recall, predictions and beliefs. (Research paper No. 520). Graduate School of Business, Stanford University, June 1979. Portions presented at the meetings of the Western Psychological Association, San Diego, Calif.: April 1979.

Martin, J., Patterson, K., Harrod, W., & Siehl, C. Memory for the content of scripts presented at varying levels of abstraction. Paper presented at the meeting of the American Psychological Association, Montreal, Canada, September 1980.

Meyer, M. W., & Rowan, B. The structure of educational organization. In M. W. Meyer & Associates, *Environments and organizations: Theoretical and empirical perspectives*. San Francisco, Calif.: Jossey-Bass, 1978, 78 –109.

Milgram, S. *Obedience to authority*. New York: Harper & Row, 1974.

Minsky, M. A framework for representing knowledge. In P. H. Winston (Ed.), *The psychology of computer vision*. New York: McGraw-Hill, 1975.

Neisser, V. *Cognition and reality: Principles and implications of cognitive psychology*. San Francisco, Calif.: Freeman, 1976.

Nelson, K. Children's long-term memory for routine events. Paper presented at the meetings of the American Psychological Association, New York, September 1979.

Nelson, K, & Gruendel, J. From personal episode to social script: Two dimensions in the development of event knowledge. Paper presented at the biennial meetings of the Society for Research in Child Development, San Francisco, Calif.: March 1979.

Nisbett, R. E., & Borgida, E. Attribution and the psychology of prediction. *Journal of Personality and Social Psychology*, 1975, *32*, 932 –943.

Nisbett, R. E., & Ross, L. *Human inference: Strategies and shortcomings of social judgment*. Englewood Cliffs, N.J.: Prentice-Hall, 1980.

Nisbett, R. E., Borgida, E., Crandall, R., & Reed, H. Popular induction: Information is not necessarily informative. In J. S. Carroll & J. W. Payne (Eds.), *Cognition and social behavior*. Hillsdale, N.J.: Erlbaum, 1976.

Ouchi, W. G., & Johnson, J. B. Types of organizational control and their relationship to emotional well being. *Administrative Science Quarterly*, 1978, *23*, 292 –317.

Ouchi, W. G., & Price, R. L. Hierarchies, clans and theory Z: A new perspective on organizational development. *Organizational Dynamics*, Autumn 1978, 25 –44.

Paivio, A. Mental imagery in associative learning and memory. *Psychological Review*, 1969, *75*, 241 –263.

Pfeffer, J. Management as symbolic acation: The creation and maintenance of organizational paradigms. In L. Cummings & B. Staw (Eds.), *Research in organizational behavior*, Vol. 3. Greenwich, Conn.: JAI Press, 1981.

Polanyi, M. *Tacit dimensions*. Garden City, N.Y.: Doubleday, 1967.

Posner, M. I., & Snyder, C. R. Attention and cognitive control. In R. I. Solso (Ed.), *Information processing and cognition: The Loyola symposium*. Hillsdale, N.J.: Erlbaum, 1975.

Reyes, R. M., Thompson, W. C., & Bower, G. H. Judgmental biases resulting from differing availabilities of arguments. *Journal of Personality and Social Psychology*, 1980, *39*, 2 –12.

Rodgers, W. *Think: A biography of the Watsons and IBM.* New York: Stern & Day, 1969.

Rosch, E., Mervis, C. B., Gray, W. D., Johnson, D. M., & Boyes-Braem, P. Basic objects in natural categories. *Cognitive Psychology*, 1976, *8*, 382 –439.

Rumelhart, D. E., & Ortony, A. The representation of knowledge in memory. In R. C. Anderson, R. J. Spiro, & W. E. Montague (Eds.), *Schooling and the acquisition of knowledge.* Hillsdale, N.J.: Erlbaum, 1977.

Schank, R., & Abelson, R. *Scripts, plans and knowledge.* Hillsdale, N.J.: Erlbaum, 1977.

Scott, W. G. Organization theory: An overview and appraisal. *Academy of Management Journal*, 1961, *4*, 7 –26.

Selznick, P. *Leadership and administration*. Evanston, Ill.: Row, Peterson, 1957.

Smith, E. E., & Medin, D. Representation and processing of lexical concepts. Paper presented at the Sloan Conference, University of California, San Diego, March 1979.

Staw, B. M., & Ross, J. Commitment in an experimenting society: An experiment on the attribution of leadership from administrative scenarios. (Working paper series No. 79 –15). College of Business Administration, University of Iowa, Iowa City, October 1979.

Taylor, S. E. The interface of cognitive and social psychology. In J. Harvey (Ed.), *Cognition, social behavior and the environment.* Hillsdale, N.J.: Erlbaum, 1980.

Taylor, S. E., & Crocker, J. Schematic bases of social information processing. In L. Berkowitz (Ed.), *Advances in experimental social psychology*, Vol. 12. New York: Academic, 1979.

Thompson, J. D., & Tuden, A. Strategies, structures, and processes of organizational decision. In J. D. Thompson et al. (Eds.), *Comparative studies in administration*. Pittsburgh, Pa.: University of Pittsburgh Press, 1959.

Tversky, A., & Kahneman, D. Availability: A heuristic for judging frequency and probability. *Cognitive Psychology*, 1973, *5*, 207 –232.

Watson, Jr., T. J. *A business and its beliefs: The ideas that helped build IBM.* New York: McGraw-Hill, 1963.

Weick, K. Educational organizations as loosely coupled systems. *Administrative Science Quarterly*, 1976, *21*, 1 –19.

Wells, G. L., & Harvey, J. J. Do people use consensus information in making causal attributions? *Journal of Personality and Social Psychology*, 1977, *35*, 279 –293.

Wilkins, A. Organizational stories as an expression of management philosophy: Implications for social control in organizations. Unpublished doctoral dissertation, Stanford University, Stanford, Calif., 1978.

Wilkins, A., & Martin, J. *Organizational legends* (Research paper No. 521) Graduate School of Business, Stanford University, Stanford, Calif., 1979.

Yuille, J. C., & Paivio, A. Abstractness and recall of connected discourse. *Journal of Experimental Psychology*, 1969, *82*,467 –471.

Zajonc, R. B. Thinking and feeling: Preferences need no inferences. Paper presented at the meeting of the American Psychological Association, New York, September 1979.

Zajonc, R. B. Cognition and social cognition: A historical perspective. In L. Festinger (Ed.), *Four decades of social psychology*. London: Oxford University Press, 1980.

ANDREW BAUM JEROME E. SINGER

PSYCHOSOCIAL ASPECTS OF HEALTH, STRESS, AND ILLNESS

For one reason or another, cognitive aspects of social behavior have long been a focus of applied social psychology. The action research advocated by Lewin (1948) was firmly grounded in the perceptual theory of the Gestalt psychologists in Europe and in Lewin's own field theory. This research was conducted amidst a movement toward application of what psychologists were learning about cognition and attitudes to the needs of the late 1940s and early 1950s. At this time issues such as persuasibility and inoculation against brainwashing were highly relevant, and research based on what was known about cognitive and social determinants of attitude change was conducted. This cognitively oriented framework was applied to real problems, including wartime needs such as having people shift from eating usual cuts of meat to eating internal organs (Lewin, 1943), facilitating integration in biracial housing projects (Deutsch & Collins, 1951), or improving employee morale in a pajama factory (Coch & French, 1948). This set of applications stood in marked contrast to the almost exclusively laboratory (primarily animal) investigations of the predominant S–R (stimulus–response) learning theories of the day.

The last two decades have seen learning theory become both cognitive and applied: it is used as a basis for theories and practices of instruction. But in some senses the cognitive social psychologies have not lived up to the potential many thought they had for the solution of social problems. Social psychology held greater promise for potential application because of both its subject matter and its earlier success in action research. Social engineering approaches to social issues have met with some success (e.g., Varela, 1969), and other endeavors have been successfully applied. Yet these instances are not the rule, and for a number of reasons this promise has not always been fulfilled.

Some of these reasons for this are related to the structures and restrictions of academic psychology. The professional needs of young Ph.D.s, for example, may not augur well for the long-term research required for adequate social application. Psychologists may not always recognize a problem that is amenable to study and intervention, and they may be unaware of the contributions they can make. At the same time other fields are not always receptive to the research that social psychologists have done; much of the work conducted by environmental psychologists, for example, has not been applied because architects and policy-makers have been reluctant to use this research, and it is not framed in a manner convenient for them to use. However, instances of successful psychological input in work on social problems are increasing. Studies of heuristics and cognitive aspects of behavior, for example, are included in work on the psychological impact of nuclear power, and social support and cognitive style have been used to explain some of the effects of stress (e.g., Cobb, 1976; Mehrabian, 1976).

One area presently of great potential for application is the social psychological study of medically related outcomes, and, not surprisingly, cognitive and social perspectives are in the forefront of this effort as well. The application of social and personality theories to health and health care problems has already led to important work on coronary-prone behavior (e.g., Glass, 1976), surgical and medical stress (e.g., Johnson, 1973; Johnson & Leventhal, 1974), and other aspects of health. Potentially valuable work has also appeared on aspects of patient compliance with medical regimens, attitudinal bases of health care preferences, and the psychological aspects of a number of illnesses (e.g., Dimateo, DiNicola, & Flynn, 1979; Krantz, Baum, & Wideman, 1980; Krantz & Schulz, 1980; Korsch & Negrete, 1972; Wallston, Wallston, Kaplan & Maides, 1976).

Social and cognitive approaches to mental and physical health are not new. However, they are enjoying a renewal of focus and have recently become an important aspect of the study of health. Thus cognitive perspectives on depression, anger, the regulation of pain, eating disturbances, and smoking (e.g., Beck, 1976; Novaco, 1979; Turk, 1978; Schachter & Rodin, 1976) have been accepted and have formed the basis for more advanced work in these areas.

For the purposes of this volume, we thought it best to consider some examples of the study of health and illness that involve a social-cognitive perspective. Central to most of these examples is the notion of stress, which we consider in some detail. Subsequently, we review research in the areas of medical stress, mass psychogenic illness, and behavioral causes of illness to demonstrate more explicitly the applicability of basic research in this area.

STRESS

Stress is a pervasive concept in our society. There are few terms that have been so well imbedded into our common assessment of our response to life or that have received so much attention by the press. Articles on controlling stress are common, television shows about how to cope or deal with the stress common to life are widely viewed, and stress is often blamed for physical and mental ills that otherwise seem to defy explanation. Yet, despite the widespread use of this term, stress remains an only partially understood phenomenon, and it is an underestimated determinant of health and well-being.

Stress is best thought of as a process, rooted in the physiological mechanisms of the body. It is an interactive process; however, while responses may be based on the activation of physiological response patterns, the source and transmission of stress may be psychosocial in nature. For our purposes the stress process is that process by which environmental events, or stressors, threaten an organism's existence and well-being and by which the organism responds to this threat. Three clearly discernible parts of this process can be identified, and the consideration of these stages can demonstrate the social and cognitive mediation of stress. The degree to which many stressors will evoke a stress response and, ultimately, produce negative effects on an organism will depend on those social and psychological variables that mitigate or intensify the impact of the sources of stress or our ability to deal with them.

Selye (1956) is generally credited with the first systematic treatments of stress. His work suggested that stress was a process resulting in a triad of physiological changes accompanying physiological challenge—hypertrophy of the adrenal glands, shrinkage of the thymus and lymphatic tissue, and gastrointestinal ulceration. Thus injection of a pathogen into healthy tissue evoked adrenal gland activity and general activation of the adrenal–pituitary axis to initiate the process. These responses were interpreted as reflective of the body's natural defenses against noxious elements and gave rise to Selye's postulation of a General Adaptation Syndrome.

The General Adaptation Syndrome suggests that the body is capable of coping with stressors, and the physiological responses evoked by the introduction of a pathogen are symptomatic of this coping process. However, Selye also noted that our ability to cope is limited. Coping has costs for subsequent resistance; chronic or repeated exposure to stressors depletes the body's adaptive reserves and produces physical dysfunction. When first exposed to a stressor, the body responds by mobilizing its coping abilities; this alarm reaction represents preparation for resistance. This stage of alarm is one of readiness—if the stressor is only briefly encountered, response may go no further. When the stressor persists, the body begins to resist, coping with the stressor through various mechanisms and typically achieving suitable adaptation. Sometimes, however, coping is not successful; if a person's coping abilities or adaptive resources are sufficient merely to resist but not eliminate a stressor, or if the noxious agent is strong enough to overwhelm or outlast efforts to cope, adaptive reserves are depleted. When this occurs, the organism enters a state of exhaustion; coping is no longer possible, resistance declines, physiological breakdown occurs, and the body becomes more susceptible to disease.

This pathogen model of stress is based on mobilization by the body to fight off infection or disease. As the presence of a pathogen is recognized, the endocrine system responds. Adrenal compounds secreted into the blood increase levels of bodily activity and mobilization. In a state of arousal, the organism is better able to combat threats posed by invading pathogens. As resistance overcomes the threatening substance, adaptation is achieved, and steroid and catecholamine production return to normal levels. When adaptation is not achieved, the organism will remain in a state of arousal. This arousal may then yield to exhaustion when the adaptive reserves are depleted.

The work of Selye and his associates was directed toward a focus on simple pathogens, such as bacteria, physical damage, or chemical irritants, acting on infrahuman species, most frequently the laboratory rat. The picture for humans is more complicated. Even the simplest of physical stressors may produce not only direct stress effects but also cognitive representations of the stressor and its consequences. These representations may also be stressors. For example, a new mother with a case of influenza experiences both the nonspecific stress reaction to the virus and the nonspecific stress of her worry that her infant will contract the disease from her. Thus, while Selye's and others' interest in physiological response to bodily threat or harm (e.g., Mason, 1968) provides an important biological context for stress, the impact of psychological variables not explict in the general theory of stress is also important. Psychological variables are instrumental in the onset of stress and form the basis of the appraisal of environmental events (e.g., Lazarus, 1966). In some instances these variables mediate response to stressors, and in other cases, appraisal of events leads directly to stress. Thus psychological evaluation of one's loss of employment or of the demands of one's daily work may generate stress (e.g., Frankenhaeuser, 1978; Kasl & Cobb, 1970). These cognitive appraisals are also instrumental in the selection of coping strategies.

These kinds of interpretive functions also suggest reasons for our seemingly endless susceptibility to stress; people respond not only to dangers or threats but to the expectation of threatening events and to symbols of danger as well (Wolf & Goodell, 1968). Lazarus (1966) has proposed that stress is determined by the interpretation of environmental events. If an event is appraised as threatening (either as dangerous, challenging, or threatening harm or loss), stress is evoked. The evaluation of each event will depend on a number of psychosocial variables, and coping will be directed toward the appraised threats and their perceived origins. The importance of this multilevel mediation is underscored by the consistent finding that people differ in what they appraise as stressful or in their susceptibility to stress (e.g., Antonovsky, 1971; Glass, 1976; Jenkins, 1979). Not all environmental events will elicit responses, nor do all people respond to the same events. To the extent that an event is interpreted as threatening, however, stress responding will follow.

Thus people exposed to a potentially stressful situation appraise the setting and judge how threatening it is. If threatening, a secondary appraisal is made. Here the focus is not assessment of danger but rather evaluation of different coping strategies. The perception of danger motivates a search for coping responses that will reduce this threat. Coping may involve direct action, where the individual tries to manipulate or alter his or her relationship to the stressful situation. Thus action directed toward terminating a stressor would be considered direct action (Lazarus, 1966). People may change the setting, flee, or otherwise remove the physical presence of the stressor. However, this is not always feasible. People who feel crowded may not be able to escape and are generally not capable of changing physical density. In such a case, Lazarus (1966) considers palliative coping to be that which is directed toward altering the "internal environment," accommodating a stressor by taking drugs, using alcohol, creating or using psychological defense mechanisms, or engaging in mediation.

Jenkins (1979) has recently proposed an account of psychosocial modifiers of stress that considers both psychological and physiological perspectives. Stressors are viewed in terms of both direct biological threat and perceptions or interpretations of threat, loss, or challenge, and the three-stage response set described by Selye (1956) is also included. The alarm reaction is characterized by arousal and, depending on the nature of the stressor, by feelings of grief, fear, shock, rejection, or anxiety. Defensive reactions, marking resistance to the stressor, range from increased adrenal activity on a biological level to the use of ego defenses, avoidance, or behaviors that will reduce the impact of the stressor at more psychological or interpersonal levels. When these defenses or coping responses do not reduce the threats posed by a stressor, or when danger persists over long periods of time, a pathological end-state is likely. Here the individual ceases in purposive coping and may become helpless, anomic, or exhausted, or may suffer physiological dysfunction.

Jenkins goes further, however, in an effort to deal with differential susceptibility to stress in more detail. He suggests that individuals have different adaptive capacities that may be likened to the notion of "host resistance" as used to account for differential vulnerability to infectious disease. Just as immunities to certain diseases allow us to resist these illnesses without serious consequences, adaptive capacities at a number of levels can help us to cope with or avoid disruption from stressors. Further, these capacities can influence the magnitude of the stress response when an event is interpreted as threatening. An individual's perceptions of how well he or she will be able to deal with threat or danger will determine the extent of alarm and defense that is experienced. Thus adaptive capacities, including resources and skills at biological, psychological, interpersonal, and sociocultural levels, are important determinants of the stress response (Jenkins, 1979).

Similar to Lazarus' (1966) conceptualizations, we believe that the appraisal of environmental events, in terms of both threat and coping, is the key to stress. While some stressors are nearly universal in their power to threaten, most are not, and their effects will be mediated by a constellation of psychosocial variables characterizing a setting. This of course complicates the issue; it is no longer sufficient to identify a stressor and chart responses. The appraisal of threat and where it comes from will determine not only *whether* stress is experienced, but *how* people will cope. We also believe that, consistent with Jenkins (1979), characteristics of stressors as well as adaptive resources and coping predispositions will influence the way in which stress is experienced. Thus three specific domains emerge as characteristics of the stress response, each of which must be understood in order to make sense of stress.

Stressors

Stressors can be considered to be any environmental event or psychological representation of such an event that may be perceived as threatening. Generally, all stressors are linked in some way to an environmental (physical or social) event that has occurred, is occurring, or will occur. The death of a loved one is stressful, and memories long after bereavement can constitute stressors to some degree. Similarly, thinking about the future death of a parent can be a highly stressful experience. The event need not have actually occurred for it to be reflected in stress, or it may have occurred long ago. Our ability to remember and to think of the future releases stress from the temporal restriction of the here and now.

Stressors vary on a number of dimensions, including magnitude of adaptation required, duration and chronicity, extent of impact, and controllability, although, as we have noted, the value of many of these dimensions will depend upon the prior stress experience and the adaptational state of the person. Lazarus and Cohen (1977) have organized them into three types, dividing them along several dimensions. The first type, cataclysmic events, demands a great deal of adaptive energy and has an impact upon a large number of individuals. These events are sudden upheavals such as storms, tornadoes, earthquakes, wars, and other large-scale disasters. These events are not of long duration, but are generally powerful acute stressors. Though they may have long-term or far-reaching consequences, they are generally not chronic.

Stressors that impact fewer people, exert strong adaptive demands, and present more chronic problems are included in a second class of stressor. Imprisonment, relocation, illness, death, divorce, or giving birth can be seen as stressful. The stressors in this class require a good deal of coping but impact fewer people at one time. This distinction is important, since affiliative coping strategies may be of great value when there are many people sharing the same misfortune. In considering this second type of stressor, there are fewer people affected, and thus fewer to work with or to share. In some cases there will be only one individual affected, making coping more difficult.

The more chronic nature of these kinds of stressors is also important. In the case of illness, for example, adaptive challenge may increase over time as opposed to decreases following more acute problems. Although the long-term effects of a tornado may be in the present, the major adaptive effort involved will pass once the storm is past and "normalization" under way. Illness, however, may not follow this course and may create problems simply because stress is so prolonged.

A third group of stressors includes all the everyday, routine, and mundane events that bother us. Lazarus and Cohen (1977) refer to these as "daily hassles," and we have referred to them as background stressors (Baum, Singer, & Baum, 1981). These stressors generally do not require the adaptive energy required by disasters, death, illness, or the like. They also do not have an impact on many people as a group; though millions are affected by transportation noise in their homes, they do not share this stress. Rather, each experiences it individually or in neighbor or family groups. Finally, these are generally not acute stressors. Some are clearly chronic, but most are a repetitive series of acute events that are linked by a common cause. In other words, each daily hassle is typically short-lived but recurs frequently. Exposure to stress of this type is chronic, but is made up of many acute instances. This makes the true cost of background stress deceptive. The energy required to adapt to a specific instance of a stressor may be small, but the cumulative cost may be very high. Thus the daily experiences of racial and ethnic prejudice, job dissatisfaction, poverty, noise, crowding, or commuting may be much more stressful over the long haul than more dramatic disruptions of life.

There are a number of other ways to classify stressors, including those based on judgments of controllability, whether they are gain or loss experiences, or whether they are unusual or common (e.g., Kiretz & Moos, 1974). One thing that becomes apparent, however, is that some stressors are more intrusive, physical, and universally threatening (such as natural disaster) than others, and some stressors are more culturally determined and more psychosocial in nature (such as occupational stress). In a series of studies Frankenhaueser and Gardell (1976) found that occupational variables such as control over work, responsibility, or redundancy in the job represent stressors. They are clearly more imbedded in the psychological processes involved in appraisal and less universal than such things as earthquakes or floods. The psychosocial medium in which these events are conveyed render them different.

One other way to classify stressors might be the extent to which they have physical and cognitive components. Some noxious agents or pathogens might be unobtrusive to the extent that the person undergoing them is not aware of being stressed. These stressors short-circuit the cognitive mediation/appraisal process. Other stressors may have no physical representation. People may be stressed by the worry over the consequences of hypothetical events. By far, the most common stressors will be those that have a palpable cause, irrespective of whether it is a bacterium, a social interaction, or a cognitive representation. Almost all of our discussion is directed to this latter class of stressors.

Appraisal of Stressors

The interpretation of the degree to which an event (experience remembered or anticipated) is threatening or dangerous provides the link between stressors and stress responses. For example, if we have many resources with which to cope with a stressor at our disposal, threat will not be perceived as very great. Individuals with a great wealth of resources for coping (e.g., money, friends, material) may be less likely to appraise events as threatening and, as a result, may be less affected by the stressor. Familiarity with a stressor may also reduce its judged danger, either because we know how to cope successfully from past experience or because we know how dangerous it really is (or is not). Attitudes toward the sources of stress will also mediate responses; if we believe that a stressor will cause us no permanent harm, our response will probably be less extreme than if its danger carries the threat of lasting harm. Perceptions of control, social support, and other characteristics of the person exposed to the stressor can also affect the appraisal of different events.

The importance of the appraisal process has already been noted, and, not unexpectedly, it is the phase of the stress process that has received most attention from social psychologists. Since the studies reported by Lazarus and colleagues (e.g., Lazarus, Speisman, Mordkoff, & Davison, 1962; Speisman, Lazarus, Mordkoff, & Davison, 1964) demonstrated mediation of stressful material, many investigations have examined social and psychological mediators of stress. Some have considered cognitive interpretation of events, attempting to understand or intervene in actual appraisal process so as to change interpretation of the event. These include studies of environmental events such as crowding (e.g., Saegert, 1978; Worchel, 1978) and transportation noise (e.g., Cederlöf, Jonsson, & Sorenson, 1967), as well as interventions designed to control pain or anxiety (see Kendall & Hollon, 1979). In a later section we show that these kinds of studies form the basis of efforts to reduce stress in a number of settings.

Other research has addressed the relationship between a person's attitudes and his or her susceptibility to stressful interpretation of environmental events. Perhaps the best example of this is in the consideration of attitudinal mediation of noise annoyance (e.g., Leonard & Borsky, 1973; Wilson, 1963). Though noise is clearly aversive and has been linked to a number of deleterious effects on health and behavior (Glass & Singer, 1972; Cohen, Evans, Krantz, & Stokols, 1980), studies have also indicated that the direct relationship between noise and associated annoyance is statistically weak (Wilson, 1963). The addition of attitudinal variables, however, has led to severalfold increases in accountable variance (Tracor, 1971; Leonard & Borsky, 1973). Fear, positive or negative attitudes about the source of noise, judgments as to the necessity of the noise, and cost–benefit analyses of the source of the noise may all exert an influence on whether the noise is perceived as annoying.

Cederlöf and associates (1967) reported a study in which attitudes were actually shaped so that annoyance could be reduced. Some of the residents of an area near a Swedish Air Force base were given a "positive induction," consisting of filling out a questionnaire that asked interesting questions, reading a positively worded report on the results of the questionnaire, and receiving a commemorative book about the air force. This treatment was designed to improve residents' attitudes about the nearby base. In later interviews this goal appeared to have been accomplished. Residents receiving the positive treatment reported less annoyance from the base than did residents who were not given a treatment. A similar study (Jonsson & Sorenson, 1967) provided both positive and negative inductions and obtained results consistent with Cederlöf et al.

Risk perception is another cognitive variable that can affect interpretation of stressors. Using heuristics such as availability, people can calculate the riskiness of an event and determine "statistically" whether there is cause for alarm. Activities or events that are judged to be risky may lead to stress, while those believed to be safe probably will not. However, people are often in error when they make these calculations; the inferential rules that people use are susceptible to a number of biases and, by reducing a great deal of information, may cause loss of important data (Simon, 1957; Singheimer, 1971; Slovic, Fischhoff, & Lichtenstein, 1981; Taylor & Fiske, 1978). As a result, appraisal of stressors may not always be accurate, even though people continue to behave as if they are correct. For example, people may repeatedly rebuild houses in earthquake-prone areas, discounting not only technical information but their own disastrous experiences.

Control, perceived or otherwise, is also an important mediator of stress. If a stressor is seen as controllable or predictable, it may be judged less threatening; if it is uncontrollable or unpredictable, it may be judged as more threatening. This seems to be borne out by the results of many studies (e.g., Glass & Singer, 1972; Sherrod, 1974; Singer, Lundberg, & Frankenhaeuser, 1978). Control may also pertain to ability to cope. Regardless of how one perceives the stressor, the knowledge that one can successfully control other aspects of his or her environment should increase coping efficacy and decrease the threat posed by a stressor. If, on the other hand, an individual lacks this confidence or is explicitly aware of specific noncontingencies in the environment, stressors may be seen as more dangerous. Indeed, the choice of various stressful pastimes such as ski jumping or auto racing can be viewed in part as people's attempts to demonstrate to themselves the extreme extent to which they have control over dangerous environmental events.

Social support, or the sense of belonging and feeling that one is a valued member of some group, has also been identified as an important determinant of stress (e.g., Cobb, 1976). Either because the feelings derived from close association with others facilitates feelings of control or because group membership provides resources and protection from harm, individuals who perceive themselves as having social support tend to be more resistant to the disruptive influences of stressors. Social support can provide others with whom to share distress, additional resources with which to combat the stressor, and more confidence in one's ability to fight it off. These benefits are apparent in fairly dramatic ways. Social support (or perceptions of it) is associated with reduction of medical complications and death rates in stressful situations (e.g., Burch, 1972; Nuckolls, Cassel, & Kaplan, 1972; Whitcher & Fisher, 1979). Low social support seems to increase suseptibility to illness (e.g., Chambers & Reiser, 1953; Brown, 1975), while high social support aids people in coping with stressors (e.g., Cobb, Kasl, French, & Norstebo, 1969).

Akin to social support and control are other skills or perspectives that people can obtain from the social milieu. Cobb (1976) refers to flexibility and role multidimensionality that are associated with membership in social networks. These characteristics should reduce the effects of stress appraisals judged as threatening by virtue of their salutary effect on coping. Social belonging may also affect appraisal as a result of the strength and encouragement one can obtain from a group (Cobb, 1976). Thus group-based variables may also affect the appraisal of stressors.

There are a number of dispositional variables as well as additional social factors that can affect the appraisal process. Because we are not attempting a review here, but rather are interested in organizing research on stress, we will not deal with these other elements. Suffice it to say that any variable or set of variables that affects the degree to which an individual feels he or she can adequately cope with a stressor, the degree to which harm or threat is perceived as real and unavoidable, the degree to which a stressor seems necessary, or the extent to which the individual feels better or worse in comparison to others will influence the appraisal of stressors.

The Stress Response

The nature of stress response ranges widely over a number of subjective physiological and psychological reactions as well as a good portion of our social repertoire and cognitive abilities. Thus stress may have the common anxietylike symptoms many attribute to it, but may also involve unexpected physiological reactivity, inhibition of social behavior, aftereffects, and cognitive or motivational deficits. To some extent the responses will be determined by the nature of the stressor in conjunction with the appraisal of it and the individual's coping skills, history, or preferences. On some levels, however, there is less specificity as the body responds to threat.

At a basic level stress involves the enhancement of response by both the adrenal medulla and cortex. The resulting increases in circulating blood levels of catecholamines and corticosteroids can be measured (Frankenhaeuser, 1976) or can be presumed by observing their effects on heart rate, blood pressure, muscle tension, and the like. At this level the stress response is fairly nonspecific; increased catecholamine secretion has been observed following exposure to examinations, dental treatment, hospital admission, sensory deprivation, pleasant or unpleasant films, or space flights (e.g., Cohen, Silverman, & Shmavonian, 1961; Hale, 1965; Levi, 1965, 1979; Nelson, Masuda, & Holmes, 1966; Uldeval, Smith, & Welch, 1963). Other studies have also found fairly consistent responses to stressors at this level—physiological arousal and related somatic change seem similar for most types of stressors. Some of the responses to psychosocial stressors, for example, are virtually indistinguishable from those generated by direct pathogen attack on body tissue. Challenge, loss of control, and emotional distress have been linked to the same sympathoadrenomedullary reactions as infection (e.g., Euler, 1966; Frankenhaeuser, 1978; Glass, 1976; Konzett, 1975). Based upon a great deal of evidence, then, one could argue that, despite differences among individuals, psychosocial stimuli are capable of arousing adrenal medullary activity in ways similar to direct pathogen assault, and, at this level, response to stressors is fairly unspecific.

Other aspects of the stress response are more specific to the stressor. Mason (1968), for example, has made a case for patterning of corticosteroids secreted by the adrenal cortex, and these patterns have been identified in a number of situations (e.g., Freeman, Pincus & Glover, 1944; Bliss, Migeon, Branch & Samuels, 1956).

Somatic consequences of stress are important for several reasons. Enhanced catecholamine and corticosteroid secretion is associated with a wide range of other physiological responses including increased heart rate, blood pressure, muscle potential, breathing, and other autonomic functions. Thus the secretion of catecholamines plays a readying role, increasing the body's capability to react or avoid danger (see below). However, if elevation of circulating catecholamines is prolonged or repeated often, functional disturbances in mood and organ function may occur. Cardiovascular damage and permanent structural change may occur if stress is long-term (Levi, 1979; Raab, 1966).

Catecholamines appear to enhance cognitive and emotional functioning, at least to a point. Once again, some stress seems to be salutary, but prolonged or repeated arousal may not be. Cannon (1929, 1931) initially suggested that catecholamines have salutary effects on adaptation; by arousing the organism, they provide biological advantages, enabling it to respond more rapidly to danger. Stress-related increases in catecholamines may facilitate adaptive behavior. Supportive of this, some studies have shown superior performance on tasks following epinephrine infusion (Frankenhaeuser, Jarpe & Mattell, 1961) and among people with higher catecholamine output in the face of challenge (e.g., Frankenhaeuser, 1971).

While it is clear that there are some cognitive benefits of stress, it is also evident that the "fight or flight" model derivable from Cannon's work is no longer adequate for predicting response to danger in our complex society. Aside from the "wear and tear" on our bodies generated by repeated or prolonged stress, a number of less desirable outcomes are likely when stress does not readily abate. Most of the research that finds support for the facilitating aspects of stress has considered acute situations in which adjustment leads to reduction of stress. Unabated or repeatedly provoked stress, as in the case of exposure to background stressors, may exert a toll that has yet to be fully comprehended. We know that adaptation to stress has some cost; people appear less able to cope with subsequent stressors following adaptation, and aftereffects of cognitive and physiological origin appear following adaptation to a number of stressors. A similar point has been raised by Benson (1975) in his discussion of the relaxation response.

Cognitive deficits, motivational deficits, and general mood suppression have also been noted as consequences of stress. Cognitive problems may be by-products of coping choices—the person who copes with noise by "tuning out" may also fail to hear important information—or this may be the result of overload or narrowing attention (e.g., Cohen, 1978). Motivational changes may accompany uncontrollable stressors as the individual learns that he or she cannot control what is happening. A helplessness of sorts may thus be learned and may shape behavioral response (or lack thereof) to stress (e.g., Seligman, 1975). Finally, anger, hostility, tension, and generally unpleasant somatic sensations may accompany stress; these feelings are less related to behavioral response than to physiological reactivity but may in some cases be manifestations of coping.

In general, behavioral responses or coping strategies tend to be directly related to the perceived nature of the stressor. For example, Baum and Koman (1976) studied people anticipating crowding stress. For some subjects, spatial problems were made salient, leading them to expect cramped space and interference with intimacy regulation. For other subjects, social problems were emphasized so that these people would expect frequent and uncontrollable interaction with the others in the session. A great deal of response specificity was observed. When expecting crowding stress as a result of spatial restriction, subjects were more likely to be aggressive, choosing central seating positions and behaving more dominantly. When social problems were expected, subjects were more likely to withdraw, sitting on the periphery and avoiding contact with others. Thus the same stressor (crowding) with different aspects made salient (spatial, social) elicited different coping responses (aggressive, withdrawn).

This kind of specificity is reasonable if one remembers that coping may be directed toward alteration of the stressor or situation. When people respond directly, their behaviors will be aimed at what they believe is responsible for their distress. Part of Lazarus' (1966) secondary appraisal notion must include this kind of rational target evaluation. Once a source has been identified, appropriate behavioral or cognitive strategies can be analyzed. However, this is not to say that the real cause is always discernible; target identification may be susceptible to the same cognitive biases and distortions as perception of risk. When the use of inferential rules is necessary, people may incorrectly identify an event as the source of stress and therefore evaluate coping strategies along irrelevant dimensions. People may respond to job loss, for example, by increasing their effort in subsequent jobs or by improving their abilities through training. When job loss is seen as a result of environmental or social pressures (recession, the boss wanted to hire his nephew) this kind of response is less likely. If job loss caused by lack of ability is attributed to these external factors, the "proper" coping strategies may be less likely. Judgments of helplessness are also apparently determined by these kinds of phenomena (e.g., Abramson, Seligman, & Teasdale, 1978; Baum & Gatchel, 1981). Similarly, coping with victimization or serious injury appears to be specific to different levels of self-blame (e.g., Bulman & Wortman, 1977).

Aftereffects, defined as consequences that are experienced after exposure to a stressor has terminated, are not as specific to certain stressors. Conceptually, these effects are consistent with Selye's (1976) notion of limited adaptive energy; as exposure to stress draws on or recurs often, adaptive reserves are depleted and aftereffects are made more likely at the cost of subsequent coping ability. Evidence for these poststressor effects has been reported in studies of a number of stressors, including research on the effects of noise (e.g., Glass & Singer, 1972; Rotton, Olszewski, Charleton, & Soler, 1978; Sherrod & Downs, 1974; Sherrod, Hage, Halpern, & Moore, 1977), crowding (Sherrod, 1974), and electric shock (Glass, Singer, Leonard, Krantz, Cohen, & Cummings, 1973). They appear fairly similar across these stressors, but explanations for these effects are not as clear.

Aftereffects that have been associated with stress include decreases in cognitive functioning and reduced tolerance for frustration, aggressiveness, helplessness, decreased sensitivity to others, and withdrawal (Baum & Valins, 1977; Donnerstein & Wilson, 1976; Glass & Singer, 1972; Rodin, 1976; Rotton et al., 1978; Sherrod & Downs, 1974). However, evidence for these aftereffects as costs of adaptation is equivocal (Cohen, 1980). More detailed consideration of effort expended during adaptation may better reflect this relationship. In addition to psychic costs, aftereffects may represent persistent coping responses (Baum & Valins, 1979) or the effects of narrowing of attention or restricted and overloaded information capacity (e.g., Cohen, 1980; Deutsch, 1964; Easterbrook, 1959). They may also reflect symptoms of learned helplessness (Glass & Singer, 1972).

Most important is the effect of stress on our ability to cope with subsequent exposure to threat or danger. Several studies have suggested that repeated or prolonged exposure to stress can reduce subsequent coping ability. Physiological systems may become exhausted or may simply require refraction so as to recover full functioning, just as cognitive and social skills may fatigue or give out. For example, studies of adjustment to life change (e.g., Dohrenwend & Dohrenwend, 1974; Holmes & Rahe, 1967) suggest that there are physiological and social costs associated with adaptation to most things, but these costs seem particularly high when life changes are clustered together in time.

Psychosocial Determinants of Coping and Adaptation

People can adapt to most stressors. The media have provided us with numerous examples of the human spirit indomitably coping with the most disruptive of physical and social upheaval, and research has shown that people can adapt quite readily to many events (e.g., Freedman, 1975; Glass & Singer, 1972). Studies of residential crowding have indicated that people can adapt to uncontrollable environments by withdrawing from them and investing energy in more easily managed settings (e.g., Baum & Valins, 1977), and most studies of noise stress suggest that adaptation occurs fairly quickly (Glass & Singer, 1972). However, evidence also suggests that the short-term costs of stress, that is, those that occur prior to adaptation, may represent only part of the overall impact of many stressors. Aftereffects or long-term consequences of cumulative episodes with stressors may be more extensive.

A study by Cohen, Glass, and Singer (1973) illustrates this. They studied the effects of living in apartments built directly over congested highways in New York City. These highways are busy 24 hours a day, seven days a week and produce a fairly intense noise level within the apartment buildings. Yet, despite the relatively higher noise levels on lower floors of the buildings, residents of lower floors did not differ from neighbors on upper floors in ratings of noise level or annoyance. These residents appeared to have adapted to the unusual noise levels to which they were exposed.

However, the ability of children living on lower floors to discriminate between similar sounds was lower than that displayed by children living on upper floors. While adaptation to the disruptive or annoying properties of the highway noise had occurred, these children showed a continuing deficit in their skill in verbal discrimination. Apparently, children on lower floors adapted to the noise by "tuning out" sounds. They were less responsive to differences in spoken words, and their reading ability suffered as a result. Thus, despite the comparability of ratings of noise, the effects of close proximity to the source of the noise were apparent in long-term reading impairment.

The role of predisposing or protective mediating variables in determining the means and costs of adaptation has also been studied. Glass and Singer (1972) found that predictability and controllability were important determinants of ease of adaptation and severity of aftereffects during exposure to noise. These effects were particularly evident in a study of commuting reported by Singer, Lundberg, and Frankenhaeuser

(1978). In this study, when train commuters in Stockholm were considered, the length of commute was found to be unrelated to the stressful effects of the daily commute. Passengers who boarded the train at its first stop traveled for about an hour and a half. Those getting on halfway to Stockholm rode for only 43 minutes. Yet, these midline passengers experienced more stress than did those riding all the way. Indices of stress included assays of catecholamine excretion and ratings of discomfort, which varied with the density of the passengers on the train but not with length of exposure.

This surprising finding was explained by noting social and ecological circumstances of the train ride. Those passengers boarding the train at its first stop could choose seats freely, arrange coats, briefcases, packages, and the like as they wished and otherwise structure their surroundings because they boarded an empty train. Thus they were able to exercise control over the train car environment. Groups of commuters wishing to travel together could occupy adjacent or facing seats, lone commuters who wanted window seats could have them, etc. Passengers boarding halfway to Stockholm, however, did not have as much of an opportunity to exercise control—they boarded a partially filled train and were forced to "fit into" the structure created by those already on the train. Groups of commuters might not be able to find seats together, and individuals might not have as good a choice of seats. In general, the passengers boarding at the train's origin, though exposed to a longer trip, were able to exercise a good deal more control over the experience of commuting.

A study by Baum, Davis, and Aiello (1978) provides another example of this kind of mediation of stress. They studied urban neighborhoods in which residents reported stress resulting from frequent contact with neighbors and strangers in the areas outside of their homes. This stress was labeled as crowding and led to a reluctance to use outside areas. Residents withdrew into their homes and did not use their yards, porches, or local parks as much as did residents of neighborhoods in which contact with neighbors and strangers was less frequent.

An interesting consequence of this was that residents of stressful neighborhoods were less likely to belong to local neighborhood groups. Membership in these informal friendship networks served two protective functions: residents who did belong to local groups reported more perceived control over what happened in the neighborhood and greater perceived social support from neighbors. These functions have been associated with reduction of stress, and, not surprisingly, residents who reported membership in local groups were less susceptible to the effects of frequent contact with others. They reported a greater sense of control over what happened in the neighborhood and were more likely to share spaces with their neighbors. Thus residents who were friendly with their next-door neighbors might jointly use their yards for neighboring and derive greater control over these spaces than residents using only their own yards by themselves.

Subsequent research (Baum, Aiello, & Davis, 1979) identified some health-related effects of group membership and residence in stress-enhancing surroundings. When contact with others was frequent, group membership mediated both perceptions of health and willingness to seek medical attention. Residents who reported relatively high levels of social support also reported fewer symptoms of illness. At the same time, residents who perceived themselves as having control over what happened in the neighborhood were more likely to seek medical attention when they felt sick. Social support appeared to mediate symptom perception and perceived control influenced willingess to take action when these symptoms were perceived. This was associated with seemingly maladaptive behavior on the part of residents who were not members of local groups. Since they were less likely to report having social support or control, they were more likely to perceive symptoms and less likely to seek medical attention. Group members, who reported fewer symptoms, were more likely to seek help when they did feel ill.

This kind of mediation of stress has also been reported in other studies. Social structures such as those that group membership supplies appear to be an effective mediator of stress (e.g., Baum & Davis, 1980; Schopler & Walton, 1974). Cognitive variables such as expectations also affect the impact of stress; expectations for control, for example, have been shown to mediate the effects of stress and helplessness (Baum, Aiello, & Calesnick, 1978; Wortman & Brehm, 1975).

THE STRESS PROCESS

Stress, then, can be viewed as a fairly complex process involving the evaluation of stressors and coping strategies and the implementation of those behaviors deemed appropriate. The effects of stressors are intensified by certain predisposing situational or psychological variables (e.g., loss of control, loneliness, poor or inadequate past experience with the stressor) or can be moderated by protective mediating variables (group membership or social support, control, familiarity with the stressor). The role of stress in physiological dysfunction has been identified, and a number of studies have linked stress to illness or death (e.g., Eliot & Buell, 1979; Paulus, McCain, & Cox, 1978). By the same token, the role of stress in psychological dysfunction has been shown, and stress has been related to the incidence of mental illness and maladaptive responding (Kagan & Levi, 1974; Levi, 1979).

Not unexpectedly, the prevention, management, and reduction of stress has received a great deal of attention. As Levi (1979, p. 22) notes, the "misfit between environmental demands and opportunities on the one hand and man's genetically determined abilities and needs on the other" is of great importance in understanding psychological and biological reactions to the world. Researchers have considered a number of interventions designed to deal with this kind of problem, attempting to provide protective skills or situational supports, management skills, and more benign environmental settings. The following sections of this chapter deal with some of these attempts.

Cognitive-Behavioral Intervention

Given that stress and other medically relevant processes are at least in part psychologically driven, it is not surprising that a number of cognitive-behavioral strategies for intervention have appeared. Pain, obesity, dental anxiety, alcoholism, and the like have been considered in light of these interventions (e.g., Gatchel, 1980; Leon, 1979; Nathan, 1976; Rodin, 1978; Turk & Genest, 1979), and for the most part these treatments have been more successful than strictly behavioral, cognitive, or medical interventions (Hollon & Kendall, 1979). Part of this success has been due to recognition of the role of different cognitive styles and coping abilities (e.g., Kagan, 1966) in response to stress or other aspects of life. In addition, the function of cognition in the appraisal of events and treatments has been considered in these interventions, both in terms of its effects on autonomic response and subsequent psychological events (Kendall & Hollon, 1979).

Social psychologists have considered a number of intervention strategies. One of the most thoroughly researched has been the effort to reduce or minimize stress in medical settings. Treatment is not directed toward change in lifestyle or habit. Rather, it is aimed at minimizing the distress and anxiety of patients anticipating or undergoing fear-evoking procedures or surgery. Since anxiety and stress appear to be related to the experience of pain and the appraisal of the event is ultimately related to the success of the operation, this topic has received a great deal of attention.

Reducing Surgical Stress. Perhaps the first systematic attempt to examine stress associated with surgery was reported by Janis (1958). By interviewing patients following recovery from surgery, he found that those who had been moderately fearful prior to surgery recovered more rapidly. Those who had been extremely fearful showed poor coping during recovery, and those who were not fearful at all were also not as successful in coping with recovery. He reasoned that those patients who were moderately fearful were able to act on their fear by seeking out information about postsurgical experience and by rehearsing these anticipations. This "work of worrying" resulted in better preparation for the recovery period; these patients were able to predict what they might experience and had appropriate labels and explanations for the discomforts they felt. Patients who were extremely fearful, however, were not able to engage in constructive worry and rehearsal because their fear led them to avoid considering these aspects of the surgery. Low-fear patients were presumably denying what was about to happen, and this also led to a failure to worry and rehearse what might happen.

Janis suggested that the combination of having information about the recovery period and being motivated to consider this information by moderate levels of fear led to more adequate preparation. Implicit in this formulation is the notion that if people have an idea of what is going to happen to them and can somehow prepare for these occurrences, they will fare better when they actually encounter them. Fear, in this instance, is a source of motivation assuring that information is adequately considered. Thus fear is probably less important in and of itself; information about what will occur is the primary component of preparation for surgery and recovery, while fear serves the role of motivating the patient to address or seek it out. Information appears necessary, but fear seems to be only one of many ways of considering motivation to prepare and rehearse.

However, these relationships quickly proved to be fairly complex. Cohen and Lazarus (1973) studied postsurgical recovery among patients who shunned information about what they might experience, those who sought out information and were willing to consider it, and those who were extremely vigilant and "overly" concerned. Surprisingly, those who avoided information, relying primarily on denial as a coping strategy, showed the best recovery. These patients recovered more rapidly, had fewer postsurgery complications, and were more positive about their recovery. In contrast to Janis' (1958) findings, denial was associated with better recovery. Similarly, the most vigilant subjects showed the poorest recovery, remaining in the hospital longer, developing more complications, and expressing more negative affect during recovery.

Additional research has suggested that denial is generally associated with more difficult recovery, bearing out the findings that Janis (1958) reported. Of course, we do not know how much information patients have prior to hospitalization, and it is possible that the denial patients in Lazarus and Cohen's study had done some rehearsal before involvement in the study. Patients were classified as deniers if they showed a reluctance to receive information about their condition or postsurgical sensations. These patients may have felt that they already knew enough about these events or that additional information would make them uncomfortable. Vigilant subjects who seemed more neurotic in their desire for information may have, in fact, had little at the time of classification. This interpretation is somewhat supported by Burstein and Meichenbaum's study (1977) of children undergoing surgery. These children presumably had little knowledge of surgery prior to entering the hospital, and, consistent with Janis' findings, the children who were classified as deniers showed more postsurgical distress than did those who sought out information.

Additional research has also indicated that the events mediating surgical distress and recovery are extremely complex. Andrew (1970) investigated the recovery success of surgical patients who differed in their receptivity to information but actually provided information to patients rather than simply measuring how willing they were to receive it. Patients were grouped on the basis of preferred coping styles, and, similar to Cohen and Lazarus' (1973) classification, three groups were derived. Some subjects indicated that they preferred not to receive information (denial group), some indicated that they preferred vigilant strategies (vigilant group), and the rest were characterized as preferring a combination of these styles (vigilant–denial group). Patients in the denial group, when actually presented with information about their consideration, required more medication during recovery than did denial subjects who were not given information. Consistent with Janis' results, denial was associated with poor recovery. The vigilant group was not affected by the information provided, and the vigilant–denial group showed the best recovery.

Studies by DeLong (1970) and by Williams, Jones, Workhoven, and Williams (1975) have also indicated that providing information to patients who do not want it can have an adverse effect on their recovery from surgery. Research on other aspects of health-related behavior also provides evidence of mediation by preferences or coping styles (e.g., Glass, 1976; Krantz, Baum, & Wideman, 1980; Wallston & Wallston, 1978). Receptiveness to information appears to play a significant role in responses to surgical or medical procedures. But what is it about information that influences their response? How does information facilitate or inhibit recovery from surgery or distress while undergoing medical examination?

Most studies of reducing stress associated with surgery have focused on two functions of information. First, research has considered the degree to which information affects the cognitive appraisal of threat. Thus some work has been directed toward helping patients perceive their surgery as less fearful and threatening. The second approach has been to provide patients with the opportunity to engage in anticipatory coping. By giving patients information about the surgery, researchers have attempted to help them work out impending events and dangers, derive expectations, and rehearse these anticipated threats or discomforts. Of course, these two approaches are very much related. For example, studies that provide patients with coping instructions or information about specific sensations that they will experience can be seen as accomplishing both of these goals. The patients who know what they will feel following surgery and have prepared themselves for these sensations through anticipatory coping will also appraise them as less threatening than would be the case with no forewarning. We will return to this point later; first, however, we will consider some of the research that has been reported.

One way of facilitating anticipatory coping with surgical events and reducing the likelihood that appraisal will yield stress has been to provide patients with information about coping strategies/behaviors that they can use to ease the discomfort of recovery or that will otherwise allow them to affect their condition. Frequently, this kind of information is provided along with reassurance, supportive messages, or descriptions of the surgical experience (e.g., Egbert, Battit, Welch, & Bartlett, 1964), and in general it appears that this kind of preparation for surgery, when given in addition to some other information, can be effective (e.g., Lindeman & Van Aernam, 1971; Schmitt & Wooldridge, 1973; Wolfer & Vistainer, 1975). By teaching patients to use techniques such as relaxation, deep breathing, and body maneuvers that relieve discomfort and by informing them of some of the sensations that would follow surgery and procedures that would be used, Egbert et al. (1964) were able to reduce patients' use of narcotics after surgery as well as decrease the number of days required for recovery. Similarly, Doering and Entwisle (1975) found that descriptive and coping information was more effective than descriptive information alone in reducing the pain of childbirth. Consistent with theoretical considerations of the usefulness of providing behavioral alternatives with fear-inducing stimuli to affect greater attitude change (cf. Leventhal, 1970), the provision of instructions that might help a patient reduce the aversiveness of surgery seems to facilitate recovery.

However, the fact that the effectiveness of coping information appears to depend on the coincident provision of descriptive information raises questions about the usefulness of coping information. As a result, two kinds of descriptive information have been considered. Some studies have provided patients with situational or procedural information, including objective descriptions of procedures that will be followed or of the physical or social properties of the operation and hospitalization. By giving patients details about what would happen to them, researchers hoped to reduce the threats inherent in unknown surgical procedures (e.g., Andrew, 1970; Melamed & Siegel, 1975; Vernon & Bigelow, 1974; Williams et al., 1975). Thus information about the origin and treatment of an illness or inquiry, the procedures involved in treating it, and the consequences of that treatment can reduce required medication, the length of recovery, or otherwise improve surgical outcomes (e.g., Andrew, 1970; Melamed & Siegel, 1975). However, support for the value of procedural information as a determinant of stress appraisal has been equivocal (Turk & Genest, 1979). Further, when Egbert et al. (1964) compared the recoveries of patients receiving procedural information with those receiving both procedural and coping information, the procedural message alone was not very effective. The reasons for relatively weak support for the effectiveness of procedural information are not clear, but we attempt to develop a rationale for this later in this chapter.

A second approach to reducing pre- and postoperative stress has been to provide sensory information. These attempts typically involve describing the location and severity of pain that may be experienced as well as the discomforts or other sensations that may accompany or follow surgery (e.g., Johnson, Rice, Fuller, & Endress, 1977; Langer, Janis, & Wolfer, 1975; Skipper & Leonard, 1968). However, the research based on this kind of intervention has been inconsistent in its findings. Johnson et al. (1977) provided patients with information about the effects that the preoperative medication might have, the pains that they might feel after surgery, and their general feelings after the operation, and found that this intervention improved recovery from one type of surgery but not from another type. Langer et al. (1975) found that sensory information increased preoperative distress and that the information was not related to recovery.

The strongest evidence for the effectiveness of sensory information, however, comes from a series of studies by Johnson, Leventhal, and their colleagues (e.g., Johnson, 1973; Johnson & Leventhal, 1974; Johnson, Morrissey, & Leventhal, 1973). These studies do not consider surgical patients but rather study the effects of information on distress exhibited by patients undergoing painful or uncomfortable medical examinations. Thus patients having endoscopic examinations (in which they must swallow a fiberoptic tube and maintain it in the gastrointestinal tract for more than 30 minutes), having gynecological examinations, undergoing ischemic pain, or subjected to other stressful procedures were provided with one or another type of message, and their distress during the examination was measured. While not based on surgical situations, these studies are generally considered to be consistent with that literature and have greatly amplified the relationship between information and stress reduction.

These studies have not only provided support for the use of sensory-based messages, but have also compared their efficacy with that of procedural information. Johnson (1973) studied subjects experiencing pain and discomfort produced by an inflated blood pressure cuff, providing some of them with information about what they would feel (tingling, aching, numbness, etc.) and others with information about procedures of inflating the cuff and the like. Sensory-based messages proved more successful in reducing the aversiveness of this situation. Similarly, Johnson et al. (1973) studied patients undergoing endoscopic examinations, providing some patients with procedural information and others with both sensory and procedural information. Both information pretreatments reduced the amount of medication (sedatives) requested during the examination. However, patients receiving only procedural information were more tense, restless, and anxious during the session than were patients receiving sensory information as well. Further, procedural information patients had more heart rate acceleration during the examination than did the other information subjects. Thus, hearing about the procedures involved in the examination, and therefore being able to predict what would happen and to recognize what was being done at each step, did reduce need for sedation during the examination. Yet this procedural familiarity was not as effective as hearing about procedures and how each step might make them feel.

At this point the evidence suggests that providing patients with sensory information in combination with coping suggestions can reduce the stress of surgery or medical examinations. Procedural information alone may not be as effective, at least in some cases. Several explanations of these phenomena have been proposed, centering around cognitive control (e.g., Fuller, Endress, & Johnson, 1978) and its relation to the two-stage appraisal and coping formulation noted earlier. Cognitive control refers to "the way a potentially harmful event is interpreted" and is therefore relevant to the notion that stress can be reduced by modifying appraisals of potentially threatening events. By facilitating cognitive control, researchers have attempted to alter the way in which potentially stressful information is processed so as to reduce the aversiveness of the information. This is consistent with a great deal of research conducted in laboratory or nonmedical settings that indicates that providing information that increases cognitive control can reduce the impact of stressful stimulus material (e.g., Averill, 1973; Averill & Rosenn, 1972; Lazarus et al., 1962; Speisman et al., 1964).

Cognitive appraisal of medical events depends on a number of factors. As we have already suggested, anticipatory coping (Janis, 1958), the kind of rehearsal that allows for prediction and explanation of events, can affect appraisal of potential stressors. The patient in the recovery room following surgery may experience pain and discomfort that can be interpreted as danger signals. With prior knowledge that these sensations are normal and to be expected, the likelihood that they will be seen as abnormal or threatening is reduced. Without such anticipatory coping, the sensations may be frightening and patients may interpret them as danger signals. Thus, having accurate expectations of what will occur can reduce the likelihood that sensations or events will be appraised as threatening and stressful.

This is not to suggest that providing expectations is the only way that appraisals can be influenced or that alteration of perceptions of potential stressors is the only way to reduce distress. Some studies have indicated that reassurance and socially supportive preparations can alter appraisal of a stressor and improve recovery (e.g., Cobb, 1976; Langer et al., 1975). For example, Langer et al. (1975) found that combining procedural and sensory information and reassurance with distracting information or with instruction about how patients could reappraise stressful events was successful in reducing requests for pain killers and sedatives following surgery. Further, the consistent finding that providing combinations of information that detail expectations and possible coping strategies can also reduce distress suggests that the aversiveness of medical procedures can also be minimized by facilitating secondary appraisals of coping possibilities. By helping subjects choose the "best" way to deal with what they expect to occur, stress can also be affected.

These combined approaches have varied in the extensiveness of the information provided, but have tended to combine procedural, sensory, and coping material in the message given to the patient. For example, Johnson and Leventhal (1974), again studying patients undergoing endoscopic examination, provided procedural and sensory information, procedural and coping information, or a combined message detailing all of this instruction. Results indicated that both procedural/sensory and procedural/coping instructions reduced distress, but that the combination of these messages was more effective than either one alone.

Thus it can be concluded that providing patients with some combination of sensory, procedural, supportive, and coping information results in a reduction of distress associated with surgery or medical examination. The benefits of such reductions include greater comfort, more efficient procedures, more rapid recoveries, fewer postsurgical complications, and less need for analgesics or sedatives. However, as we noted

sick for no apparent reason, may be reasonably explained in terms of factors that heighten stress experienced in the workplace.

Colligan and Murphy (1979) have suggested five factors that are common to settings in which mass psychogenic illness has occurred. The first of these is the presence of a physical stressor (such as noise) or subjective discomfort experienced as a result of physical conditions such as temperature or lighting. Boredom or highly repetitive work is also characteristic of these settings. The other three factors address job-related precursors of psychogenic illness; outbreak settings are usually characterized by perceived pressures toward increased productivity or increases in workload, conflict with supervisors, and limitations on communication between workers.

Clearly these factors can be considered contributors to stress and may thereby be linked to physiological reactions such as increased secretion of cortisol and catecholamines and consequent increases in blood pressure, heart rate, and the like. In addition, job-related stress has been linked to illness and sudden death (e.g., Eliot & Buell, 1979; House, 1974). Stress can also induce greater perception of bothersome or uncomfortable symptoms (e.g., Pennebaker, 1979; Baum et al., 1979). When these symptoms are experienced, people will not only seek to understand their meaning but will also seek causes for their awareness of physiological changes such as palpitation, sweating, flushing, muscle tension or "butterflies in the stomach." The process by which workers go about explaining and labeling these internal sensations may have implications for mass psychogenic illness.

Stress in Occupational Settings

Physical stressors such as noise (Colligan, 1978; Shepard & Kroes, 1975; Stahl & Lebedun, 1974), air contamination (Shepard & Kroes, 1975) and noxious odors (Colligan, 1978; Colligan et al., 1978; Folland, 1975; Kerckhoff & Back, 1968; Phillips, 1974; Shepard & Kroes, 1975) have been observed as antecedents of outbreaks of mass psychogenic illness. These stressors have been linked to discomfort, illness, and a range of other problems (e.g., Frankenhaeuser, 1976). Compounding the effects of these stressors is the fact that most of the labor performed by workers involved in mass psychogenic illness outbreaks has been assembly-line work consisting of monotonous repetitive tasks. In their study of sawmill workers, Frankenhaeuser and Gardell (1976) found that people who did machine-paced short-cycle tasks exhibited stress reactions as measured by increased ratings of strain and ill health as well as by heightened catecholamine production. As Frankenhaeuser and Gardell note:

> The quest for increased productivity in industrial countries has been most intense in industrial manufacturing. This has enhanced the pressure on industrial workers as expressed in ever-increasing demands on pace and

> effective use of working time, and in decreasing options for variety, relaxation and social interaction at work. To some extent, the growing demands on the workers emanating from this development tend to be reflected in more frequent dispensary visits, sick leaves and early retirements. (p. 43)

Thus stressful work environments can have health outcomes, and those characterized by low levels of responsibility, variation, and satisfaction have been associated with heart disease and mortality (e.g., Caplan, Cobb, & French, 1975).

It is interesting to note that in commenting on stressful environments, Frankenhaeuser and Gardell list three of the five common characteristics of settings in which mass psychogenic illness occurs. Boredom, increased pressure towards production and limited contact with co-workers are indicated as stressors with health-related consequences. It should not be surprising, then, that environments in which these problems are confounded by environmental stressors and strained relations with management should be characterized by increased perception of illness symptoms. Thus workers in outbreak settings have probably experienced physiological symptoms of stress. Exposure to environmental stressors, boring repetitive tasks, and increased pressure all can predispose an individual to experience headaches, dizziness, nausea, fatigue, and the like, many of which are the same as symptoms found in cases of mass psychogenic illness. It is possible, therefore, that the ways in which workers attribute these symptoms will be of great importance in predisposing them to psychogenic illness and hysteria.

Social Comparison and Occupational Stress. Social comparison theory (Festinger, 1954) suggests that people tend to evaluate their beliefs and their abilities through comparison with both social and nonsocial standards. In the absence of objective or nonsocial standards, individuals will seek to compare themselves with others who are similar to them. In such cases we would expect a greater amount of comparison with others. Although the general case for social comparison is usually made in terms of attitudes, the process seems equally applicable to emotions (cf. Schachter & Singer, 1962). Reactions to stress or anxiety may be especially difficult for an individual to evaluate objectively. Thus comparison processes may be particularly important in the appraisal of threatening events or the labeling of physical symptoms and sensations.

Studies of affiliation indicate that some individuals seek the company of others when they are in an anxious state. Additional studies established that this selective affiliation was used to evaluate the relative degree of individuals' own arousal and its appropriateness for their situation. In these studies, however, subjects were aware of the reason for their anxiety: the instructions quite explicitly indicated the source of arousal and reasons for subjects' anxiety. The source of arousal outside of the laboratory may not always be so immediately recognizable. In such cases individuals should search their environments for an explanation of their arousal.

To investigate the role of social comparison processes in evaluating physiological arousal, Schachter and Singer (1962) injected subjects with epinephrine, a drug that has sympathomimetic qualities. Some subjects (informed group) were given an objective referent for their arousal as the effects of the drug were fully explained to them. Remaining subjects (some uninformed as to the drug s effects, others misinformed as to its true effects) were told that the injection was a simple vitamin and were not led to expect the effects that were actually produced (e.g., palpitation and tremor). All subjects were then placed in a room with an experimental confederate who played one of two roles in this situation, becoming either increasingly euphoric or angry as the experimental session unfolded.

The results of this study indicated that social comparison had a strong influence on the interpretation of physiological arousal. Informed subjects were relatively unaffected by the confederate's behavior, but other subjects, uninformed or misinformed, interpreted their arousal in terms of the behavior of the other person. Uninformed subjects placed with a euphoric confederate rated themselves as being in a euphoric state, while those with any angry confederate reported feeling a significant amount of anger, and behavioral observations paralleled these findings.

These results seem to indicate that two factors are involved in the identification of emotion: (1) physiological arousal and (2) cognitive labeling of that arousal. Labeling occurs as a function of establishing a cause and effect relationship between environmental stimuli and perceived arousal. New or ambiguous physical states, such as those associated with stress, will create pressure for people experiencing them to determine what it is they feel and what is responsible for their discomfort. It is possible, then, that mass psychogenic illness involves the perception of physical symptoms (induced by the stress characteristic of affected settings), and the way in which workers explain them. As Kerckhoff and Back (1968) point out, "To the extent that the new label 'makes sense' and is thus easily accepted, it will be adopted readily by all those who have the experience but have been unable to conceptualize it satisfactorily."

Thus it can be argued that work settings in which mass psychogenic illness has occurred are characterized by multiple stressors, that these stressors are responsible for physiological changes or arousal among workers, and that many of these symptoms are the same as those reported in mass psychogenic illness outbreaks. Workers will seek to understand their changed feelings or symptoms, and the others working with them are a primary source of information for such understanding. Stressed workers may therefore engage in social comparison in order to label their sensations, and, under normal circumstances, workers should discuss these conditions and their reactions to them. By comparing their symptoms and their interpretations of them, workers could thereby derive accurate appraisals of stressful aspects of their jobs and their reactions to these stressors (Singer, Baum, Baum, & Thew, in press).

In comparing epidemic hysteria with panics and riots, Sirois (1974) has noted that the conflictual object in the former is much less obvious. The "conflict object" is often unknown or not dealt with directly, and it is frequently difficult or impossible for workers to openly acknowledge and deal with the conflict. Colligan and Murphy (1979) have also noted little informational support prior to the outbreak of mass psychogenic illness, and Kerckhoff and Back (1968) observed a greater reluctance among affected individuals to discuss job-related problems and work dissatisfaction with co-workers. Similarly, Colligan et al. (1978) found that workers affected by a mass psychogenic illness outbreak were more introverted than workers who were not affected. These findings are consistent with the fifth characteristic of outbreak settings and suggests that conditions facilitating comparison of symptoms may be lacking in these settings.

This fifth characteristic refers to general limitations on opportunities for communication between workers. Such limitations may be due to a number of factors, including scheduling of lunch and break times (Stahl & Lebedun, 1974) or ambient noise levels that make interaction difficult (Colligan, 1978; Folland, 1975; Kerckhoff & Back, 1968; Phillips, 1974; Shepard & Kroes, 1975). When experiencing unusual symptoms or sensations, curtailment of communication might hinder workers' efforts to properly attribute their somatic complaints to appropriate job-related stimuli. The question then becomes one of process: how is it that the blocking of normal comparison opportunities can lead to an outbreak of psychogenic illness?

First, consider that, although social comparison can be facilitated by direct verbal communication, even in the absence of the ability to converse people can shape their own behavior from their inferences about other people's emotions and beliefs (Horwitz, 1953). In exploring the reasons for affiliation among anxious people, Schachter (1959) demonstrated that social comparison processes operate even when direct communication is ruled out. One of the keys to social comparison is the choice of appropriate reference to others. Festinger (1954) noted that, when evaluative needs are aroused, people want comparison to others who are both like themselves and in the same set of circumstances. The settings for mass psychogenic illness provide for both of conditions being met. The worker or student with symptoms to evaluate sees in the index case someone else obviously in distress. The response of the index or subsequent case, be it nausea, fainting, dizziness, or whatever, becomes a benchmark for the person's own reactions. In addition, as Colligan and Murphy (1979) report, there is increased susceptibility to mass psychogenic illness among friends, who may be presumed to see each other as similar (Newcomb, 1961). Although those affected by the index case tend to be physically clustered around the case, those at points removed who also become affected are almost invariably friends of the earlier affecteds. In studies of mass psychogenic illness in Singapore, Chew, Phoon, and Mae-Lim (1976) report outbreaks in which all the affecteds were of a single racial-ethnic group, despite their being scattered among two other groups.

In order to better understand this process, it is necessary to consider the actual precipitating factors of an outbreak. Most cases of mass psychogenic illness are characterized not only by a series of stressors but also by a triggering event and an index case or cases. Though precipitating triggering events are not always present in outbreaks, they are generally present in industrial settings in the form of strange odors, gases, and the like. An index case, or an initial individual reporting symptoms, provides a model that indicates a potential link between the triggering event and other workers' physiological reactions to the stressful environment. As stated by Colligan et al. (1978) "the detection of a strange odor . . . or witnessing others become ill may have provided the affected workers with an explanation of their discomfort and triggered a contagion reaction."

Thus the presence of a triggering event provides a plausible environmental attribution for symptoms and index cases provide comparison-based rationale for linking symptoms to the trigger and concluding that one is ill. Because normal channels of comparison are not available, unexplained symptoms or arousal may be explained as illness based on comparison with index cases, and the incidence of illness may spread geometrically through the worker population. This is consistent with findings suggesting that social networks affected the likelihood that individual workers would be affected by an outbreak, and with Colligan et al.'s (1978) observation that affected workers were more likely to have directly witnessed an index case, while unaffected workers were more likely to have heard of such a case. Direct experience provides a greater opportunity for labeling symptoms by comparing with others. Observation of others who are experiencing illness and attributing it to some environmental event can be a potent standard for comparison with one's own somatic complaints.

This interpretation is bolstered by findings concerning individual workers and the likelihood that they may be affected by an outbreak of mass psychogenic illness. For example, prior work histories among those affected by outbreak indicate higher absenteeism (Colligan & Murphy, 1979). This absenteeism describes behavior prior to actual outbreak and indicates that those workers who were affected may have had even less opportunity for communication with workers by virtue of their uneven attendance. In addition to already restricted opportunities for social comparison, absenteeism may have put these individuals at a further disadvantage in labeling of job-related stressors and somatic complaints.

It is of course possible that those with less frequent attendance may have been experiencing stronger physical reactions to stressors in the work situation. Smith, Colligan, and Hurrel (1978) have noted that affected workers are more likely to report being bothered by environmental factors such as noise, poor lighting, irritating odors, and temperature variations in the workplace, and indicated higher levels of job-related stress as a result of such factors as work pace, task repetition, job insecurity, and lack of supervisory support. While the affected workers surveyed by Smith et al. (1978) reported poorer general health than unaffecteds, some studies using more ojective measures of general health (i.e., previous health complications, reported medicine usage) have found no differences (Colligan et al., 1978; Colligan, 1978). Kerckhoff and Back (1968) found that affecteds were more likely to have been taking pills or other medication prior to the outbreak but were not more likely to have "had to stay home because of organic sickness only during the past year."

Alternatively, it is possible that these individuals are simply more prone to symptom reporting. Research has indicated that affecteds have a greater tendency toward somatization (Knight, Friedman, & Sulanti, 1965), score higher on the Hysteria scale of the MMPI (Colligan et al., 1978; Colligan, 1978), and are more likely to seek medical attention (Kerckhoff & Back, 1968). In a follow-up study conducted 25 years after an outbreak of epidemic hysteria in Tristan de Cunha, Rawnsley and Loudon (1964) found that affected women were later characterized by frequent medical consultations.

If the differential absenteeism rate is a function of greater symptom reporting or help-seeking, this could reflect a stronger need to evaluate physical reactions among affected individuals. This notion is supported by Kerckhoff and Back (1968), who found that affecteds tended to focus on emotive or physiological responses rather than potential external sources. If this is the case, such individuals should engage more actively in social comparison in an attempt to evaluate their physical distress and would thus be more susceptible to mass psychogenic illness.

The causes and processes underlying mass psychogenic illness are by no means clear. The study of outbreaks of these epidemics is inhibited by the necessarily retrospective nature of most research and by the fact that psychogenic causes are not usually considered until the presence of a toxin has been ruled out. The search for pathogens may take weeks, and, as a result, psychological explanations are often applied quite late in the progress of the illness. However, the usefulness of applying research and theory from social psychology to such problems appears to be significant.

COGNITIVE AND SOCIAL DETERMINANTS OF ILLNESS

In preceding sections we have considered the role of psychosocial processes in the appraisal of stress, in coping with and adapting to stress, and in determining the impact of stress. Cognitive and social variables have proven useful in reducing anticipatory stress and improving medical outcomes as well as in explaining the ways in which stress may be interpreted as illness. We now turn to the role of these variables in the etiology of disease and in mediating the relationships between stress and illness.

Traditionally, illness has been viewed as a biological phenomenon, regulated by genetic, pathogenic, and physiological factors. Such a perspective resulted in general disregarding of variables such as an individual's physical and social environments, lifestyles, and the like.

Rather, illness was considered as a product of specific agents or pathogens and bodily dysfunction. This model of illness, however, has simply not proven capable of accounting for all illness states. Further, the traditional biological perspective has not yielded satisfactory explanations for selective susceptibility and the fact that certain diseases are manifest in some people but not in others. Many major medical problems are neither contagious nor necessarily linked to "germs" or noxious agents. Rather, a number of illnesses, including some of the most common in modern society, appear to be caused, at least in part, by psychosocial variables such as lifestyle or coping proclivity. Thus psychosomatic medicine has considered a number of psychophysiological disorders such as migraine headache, dysmenorrhea, allergy, and ulceration of the gastrointestinal tract. In addition, diseases of "lifestyle," such as hypertension and coronary heart disease, have been studied as products of behavioral and psychological factors rather than pathogens and physiological breakdown.

Stress and different modes of coping with it are now considered to be important in the etiology of illness. Levi (1972) and Kagan and Levi (1974) have developed an ecological "diathesis-stress" model (see Figure 2) that attempts to incorporate stress as well as psychosocial mediation of it into the origins of many illnesses. The model simply posits that the environment (physical and social) produces psychosocial stimuli that interact with psychological and physiological predispositions to produce psychological and physiological responses. These responses may lead to precursors of disease and, on occasion, to disease states. Thus, at a number of levels, physical, social, and psychological events may affect the onset of disease.

"Psychosocial stimuli," according to Kagan and Levi (1974), refer to events or cognitions that are "suspected" of being related to disease, that "originate in social relationships or arrangements (i.e., the envi-

FIGURE 2 The diathesis-stress model. (From L. Levi, "Evolutionary and Ecological Approach" in L. Levi, *Emotions: Their Parameters & Measurement*, New York: Raven Press, 1975).

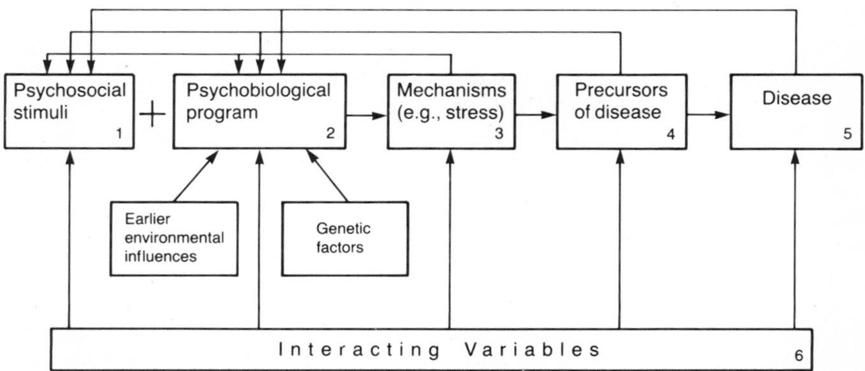

ronment)'' and are transmitted by the nervous system. Thus stimuli such as stress may be produced by the environment and one's appraisal of the environment. These stimuli, in turn, interact with the ''psychobiological program,'' defined as predispositions or propensities to respond in specific psychophysiological patterns. These predispositions are derived from genetic factors, environmental influences, and relationships that have been learned throughout one's life. The interaction of these stimuli and predispositions results in what Kagan and Levi (1974) call ''mechanisms,'' or the actual psychological and physiological reactions to psychosocial events. These responses are directed by learned or inherited response patterns. Responses or mechanisms may subsequently, under some conditions, lead to ''precursors of disease,'' or psychological or physiological breakdown. When this occurs, disease states may ensue.

This system of relationships is mediated by underlying ''interacting variables,'' defined as ''intrinsic or extrinsic factors, mental or physical, that alter the action of 'causative' factors at the mechanism, precursor or disease stage'' (Levi, 1975). These cognitive, social, or environmental variables are seen as promoting or inhibiting specific types of responding, determining whether or not response patterns ultimately lead to illness, and generally affecting the impact of psychosocial stimuli on the system. Thus psychosocial variables are considered as contextual determinants of illness.

By incorporating psychosocial stimuli, response predispositions, and underlying interacting factors into a model of disease state, this diathesis-stress model does not rule out the more traditional biological model in all cases. The term *diathesis* refers to genetic or constitutional predispositions toward certain kinds of pathology, and, in some cases, one might be able to trace a relationship between such predispositions and illness. In most cases, however, these biological weaknesses are considered necessary but insufficient conditions for disease onset. Thus biological predispositions typically cannot explain the onset of illness nor adequately predict likelihood that one person may become ill while another will not. Triggering events, such as stress, are needed in order to explain whether a disease will be manifest in an individual who may show constitutional tendencies toward that illness. The diathesis-stress model allows for this determination, providing not only for a psychosocial trigger, but also for consideration of prior learning, appraisal, coping, and the like in the etiology of illness.

The implications of this way of viewing illness are vast and vitally important. At a number of levels, this perspective can better explain the onset of a disease and provide for more effective preventive and treatment procedures. Consider the following description of psychosomatic disorders:

> Certain environmental stimuli provoke in certain, say, anxiety-prone individuals an emotional response, say, anxiety. This response implies central and peripheral physiological concomitants, part of which, say, tachycardia

> and palpitations, may generate proprioceptive signals. If perceived and interpreted by the individual as something unpleasant and/or dangerous, this may augment his anxiety reaction. In some individuals and under certain circumstances, even perfectly 'normal' proprioceptive signals may be interpreted by the individual as a threat or as symptoms of disease, as in the case of *hypochondriasis*. If the environmental stimulation becomes pronounced, prolonged, or often repeated, or if the organism is predisposed to react, or because of the presence or absence of certain interacting variables, the result may be a prolonged or often repeated hyper-hypo-, or dysfunction in one of more organs and organ systems, i.e., a functional disorder. (Levi, 1975, p. 708)

A growing body of research has examined the relationships that are stated or implied by this model, ranging from studies of the role of intense, prolonged, or repeated stressors on illness to the mediating influences of coping styles or patterns of response. Research has suggested that the number and severity of life changes and psychophysiological responses to them interact to influence health, affect biochemical processes related to vulnerability to various diseases, and to determine the onset and course of an illness (e.g., Engel, 1977; Holmes & Masuda, 1974; Holmes & Rahe, 1967; Johnson & Sarason, 1979; Theorell & Rahe, 1971; Wyler, Masuda, & Holmes, 1971). Additional research has suggested that culturally determined conflict and occupational stress can contribute to illness (e.g., Eliot & Buell, 1979; Frankenhaeuser & Gardell, 1976; House, 1974).

Evidence for Psychosocial Determinants of Illness

There are several ways in which the diathesis-stress notion of the etiology of disease can focus research. Three general areas of concern have emerged, considering cognitive and social mediation of stress, predispositions or personality characteristics related to susceptibility to illness, and psychosocial interacting variables that may heighten or supress one's vulnerability to or interpretation of stress or reactions to stress.

A number of studies have considered the general relationship between stress and health. Some have shown a greater likelihood of individuals under stress to develop some form of illness (e.g., Hinkle, 1961). One of these studies considering highly stressed air controllers (Cobb, 1972) reported increased incidence of "every psychosomatic disease that could be studied." Specific stressors have been linked to illness as well, including pressures, job dissatisfaction, uncontrollability, exposure to rapid change, loss or bereavement, and life changes that require readjustment or a great deal of adaptation (e.g., Greene, 1966; Holmes & Rahe, 1967; House, 1974; Paulus, McCain & Cox, 1978).

In relating stress to an illness state, many studies have considered appraisal processes and responses to stress as determinants of illness. In the case of ulcers, for example, research has suggested that one response to stress, increased secretion of gastric acid, is a direct cause of gastrointestinal ulceration (e.g., Wolf & Wolff, 1947). In other cases, the appraisal of stressors has been found to be important in disease onset. Perceived pressures, incongruity between occupational expectations and realities, and uncontrollability have been considered as psychosocial precursors of coronary heart disease and hypertension (e.g., Friedman, Rosenman, & Carroll, 1957; Glass, 1976; House, 1974; Jenkins, 1971; Kasl & Cobb, 1970). Thus, when considering stress as a psychosocial determinant of illness, the entire stress process (as outlined earlier) provides a more complete picture than any single aspect of it.

Perhaps the most important aspect of the diathesis-stress notion is its emphasis on the interaction of psychosocial stimuli and individual predispositions. As we have noted, the way in which an individual copes with stress may ultimately prove more important than the stressor alone. Thus personality dimensions related to the onset of disease have been reported, and research has considered general orientations toward health or health care (e.g., Krantz et al., 1980; Mechanic & Newton, 1965; Hinkle, Christenson, Kane, Ostfeld, Thefford, & Wolff, 1958). Studies have found relationships between the onset of cancer and emotionality, extraversion, repression, and an inability to express hostility (Bahnson & Bahnson, 1969; Hagnell, 1966; Solomon, 1969). Similarly, hypochondriasis has been linked to the onset of coronary heart disease (Ostfeld, Lebovitz, Shekelle, & Paul, 1964). A number of personality variables have been postulated as potential determinants of response to stress.

More importantly, several syndromes or behavior patterns that seem to predispose individuals to respond in ways that facilitate the development of illness have been studied. For example, giving up or being helpless has been considered as a means of coping with stress that may lead to illness or sudden death. Schmale (1972) and Engel and Schmale (1967) have suggested that giving up in response to loss is a precursor of disease. Giving up is a response mechanism caused by an individual, predisposed to helplessness or giving up, who encounters stressful loss. Thus people who had experienced real or apparent loss and had expressed feelings of helplessness in the face of this loss were more likely to develop cancer than were those responding in other ways (Schmale & Iker, 1971). Further study of the "giving up" predisposition is warranted, especially in light of the burgeoning literature on learned helplessness and its cognitive and social determinants (e.g., Abramson et al., 1978; Seligman, 1975; Wortman & Dintzer, 1978).

A somewhat different perspective on predispositions has been developed by Graham (1962; Graham, Stern, & Winokur, 1958). In proposing a specific attitudes theory, it was postulated that attitudes toward stressful life situations or tendencies to interpret distressing events in certain ways is linked to the development of specific disorders. On the basis of clinical interviews with patients suffering from psychophysiological illnesses, Grace and Graham (1952) were able to associate different ways of interpreting what was happening with different illnesses; the tendency to appraise life events as evidence of ever-present danger requiring constant vigilance was linked to the development of hypertension, while interpretation of events as deprivation and cause for revenge was more common among patients with ulcers. In a series of intriguing studies evidence for this view of illness etiology was obtained. By hypnotizing subjects and inducing some of the specific feelings associated with specific illnesses, Graham and colleagues were able to elicit physiological symptoms of these disorders. In one study, induction of feelings of ever-present threat and the need to be vigilant, supposedly associated with hypertension, resulted in an increase in blood pressure (Graham, Kabler, & Graham, 1962).

Although some studies have failed to confirm the specific attitude-illness relationship (e.g., Buss, 1966), some evidence for such a relationship remains. The idea that tendencies to interpret or appraise stress should be related to illness is not all that surprising. Such tendencies should moderate actual response to stress and, as a result, have the potential to determine whether responses will lead to disease. This kind of reasoning forms the basis for work on other predispositions, such as Glass' (1976) elaboration on the Type A behavior pattern. Part of this pattern, argues Glass, is the tendency to view stress as threatening to one's sense of control.

The Type A behavior pattern, or coronary-prone behavior, was originally developed by Friedman and Rosenman (1974). This pattern, characterized by aggressive, time-urgent, and competitive response to challenge or stress, has been associated with incidence of coronary heart disease (e.g., Glass, 1976; Jenkins, 1971). In the Western Collaborative Group Study, a major attempt to study coronary-prone behavior, Type A pattern men were more than six times more likely to develop heart disease between the ages of 39 and 49 than were Type B individuals (defined as those with an absence of Type A characteristics). For men in their fifties, Type A men were almost twice as likely to develop heart disease (e.g., Rosenman, Brand, Jenkins, Friedman, Straus, & Wurm, 1975).

Glass (1976) has suggested that the link between Type A behavior and heart disease is best viewed as a control-oriented coping style that involves both physiological and psychological reactivity. Type A individuals are concerned with maintaining control over aspects of different situations, and in order to do this, they must strive harder, accelerate their activities, and assert themselves. Events that threaten control should evoke even more striving and aggressiveness as well as responses involving corticosteroids and catecholamines. Thus the Type A pattern involves both the tendency to interpret events in certain ways and to respond to psychosocial stimuli in characteristically hard-driving ways.

Research has also addressed the general category of "interacting variables" in Kagan and Levi's (1974) account of stress and illness. Recall from an earlier section that variables such as social support, perceived control, or attitudes toward stressors have shown relationships to stress and seem to have an effect on whether stressful events will lead to illness. At any stage of the process, these and other conditioning variables may alter or end the progression of illnesses. Just as the presence of a treatment that can prevent a disease (e.g., a vaccine) can negate the effects of stress in causing some illnesses, social and psychological prophylaxis can also reduce the likelihood of stress-induced disease. By the same logic, physical, social, and psychological factors may facilitate the development of illness.

SOCIAL PSYCHOLOGY IN MEDICAL SETTINGS

The implications of what we have considered in this chapter are numerous. They suggest new ways of viewing illness, preventive strategies concerned with stress management and reduction, and a number of interesting and potentially useful ways of improving health. At the same time, we believe that they underscore both the many aspects of health and illness that are psychologically based or mediated and the opportunity for psychologists to provide valuable data and insight for their medical colleagues. The contributions that psychologists can make, both in terms of a methodological approach and a theoretical orientation, are potentially great. What, then, are the quids and quos associated with psychology's entry into behavioral medicine?

Paramount is the fact that social psychology, particularly the sort focusing on individual cognitive processes, is in a healthy symbiotic relationship with biomedical research. Social psychology has several important contributions to make to the research, and it receives several important benefits.

What Social Psychology Brings to Medicine

The contributions psychology makes can be viewed on at least three different levels. First, the past three decades of social psychology have witnessed extraordinary increases in experimental sophistication in both the methodology as well as the design and analysis of studies. One need only reread some of the classic studies from the post-World War II Group Dynamics Center at Michigan or the attitude group at Yale and contrast their characteristics with most of the studies routinely published in the *Journal of Personality and Social Psychology* to see how the field has advanced. The general skills of social psychologists as complex human experimenters are often not appreciated by our field: it is easy to take for granted that which "everyone" knows. Yet these very skills are exceptionally valuable to a biomedical research team. Although the general principles of research are probably the same for all the sciences, the day-to-day practices are not always obvious. Just as every bench scientist knows that centrifuge rotors must be counterbalanced, so does every attitude measurer realize that the same is true for attitude scales. What is routine procedure in one field can save time and trouble in another. There are a limited number of times the wheel must be invented. As biomedical researchers study the concomitant behavioral problems that accompany their primary interests, the general skills of the social psychologist become useful.

Second, social psychologists have a variety of theories and concepts to explain social and individual behaviors. These theories can be applied to problems in medical settings to clarify situations rather recalcitrant to informal or common sense speculation. While our discussion of mass psychogenic illness and social comparison may provide one illustration of this point, some other specific examples may be helpful. The concept of a coronary-prone Type A behavior pattern had been studied for about ten years by clinicians in both prospective and retrospective studies. Many behaviorists were still uneasy about the concept; it was all too similar to a variety of previous distinctions that had not lived up to advance billing. The meticulous set of studies by Glass (1976), providing laboratory analogs for the component behaviors of Type A and using these analogs to explore the mechanisms by which behaviors are linked to the pathogenesis of artherosclerosis, have proven instrumental in helping to solidify the construct.

As useful as the traditional social psychological laboratory is, the same utility can also serve in the field. Consider the question of how patients should be treated in a hospital. Some modes of patient management will obviously make it easier for the institution to go about its daily routine, but what effect does this have on the patient? Taylor (1979) has analyzed this situation in social psychological terms and pointed out that extremes of control or independence produce excessively dependent or reactant patients. Even if these extreme states make it easier for staff to handle the patient (in one case they are docile, in the other they fend for themselves), there are deleterious consequences in both conditions that carry with them unfortunate outcomes, both behavioral and medical. Yet another example: to some, at first glance attribution theory may seem as arcane and nonapplied as any theory in social psychology. Yet Bulman and Wortman (1977) were able to demonstrate that, among victims of spinal cord accidents, the answers to the attributional questions of blame and responsibility for their condition were indicative of their rehabilitative progress. Similar aspects of attribution theory (combined with reactance and social comparison) have been extended with equal success to the general state of health of cancer patients.

Third, social psychologists are also psychologists. As members of that profession, they have been socialized by their training to view the world in a particular way. It is not necessarily better or more insightful than that of other professions, just different. We view the world with Wundt-colored glasses, so to speak. For example, just as physicians may routinely think and talk in terms of pathogens and titers, psychologists may think and talk of learning and conditioning. Even when working on a familiar problem, the different perspective of the psychologist may bring new facets of it into view. The problem of obesity, for instance, is one of concern to medicine as well as being of psychological interest. Biomedical studies have tended to focus on metabolic processes or developmental growth of lipid cells. On the psychological plane, the recent work of Rodin (1978) demonstrated that in moderately obese people secretion of insulin into the bloodstream occurs in response to the sight and description of food prior to its ingestion. This pattern of secretion does not occur in people of normal weight. The notion of looking for this pattern and the ideas for following studies are facilitated by a general psychological background and a socialized predisposition to conceive of phenomena as conditionable.

What Medicine Can Bring to Social Psychology

Obviously, the social psychology nexus with medical science is a two-way link. There are several benefits to social psychology that come from working in medical settings. These range from the mundane economic considerations to sources of ideas.

First, the financing and support of research has seemingly become more and more mission oriented. Foundations, health agencies, and even agencies that finance basic research, such as the National Science Foundation, are applying a criterion of utility and applicability in addition to their normal criteria of scientific and scholarly merit. The biomedical arena offers a wide range of problems, of different interests and appeals, most of which offer the cachet of immediate utility. We are not suggesting that behavioral factors in biomedical research provide a crass and opportunistic home for the research of social psychologists who would otherwise not receive funding, but rather that in addition to being interesting, such research is also useful. Why should attribution theory be any less fascinating for social psychologists for being conducted among cancer patients than among college sophomores? Indeed, almost by definition, one of the hallmarks of "useful" research is that it deals with outcomes that matter. Most of the investigators we know at some time or other have been willing to downgrade the statistical significance of their research in favor of "external validity," "variance accounted for," or "a real-life effect." Morbidity and mortality are by consensus useful, important, and externally valid outcomes.

Second, biomedical settings provide a variety of useful field settings in which to conduct research. Social psychology has had a history of shuttling between an emphasis on laboratory studies and an emphasis on field studies. It is true that both settings have had their doctrinaire proponents, e.g., "All lab studies are artificial" and "All field studies are uncontrolled" are not unfamilir refrains. Our hunch is that if the pendulum in the last generation was on the laboratory side, it was because of the difficulties in finding appropriate field settings rather than for theoretical reasons (cf. Singer & Glass, 1975). The problems of ethics, logistics, and access often seemed insurmountable. Consider the attitude-change literature. Most of the work was laboratory-based, and when it dealt with attitudes of importance to the subjects, these were often college-related—tuition increases, for example. Political questions asked of undergraduates (at least in the days before the 18-year-old vote) always seemed a little uninvolving, yet what right did researchers have to go into the community to persuade people to vote for or against particular candidates? Similarly, health issues that may seem forced in a classroom are natural explorations in a clinic or hospital. The study of such issues as what characteristics of the physician's interview elicit the most valid background information are not only ethical, but valued and supported by those with access to the setting and by potential subjects. In brief, behavioral or social psychological investigations in biomedical settings may give investigators an unparalleled opportunity to combine both impact and control. The range of situations and issues available is so wide that an appropriate arena can be found for practically every social psychological theory.

Third, social psychological theories can pick up a type of "hybrid vigor" from a medical setting. Biomedical research, as with most applied research, is often problem oriented. It has been pointed out before that problem-oriented research is often interdisciplinary by necessity (Singer & Glass, 1975). The boundaries of the point at issue are resistant to partial solutions; i.e., the "operation was successful but the patient died" philosophy is as inappropriate for social psychology as it is for surgery. The social psychologist working on biomedical problems must collaborate with a variety of other people, many of whom have skills and perspectives not found in the psychologist's training or experience. Just as the psychologist's Weltanschauung illuminates the medical researchers, so the Weltanschauung of the medical researchers illuminates the psychologists. A psychologist interested in the effects of perceived control on competence and self-esteem may choose to study a group of teenagers with juvenile-onset diabetes, seeking to relate their perceptions to disease management and general social and scholastic adjustment. The researcher would quickly find that the patients could not be studied independently of the nature of the disease. Diabetes may affect growth, physical activity, and the ability of the teenager to participate in some selected activities—such a patient does not casually go to McDonald's for a snack. As a consequence, the psychologist may alter his or her views of the role of physical and somatic factors in the formation of personality and the expression of social behavior. Even further, the investigator, although attracted to the problem for theoretic reasons deriving from social psychology, may begin to appreciate previously neglected other areas of psychology. The observation that the parents of juvenile-onset diabetics ambivalently push their children toward independence and self-care while simultaneously keeping them under detailed surveillance may pique the psychologist's interest in parent–child interactions and general developmental issues. Necessity does not always breed invention. Neolithic man, after all, did not develop the shotgun. But we do not see how a well-trained researcher with merely a modicum of curiosity could fail to be intrigued by the staggering variety of medical problems with basic social psychological implications.

CONCLUSION

Social psychology has of late turned to investigations in biomedical settings. These settings have proven to be useful arenas of research for testing social psychological propositions; they have offered a series of theoretical problems that have been shown to be amenable to social psychological interpretation; they have suggested to social psychologists a number of interesting practical problems toward whose solution social psychology can contribute. In this chapter we have sought to illustrate several of these areas by examining them in case-study fashion and proceed from there to draw a number of conclusions about the mutually beneficial effects of applying social psychology in the field of heath and disease.

REFERENCES

Abramson, L. Y., Seligman, M., & Teasdale, J. Learned helplessness in humans: Critique and reformulation. *Journal of Abnormal Psychology*, 1978, *87*, 49 –74.

Andrew, J. M. Recovery from surgery, with and without preparatory instruction, for three coping styles. *Journal of Personality and Social Psychology*, 1970, *15*, 223 –226.

Antonovsky, A. Twenty-five years later: A limited study of the sequelae of the concentration camp experience. *Social Psychiatry*, 1971, *6*, 186 –193.

Averill, J. R. Personal control of aversive stimuli and its relationship to stress. *Psychological Bulletin*, 1973, *80*, 286 –303.

Averill, J. R., & Rosenn, M. Vigilant and non-vigilant coping strategies and psychophysiological stress reactions during the anticipation of electric shock. *Journal of Personality and Social Psychology*, 1972, *23*, 128 –141.

Bahnson, M. B., & Bahnson, C. B. Ego defenses in cancer patients. *Annals of the New York Academy of Sciences*, 1969, *164*, 546 –557.

Baum, A., & Davis, G. E. Reducing the stress of high density living: An architectural intervention. *Journal of Personality and Social Psychology*, 1980, *38*, 471 –481.

Baum, A., & Gatchel, R. J. Cognitive determinants of reaction to uncontrollable events: Development of reactance and learned helplessness. *Journal of Personality and Social Psychology*, 1981, *40*, 1078 –1089.

Baum, A., & Koman, S. Differential response to anticipated crowding: Psychological effects of social and spatial density. *Journal of Personality and Social Psychology*, 1976, *34*, 526 –536.

Baum, A., & Valins, S. *Architecture and social behavior: Psychological studies of social density.* Hillsdale, N.J.: Erlbaum, 1977.

Baum, A., & Valins, S. Architectural mediation of residential density and control: Crowding and the regulation of social contact. In L. Berkowitz (Ed.), *Advances in experimental social psychology*, Vol. 12. New York: Academic, 1979.

Baum, A., Aiello, J. R., & Calesnick, L. E. Crowding and personal control: Social density and the development of learned helplessness. *Journal of Personality and Social Psychology*, 1978, *36*, 1000 –1011.

Baum, A., Davis, G. E., & Aiello, J. R. Crowding and neighborhood mediation of urban density. *Journal of Population*, 1978, *1*, 266 –278.

Baum, A., Aiello, J. R., & Davis, G. Neighborhood determinants of stress and symptom perception. Paper presented at the meeting of the American Psychological Association, New York City, September 1979.

Baum, A., Fisher, J. D., & Solomon, S. K. Type of information, familiarity, and the reduction of crowding stress. *Journal of Personality and Social Psychology*, 1981, *40*, 11 –23.

Baum, A., Singer, J. E., & Baum, C. S. Stress and the environment. *Journal of Social Issues*, 1981, *37*, 4–35.

Beck, A. T. *Cognitive therapy and the emotional disorders.* New York: International Universities Press, 1976.

Benson, H. *The relaxation response.* New York: Morrow, 1975.

Benson, J. S., & Kennelly, K. J. Learned helplessness: The result of uncontrollable stimuli. *Journal of Personality and Social Psychology*, 1976, *34*, 138–145.

Bliss, E. L., Migeon, C. J., Branch, C. H., & Samuels, L. T. Reaction of the adrenal cortex to emotional stress. *Psychosomatic Medicine*, 1956, *18*, 56–76.

Brown, B. *New mind, new body.* New York: Harper & Row, 1975.

Bulman, R., & Wortman, C. B. Attributions of blame and coping in the "real world": Severe accident victims react to their lot. *Journal of Personality and Social Psychology*, 1977, *35*, 351–363.

Burch, J. Recent bereavement in relation to suicide. *Journal of Psychosomatic Research*, 1972, *16*, 361–366.

Burstein, S., & Meichenbaum, D. The work of worrying in children undergoing surgery. Unpublished manuscript, cited in B. Melamed, Psychological preparation for hospitalization. In S. Rachman (Ed.), *Contributions to medical psychology*. New York: Pergamon, 1977.

Buss, A. H. *Psychopathology*. New York: Wiley, 1966.

Cannon, W. B. *Bodily changes in pain, hunger, fear and rage.* Boston, Mass.: Branford, 1929.

Cannon, W. B. Studies on the conditions of activity in the endocrine organs. XXVII. Evidence that the medulliadrenal secretion is not continuous. *American Journal of Physiology*, 1931, *98*, 447–452.

Caplan, R. D., Cobb, S., & French, J. R. P., Jr. Relationships of cessation of smoking with job stress, personality, and social support. *Journal of Applied Psychology*, 1975, *60*, 211–219.

Cederlöf, R., Jonsson, E., & Sorenson, S. On the influence of attitudes toward the source on annoyance reactions to noise: A field experiment. *Nordisk hygienesk tidskrift*, 1967, *48*, 46–55.

Chambers, W. N., & Reiser, M. F. Emotional stress in the precipitation of congestive heart failure. *Psychosomatic Medicine*, 1953, *15*, 38–60.

Chew, P. K., Phoon, W. H., & Mae-Lim, H. A. Epidemic hysteria among some factory workers in Singapore. *Singapore Medical Journal*, 1976, *17*, 10–15.

Cobb, S. A report on the health of air traffic controllers based on aeromedical examination data. Unpublished report to the Federal Aviation Agency. University of Michigan, Ann Arbor, 1972.

Cobb, S. Social support as a moderator of life stress. *Psychosomatic Medicine*, 1976, *38* (5), 300–314.

Cobb, S., Kasl, S. V., French, J. R. P., Jr., & Norstebo, G. The intrafamilial transmission of rheumatoid arthritis. VII. Why do wives with rheumatoid arthritis have husbands with peptic ulcer? *Journal of Chronic Diseases*, 1969, *22*, 279–293.

Coch, L., & French, J. R. P., Jr. Overcoming resistance to change. *Human Relations*, 1948, *1*, 512–532.

Cohen, F., & Lazarus, R. S. Active coping processes, coping & dispositions, and recovery from surgery. *Psychosomatic Medicine*, 1973, *35*, 375–389.

Cohen, S., Silverman, A., & Shmavonian, B. Neurophysiological, humoral and personality factors in the response to sensory deprivation. *Proceedings of the World Congress of Psychiatry*. Montreal, 1961.

Cohen, S. A. Environmental load and allocation of attention. In A. Baum, J. E. Singer, & S. Valins (Eds.), *Advances in environmental psychology*. Hillsdale, N.J.: Erlbaum, 1978.

Cohen, S. A. The aftereffects of stress on human performance and social behavior: A review of research and theory. *Psychological Bulletin*, 1980, *88*, 82–108.

Cohen, S. A., Evans, G. W., Krantz, D. S., & Stokols, D. Physiological, motivational and cognitive effects of aircraft noise on children: Moving from the laboratory to the field. *American Psychologist*, 1980, *35*, 231 –243.

Cohen, S. A., Glass, D. C., & Singer, J. E. Apartment noise, auditory discrimination, and reading ability in children. *Journal of Experimental Social Psychology*, 1973, *9*, 407 –422.

Colligan, M. J. An investigation of apparent mass psychogenic illness in a furniture assembly plant. Unpublished NIOSH evaluation report, 1978.

Colligan, M. J., & Murphy, L. R. Mass psychogenic illness in organizations: An overview. *Journal of Occupational Psychology*, 1979.

Colligan, M. J., Urtes, M. A., Wisseman, C., Rosenstell, R. E. & Anania, T. L. An investigation of apparent mass psychogenic illness in an electronics plant. Unpublished NIOSH evaluation report, 1978.

DeLong, D. R. Individual differences in patterns of anxiety arousal stress-relevant information and recovery from surgery. Unpublished doctoral dissertation, University of California, Los Angeles, 1970.

Deutsch, C. P. Auditory discrimination and learning: Social factors. *The Merrill-Palmer Quarterly of Behavior and Development*, 1964, *10*, 277 –296.

Deutsch, M., & Collins, M. E. *Interracial housing: A psychological evaluation of a social experiment*. Minneapolis, Minn.: University Minneapolis Press, 1951.

Dimateo, M. R., DiNicola, D. D., & Flynn, D. P. The art of medicine: How to use motivating power for better patient management. *Behavioral Medicine*, October 1979, 20 –26.

Doering, S. G., & Entwisle, D. R. Preparation during preganancy and ability to cope with labor and delivery. *American Journal of Orthopsychiatry*, 1975, *45*, 825 –837.

Dohrenwend, B. S., & Dohrenwend, B. P. (Eds.), *Stressful life events: Their nature and effects*. New York: Wiley, 1974.

Donnerstein, E., & Wilson, D. W. Effects of noise and perceived control on ongoing and subsequent aggressive behavior. *Journal of Personality and Social Psychology*, 1976, *34*, 774 –781.

Easterbrook, J. A. The effects of emotion on cue-utilization and the organization of behavior. *Psychological Review*, 1959, *66*, 183 –201.

Egbert, L. D., Battit, G. E., Welch, C. E., & Bartlett, M. K. Reduction of postoperative pain by encouragement and instruction of patients. *New England Journal of Medicine*, 1964, *270*, 825 –827.

Eliot, R., & Buell, J. Environmental and behavioral influences in the major cardiovascular disorders. Presented at the annual meeting of the Academy of Behavioral Medicine Research. Snowbird, Utah, 1979.

Engel, G. L. The need for a new medical model: A challenge for biomedicine. *Science*, 1977, *196*, 129 –136.

Engel, G. L., & Schmale, A. H. Psychoanalytic theory of somatic disorder. *Journal of the American Psychoanalytic Association*, 1967, *15*, 344 –363.

Euler, U. S. von. Twenty years of noradrenaline. *Pharmacol. Rev.*, 1966, *18*, 29.

Festinger, L. A theory of social comparison processes. *Human Relations*, 1954, *7*, 117 –140.

Fisher, J. D., & Baum, A. Situational and arousal-based messages and the reduction of crowding stress. *Journal of Applied Social Psychology*, 1980, *10*, 191 –201.

Folland, D. S. Suspect toluene exposure at a boat factory. Internal report, Tennessee Department of Health, Nashville, Tennessee, 1975.

Frankenhaeuser, M. Behavior and circulating catecholamines. *Brain Research*, 1971, *31*, 241 –262.

Frankenhaeuser, M. The role of peripheral catecholamines in adaptation to understimulation and overstimulation. In G. Serban (Ed.), *Psychopathology of human adaptation*. New York: Plenum, 1976.

Frankenhaeuser, M. Coping with job stress: A psychobiological approach. *Reports from the Department of Psychology*, 1978 (532).

Frankenhaeuser, M., & Gardell, B. Underload and overload in working life: Outline of a multidisciplinary approach. *Journal of Human Stress*, 1976, *2*(3), 35 –46.

Frankenhaeuser, M., Jarpe, G., & Mattell, G. Effects of intravenous infusions of adrenaline and noradrenaline on certain psychological and physiological functions. *Acta Physiologica Scandinavia*, 1961, *51*, 175 –186.

Freedman, J. L. *Crowding and behavior.* San Francisco, Calif.: Freeman, 1975.

Freedman, J. L. Theories of contagion. Paper presented at the NIOSH Symposium on Mass Psychogenic Illness, Chicago, Ill., 1979.

Freeman, W., Pincus, G., & Glover, E. D. The excretion of neutral urinary steroids in stress. *Endocrinology*, 1944, *35*, 215.

Friedman, M., & Rosenman, R. H. *Type A behavior and your heart.* New York: Knopf, 1974.

Friedman, M., Rosenman, R. H., & Carroll, V. Changes in the serum cholesterol and blood clotting time of men subject to cyclic variation of occupational stress. *Circulation*, 1957, *17*, 852 –961.

Fuller, S., Endress, M., & Johnson, J. E. The effects of cognitive and behavioral control on coping with an aversive health examination. *Journal of Human Stress*, 1978, 18 –25.

Gatchel, R. J. Perceived control: A review and evaluation of therapeutic implications. In A. Baum and J. E. Singer (Eds.), *Advances in environmental psychology* (Vol. 2). Hillsdale, N.J.: Erlbaum, 1980.

Glass, D. C. *Behavior patterns, stress and coronary disease.* Hillsdale, N.J.: Erlbaum, 1976.

Glass, D. C., & Singer, J. E. *Urban stress: Experiments on noise and social stressors.* New York: Academic, 1972.

Glass, D. C., Singer, J. E., Leonard, H. S., Krantz, D. S., Cohen, S., & Cummings, H. Perceived control of aversive stimulation and the reduction of stress responses. *Journal of Personality*, 1973, *41*, 577 –595.

Grace, W. J., & Graham, D. T. Relationship of specific attitudes and emotions to certain bodily diseases. *Psychosomatic Medicine*, 1952, *14*, 242 –251.

Graham, D. T. Some research on physiologic specificity and its relation to psychosomatic disease. In R. Roessler and N. S. Greenfield (Eds.), *Physiological correlates of psychological disorders.* Madison, Wis.: University of Wisconsin Press, 1962.

Graham, D. T., Kabler, J. D., & Graham, F. K. Physiological response to the suggestion of attitudes specific for hives and hypertension. *Psychosomatic Medicine*, 1962, *24*, 159 –169.

Graham, D. T., Stern, J. A., & Winokur, G. Experimental investigation of the specificity of attitude hypothesis in psychosomatic disease. *Psychosomatic Medicine*, 1958, *20*, 446 –457.

Greene, W. A. The psychosocial setting of the development of leukemia and lymphoma. *Annals of the New York Academy of Sciences*, 1966, *125*, 794 –801.

Hagnell, L. The premorbid personality of persons who develop cancer in a total population investigated in 1947 and 1957. *Annals of the New York Academy of Sciences*, 1966, *125*, 846 –855.

Hale, H. B. Plasma corticosteroid changes during space-equivalent decompression in partial pressure suites and in supersonic flight. *Proceedings, First International Congress on Hormonal Steroids*, 1965, 527.

Hinkle, L. E., Jr. Ecological observations on the relation of physical illness, mental illness, and the social environment. *Psychosomatic Medicine*, 1961, *23*, 289 –297.

Hinkle, L. E., Jr., Christenson, W. N., Kane, F. D., Ostfeld, A. M., Thefford, W. N., & Wolff, H. G. An investigation of the relationship between life experience, personality characteristics and general susceptibility to illness. *Psychosomatic Illness*, 1958, *20*, 278 –295.

Hollon, S. D., & Kendall, P. D. Cognitive-behavioral interventions: Theory and procedure. In P. C. Kendall and S. D. Hollon (Eds.), *Cognitive-behavioral interventions*. New York: Academic, 1979.

Holmes, T. H., & Masuda, M. Life changes and illness susceptibility. In B. S. Dohrenwend and B. P. Dohrenwend (Eds.), *Stressful life events: Their nature and effects*. New York: Wiley, 1974.

Holmes, T. H., & Rahe, R. H. The social readjustment rating scale. *Journal of Psychosomatic Research*, 1967, *11*, 213 –218.

Horwitz, M. The recall of interrupted group tasks: An experimental study of individual motivation in relation to group goals. In D. Cartwright and A. Zander (Eds.), *Group dynamics: Research and theory*. New York: Harper & Row, 1953.

House, J. S. Occupational stress and coronary heart disease: A review and theoretical integration. *Journal of Health and Social Behavior*, 1974, *15*, 12 –27.

Janis, I. *Psychological stress*. New York: Wiley, 1958.

Jenkins, C. D. Psychologic and social precursors of coronary disease. *New England Journal of Medicine*, 1971, 284 –255 and 307 –317.

Jenkins, C. D. Psychosocial modifiers of response to stress. *Journal of Human Stress*, 1979, *5*(4), 3 –5.

Johnson, H. J., & Sarason, I. G. Recent development in research on life stress. In V. Hamilton and D. M. Warburton (Eds.), *Human stress and cognition: An information processing approach*. Chichester, England: Wiley, 1979.

Johnson, J. E. Effects of accurate expectations about sensations on the sensory and distress components of pain. *Journal of Personality and Social Psychology*, 1973, *27*, 261 –275.

Johnson, J. E. Stress reduction through sensory information. In I. G. Sarason and C. D. Speilberger (Eds.), *Stress and anxiety*, Vol. 2. New York: Wiley, 1975.

Johnson, J. E., & Leventhal, H. Effects of accurate expectations and behavioral instructions on reactions during a noxious medical examination. *Journal of Personality and Social Psychology*, 1974, *29*, 710 –718.

Johnson, J. E., Morrissey, J. F., & Leventhal, H. Psychological preparation for an endoscopic examination. *Gastrointestinal Endoscopy*, 1973, *19*, 180 –182.

Johnson, J. E., Rice V. H., Fuller, S. S., & Endress, M. P. Sensory information, behavioral instruction, and recovery from surgery. Paper presented at the annual meeting of the American Psychological Association, San Francisco, Calif.: August 1977.

Jonsson, E., & Sorenson, S. On the influence of attitudes toward the source on annoyance reactions to noise: An experimental study. *Nordisk hygienesk tidskrift*, 1967, *48*, 35 –45.

Kagan, A. R., & Levi, L. Health and environment—Psychosocial stimuli. *Social Science and Medicine*, 1974, *8*, 225 –241.

Kagan, J. Reflection—impulsivity: The generality and dynamics of conceptual tempo. *Journal of Abnormal Psychology*, 1966, *71*, 17 –24.

Kasl, S. V., & Cobb, S. Blood pressure changes in men undergoing job loss: A preliminary report. *Psychosomatic Medicine*, 1970, *32*, 19 –38.

Kendall, P. C., & Hollon, S. D. Cognitive behavioral interventions: Overview and current status. In P. C. Kendall and S. D. Hollon (Eds.), *Cognitive-behavioral interventions: Theory, research, and procedures*. New York: Academic, 1979.

Kendall, P. C., Williams, L., Pechacek, T. F., Graham, L. G., Shisslak, C. S., & Herzoff, N. Cognitive-behavioral and patient education interventions in cardiac catheterization procedures: The Palo-Alto medical psychology project. *Journal of Consulting and Clinical Psychology*, 1979, *47*, 49 –58.

Kerckhoff, A. C., & Back, K. W. *The June Bug: A study of hysterical contagion*. New York: Appleton-Century-Crofts, 1968.

Kiretz, S., & Moos, R. H. Physiological effects of social environments. *Psychosomatic Medicine*, 1974, *36*, 96 –114.

Knight, J. A., Friedman, T. S. & Sulanti, J. Epidemic hysteria: A field study. *American Journal of Public Health*, 1965, *55*, 858 –865.

Konzett, H. Cardiovascular parameters and methods of measuring emotions. In L. Levi (Ed.), *Emotions—Their parameters and measurement*. New York: Raven Press, 1975.

Korsch, B., & Negrete, V. Doctor–patient communication. *Scientific American*, 1972, 66–73.

Krantz, D. S., & Schulz, R. Life crisis, control, and health outcomes: A model applied to cardiac rehabilitation and relocation of the elderly. In A. Baum and J. E. Singer (Eds.), *Advances in environmental psychology*, Vol. 2. Hillsdale, N.J.: Erlbaum, 1980.

Krantz, D. S., Baum, A., & Wideman, M. v. Assessment of preferences for self-treatment and information in medical care. *Journal of Personality and Social Psychology*, 1980, *39*, 977–990.

Langer, E. J., Janis, I. L., & Wolfer, J. A. Reduction of psychological stress in surgical patients. *Journal of Experimental Social Psychology*, 1975, *11*, 155–165.

Lazarus, R. S. *Psychological stress and the coping process*. New York: McGraw-Hill, 1966.

Lazarus, R. S., & Cohen, J. B. Environmental stress. In I. Attman and J. F. Wohlwill (Eds.), *Human Behavior and Environment*, Vol. 2, New York: Plenum, 1977.

Lazarus, R., Speisman, J., Mordkoff, A., & Davison, L. A laboratory study of psychological stress produced by a motion picture film. *Psychological Monographs*, 1962, *76* (Whole No. 553).

Leon, G. Cognitive-behavior therapy for eating disorders. In P. Kendall and S. Hollon (Eds.), *Cognitive-behavioral interventions*. New York: Academic, 1979.

Leonard, S., & Borsky, P. N. A causal model for relating noise exposure, psycho-social variables and aircraft noise annoyance. In W. Ward (Ed.), *Proceedings of the international congress on noise as a public health problem*. Washington, D.C.: Environmental Protection Agency, 1973.

Leventhal, H. Findings and theory in the study of fear communication. In L. Berkowitz (Ed.), *Advances in experimental social psychology*, Vol. 5. New York: Academic, 1970, 119–186.

Levi, L. The urinary output of adrenalin and noradrenalin during pleasant and unpleasant emotional stress. *Psychosomatic Medicine*, 1965, *27*, 80–85.

Levi, L. Stress and distress in response to psychosocial stimuli. Laboratory and real life studies on sympathoadrenomedullary and related reactions. *Acta Medica Scandinavia Supplement*, 528, 1972.

Levi, L. Parameters of emotion: An evolutionary and ecological approach. In L. Levi (Ed.), *Emotions—Their parameters and measurement*. New York: Raven Press, 1975.

Levi, L. Psychosocial factors in preventive medicine. In *Healthy people: The surgeon general's report on health promotion and disease prevention*. Washington, D.C.: U.S. Dept. of Health, Education, and Welfare, 1979.

Lewin, K. Forces behind food habits and methods of change. *Bulletin National Research Council*, 1943, *108*, 35–65.

Lewin, K. *Resolving social conflicts*. New York: Harper, 1948.

Lindeman, C. A. & Van Aernam, B. Nursing intervention with the presurgical patient—The effects of structured and unstructured preoperative teaching. *Nursing Research*, 1971, *20*, 319–332.

Mason, J. W. A review of psychoendocrine research on the pituitary-adrenal cortical system. *Psychosomatic Medicine*, 1968, *30*, 576–607.

Mechanic, D., & Newton, M. Some problems of the analysis of morbidity data. *Journal of Chronic Diseases*, 1965, *18*, 569–580.

Mehrabian, A. A questionnaire measure of individual differences in stimulus screening and associated differences in arousability. *Environmental Psychology and Nonverbal Behavior*, 1976, *1*, 89–103.

Melamed, B., & Siegel, L. Reduction of anxiety in children facing surgery by modeling. *Journal of Consulting and Clinical Psychology*, 1975, *43*, 511–521.

Mills, R. T., & Krantz, D. S. Information, choice and reactions to stress: A field experiment in a blood bank with laboratory analogue. *Journal of Personality and Social Psychology*, 1979, *37*, 608 –620.

Nathan, P. W. The gate-control theory of pain: A critical review. *Brain*, 1976, *99*, 123 –158.

Nelson, G. N., Masuda, M., & Holmes, T. H. Correlation of behavior and catecholamine metabolite excretion. *Psychosomatic Medicine*, 1966, *28*.

Newcomb, T. M. *The acquaintance process*. New York: Holt, Rinehart & Winston, 1961.

Novaco, R. The cognitive regulation of anger and stress. In P. Kendall and S. Hollon (Eds.), *Cognitive-behavioral interventions*. New York: Academic, 1979.

Nuckolls, K. B., Cassel J., & Kaplan, B. H. Psychosocial assets, life crisis, and the prognosis of pregnancy. *American Journal of Epidemiology*, 1972, *95*, 431 –441.

Ostfeld, A. M., Lebovitz, B. Z., Shekelle, R. B., & Paul, P. A prospective study of the relationship between personality and coronary heart disease. *Journal of Chronic Diseases*, 1964, *17*, 265 –276.

Paulus, P., McCain, G., & Cox, V. Death rates, psychiatric commitments, blood pressure and perceived crowding as a function of institutional crowding. *Environmental Psychology and Nonverbal Behavior*, 1978, *3*, 107 –116.

Pennebaker, J. Environmental determinants of symptom perception. Paper presented at the meeting of the American Psychological Association, New York City, September 1979.

Phillips, P. E. Internal report prepared for the Division of Health of the State of Missouri, 1974.

Raab, W. *Preventive cardiology*. Springfield, Ill.: Thomas, 1966.

Rawnsley, K., & Loudon, J. Epidemiology of mental disorder in a closed community. *British Journal of Psychiatry*, 1964, *110*, 830 –839.

Rodin, J. Density, perceived choice, and response to controllable and uncontrollable outcomes. *Journal of Experimential Social Psychology*, 1976, *12*, 564 –578.

Rodin, J. Has the distinction between internal versus external control of feeding outlived its usefulness? In G. A. Bray (Ed.), *Recent advances in obesity research* (Vol. 2). London: Newman, 1978.

Rosenman, R. H., Brand, R. J., Jenkins, C. D., Friedman, M., Straus, R., & Wurm, M. Coronary heart disease in the Western Collaborative Group Study: Final follow-up experience of 8½ years. *Journal of the American Medical Association*, 1975, *233*, 872 –877.

Rotton, J., Olszewski, D., Charleton, M., & Soler, E. Loud speech, conglomerate noise, and behavioral aftereffects. *Journal of Applied Psychology*, 1978, *63*, 360 –365.

Saegert, S. High density environments: Their personal and social consequences. In A. Baum and Y. Epstein (Eds.), *Human Response to Crowding*. Hillsdale, N.J.: Erlbaum, 1978.

Schachter, S. *The psychology of affiliation*. Stanford, Calif.: Stanford University Press, 1959.

Schachter, S., & Rodin, J. *Obese humans and rats*. Hillsdale, N.J.: Erlbaum, 1976.

Schachter, S., & Singer, J. E. Cognitive, Social, and physiological determinants of emotional state. *Psychological Review*, 1962, *69*, 379 –399.

Schmale, A. H., Jr. Giving up as a final common pathway to changes in health. *Advances in Psychosomatic Medicine*, 1972, *8*, 20 –40.

Schmale, A. H., Jr., and Iker, H. P. Hopelessness as a predictor of cervical cancer. *Social Science and Medicine*, 1971, *31*, 699 –714.

Schmitt, F. E., & Wooldridge, P. J. Psychological preparation of surgical patients. *Nursing Research*, 1973, *22*, 108 –116.

Schopler, J., & Walton, M. The effects of expected structure, expected enjoyment, and participant's internality –externality upon feelings of being crowded. Unpublished manuscript, University of North Carolina, 1974.

Seligman, M. E. P. *Helplessness: On depression, development, and death*. San Francisco, Calif.: Freeman, 1975.

Selye, H. *The stress of life*. New York: McGraw-Hill, 1956.

Selye, H. *The stress of life* (rev. ed.). New York: McGraw-Hill, 1976.

Shepard, R. D., & Kroes, W. H. Report of an investigation at the James plant. Internal report prepared for the National Institute for Occupational Safety and Health: Cincinnati, Ohio, 1975.

Sherrod, D. R. Crowding, perceived control and behavioral aftereffects. *Journal of Applied Social Psychology*, 1974, *4*, 171 –186.

Sherrod, D. R., & Downs, R. Environmental determinants of altruism: The effects of stimulus overload and perceived control on helping. *Journal of Experimental Social Psychology*, 1974, *10*(5), 468 –479.

Sherrod, D. R., Hage, J. N., Halpern, P. L., & Moore, B. S. Effects of personal causation and perceived control on responses to an aversive environment. The more control, the better. *Journal of Experimental Social Psychology*, 1977, *13*, 14 –27.

Simon, H. A. *Models of man: Social and rational.* New York: Wiley, 1957.

Singer, J. E., & Glass, D. C. Some reflections upon losing our social psychological purity. In M. Deutsch and H. A. Hornstein (Eds.), *Applying social psychology: Implications for research, practice, and training.* Hillsdale, N.J.: Erlbaum, 1975.

Singer, J. E., Lundberg, U., & Frankenhaeuser, M. Stress on the train: A study of urban commuting. In A. Baum, J. E. Singer, and S. Valins (Eds.), *Advances in environmental psychology*, Vol. 1. Hillsdale, N.J.: Erlbaum, 1978, pp. 41 –56.

Singer, J. E., Baum, C. S., Baum, A., and Thew, B. D. Mass psychogenic illness: The case for social comparison. In M. Colligan and J. Pennebaker (Eds.), *Mass psychogenic illness.* Hillsdale, N.J.: Erlbaum, in press.

Singheimer, R. F. The brain of Pooh: An essay on the limits of the mind. *American Scientist*, 1971, *59*, 20 –28.

Sirois, F. Epidemic hysteria. *Acta Psychiatrica Scandinavica Supplementum*, 1974, *252*, 5 –46.

Skipper, J. R., Jr., & Leonard, R. C. Children, stress, and hospitalization: A field study experiment. *Journal of Health and Social Behavior*, 1968, *9*, 275 –287.

Slovic, P., Fischhoff, B., & Lichtenstein, S. Images of disaster: Perception and acceptance of risks from nuclear risks. In G. Goodman (Ed.), *Impacts and risks of energy strategies: Their analysis and role in management.* New York: Academic, 1981.

Smith, J. J., Colligan, M. J., & Hurrel, J. J. Three incidents of industrial mass psychogenic illness. *Journal of Occupational Medicine*, 1978, *20*, 399 –400.

Solomon, G. F. Emotions and immunity. *Annals of the New York Academy of Sciences*, 1969, *164*, 461 –462.

Speisman, J., Lazarus, R., Mordkoff, A., & Davison, L. Experimental reduction of stress based on ego defense theory. *Journal of Abnormal and Social Psychology*, 1964, *68*, 367 –380.

Stahl, S. M., & Lebedun, M. Mystery gas: An analysis of mass hysteria. *Journal of Health and Social Behavior*, 1974, *15*, 44 –51.

Taylor, S. E. Hospital patient behavior: Reactance, helplessness, or control? *Journal of Social Issues*, 1979, *35*(1).

Taylor, S. E., & Fiske, S. T. Salience, attention, and attribution: Top of the head phenomena. In L. Berkowitz (Ed.), *Advances in experimental social psychology*, Vol. 11. New York: Academic, 1978.

Theorell, T., & Rahe, R. H. Psychosocial factors and myocardial infarction I: An inpatient study in Sweden. *Journal of Psychosomatic Research*, 1971, *15*, 25.

Tracor, Inc. *Community reaction to aircraft noise*, Vol. 1. Washington, D.C.: National Aeronautics and Space Administration, *NASA Report CR-1761*, 1971.

Turk, D. C. Cognitive-behavioral techniques in the management of pain. In J. P. Forey and D. J. Rathgen (Eds.), *Cognitive behavior therapy: Research and application.* New York: Plenum, 1978.

Turk, D. C., & Genest, M. Regulation of pain: The application of cognitive and behavioral techniques for prevention and remediation. In P. C. Kendall and S. D. Hollon (Eds.). *Cognitive-behavioral interventions.* New York: Academic, 1979.

Uldeval, F., Smith, W. R., & Welch, B. E. Steroid and catecholamine studies on pilots during prolonged experiments in a space cabin simulator. *Journal of Applied Physiology*, 1963, *18*, 1257.

Varela, J. A. *Psychological solutions to social problems.* New York: Academic, 1969.

Vernon, D. T. A., & Bigelow, D. A. The effect of information about a potentially stressful situation on responses to stress impact. *Journal of Personality and Social Psychology*, 1974, *29*, 50 –59.

Wallston, B. S., & Wallston, K. A. Locus of control and health: A review of the literature. *Health Education Monographs*, 1978, *6*, 107 –117.

Wallston, B. S., Wallston, K. A., Kaplan, G. D., & Maides, S. A. Development and validation of the health locus of control scale. *Journal of Consulting and Clinical Psychology*, 1976, *44*, 580 –585.

Whitcher, S. J., & Fisher, J. D. Multidimensional reaction to therapeutic touch in a hospital setting. *Journal of Personality and Social Psychology*, 1979, *37*, 87 –96.

Williams, G. L., Jones, J. R., Workhoven, M. N., & Williams, B. The psychological control of preoperative anxiety. *Psychophysiology*, 1975, *12*, 50 –54.

Wilson, A. H. *Noise: Final report of the committee on the problem of noise.* London: Her Majesty's Stationary Office, Cmnd. 2056, 1963.

Wolf, S., & Goodell, H. *Stress and disease.* Springfield, Ill.: Thomas, 1968.

Wolf, S., & Wolff, H. G. *Human gastric function*, 2nd ed. New York: Oxford University Press, 1947.

Wolfer, J. A., & Vistainer, M. A. Pediatric surgical patients' and parents' stress responses and adjustment as a function of psychologic preparation and stress-point nursing care. *Nursing Research*, 1975, *24*, 244 –255.

Worchel, S. The experience of crowding: An attributional analysis. In A. Baum and Y. M. Epstein (Eds.), *Human response to crowding.* Hillsdale, N.J.: Erlbaum, 1978.

Wortman, C. B., & Brehm, J. W. Responses to uncontrollable outcomes: An integration of reactance theory and learned helplessness model. In C. Berkowitz (Ed.), *Advances in experimental social psychology*, Vol. 8. New York: Academic, 1975.

Wortman, C. B., & Dintzer, L. Is an attributional analysis of the learned helplessness phenomenon viable?: A critique of the Abramson –Seligman –Teasdale reformulation. *Journal of Abnormal Psychology*, 1978, *87*, 75 –90.

Wyler, A. R., Masuda, M., & Holmes, T. H. Magnitude of life events and seriousness of illness. *Psychosomatic Medicine*, 1971, *33*, 115 –122.

INDEX

C

D

E